DANWEI

★ SOCIALISM AND ★
SOCIAL MOVEMENTS

Series Editor: Mark Selden

DANWEI

the changing chinese workplace in historical and comparative perspective

Edited by
Xiaobo Lü and Elizabeth J. Perry

An East Gate Book

M.E. Sharpe
Armonk, New York
London, England

An East Gate Book

Copyright © 1997 by M. E. Sharpe, Inc.

Library of Congress Cataloging-in-Publication Data

Danwei: the changing Chinese workplace in historical and
comparative perspective
Xiaobo Lu and Elizabeth J. Perry, editors.
p.   cm.
"An East Gate book."
ISBN 0-7656-0075-7 (cloth : alk. paper).—ISBN 0-7656-0076-5 (pbk. : alk. paper)
1. Communism—China.
2. Danwei.
3. Industrial sociology—China.
4. Sociology, Urban—China.
5. Working class—China—Political activity.
6. Labor mobility—China.
I. Lü, Hsiao-po.
II. Perry. Elizabeth J.
HX418.5.D38   1997
306.3′6′0951—dc21
97-9979
CIP

Printed in the United States of America

The paper used in this publication meets the minimum requirements of the
American National Standard for Information Sciences—
Permanence of Paper for Printed Library Materials,
ANSI Z 39.48-1984.

BM (c)   10   9   8   7   6   5   4   3   2   1
BM (p)   10   9   8   7   6   5   4   3   2   1

Contents

Acknowledgments

This book originated in a panel at the annual meeting for the Association for Asian Studies in March 1994 and then a symposium held at the Center for Chinese Studies of the University of California at Berkeley in April of 1994. The main questions that guided our discussions at the panel and symposium were: What are the origins of the *danwei* and how and when did the *danwei* system become institutionalized? Is the institution of the *danwei* unique to China, or docs it have close counterparts elsewhere in the world? What functions does the *danwei* serve, and how have these changed since the launching of the post-Mao reforms? The present volume, which includes revised symposium papers as well as several other solicited contributions, attempts to address these issues both historically and comparatively.

The editors express their gratitude to the institutions and people who have offered assistance: the Center for Chinese Studies at the University of California at Berkeley for its logistical and financial support for the symposium; Thomas Gold, then the chair of the Center, for his personal support in making the symposium possible; Mark Selden, who not only participated in the AAS panel but also provided valuable suggestions and assistance on the project; and Susan Greenwell, for her editorial assistance.

Xiaobo Lü
Elizabeth J. Perry

Contributors

Yanjie Ban is Assistant Professor of Sociology at the University of Minnesota. He is author of *Work and Inequality in Urban China* (1994).

Anita Chan is an Australian Research Council Fellow at the China and Korea Centre of the Australian National University. She is co-editor of *The China Journal* (formerly *The Australian Journal of Chinese Affairs*) and editor of the translation journal *Chinese Sociology and Anthropology*. She is the author of *Children of Mao* and joint author of *Chen Village under Mao and Deng*, and a book in Chinese, *Symbolism and Undercurrents: The 1989 Mass Movement*. Her current research focuses on changing industrial relations in the People's Republic of China.

John R. Logan is Professor of Sociology at the University of Albany, SUNY. He is co-author of *Urban Fortunes: The Political Economy of Place* (1987) and *Family Ties: Enduring Relationships between Parents and Their Grown Children* (1996).

Hanlong Lu is Director of the Institute of Sociology, Shanghai Academy of Social Sciences.

Xiaobo Lü is Assistant Professor of Political Science at Barnard College, Columbia University, and a member of the East Asian Institute of Columbia University. He has written and published on political corruption, informal politics, Chinese foreign policy, and political economy of enterprise reform.

Barry Naughton is Associate Professor of Economics at the Graduate School of International Relations and Pacific Studies, University of California at San Diego. His book, *Growing Out of Plan: Chinese Economic Reform, 1978–1993*, recently won the Masayoshi Ohira Memorial Prize. He has published on Chinese foreign trade and investment, state-owned enterprises, and economic reforms in China. His current research interests include the economic transition, Chinese industry, and macroeconomics in China.

Yunkang Pan is Director of the Institute of Sociology, Tianjin Academy of Social Sciences, where Ying Guan is a research associate.

Elizabeth J. Perry is Professor of Government at Harvard University. She has also taught at the universities of Arizona, Washington, and California-Berkeley. She is the author of *Rebels and Revolutionaries in North China, 1845–1945*; *Shanghai on Strike: The Politics of Chinese Labor*; and co-author of *Proletarian Power: Shanghai in the Cultural Revolution*. Her edited or co-edited volumes include: *The Political Economy of Reform in Post-Mao China*; *Popular Protest and Political Culture in Modern China*; *Urban Spaces in Contemporary China*; and *Putting Class in Its Place: Worker Identities in East Asia*.

Rudra Sil is Assistant Professor in the Department of Political Science at the University of Pennsylvania. His current research interests include the interactions between state institutions, historical legacies and privatization in post-communist and late-industrializing societies. He is also interested in the general problems of epistemology in the social sciences as well as the comparative method.

Dorothy J. Solinger is Professor in the Department of Politics and Society, School of Social Sciences, University of California. She is the author of *Chinese Business under Socialism*; *From Lathes to Looms: China's Industrial Policy in Comparative Perspective*; and *China's Transition from Socialism*. She is currently completing a study of the movement of migrants into the large cities of China.

Kenneth M. Straus is an Assistant Professor of History at Binghamton University. His forthcoming study, *Factory and Community in Stalin's Russia: The Making of an Industrial Working Class* will be published by the University of Pittsburgh Press.

Wen-hsin Yeh is Professor of History at the University of California, Berkeley. Her most recent work is *Provincial Passages: Culture, Space, and the Origins of Chinese Communism, 1919–1927*, published by University of California Press, 1996.

DANWEI

Introduction

The Changing Chinese Workplace in Historical and Comparative Perspective

Xiaobo Lü and Elizabeth J. Perry

China today is in the throes of momentous socioeconomic change. The post-Mao reforms have wreaked havoc on such socialist institutions as the household registration system that once enforced a strict separation between city and countryside. That division bespoke a gap between the standard of living in urban and rural China that favored city-dwellers by a ratio of at least three-to-one toward the end of the Maoist period.

The superior living standard found in Chinese cities was largely due to the *danwei* system, a hierarchy of state-owned workplace units (schools, factories, hospitals, government agencies, and the like) whose employees were guaranteed a variety of perquisites denied to peasants in the countryside: secure jobs, affordable housing, inexpensive medical care, a range of subsidies for everything from transportation to nutrition, and generous retirement pensions. Along with these economic benefits went political controls; the party branch at the work unit closely monitored its employees' public and personal activities, wielding an assortment of rewards and sanctions to encourage politically acceptable behavior. Such incentives, in turn, contributed to a relatively high level of urban social order. Moreover, when popular protests did erupt, they were usually delimited by the confines of the *danwei*.

The work unit was once so essential to daily life in urban China that people would say one could be without a job, but not without a *danwei*. Unless one gained the approval of one's *danwei*, a person could not freely transfer to a different unit. Until recently, one could not buy an airline ticket or check into a hotel without a written letter of introduction from his or her work unit. The *danwei* was the center of social activities. An individual *belonged* to a *danwei*, which was responsible for the political and social well-being of its members.

The significance of the Chinese work unit has attracted attention from journalists and scholars alike. Thus former *New York Times* correspondent Fox Butterfield as well as sociologists Martin Whyte and William Parish constructed their influential descriptions of urban China around a discussion of the *danwei*.[1] Impressive studies of industrial, medical, and technical units are also readily available.[2]

Despite widespread recognition of the importance of the *danwei* system, however, there remain several unanswered questions. First is the issue of origins: Where did the *danwei* come from? Previous accounts assumed that the *danwei* was either the product of Soviet inspiration in the 1950s or a continuation of long-standing Chinese practice as exemplified in the *baojia* household registration system of imperial days. Yet until recently, little research was actually directed at tracing the roots of this key institution. Part I of this volume, based upon new explorations into the historical antecedents of the *danwei*, presents three different answers to the intriguing question of origins. Second is the matter of operations: What functions has the *danwei* actually served in China, and how do these replicate or differ from the role of work units in other socialist and East Asian countries? Part II of this volume puts the *danwei* in comparative perspective through explicit comparisons with the Soviet Union and Japan. Third is the question of change: How is the *danwei* faring under the contemporary reforms? Are we witnessing the decline, maintenance, or transformation of this critical institution? Part III addresses the issue of continuity and change with particular attention to economic functions, housing provisions, and labor mobility.

As an integral part of the state socialist system in China, the *danwei* is not merely a subject for scholarly inquiry; it is also the target of practical reform policies. The state enterprise reform currently under way touches on a host of issues relating to the *danwei* system; for example, property rights, social welfare, unemployment insurance, and labor mobility. Reforming the socialist work unit is deemed, by general consensus among Chinese officials and scholars alike, one of the most pressing tasks of enterprise reform.[3]

Another significant component of *danwei* reform is targeted at nonenterprise, administrative units. This type of *danwei* has been largely overlooked in the literature on the Chinese workplace. It is by no means insignificant, however. The *shiye* (nonproduction) or *xingzheng* (administrative) *danwei* comprise a very large sector of China's political economy. Parallel to enterprise reform, but with less momentum and fanfare, an overhaul of these units has also been launched.[4] Heated debates over whether nonproduction units should be allowed to engage in economic activities have been raging for some time, resulting in ambiguous and changing government policies. Following a wave of setting up profit-making firms by *xingzheng danwei*, such registered firms numbered 487,000 by the end of 1992, an increase of 88 percent over the previous year. Most of the new firms were established after an official call in June 1992 to downsize administrative agencies by channeling more personnel into business.[5]

In short, an understanding of the *danwei* is essential not only in analyzing the foundations of Chinese socialism but also in appraising the prospects for change. As Perry and Chan note in chapters 2 and 4, labor unrest has escalated since the announced industrial reforms of the mid-1980s. Workers have registered unhappiness over the threat to their "iron rice bowl" through covert resistance and overt protest alike. Whether the Chinese leadership proves able to implement its ambitious reforms will hinge upon a successful handling of labor's concerns. With economic production, social welfare, and political control so thoroughly intertwined in the institution of the *danwei*, change entails unusually complicated challenges.

What Is the *Danwei*?

Surprisingly, considering its everyday use, the concept of the *danwei* is not clearly defined in China. According to one of the most authoritative contemporary Chinese dictionaries, *Cihai*, the word *"danwei"* has two basic meanings: First, it refers to a measurement unit; second, "it refers to agencies, organizations, or departments within an agency or an organization."[6] Other dictionaries offer similar definitions.[7] In common parlance, however, the word *"danwei"* carries a much broader meaning. It refers not only to administrative units but also to other work units—including enterprises, retail shops, hospitals, and schools.

Because of these broad connotations, a practical problem for analysis arises: When someone belongs to a factory with a hierarchy of shops and teams, which level constitutes his or her *danwei*? The factory? The shop? Or the team? Obviously size is not a good criterion, for *danwei* vary greatly in size. A large *danwei* can have several thousand employees, encompassing a number of smaller units. More promising is a functional definition. A *danwei*, we suggest, is a work unit that exhibits the following attributes:

1. *Personnel power*—usually including the right to hire, fire, and arrange transfers. A *danwei* controls the dossiers of its employees, which play a key role in personnel-related matters. Sometimes, however, even when a lower unit controls dossiers, important personnel decisions are made by its superior unit.

2. *Communal facilities* (often in the form of a compound with living quarters physically separated from the outside by walls)—including residential housing, dining hall, health clinic, fleet of cars, and other basic service facilities.

3. *Independent accounts and budgets.* Small units within a large *danwei* are not generally regarded as *danwei* if they do not (legally) maintain separate books.

4. *Urban or nonagricultural purview.* A rural commune or village was never regarded as a *danwei*. On the other hand, a state-owned industrial plant located in a rural area is considered a *danwei*.

5. *Public sector.* The original meaning of the *danwei* encompassed only work units that were government agencies or official organizations. Later the term was extended to all types of units in the public sector. Although the distinction became somewhat meaningless when private businesses virtually disappeared during the Maoist era, in the post-Mao reform period it is clear that some of the functions performed by traditional *danwei* are not fulfilled by private businesses.

Taxonomy of the *Danwei*

China's workplaces are organized in a rather complex fashion. They form the most basic component of the often confusing *tiaotiao* (vertical) and *kuaikuai* (horizontal) relations for which the Chinese bureaucracy is famous.[8] Their organizational fluidity (frequent mergers or elimination of units, creation of new units, etc.), has prevented the compilation of accurate official statistics on the number of work units in China. The government announced that it would conduct the first comprehensive national survey of basic work units on December 31, 1996.[9]

The ambiguity surrounding the status of the *danwei* is heightened by sectoral variation. For example, a 1991 study found a significant correlation between ownership differences in work units and employees' social status and material benefits. Resources varied substantially among state, collective, and private sectors, while higher status and benefits were enjoyed by employees at state administrative agencies.[10]

Further confusing the position of the *danwei* is the fact that all work units are assigned certain administrative ranks by higher authorities. The ranking confers particular privileges and treatment. For example, access to government or party circulars and internal directives is limited by such ranks. The factory manager of a lower-ranked enterprise is not permitted to read circulars that are available to upper levels of the administrative hierarchy. Under the reforms, this ranking also affects the ability of various *danwei* to compete successfully for markets, raw materials, and low-interest loans from the state. Units that enjoy higher administrative rank or are affiliated with a higher government bureau generally fare better than those of lower rank.[11] To redress some of the problems associated with administrative rank designations, it was decided in 1995 temporarily to replace unit-based ranks with personal ranks assigned to the unit's main leaders; eventually these are to be supplanted by functional classifications.[12]

In an effort to cut through some of these ambiguities, we propose a crosscutting taxonomy of Chinese work units classified along lines of operation and status in the administrative hierarchy.

Operations

1. *Qiye danwei,* or enterprise units. This category covers all units engaged in production or profit-making. Factories, retail shops, trading firms, and so on

belong to this category. According to one set of official figures, there were 316,875 units of this sort in 1990.[13] At the end of 1994, the enterprise units employed 113.7 million people.[14]

2. *Shiye danwei*, or nonproduction, nonprofit units. This designation includes scientific research institutes, educational institutions, as well as government-sanctioned social and professional organizations (e.g., the Consumer Rights Association), health services, cultural organizations, and athletic organizations. By official figures, as of 1995 there were more than 1.3 million units in this category.[15] This remains the largest of all three main types of units, employing more than 24 million people.[16] Before the fiscal reforms of the 1980s, the budgets of these units were allocated by the state (Ministry of Finance). Since the reforms, however, the Ministry of Finance no longer provides budgetary funds to local *shiye danwei*. This is thus a sector in flux. It has been shrinking because of the conversion of many *shiye danwei* into self-supporting, profit-generating entities no longer dependent upon the state budget or subsidies. Many banks, post offices, and railroads and some research institutions have been converted to *qiye danwei* in this process. Such reforms have achieved mixed results, however. While some nonproduction units were able to convert fully to *qiye danwei*, others have either shed their previous service wing entirely or have been relegated to "tertiary production" (*disan chanye*) still affiliated with the mother unit in one way or another. Despite these developments, the size of *shiye danwei* functionaries has outpaced the growth in other types of units. In Henan province, for example, between 1986 and 1991 the number of staff in the *shiye danwei* increased 21.1 percent while staff in administrative units grew by 17.7 percent and nonproduction staff in enterprise units increased by only 3.2 percent.[17]

3. *Xingzheng danwei*, or administrative units. In 1990, there were 253,587 such units.[18] At the end of 1994, 10 million people were employees of administrative units.[19] This category is often confused with *shiye danwei* for an obvious reason: Administrative units are also nonproduction and nonprofit entities. Sometimes they are regarded as a subcategory of the *shiye danwei*. But because administrative units have their own characteristics and involve state power, they should be treated as a separate type. Included under this rubric are government agencies, mass organizations (e.g., the Women's Federation, Communist Youth League, Federation of Trade Unions), and other organizations that receive regular budgets from the state.

Hierarchical Status

1. *Zhongyang danwei*, or central units. These units may be located in Beijing or in any province. What distinguishes them from local units is that their initial investment came from the central government (hence their revenues were remitted to the central government), and their operations are usually under the supervision of a certain ministry (or ministries) in Beijing. Although the reforms have

changed some previously existing arrangements, there were 52,058 such units in 1990.

2. *Difang danwei,* or local units. Unlike the centrally controlled units, these units were set up by and controlled by local governments. Before the reforms, the fiscal and financial treatment of local and central units were quite different. There were 276,758 local production units, 820,752 nonproduction units, and 251,293 administrative units in 1990.[20]

3. *Jiceng danwei,* or basic units. This is a generic term applied to all units at the bottom end of the command chain in the Chinese political hierarchy. Grass-roots policy implementation and political mobilization were carried out by these lower-level units (referred to in the literature on the Soviet Union as "cells").

Functions and Characteristics of the *Danwei*

The *danwei* is not merely a type of workplace, but a long-standing and multifaceted institution that has served many purposes for the regime. Because it is so embedded in the larger sociopolitical system, any change in its operations inevitably affects other aspects of the system. The functions of the *danwei* can be divided into two main areas: political and social. These two functions may be characterized as "paternalistic" and "maternalistic" respectively. As in a traditional family, the *danwei* acts as a patriarch who disciplines and sanctions his children, while at the same time serving as a maternal provider of care and daily necessities.[21]

Political Functions

The *danwei* operates as a tool of the state for organizing and controlling urban society. It was through the *danwei* that the state mobilized the working population for political participation. With the notable exception of the Cultural Revolution, urban political campaigns have generally been organized and carried out at the unit level. Other public policies are also implemented through work units. For example, the family planning program has operated most effectively at the unit level. Among people without a regular *danwei,* by contrast, the program has proved difficult to enforce.

The *danwei* allowed the Maoist state to monitor the political loyalty of its citizens, particularly party members. Each unit was responsible for its members; the activities of members when outside their units were also reported back to the unit. In this way, the regime was able to inhibit (albeit not entirely prevent) large-scale organized opposition. Protests in China during the Maoist period were mainly what David Strand has termed "cellular protests," because of the limited contact across unit boundaries.[22] Only at a few critical junctures (e.g., the Hundred Flowers campaign, the *chuanlian* phase of the Cultural Revolution, the "Campaign to Criticize Lin Biao and Confucius") did cross-*danwei* collective actions pose a serious threat to the regime. For the most part, "cellular protests" demonstrated the key role of the *danwei* system in structuring and restraining mass mobilization.[23] However, it is clear that recent market reforms have greatly reduced the effectiveness of such political controls by the *danwei*.[24]

Work units have also limited the mobility of their employees. Without proper permission duly noted in their dossiers (*dang'an*), employees could only dream about a job transfer. The importance of the personal dossier can hardly be over-estimated. One report suggests that there are at least forty different kinds of activities—ranging from quitting a job to opening one's own business to taking part in an examination—that require reference to one's dossier.[25] Even after the market reforms began to take hold, one still needed "proof of resignation" from one's previous employer to obtain a license to operate a private business. Personnel power remains one of the most potent weapons in the *danwei*'s arsenal of political controls.

Social Functions

The danwei also serves important socioeconomic needs by offering permanent employment and attendant benefits. The welfare provisions of the danwei have become so comprehensive over the years that work units operate as self-sufficient and multifunctional social communities. Each danwei came to constitute a "small society" (*xiao shehui*) with little need for interunit exchanges. The danwei was instrumental in reducing the pressure of urban unemployment by absorbing the new working population internally. It also provided benefits for retirees. In general, it helped to lighten the state's burden of social welfare and entitlement provisions.

Xiaobo Lü and Wen-hsin Yeh in chapters 1 and 3 in this volume trace the development of communal welfare functions back to the wartime period, explaining it as a response to economic exigencies. Others, like Elizabeth Perry, stress the political considerations behind the Chinese Communist Party's (CCP's) effort in the 1950s to assume the welfare and insurance functions of traditional labor organizations and thereby displace their authority.[26] Whatever the origins, it is clear that the welfare functions became increasingly systematized after the establishment of the People's Republic of China (PRC) in 1949, as social services were gradually extricated from market forces.

The welfare functions of work units are not unique to China. As Anita Chan, Rudra Sil, and Kenneth Straus point out in chapters 4, 5, and 6, analogues can be found in Japanese and Soviet enterprises. Barry Naughton in chapter 7 proposes that the provision of welfare should be seen as a defining feature of socialist firms, which engage in a horizontal "bundle of activities," in contrast to market-oriented firms, which operate on the premise of a vertical chain of activities. In the socialist firm, a production organization is transformed into a social community. But comparison to the Soviet industrial units, which many Chinese enterprises were modeled after, also reveals some major differences. One area of divergence is in real-estate property rights. Unlike in the Soviet Union, where urban housing was controlled by municipal governments, Chinese work units controlled 90 percent of urban public housing—despite the fact that before 1978 most investment in urban housing came from the state. In the Chinese case, only 10 percent of urban public housing was managed by local governments.[27] After the reforms began, the pressure for units to allocate funds to build new housing actually increased because of a reduction in direct state appropriations for this purpose. Between 1979 and 1986, self-raised funds by units to build housing accounted for 60 percent of the total investment in new housing.[28] Since the mid-1980s, units have been even more pressed to come up with their own housing funds.

The housing issue touches on a long-standing problem in socialist China—the muddled distinction between the state and the *danwei*. In Chinese society, "public" (*gong*) is regarded as anything that is outside the private domain (*si*) of the individual or family. The state is not distinguished from the public: It *is* the public. However, the "minor public" of the *danwei* constituted a different kind of *gong,* which was in some ways at odds with the state, or "greater public." The "minor public" is not simply an abstract concept. It is possessed of both a superstructure—a "minor public mentality" (at times referred to as "small groupism," "departmentalism," "unitism," or "dispersionism")—and an infrastructure—assets and retained revenues.

Ever since the 1950s, the state has launched a continuing series of inspections and investigations of the revenues retained by work units. "Small coffers," as they are called, continue to flourish, however. The actual control of assets and revenues by the *danwei* is so extensive that one might argue that the main form of property rights in China has long been "work unit ownership," rather than state ownership. According to official statistics from the Bureau of State Property Management, the assets controlled by administrative and nonproduction units that should actually belong to the state amounted to 892 billion yuan by the end of 1993.[29] Currently the government is pushing for a clear accounting and systematic registration of work unit assets.[30] If successful, this effort would mark the first time in PRC history that a legally defined distinction between state and *danwei* assets in a *public unit* has been enforced.

Because of its reliance on work units for both political control and welfare, the state has to date been unable to control the finances of work units. The state's delegation of public goods provision to the units has proved both facilitative and obstructive in the transition to a market economy. The relative autonomy of the *danwei* encouraged units to take the initiative in adapting to new market conditions and allowed the state to reduce drastically its budgetary support for many projects. At the same time, the lack of a centralized welfare system and dwindling state financial support created bottlenecks, forcing the state to delay its much-publicized state-owned enterprise reform program and inclining work units to seek additional extrabudgetary revenues. Caught in between diminishing state funding and pressure from an increasingly mobile labor population (including people leaving their *danwei* and nonurban residents coming to the city in search of work), municipal authorities find themselves unable to provide needed social services. This has generated new tensions between urban dwellers and the so-called floating population, as Dorothy Solinger indicates in chapter 8.

Perhaps the most distinctive feature of the *danwei* is its encapsulation as a community and social cell. In some cases, the physical separation by brick walls is matched by an invisible segregation as well. As one geographer has noted,

> [W]hen a new *danwei* is started, wall-building is the first step in construction, not the last as is common in North America. Buildings relating to it are faced inward rather than outward, either by making a separate wall or by arranging the individual parts to achieve the same effect. Such spatial arrangements create a protected area within, a boundary effect, and a means of excluding outsiders. From the Chinese point of view, the enclosure of place makes it proper and secure—conducive to effective social interaction and to organization of activities within. . . . It excludes those who are not members, while at the same time it provides a basis for integrating those within it into an effective social, economic, and political unit.[31]

The consequences of such cellularization of Chinese society are both internal and external. Inside, as Andrew Walder noted in his study of urban industrial units, members become dependent on the unit for both political and economic resources.[32] Externally, urban units are separated from one another and from rural communities. Because these enclosed entities resemble traditional agricultural communities, urban *danwei* are sometimes referred to as "villages within a city"—the title of a popular movie in the early 1980s.[33]

In the "Third Front" effort to relocate defense industry to the interior during the Cultural Revolution,[34] the basic character of the *danwei* was not altered by the rural setting. Nor did these transplanted enterprises make much of an impact on their new environment. Consider the case of a large state-owned weapons factory with some five thousand employees, which was first established in the remote mountains of Shaanxi province in 1968. The factory was situated in a poor agricultural area surrounded by three villages. Under normal circumstances, a large industrial establishment of this sort would stimulate the local economy. However, in this case the factory was entirely self-sufficient. Not only did it operate its own entertainment facilities for employees, but it also ran its own dairy, retail shop, and vegetable and pig farms. Local peasants were given no access to these services, and any contact between the two separate communities was confined to conflict.[35]

The encysted character of the *danwei* has become an accepted feature of the system. People speak of events as occurring "out in society" (*shehui shang*), as if their own *danwei* were entirely separate from the wider social environment. To the working population, the *danwei* is seen more as a self-regenerating communal and welfare entity than as an organization that provides products and services for society at large. It is this somewhat unique situation—with the *danwei* holding independent interests that sometimes conflict with those of the state, yet remaining outside "unorganized" society—that prompts us to emphasize the ambiguous status of the work unit vis-à-vis both state and society.

Historical and Comparative Perspectives

The chapters that follow examine the Chinese work unit in historical and comparative context. Part I, focusing on the question of origins, provides three quite different—yet complementary—explanations for the derivation of the *danwei* system.

Xiaobo Lü locates historical antecedents of the *danwei* in the free supply system and related practices of economic self-reliance that emerged in the Communist base areas during the revolutionary war years. To provide for the livelihood of their members, administrative and military units were encouraged to engage in production and permitted to retain a proportion of their revenues as collective assets. This development created a realm of the "small public" that Lü sees as the "institutional foundation for units to pursue their own tangible interests, legitimately or illicitly." Lü traces the continuation of these practices into the post-1949 period, when, especially during times of economic duress, *danwei* assumed major economic and welfare responsibilities.

Wen-hsin Yeh, by contrast, highlights the urban, non-Communist forerunners of the *danwei*. Through a case study of Shanghai's Bank of China, Yeh details the development in the 1930s of a communal corporate culture in which "most boundaries between the private and the public, the personal and the professional, were erased." At the bank, work routines were supplemented by a heavy schedule of social activities, including reading clubs, group dinners, study societies, and sports. A moral philosophy that stressed paternal authority and emphasized the character and behavior of employees, in lieu of material incentives, pervaded the banking organization. Unlike the free supply system of the Communists studied by Xiaobo Lü, the Republican banking communities were concerned less with the provision of basic livelihood than with the creation of a new community culture. Although the wartime experience politicized this process and discredited the authority of the corporate patriarchs, it did not undermine the basic moralism that had come to infuse corporate life. This, according to Yeh, "eased the transition into a sort of personalized Chinese communism that combined collective leadership with institutionalized familialism."

A third interpretation is offered by Elizabeth Perry. Like Lü, Perry associates the origins of the *danwei* with pre-1949 Communist activities. Like Yeh, however, she searches for these practices not in the rural base areas but in the cities. And unlike both Lü and Yeh, she highlights the labor movement—specifically that wing of the Shanghai labor movement dominated by skilled artisans and closely linked to the Communist Party—in giving rise to the *danwei* system. Leaders of this labor movement from the 1920s on, most notably Li Lisan and Chen Yun, played a key role in putting together defining components of the *danwei* system after 1949. Yet, according to Perry, the institution of the *danwei*—like the labor movement itself—was divisive, creating "a gulf between the haves and have-nots of Chinese socialism that has fueled major strike waves in every decade of China's history since 1949."

Dissimilar as their explanations are, the chapters dealing with origins highlight specifically Chinese roots of the *danwei*. By contrast, the contributions in Part II of this volume provide a comparative context. The chapter by Anita Chan examines the Japanese experience, while the chapters by Rudra Sil and Kenneth Straus look at the Soviet exemplar.

As Sil notes, certain aspects of the *danwei* (e.g., the attempt to combine production functions with a paternalistic form of community) are commonly found in the factory systems of other late-industrializing countries. Moreover, among Communist countries—where the state enterprise was made responsible for both welfare provision and political control—additional similarities can be detected. Nevertheless, it is clear that such affinities have evolved from the exigencies of industrial development rather than from Communist theory. The writings of Marx, Lenin, Stalin, and Mao offer few guides to the organization of urban society. Both Soviet and Chinese practice emerged in improvised fashion, with similarities and differences reflecting the interaction of long-standing traditions and changing socioeconomic conditions in the two countries.

Rudra Sil stresses the carryover of rural collectivist and egalitarian values in the factory social relations of prerevolutionary Russia. Initially, according to Sil, Bolshevik leaders built upon these norms in setting up factory councils and calling for an egalitarian wage policy. Before long, however, economic difficulties convinced both Lenin and Trotsky of the need to stress factory discipline at the expense of "worker's control" and wage egalitarianism. Under Stalin, Soviet practice departed even further from communitarian norms as power became concentrated in the hands of factory directors and differential wage rates encouraged intraworker competition. Such developments, Sil argues, led to growing alienation among the work force. The lesson he draws for China is that "before replacing the entire *danwei* system with firms modeled after those in the West, Chinese reformers should pay careful attention to the legacies they inherited, that is, the attitudes, values, and behavioral norms exhibited by workers and their supervisors."

Kenneth Straus paints a somewhat different portrait of the Soviet factory, emphasizing its role as provider of food, housing, recreational facilities, health care, education, transportation, and so forth. Like Sil, Straus notes that the Stalinist factory wielded considerable disciplinary power over its work force. As a functionally specialized institution, it was a world apart from the traditional peasant commune. But Straus also notes that when managers succeeded in ful-filling the basic socioeconomic needs of their workers, "the factory realized its potential as a powerful unifying social force, a 'community organizer.' " As in the Chinese *danwei*, a clear distinction developed between "insiders" (who en-joyed the privileges available only to regular workers) and "outsiders" (e.g., temporary laborers who were denied access to quality housing, food, and other provisions). Straus concludes that among those workers who benefited from factory welfare we find not anomie but "the creation of new social solidarities."

The difference in emphasis between Sil and Straus is surely attributable in part to the particular features of the Soviet factory system on which they focus their central attention. Whereas Sil emphasizes the failure of Soviet managerial elites to "capture" the work force through hierarchical control and differential rewards, Straus seeks to provide a more nuanced appreciation of the Soviet factory by highlighting the role of welfare provision in recreating solidarity at the workplace. Whether we prefer Sil's stress on managerial hierarchy and worker alienation or Straus's somewhat more positive assessment of the Soviet factory as "community organizer," we still do not find in the Soviet case the degree of either control or community that is characteristic of the Chinese *dan-wei*. The differences, as Barry Naughton suggests in chapter 7, have much to do with the distinctive economic foundations of work units in the two countries.

Anita Chan points out that the Chinese *danwei* departs in important respects from both the "market-oriented" system of most Western economies (in which skill is seen as a demand-driven asset adhering to individual workers who are potentially mobile) and the "organization-oriented" Japanese model (in which firms compensate their workers according to criteria other than skill, expecting in return a high degree of permanency and loyalty). As in Japan, the Chinese work unit is marked by job security, low turnover, and wages rates pegged to the personal attributes of the worker rather than to skill levels per se. But, as Chan notes, in China the system was intended to facilitate identification with the state rather than with the enterprise.

This state-oriented employment system, she argues, had deleterious social and economic consequences that helped set the stage for recent reform efforts. As the reforms work to extricate Chinese enterprises from the constraints of the com-mand economy and the restraints of party control, Chan detects the possibility of a growing convergence between the Chinese and Japanese models.

Where is the *danwei* system heading under the impact of the current industrial reforms? Part III explores this question from several different, yet overlapping, angles. While Barry Naughton provides a general overview of the changing economic functions of the *danwei*, Yanjie Bian and his coauthors focus on the critical problem of urban housing, and Dorothy Solinger highlights the equally important issue of labor mobility and control.

Despite the similarities between the *danwei* and aspects of enterprise systems in the former Soviet Union and Japan, Barry Naughton emphasizes the uniqueness of the Chinese situation. In explaining the distinctive features of China's *danwei* system, as it emerged full blown in the mid-1960s, Naughton points to three factors: the virtual absence of labor mobility, substantial surpluses at the enterprise level, and a streamlined administrative command in which many types of decisions were made by the *danwei* leadership. When the post-Mao economic reforms were first implemented starting in the 1980s, the *danwei* system was actually strengthened—as retirees were replaced by their own children and work units assumed greater responsibility for housing construction. Over time, however, increased labor mobility and pressure from competing industrial firms has been forcing state-owned enterprises to reconfigure their activities. The central leadership is reluctant to abandon the *danwei* altogether because of the difficulties in imposing political control, the problems in implementing a national pension system, and the like. Yet, concludes Naughton, "the most powerful, more fundamental, and most long-lasting forces are those that tend to undermine the *danwei* and push the system toward greater marketization."

Dorothy Solinger, in examining the question of labor mobility and control, presents a complex picture in which bureaucratic, market, and personalistic forces interact to create a "transitional hybridization of the firm." In the matter of job recruitment, the market still plays little role in determining who is selected for employment in either the state or nonstate sector. Instead, bureaucratic regulations and personal connections remain the determining factors. In the matter of worker welfare, however, Solinger detects an important difference between state-owned firms, which continue to provide major benefits to their workers and township and village or foreign-owned enterprises that represent a "throwback to the totally unregulated laissez-faire capitalism of the mid-nineteenth century." Solinger does not see the decline of the *danwei* as ushering in a benevolent form of welfare state capitalism. Instead, she suggests that the floating population may be contributing to the development of an informal economy of the sort delineated by Manuel Castells and Alejandro Portes for other areas of the world: "A new society based on the relationship between unrestrained capital and primary social networks."

As Naughton acknowledges, one of the areas in which the reforms have made little headway is housing allocation. That issue is explored in detail in the paper by Yanjie Bian and his coauthors. Based on surveys of the housing situation in two major Chinese cities (Shanghai and Tianjin), Bian et al. argue that work units continue to reward their employees through the provision of housing and that "there is little reason to expect the commodification of housing to disrupt this aspect of the system's operation." Despite differences between the two cities, Bian and coauthors find that the housing reforms have not reduced the overall authority of the *danwei*. On the contrary, "work units necessarily intervene decisively in determining who has access to what kind of housing, and at what price."

In short, China's industrial reforms may be creating a situation in which unbridled capitalism and personal connections come to fill the gaps left by a retreating *danwei* system. As a recent study of the Chinese work unit under reform concludes,

> [R]eform has clearly brought with it a metastasis of informal connections of every type, for both legitimate and sub rosa (or outright criminal) activities. Among contradictory trends we are struck by the contrast between the commercialization of *guanxi* on the one hand, and the resurgence of primordial (mostly kinship-based) ties on the other. The question is whether the existing framework will be sufficient to contain this cancerous proliferation.[36]

Will the Chinese situation evolve into something resembling the Japanese prototype, as Anita Chan suggests? Or will it devolve into the "disenfranchisement" of labor characteristic of many third world economies, as Dorothy Solinger implies? It is too early to predict with confidence the outcome of the *danwei* reform effort. Whatever the end result, however, there is little doubt that the distinctive features of the Chinese socialist work unit will shape this historic transition.

Notes

1. Fox Butterfield, *China, Alive in the Bitter Sea* (New York: Times Books, 1982); Martin K. Whyte and William L. Parish, *Urban Life in Contemporary China* (Chicago: University of Chicago Press, 1984). See also Jay and Linda Matthews, *One Billion: A China Chronicle* (New York: Random House, 1983); Brantly Womack, "Transfigured Community: New Traditionalism and Work Unit Socialism in China," *China Quarterly,* no. 126 (June 1991); and Corinna-Barbara Francis, "Paradoxes of Power and Dependence in the Chinese Workplace" (Ph.D. dissertation, Columbia University, 1993).

2. See, for example, Andrew G. Walder, *Communist Neo-Traditionalism: Work and Authority in Chinese Industry* (Berkeley: University of California Press, 1986); Lowell Dittmer and Xiaobo Lü, "Personal Politics in the Chinese Danwei Under Reform," *Asian Survey* (March 1996); Mayfair Yang, "Between State and Society: The Construction of Corporateness in a Chinese Socialist Factory," *Australian Journal of Chinese Affairs,* no. 22 (1989); Gail E. Henderson and Myron S. Cohen, *The Chinese Hospital: A Socialist Work Unit* (New Haven: Yale University Press, 1984); Marc J. Blecher and Gordon White, *Micropolitics in Contemporary China: A Technical Unit During and After the Cultural Revolution* (Armonk, NY: M.E. Sharpe, 1979).

3. See Fang Weizhong, ed., *Guanyu gaohao guoyou qiye de diaocha* [Investigation on improving the operation of state-owned enterprises] (Beijing: Zhongguo wenshi chubanshe, 1995, internally circulated).

4. There have been some discussions on reforming the operation and functions of those units in the media and academic journals. See, for example, *Jingji ribao* [Economic daily], January–May 1993.

5. See *Shehui* [Society], no. 1 (1994).

6. See *Cihai* [Word ocean] (Shanghai: Shanghai cishu chubanshe, 1979), 288–89.

7. See *Hanyu da cedian* [A dictionary of Chinese] (Shanghai: Hanyu da cedian chubanshe, 1989), vol. 3, 417.

8. See Kenneth G. Lieberthal and David M. Lampton, eds., *Bureaucracy, Politics and*

Decision-Making in Post-Mao China (Berkeley: University of California Press, 1992); and Kenneth Lieberthal and Michel Oksenberg, *Policy Making in China: Leaders, Structures and Processes* (Princeton: Princeton University Press, 1988).

9. *Renmin ribao*, March 30, 1996.

10. Nan Lin and Yanjie Bian, "Getting Ahead in Urban China," *American Journal of Sociology*, 97, no. 3 (November 1991): 657–88.

11. See Zhao Chenfu, "Jiejue qiye shengzheng jibiehua wenti de gouxiang" (Ideas on solving the problem of administrative ranking of enterprises), *Dangjian yanjiu neican* [Internal references on party building], no. 6 (1993).

12. *Renmin ribao*, November 8, 1995.

13. *Zhongguo laodong tongji nianjian* (1991) [Chinese labor statistics yearbook] (Beijing: Zhongguo laodong chubanshe, 1991); figures are from 1990 and all units belong to the public sector.

14. *Chinese Statistical Yearbook* (1995) (Beijing: Zhongguo tongji chubanshe, 1995).

15. *Renmin ribao*, November 8, 1995.

16. *Chinese Statistical Yearbook* (1995).

17. *Zhongguo xingzheng guanli* [Administration and management in China] (July 1992): 36–38.

18. Ibid.

19. *Chinese Statistical Yearbook* (1995).

20. Ibid.

21. See Dittmer and Lü, "Personal Politics in the Chinese Danwei."

22. David Strand, "Protest in Beijing: Civil Society and Public Sphere in China," *Problems of Communism* (May–June 1990): 1–19.

23. See, for example, an interesting study by Sebastian Heilmann, "The Social Context of Mobilization in China: Factions, Work Units, and Activists During the 1976 April Fifth Movement," *China Information*, 8, no. 3 (winter 1993–94).

24. See Dittmer and Lü, "Personal Politics in the Chinese Danwei."

25. *Guangming ribao*, December 22, 1993.

26. For similar arguments see Kenneth Lieberthal, *Revolution and Tradition in Tientsin* (Stanford: Stanford University Press, 1980); Lü Feng, "The Origins and Formation of the Unit (Danwei) System," *Chinese Society and Anthropology*, 25, no. 3 (1993).

27. *Zhongguo chengshi jianshe nianjian* [Yearbook of urban development in China, 1986–87] (Beijing: Zhongguo jianzhu chubanshe, 1989).

28. Ibid.

29. *Renmin ribao*, December 15, 1995.

30. Ibid.

31. E.M. Bjorklund, "The Danwei: Socio-Spatial Characteristics of Work Units in China's Urban Society," *Economic Geography*, 62, no. 1 (1986), p. 21.

32. Walder, *Communist Neo-Traditionalism.*

33. Yang Zhangqiao, "Lun Zhongguo chengshi shehui de tezheng" [Characteristics of Chinese urban society], *Tansuo* [Exploration], no. 6 (1988).

34. On the Third Front, see Barry Naughton, "The Third Front: Defense Industrialization in the Chinese Interior," *China Quarterly*, no. 115 (September 1988); and Naughton, "Industrial Policy During the Cultural Revolution," in *New Perspectives on the Cultural Revolution,* ed. William Joseph et al. (Cambridge: Harvard University Press, 1991).

35. Li Zongyi, "Wo suozai de shequ" [The community I live in], *Shehui*, no. 2 (1985): 20–23.

36. Dittmer and Lü, "Personal Politics in the Chinese Danwei."

Part I

Danwei in Historical Perspective

1

Minor Public Economy: The Revolutionary Origins of the *Danwei*

Xiaobo Lü

The *danwei,* an enclosed, multifunctional, and self-sufficient entity, is the most basic collective unit in the Chinese political and social order. It plays both political (statist) and economic (societal) roles. As a basic unit in the Communist political order, the *danwei* is a mechanism with which the state controls members of the cadre corps, monitors ordinary citizens, and carries out its policies. As an economic and communal group, the *danwei* fulfills the social and other needs of its members. Many urban units have become "small societies" themselves, providing entitlements and maintaining basic services ranging from housing, car fleets, dining services, barbers, kindergartens, guesthouses, and clinics to, in some large state-owned enterprises, cremation services. Indeed, the work unit has taken over many welfare and service responsibilities the state would otherwise have to provide. Many public goods and entitlements are not provided directly by the state but by individual *danwei.* Instead of developing a social security system, for example, work units have taken on all the necessary service and welfare responsibilities even for retirees. Many of these services have been provided either free or at very low cost.

The control function exerted at the grass-roots level of a Leninist society is unique to China. In the Soviet Union and other Communist countries, similar types of "functional cells" existed through which the party-state monitored and controlled the working population.[1] Existing studies and anecdotes about the *danwei* have focused mainly on this seemingly powerful tool of an authoritarian party/state in controlling society.[2] However, it is the other dimension of the *danwei*—its comprehensive welfare and social functions—that, I contend, makes it somewhat unique and bears a more profound impact on the broader political and socioeconomic systems. As chapters 8 and 9, respectively, by Solinger and Bian and his coauthors in this volume show, some of these functions not only remain intact but have been further enhanced in some sectors even after more than a decade of reforms.

In order to understand fully the institution of the *danwei* in China, we need to trace its origins and development over the years. Surprisingly, however, not only has little been written on the *danwei* system but almost no study has been done about its origins. People generally assume that it emerged in the 1950s along with the establishment of the household registration system and other measures for the socialist transformation of urban society. Some scholars have speculated, without much data and analysis, that it originated in the revolutionary war period.[3] This chapter explores one of the most important origins of the *danwei*— the free supply system (*gongjizhi*) and related self-reliance economic activities in which Communist army and government units in the wartime base areas were involved, called at the time "agency production" (*jiguan shengchan*) or "minor public economy" (*xiaogong jingji*).[4] It was during the wartime revolutionary period that the earliest *danwei* took shape as a functional entity in the Communist political and social systems.

Guerrilla War and Free Supply System

During the long period of armed struggle, Communist forces adopted, instead of salaries, a free supply system under which essential supplies were provided at almost no cost to the members of the revolutionary rank and file, including noncombat personnel and administrative staff. To a large degree, it was as much a product of economic necessity—a salary system would have required a much stronger financial revenue base than the Communists had—as a reflection of Communist egalitarian principles. As part of the revered revolutionary tradition, this free supply system lasted well beyond the war years and was not totally replaced by a salary system until 1955.

Although the items on the supply list varied from time to time and place to place, some key items remained on it throughout the whole period. Besides regular operational funds, living allowances usually covered everything from food and miscellaneous daily allowances to a woman's health allowance, childcare subsidies, and children's clothing. All service and nonmilitary personnel also received uniforms or other clothing and other daily necessities in kind. One basic tenet of the free supply system was relatively equal treatment of officers, soldiers, officials, and staff in the Communist army and government.

In the early years, the Communists' revenue and food supply sources largely consisted of confiscations from rich landlords, apportioned funds, and donations. Later, when some base areas were established, Communist authorities also relied upon taxation and revenues from a limited number of small-scale industries run by the authorities in base the areas. When the Communists formed a united front with the Nationalists, they also received funding and some regular supplies from the Nationalist government.[5] Eventually, once all these sources became problematic—especially when the Nationalist government stopped its supplies to the Communists in 1940—revenues and supplies also came from production and commercial entities run by individual units with the aim of self-sufficiency.

One of the fundamental characteristics of the Chinese Communist revolution was its profound experience of guerrilla war fought in the country's vast hinterlands. From the late 1920s until the final takeover in 1949, Communist forces operated in "base areas" in various regions of China. Large and small contingents alike, these forces often functioned in a highly dispersed fashion. Until the late 1930s, the Communists basically operated with a decentralized supply system; their essential supplies and revenues came from local economies through the raising of revenues and their disposal by individual army units themselves (*zichou zizhi*). Revenues and supplies were raised in such an irregular fashion that local people often felt unfairly burdened. In some areas, rich peasants were squeezed; in others, poor peasants had to offer more than landlords.[6] Both politically and financially, such arrangements had negative effects on the Communist central authorities. In order to raise and dispense supplies efficiently for army units, the Chinese Communist Party's (CCP's) Central Military Commission decided to unify budgets and appropriations in 1932.[7] All the supplies and funds were to be provided by the centralized authorities of each base area with a unified supply system. The principle of "unified supply, revenue-raising, and expenditure" (*tongyi gongji, tongchou, tongzhi*) was adopted. Under such a system, individual units would not have to raise revenue to obtain the necessary supplies they required. If they did have revenue, it had to be turned over to higher-level authorities.

Economic and political conditions, however, often rendered the system less than totally effective, especially in newly established bases, where Communist governments remained highly unstable and irregular. As late as 1940, a party leader in the Shandong base area reported to the CCP Central Committee that "unified budgeting, appropriation, and supply systems have not been well established. Local forces have been raising and spending funds at will. There is no way to audit and control their finances. Squandering is shockingly high."[8]

Local economic conditions also made the centralized supply system much more difficult to implement than a fragmented one. Before the Long March in 1935–36, Communist forces operated mainly in areas such as Jiangxi and Fujian, where economic conditions were relatively good. When the Red Army moved to Yan'an and a few other, more remote base areas, things were quite different—in these poverty-stricken regions of the north, peasants were already terribly exploited by the landlords. The extra burden of sustaining a large military and administrative presence became increasingly unbearable for the local economy. In Yan'an, the number of personnel in the central party and administrative organs alone once peaked at 16,000.[9] In the most difficult year, 1941, there were some 70,000 people receiving free supplies in the base area of Shaan-Gan-Ning border region.[10] In the Jizhong (central Hebei) base area, the number of administrative personnel reached 65,000 in 1945.[11] To rely solely on extracting revenue from the local population was obviously not a good option for the Communists, who depended greatly upon peasant support. Lack of sufficient supplies also caused hardship in the daily life in the army. The supply shortage affected the army's morale and resulted in some desertions.[12] The Communist leadership found that the only sensible way to solve this problem was to produce things themselves and to let units find ways to supplement provided supplies. Thus new policies of "expanding the economy in order to guarantee supplies" and "unifying management and dispersing (economic) operation" were adopted.

Self-Reliance and the Economic Role of Units

These new policies were an attempt to remedy the economic difficulties caused by both the Japanese blockade of the Communist base regions and a lack of material supplies from the Nationalist government in the late 1930s. In 1938, some army units began experimenting with production activities such as planting vegetables, raising pigs, and making shoes, mainly to improve the soldiers' daily lives.[13] By 1939, the Communists' financial situation had worsened, due both to decreasing supplies from the Nationalists and to the increased number of government agencies and other public units and their staffs. In January 1939, Mao formally advocated the idea of "letting the army produce for itself."[14] A large-scale production movement (*da shengchan yundong*) was launched in early 1940 by the Central Military Committee, which, in a directive, called on all military units to participate in production of all kinds, including commercial businesses. The slogans at that time were to "feed and dress ourselves through self-reliance" and to "develop the economy in order to guarantee supplies."[15] Soon, it was not only army units that were mobilized to engage in production activities in order to be self-sufficient; other nonmilitary units such as government agencies, public schools, and hospitals all participated in production activities in Yan'an and the surrounding Shaan-Gan-Ning border region. Hence, such activities were called "agency production." Similar production movements were also launched in other Communist-controlled base areas in 1942–43. Although set in motion in mass campaign style, the "production movement" took on a permanent character. With encouragement from the CCP leadership, economic activities of military and administrative units not only lasted throughout the anti-Japanese resistance and civil war periods, but also after 1949. In fact, it can be argued that the contemporary commercial frenzy of "taking a plunge into the ocean (of business)"[16] by nonproduction work units and "official firms" finds its origins in this revolutionary tradition.

Economic activity by units, which Mao treated as part of the "public economy" (*gongying jingji*) in the Communist-controlled base areas,[17] was one of the two main sources of financial and grain revenues after the production movement began. The other was the "popular economy" (*minying jingji*), namely, farming and other local peasant businesses, from which some revenues were extracted by the Communist government in the form of land rent and taxes.[18] It is important to note that there were two types of enterprises and production in the "public economy": those run by the government, or "greater public family" (*da gongjia*), and those operated by individual units, or "minor public family" (*xiao gongjia*) also referred to as *xiao gong jingji* (minor public economy). For example, the textile mills run by the government produced 56 percent of the total textile output by public enterprises. Seventy percent of the paper produced by public enterprises was the output of the government-run factories.[19] The revenues from these government-run factories were wholly remitted by the government as public revenue.

What is significant for our research purposes is not this category of public enterprises, but the other—"dispersively operated" (*fensan jingying*) commercial and industrial enterprises run by individual units, whose main objective was to enrich the units and hence reduce the reliance on supplies provided by higher-level authorities. In this case, production activities and business entities were organized or operated by one or several "mess units" (*huoshi danwei*), such as a hospital in the local government or a combat company (*lian*) in the army. This is important because a "mess unit" had its own kitchen serving meals to its members, as well as a separate budget, and kept books for meals, which were the main source of financial concerns at the time. The initial goal of production activities was mainly to improve the quality of meals. Because production was run by these units, they were also referred to as "production and accounting units" (*shengchan hesuan danwei*) or "production units" (*shengchan danwei*).[20] These units varied in size. For example, a central agency could have a staff of several hundred, while an army company would have one hundred or so soldiers. The 1943 production plan of an elite army brigade—the 359th Brigade, which was the first to engage in production and later to become a symbol of the "Great Production movement"—shows that the brigade had a total of sixty-five production units.[21] Another document indicates that in the central party and governmental apparatus in Yan'an there were sixty-seven such units in 1942.[22] Each unit had a production manager and at least one accounting staff member. Besides the usual farming production, many of them also operated small factories and other lines of business.[23] Thus, even though the term *danwei* had been used before this period to refer to army or administrative units, this was perhaps the earliest usage incorporating the meaning of economic and welfare roles.

During the 1939 and 1944 period, production was one of the core tasks of the CCP. In the Taihang base area of the Shanxi-Hebei-Shandong-Henan border region, for example, local Communist Party authorities set up a special committee on self-reliant production in order to "make decisions concerning production" and "to inspect and supervise production work of all party units."[24] The achievement of the production movement was impressive. It helped greatly in solving the economic difficulties caused by the Japanese blockade and lack of sufficient local revenue. By 1942, about half the major subsistence necessities in the Shaan-Gan-Ning base area could be produced locally.[25]

Facing economic difficulties, the Communist forces survived in part because of the economic activities of the units. Such activities, in many cases, supplemented the insufficiently allocated supplies and funds to units from the central authorities. In other cases, they even generated a surplus. In 1941, the worst year the Communist forces experienced in terms of outside aid and supplies, 70 percent of all supplies came from individual units themselves.[26] The revenues from production by the twenty-one units directly under the auspices of the CCP Central Committee could meet 48 percent of these units' total expenditure in 1942. In 1943, the proportion of revenues from self-sufficient production in the Shaan-Gan-Ning base area increased to 64 percent, and in 1944, 62.8 percent of the financial revenues came from production. In 1945, unit revenues accounted for 61.4 percent of the total revenue of the region. If one added the accumulated "collective assets" owned by these units, their financial needs would be fully met by agency production.[27]

To encourage units more actively engaging in "self-reliant production," the CCP central leadership allowed units to retain a portion of their revenue as collective assets for reinvesting in new production and as funds to improve the livelihood of their members. Thereafter the production activities by units were called, tellingly, the "public family economy," which aimed at building up "collective assets" (*gao jiawu*).[28] To a great extent, the terminology reflects the needs and nature of guerrilla warfare in which armed units were scattered and somewhat independent from the central leadership. In fact, from the late 1930s to the late 1940s, many units maintained their own assets to varying degrees, as the example of the units directly affiliated with the CCP Central Committee indicates (see Table 1.1). In later years, the collective assets of units also included gold, silver, and share certificates, as well as opium.[29]

Although referred to as "production," businesses of units were not confined to farming and manufacturing. Commercial retail activities not only were common but became the dominant type of business conducted outside agriculture, as Table 1.2 indicates.[30] The Administrative Bureau of the CCP Central Committee alone operated twenty retail stores, according to 1941 statistics.[31] In 1944 commercial businesses became the second most lucrative source of revenue (see Table 1.2). By 1946 there were 348 various kinds of stores, shops, and "mobile production" (*liudong shengchan,* i.e. interregional trade) units plus some 280 consumer co-ops; roughly 2,500 staff worked in these commercial businesses, and revenue from this source increased to 30 percent of the total.[32] In addition to these commercial operations run directly by units, many large units also invested in two trading companies, which monopolized the trade of salt and "special and local products" including opium, and commissioned the trading companies to

Table 1.1

Existing Collective Assets of Units of the CCP Central Committee (1944)
(in million yuan)

Unit	Production funds	Materials	Livestock	Tools
Administrative bureau	8.34	N/A	9.90	2.82
Guest house	0.76	4.20	2.14	1.74
Medical clinic	1.97	0.69	4.06	1.01
Central hospital	5.05	14.20	5.46	1.52
Equipment team	N/A	0.21	62.30	94.30
Management office	2.40	0.67	3.05	3.59
Secretariat	47.30	15.10	19.80	7.70
General office	80.90	29.90	44.10	10.50
Military commission	8.02	4.94	24.10	6.41

Source: Chen Junqi, *Yan'an shiqi caikuai gongzuo de huigu* [Recollections of financial and accounting work in Yan'an] (Beijing: Zhongguo caizheng jingji chubanshe, 1987).
Note: The original table includes a total of twenty-one units directly under the auspices of the CCP Central Committee.

Table 1.2

Revenues by Units of the CCP Central Committee (1944) (in *dan*)

	Revenue by category	% of total revenue
Agriculture	16, 223	24.6
Livestock	1,134	1.7
Workshops	7,074	10.7
Industry	8,081	12.2
Transportation	6,653	10.1
Commerce	13,069	20.0
Private production by members	9,198	14.0
Co-ops	1,002	1.5
Other	4,415	6.7

Source: Chen Junqi, *Yan'an shiqi caikuai gongzuo de huigu* [Recollections of financial and accounting work in Yan'an] (Beijing: Zhongguo caizheng jingji chubanshe, 1987).
Note: This includes 21 units directly under the auspices of the CCP Central Committee.
1 *dan* = 2.837 bushels or 100 liters.

sell products they produced or possessed, the most lucrative one being opium.[33] The production campaign helped improve the quality of life in the base regions and reduce the financial burdens on local peasants. It played an indispensable part in the survival and expansion of the Communist troops and the base area government.[34] The campaign also trained hundreds of cadres in economic and commercial practices, many of whom later became the core of the economic and managerial elite when the Communists took power.

Not only were units allowed to retain some of the revenue they generated, but they were also given tax breaks by tax authorities even though there were no official rules stipulating any exemptions. This is revealed in a work report by the southwest regional economic and finance office in early 1943:

> [We] only laid our eyes on the violation of tax rules by some army units engaged in commercial and transportation businesses. Some of our staff made a major issue out of these activities, whose goal was to fulfill the task of production. From now on, *absolutely* [emphasis added] no tax agents are allowed to execute inspection on army equipment. Inspection has to be done with the consent of the units (including servicemen, transportation caravans, retail shops, etc.).[35]

The same report continues with self-criticism for the "overreaction" and "harsh treatment" by the tax agents of the businesses owned by administrative units:

> [Our] lack of respect for the local party and administration needs to be criticized. It reflects our attitude toward public businesses owned by party and administrative units. From now on, all tax inspection on businesses run by public units must first obtain permission from higher direct authorities or permission from the central [tax] bureau.[36]

In order to stimulate more active involvement of service personnel and administrative staff in production, some incentives were also provided to individuals in the units. Contrary to the assumption that Communist ideology and practice forbade the existence of private interests in the revolutionary ranks, the experience of the guerrilla period actually indicates that during the production campaign private interests were not only allowed but encouraged, as manifested in the policies of "attending to private interest while taking care of public interests" (*gong si jian gu*) and "prioritizing public interests first and private interests secondarily" (*xian gong hou si*).[37] These two principles were even billed as "a revolution" in cadres' attitudes toward private interests.[38] In what was later known as the "Teng–Yang Plan,"[39] the leadership of the Taihang base area actually criticized those who "took the future perspectives of communism as reality, regarding accumulation through labor as economism (*jingjizhuyi*) and the manifestation of a rich peasant mentality."[40] The plan, issued in April 1943, provided that 70 percent of income from production surplus, after fulfilling quotas for purchase by the unit, could be retained by individuals, while the rest would go to the unit's collective fund.[41]

Encouraged by this plan, the livelihood of the army and administrative units of the Taihang base area was greatly improved. In the Red Army, 9,411 people had personal savings totaling 1.67 million yuan.[42] In Yan'an, the 359th Brigade, which to this day symbolizes the spirit of the Great Production Movement, actually encouraged soldiers to participate in production by allowing them to retain one-fifth of their income, if they borrowed public tools, or one-third, if they did not.[43] During the production campaign, one of the "production models" was Guo Jin, who had been the chief of the administrative affairs section of the CCP Northern Bureau's Party School. In 1942, Guo began farming some land near his unit. By 1944, he used his fifty-thousand-yuan savings as an investment to open a small restaurant, several shops employing thirty people, and a hat factory that hired twelve people. Eventually he made over a million yuan, half of which he gave to the unit. Guo, perhaps the first "millionaire" among the Communist ranks in history, became a first-class labor hero.[44]

"Minor Public" versus "Greater Public"

The significance of allowing, and indeed encouraging, army and administrative units to engage in economic activities lies not only in its practical utility for overcoming financial hardship and supply shortages but also in its implication as to how the Communists treated the concept of the "public," and their creation of a somewhat unique realm of "minor public."[45]

By creating a new type of economic entity, the Communist Party in effect created a realm of interest that was distinctive from both the public and private realms in their conventional sense. This was the realm of the *danwei* (unit) or *xiao gong* ("minor public," as it was called in the Yan'an era) interests. Although the *danwei* as an economic entity arguably finds its origins in the decentralized supply system in the army before the Yan'an period, the production campaign appears to have provided an economic incentive and legitimate opportunity for individual units to build up *jiawu*—collective assets.[46] In many concrete aspects, the demarcation between the "greater public" and the "minor public" was clear at that time. For example, by allowing units to have their own legitimate "family economy," the distinction between what belonged to the public or "greater public" (*da gong*) and to the unit was proscribed. Ren Bishi, a CCP Politburo member who was also in charge of finance and economy at the time, spoke of the relationship between the two in 1944:

> [We] must understand that only when these localities, minor public families *[xiao gongjia]*, and the masses achieve economic development can there be a great progress in conditions and bases for courses of the greater public family *[da gongjia]*. In order to guarantee that these localities and small public families strictly follow the rules and policies, we have to help them solve problems and overcome difficulties. We must help them in expanding production.[47]

As an indication of different treatments of the two realms, there were rules regarding "graft of public property" and "graft of unit property," both of which belonged to the category of corruption, and provided for the return of recovered funds and materials to central and unit coffers respectively, according to an official directive.[48]

However, what the authorities regarded as a clearly delineated boundary between the "greater public" and the "minor public" was not always clear in practice. Nor did it avoid the tendency for units to make and retain more profits than allowed by various means. From the very beginning, the attitude of the CCP leadership toward allowing units to engage in economic activities was ambiguous. On the one hand, it was a viable option to solve the problem of supply shortages. On the other hand, the Party was wary of the negative aspects linked to the policy such as the propensity for units to underreport production revenue and collective assets, the discrepancy between rich and poor units and the resentment it caused, and illicit means—including armed smuggling, tax evasion, and dumping—by which units tried to enrich themselves.[49] As indicated in several official documents, irregularities seem to have been a particular problem associated with unit economic activities along with increasingly strong economic stakes for units and individuals. For instance, although not categorized as "graft" per se, concealment by units (of what should be reported and turned over to the authorities, such as grain seized from the enemy and fines)[50] was a common irregularity and became a main target of Communist anticorruption campaigns in the base areas.[51] It was no coincidence that in the Shanxi-Hebei-Shandong-Henan base area, an anticorruption campaign was carried out concomitantly with the production drive in 1944. The June directive required all army, administrative, and educational units to launch a three- or four-month-long "confession campaign" to expose any corrupt behavior, otherwise at a later stage they would be subjected to exposure by others.[52] What made it more than an ordinary campaign was the fact that in this campaign not only were individuals required to confess or be exposed for wrongdoing, but units faced this requirement as well. In order to encourage people to expose corruption, an incentive was created: 20 percent of the amount recovered would be rewarded to informants.[53]

Mao himself admitted that "the economy of self-sufficiency now being developed by units of the army, government, and schools is a special product under special circumstances. It would be irrational and inconceivable to exist under other historical conditions."[54] Realizing both its necessity and problems, the Communist leadership swung between "unified" and "dispersed" management of revenue and supplies. In 1941, there was a short period of time when units were asked to turn over all revenues to the central authorities. Money and supplies would then be dispersed to them. However, only three months after this policy began, it was given up because of the inability of the central authorities to appropriate funds and supplies sufficiently and in a timely manner.[55] Later in 1947, the border region government again decided to require that all commercial operation–related assets be turned over to higher-level authorities. After some units followed the decision, they found themselves in a disadvantageous position compared with those who had not done so. Those who had no revenue-generating businesses left found that their living standard suffered because of insufficient supplies allocated from above.[56] Hence the Communist leadership was faced with a dilemma that has recurred throughout the history of the People's Republic: On the one hand, it needed units to rely on their own efforts to solve the problem of insufficient funding or supplies from central sources, especially when the economy was in bad shape; on the other hand, it was also aware of the problems that unit economic activities might create.

Ye Jizhuang, who was in charge of the supply work of the Eighth Route Army, wrote about deviant actions by army units that were related to the policies of self-reliance and economic activities:

> Due to residual departmentalism [*fensan zhuyi*], the phenomenon of underreporting income and overreporting expenditure and other kinds of concealment [*da mai fu*] could not be eliminated. Although these are not corrupt acts by individuals, there exists an erroneous belief that the illegal acts of under- or overreporting can be legal if the income is retained by *the minor public of a unit,* not by individuals *privately*. This is the main source of concealment.[57]

In an important speech made at a meeting of high-ranking officials in 1943, "On Economic and Financial Problems," Mao indicated how seriously he viewed the problem:

> [U]nits[58] of lower levels run their own show separately. There is less or no unified leadership, nor coordinated plans and orchestrated inspections from above on policy guidelines and work content. Thus individual units do not know what is allowed or pretend they do not. ... Economic units not only refuse to assist each other, they fight and obstruct each other. They cheat both superiors and subordinates. Concealment and forged reports occur. ... What is especially serious is graft and gambling among some cadres. Some cadres have become totally corrupted by material things. All these evil phenomena can be found among cadres in some army units, agencies, and schools to various degrees. From now on, the superiors of all army units, administrative agencies, and schools must take measures to make sure that the general interest is attended to and policies well grasped. They must enforce integrated plans and inspections for the production activities of work units. Behavior such as autonomy-seeking, each unit pursuing its own path, breaching laws and policies, in-fighting among units, graft and gambling among cadres are absolutely prohibited. ... This is what rectification in economic work is all about.[59]

Mao's speech, which was published in 1949, indicates that irregularities and cadre corruption had much to do with agency production activities, which in turn helped shape a key institution that has lasted even to this day—the *danwei*. It also indicates that the official attitude toward the so-called minor public interests was often ambiguous, particularly when irregularities and misconduct associated with them were common.

Clearly, the policy of self-reliance and production during this period laid a policy and institutional foundation for units to pursue their own tangible interests, legitimately or illicitly. It provided units with independent economic power. Indeed, there are compelling reasons to believe that the *danwei* first took shape as a meaningful entity that embodied vested interests in the Communist hierarchy during this period. To reiterate, economic activities by Communist army and government units were instrumental in overcoming financial difficulties and, at the same time, also provided incentives and conditions conducive to engaging these units in conduct that challenged central control or violated official rules. To wit, there were conflicts of interest between the "minor public" and the "greater public."

The Yan'an Legacy Revisited

To demonstrate that the public provision of essential supplies and "self-reliant production" activities by units during wartime helped shape the *danwei* system as it exists today, we must establish that there has been some continuity in such practices as agency production and building up assets of units. The following section shows that there has indeed been such a continuity throughout the years since the Communist takeover.

The impact of the Yan'an legacy in the Maoist era and today can be seen in at least two key ways herein: first, the tendency of *danwei* to maintain a somewhat independent fiscal power and to attend to collective self-interests under a centralized financial system; and second, the significance of the role of the *danwei* in improving the livelihood of its members, especially in economically difficult times. The first was never formally approved by the authorities, and indeed was often repressed. The second was either tolerated or encouraged by the authorities.

When the Communists finally won nationwide victory in 1949, China's economy was in deep crisis. A major task for the new government was to compensate for the fiscal shortage, overcome economic difficulties, and meet the needs of the country's quickly growing number of administrative personnel. Production activities by army and administrative units remained a major source for solving the budget problem. Both continued to "build up the minor public economy" for their own welfare under poor economic conditions. Businesses ranged from the legal (construction, small mills, and farming); to the illegal (retailing, money lending, and speculation). There was a clear separation of two kinds of public industrial enterprises: the state-owned enterprises (*guoying gongye*) and the publicly owned enterprises (*gongying gongye*). However, they were both promoted by the new government.[60] In the northeastern region, the *gongying gongye*, which included 792 economic entities run by administrative agencies involving 28,096 people, contributed ten percent of the total industrial output by the public sector in 1949.[61]

Legitimate business activities by public units were in fact promoted by Mao himself. In December 1949, soon after the establishment of the People's Republic, Mao personally drafted a party directive instructing People's Liberation Army (PLA) units to launch a new production campaign in order to reduce state expenditure and to improve living standards in the military.[62] Even after the Communists had won the civil war, Mao seemed to regard the economy as still under the "special conditions" he had spoken of some years earlier. Thus the *danwei* economy was still necessary. He did, however, caution against unwarranted kinds of business activities.

It appears that, in the beginning, because of "commercial and business activities including illegal speculation by government agencies, army units, and public schools in the name of production," it was very difficult for the government to regulate the market in general and control prices in particular at a time of high inflation and severe shortages. As early as April 1950, the new government issued a directive to prohibit state agencies and army units from engaging in commercial business (*shangye jingying*).[63] Besides posing a challenge to the state control of the economy, the new government perceived that the main problem associated with such commercial activities was corruption by individuals or units. Later on, even after all economic activities by state agencies were banned during the Three Anti* campaign in 1951–52, PLA units were still allowed to continue to operate some production and businesses such as farming and mining, which were not part of regular military logistics. The economic activity by military units witnessed another surge in 1967 after Mao issued his renowned "May Seventh Instruction," in which he re-embraced the image of the army as being both a "combat corps" and a "production corps."[64]

The new government recognized the irregularities agency production had caused in this regard. In a resolution issued by the Council of Administrative Affairs (Zhengwu yuan) ordering government agencies and administrative units to close down all their businesses, it was pointed out that,

> operated in the dispersed rural environment of the revolutionary war, agency production once had a positive impact on supporting our struggle and overcoming the difficulties in staff's daily lives. However, since the nation-wide victory, such needs have been gradually reduced. The fragmentation and lack of planning in agency production have put it in conflict with the centralization and planning of the national economy. The degenerating effects of the bourgeois mentality have led state agents to immerse themselves in profit seeking and pleasure seeking. It has caused serious corruption and waste. It is a *most pervasive problem* in the current Three Anti campaign that must be resolutely dealt with.[65]

The decision, issued on March 12, 1952, required that henceforth all agricultural, commercial, manufacturing, transportation, and construction businesses

---

*Anti-graft, anti-bribery, anti-squandering.

(including all real estate, investment, and cash assets) run by state agencies, PLA units, schools, and other not-for-profit organizations had to be turned over to the Commission on the Disposition of Agency Production, an ad-hoc commission set up by the government at various levels.[66] During this campaign, the criticism of "dispersionism," a synonym of "vested-interestism" or "departmentalism," sounded very similar to what Mao and others had spoken about during the Yan'an period. An internal instruction from the Central Committee to set the campaign in motion pointed to the practices of "concealment," "feeding the minor public by encroaching on the greater public," and "agency production."[67]

Ever since the 1950s, the maintenance of *danwei* "small coffers" (*xiao jinku*) through practices reminiscent of concealment during wartime—that is, underreporting of revenue or overreporting of budgetary needs—has been a constant challenge to the country's centralized financial system. "Small coffers" are secret accounts, in violation of official financial and budgetary regulations, kept by state agencies, enterprises, and other work units. The funds retained often were used to improve the welfare of unit employees.

We have reason to believe that throughout PRC history this phenomenon has never ceased to exist, even though the government has tried many times to crack down on the "actions violating fiscal and economic discipline" (*weifan caijing jilü*) by state *danwei*. For example, a 1954 report by the Ministry of Supervision (Jianchabu) revealed that some units kept a total of 20.8 million yuan of "black coffer" funds, in addition to unreported materials.[68] In 1963, one particular investigation by the Ministry of Supervision found that "small coffers" and "small storage" were common among some government units in Heilongjiang province.[69]

In the 1970s, the government began regular "general inspections of fiscal and taxation discipline." It became virtually an annual ritual—each year millions of yuan would be uncovered and millions more escaped such inspections, while the problem only kept getting worse. In 1985, when the newly founded State Audit Bureau first inspected 66,200 *danwei* nationwide, it found 10 billion yuan worth of problematic accounts, 76 percent of which was revenue illicitly retained by these units.[70] By 1990, however, it was estimated that of the 780 billion yuan "private" savings in banks, some 15 percent, or 120 billion yuan, might actually belong to *danwei*'s "small coffers."[71] These savings accounts were usually under the names of individuals, eluding regular control mechanisms. According to Ministry of Finance figures, such illicit funds "violating fiscal discipline" during annual nationwide general inspections between 1985 and 1990 totaled 66.4 billion yuan. This figure does not even include those undiscovered funds, estimated to be even more than those actually discovered.[72]

Like its predecessor in the Yan'an period, the *danwei* in the PRC has also been a major provider of a range of materials and consumer goods in addition to many services and welfare that are generally better known. This was true even after the free supply system ceased to exist in the mid-1950s. Because China followed the Soviet model of development, consumer goods were always in short supply during the Maoist period. The practice of units making efforts to barter, purchase, or directly produce some consumer goods in order to sell or distribute them free of charge to employees first became salient in the wake of the debacle caused by the Great Leap Forward in the late 1950s. In order to overcome grain, foodstuffs, and produce shortages, some government and other nonproduction units acquired land and other production materials free of charge from local villages to establish "food production bases" (*shipin jidi*)—that is, farms that could regularly grow vegetables or grain to supplement the needs of unit members in addition to their regular rations. As a matter of fact, in the beginning units were encouraged to do so.[73] It was also revealed that during this period 312 military and *central* government agencies acquired from Hebei province a total of 1.2 million *mu* of farmland for their own production purposes. Some units even asked for seeds, fertilizer, and labor, cost-free. Another investigation found that in four counties in Gansu province, 90 percent of county governmental agencies and schools acquired land from local villages to farm. Similar phenomena occurred in many provinces.[74] Although the practice by nonproduction units of taking land and other materials from villages was later banned, some evidence indicates that, as late as 1962, many units still had these in their possession.[75] In the early 1970s, when the Sino–Soviet conflict reached its peak and the CCP leadership feared the possibility of an all-out war, many government agencies and schools in Hebei province surrounding Beijing once again set up what were called "rear bases"—facilities in mountainous areas to which these units could retreat in case of an invasion or bombing attacks. By maintaining these "bases," units could also benefit materially from close ties with local villages.[76] Factories, on the other hand, would use some of their manufactured products or parts to barter for agricultural products with peasants, or for consumer goods with retail stores. Such practices would later constitute a widespread and continuing pattern throughout the 1960s and the 1970s. Although from time to time they would be criticized during crackdowns on "speculation, profiteering," and the "black market," the authorities did not specifically endorse or prohibit such practices unless they seriously affected consumer prices. During these years, for example, trucks owned by units were very useful not only for their production but also for livelihood purposes. Units that possessed them were able to transport produce from the countryside or goods from other cities. In a strange way, these trucks and the practice of supplementing employees' daily needs helped pierce the enclosed nature of the *danwei,* urban–rural segregation, and the iron grip of central planning—if there ever was one—by mobilizing goods across regions, urban–rural lines, and units while ignoring the provisions of central planning. It also has become a standard practice that when major holidays arise members of *danwei* would always expect that their unit would distribute some goods or food items at subsidized prices or free of charge. Despite the development of consumer product markets since the reforms began, many urban units still maintain similar practices.

Conclusion

The main purpose of this study is to trace the origins of the *danwei* system. Evidence presented here indicates that units took on some significant economic and welfare functions long before 1949. Admittedly, the *danwei* may also find its origins in other practices and institutions of different historical periods, as the chapters by Perry and Yeh in this volume indicate. This evidence suggests that a key component of the *danwei* system—that is, the economic and welfare functions of work units (especially administrative and other nonproduction units) are rooted in the practices and institutions of the Yan'an era. Although the control and political functions of the *danwei* are not discussed here, it is clear that the economic and welfare functions of work units in China find their origins in the practices of the Communist base areas during wartime. In particular, this chapter highlights two such practices: the free supply system and the official endorsed (indeed encouraged) economic activities of army and administrative units. It should not be a surprise to see today's military, government, and other nonproduction units engaging in operating profit-seeking *shiti* or economic entities or to find that many state-owned enterprises and government agencies still run their own "small societies" within the confines of brick walls.

Existing studies of the *danwei* system have focused on industrial and commercial enterprises. What has been lacking thus far is an analysis of the other kind of *danwei*—administrative and nonproduction units. Although studies of Chinese industrial enterprises and industrial relations offer telling insights into how the *danwei* system functions and inform us about human relations in contemporary China, a full picture requires more attention to noneconomic units. As studies of Soviet industries (including those by some authors in this volume) have shown, the Chinese factory shares many similarities with the Soviet enterprise. However, major differences between the Chinese and the Soviet systems in this regard may be indicated by the economic and social functions played by noneconomic units in China.

It is not the intention of this study to make a normative judgment on whether the *danwei* system—its functions, and the many practices the system has adopted—are beneficial for China's present and future development. The arguments can be made, for example, that the "minor public economy" was a necessary and healthy supplement to the economy under central planning, and that it was only logical for units to conceal real revenue and assets from the higher-level authorities. Suffice it to say that as an institution functioning in different environments, the *danwei* has rendered itself both instrumental and detrimental to the centralized political, economic, and social structures.

Notes

1. See, for example, Aleksandr Zinoviev, *The Reality of Communism* (New York: Schocken Books, 1984), 85–88. Zinoviev points out, "Communist society can be differ-

entiated in many respects, but in each one of them the cell (cellular structure) forms the basis. . . . It is in the cell that the citizens' standardized behavior is established."

2. For studies of the *danwei* published in English, see Gail Henderson and Myron Cohen, *The Chinese Hospital: A Socialist Work Unit* (New Haven: Yale University Press, 1984); Marc Blecher and Gordon White, *Micropolitics in Contemporary China: A Technical Unit During and After the Cultural Revolution* (Armonk, NY: M.E. Sharpe, 1979); Mayfair Yang, "Between State and Society: The Construction of Corporateness in a Chinese Socialist Factory," *Australian Journal of Chinese Affairs*, no. 22 (1989). Andrew Walder has significantly theorized about the authority relationships in industrial work units. See Walder, *Communist Neo-Traditionalism: Work and Authority in Chinese Industry* (Berkeley and Los Angeles: University of California Press, 1986). Brantly Womack, in a critique of Walder's neotraditionalism model, emphasizes the social functionality of the *danwei* and proposes a more general model of "work unit socialism." See Womack, "Transfigured Community: Neo-traditionalism and Work Unit Socialism," *China Quarterly*, no. 126 (July 1991): 313–32.

3. See, in particular, two studies by Chinese scholars published in English: Lu Feng, "The Origins and Formation of the Unit (Danwei) System," *Chinese Sociology and Anthropology*, 25, no. 3 (1993); Li Bin, "Danwei Culture as Urban Culture in Modern China: The Case of Beijing from 1949 to 1979," in *Urban Anthropology in China,* ed. Greg Guldin and Aiden Southall (Leiden and New York: E.J. Brill, 1993), 345–52.

4. Among students of comparative communism and China scholars, only limited attention has been paid to the wartime guerrilla institutions and practices in the Communist base areas and their impact in the post-1949, particularly post-Mao, period. Only a limited amount of the literature on the wartime Communist movement has presented a case for the impact of the Yan'an legacy on post-1949 development. Two notable exceptions are Peter Schran, *Guerrilla Economy* (Albany: State University of New York Press, 1976), and Mark Selden, *The Yenan Way in Revolutionary China* (Cambridge: Harvard University Press, 1971). This chapter focuses only on the origins of the *danwei,* even though many other legacies of this period remain in Chinese society today.

5. Caizheng kexue yanjiusuo, *Geming genjudi caizheng jingji* [Finance and economy in the revolutionary base areas] (Beijing: Zhongguo caizheng jingji chubanshe, 1985).

6. Lu Shichuan, "Shandong Kang Ri genjudi caizheng de chuangjian he fazhan" [The establishment and development of financial work in Shandong anti-Japanese base area], in *Caizhengbu Kang Ri genjudi de caizheng jingji* [Finance and economy of the anti-Japanese base areas] (Beijing: Zhongguo caizheng jingji chubanshe, 1987), 235–36.

7. Zhou Zhicheng and Wu Shaohai, *E Yu Wan geming genjudi caizhengzhi* [A gazetteer of finance in the E-Yu-Wan base areas] (Wuhan: Hubei renmin chubanshe, 1987), 77.

8. Ibid, 235.

9. Chen Junqi, *Yan'an shiqi caikuai gongzuo de huigu* [Recollections of the financial and accounting work in Yan'an] (Beijing: Zhongguo caizheng jingji chubanshe, 1987), 31.

10. *Kang Ri zhanzheng shiqi Shaan-Gan-Ning bianqu caizheng jingji shiliao xuanbian* (cited as *KZSGN*) [Selected historical materials of finance and economy during the anti-Japanese war in the Shaan-Gan-Ning border region] (Xi'an: Shaanxi renmin chubanshe, 1981), vol. 1, 149.

11. Fu Shangwen, "Jizhong Kang Ri genjudi caizheng jingji fazhan qing kuang" [The development of finance and economy in the central Hebei base area] in Caizhengbu, *Kang Ri genjudi de caizheng jingji,* 212.

12. See Mao Zedong, *Jingji yu caizheng wenti* [On economic and financial problems] (Hong Kong: Xinminzhu chubanshe, 1949), 98.

13. Ibid.

14. Zhongzhengzhibu, *Zhongguo renmin jiefangjun qunzhong gongzuoshi* [The history of mass work in the PLA] (Beijing: Jiefangjun chubanshe, 1989), 77. On the launching of the production campaign, see also Selden, *The Yenan Way*, 250–51.

15. Ibid., 78. The directive did warn that the army units should take a cautious approach to operating commercial businesses.

16. This popular Chinese phrase (*xiahai*) refers to individuals or units, usually non-business types, getting into business.

17. Economic activities by the Communists were not new in the Yan'an period. The public economy also contributed an important portion of revenue during the central Chinese soviet period in the early 1930s. However, at that time the public sector was run by the central government in the base area rather than by individual agencies or units. See Qiu Songqing, "Zhongyang suqu shangye lunshu" [On the commerce in the central soviet region], *Zhongguo shehui jingjishi yanjiu*, no. 4 (1987), 68–74.

18. Mao Zedong, *Jingji yu caizheng wenti*, 7.

19. Ibid., 101–2. Running these early public sector enterprises provided the Communists with some valuable experiences when they achieved national victory.

20. See Chen Junqi, *Yan'an shiqi caikuai gongzuo*, 58.

21. Mao Zedong, *Jingji yu caizheng wenti*, 152.

22. Ibid., 16.

23. Zhao Chaogou, *Mao Zedong xiansheng fangwen ji* [Meeting with Mr. Mao Zedong] (Wuhan: Changjiang wenyi chubanshe, 1990).

24. *Kang Ri zhanzheng shiqi Jin-Ji-Lu-Yu bianqu caizheng jingji shi ziliao xuanbian* (cited as *KZJLY*) [Materials relating to the financial and economic history of the Shanxi-Hebei-Shandong-Henan border region during the anti-Japanese war] (Beijing: Zhongguo caizheng jingji chubanshe, 1992), vol. 1, 1349.

25. See Zhu De, "Jianli geming jiawu" [Build up revolutionary family economy] (May 1, 1943), in Beijing junqu houqinbu, *Houqin gongzuo shiliao* [Historical materials on logistical work] (Beijing: Junshi xueyuan chubanshe, 1985), 184–86. For a detailed discussion of the result of the production movement, see Schran, *Guerrilla Economy*, chap. 6.

26. *KZSGN*, vol. 8.

27. Caizhengbu, *Kang-Ri genjudi de caizheng jingji*, 96; Xing Guang and Zhang Yang, *Kang Ri zhanzheng shiqi Shaan-Gan-Ning bianqu caizheng jingji shigao* [A brief history of finance and economy in the Shaan-Gan-Ning border region during the anti-Japanese war] (Xi'an: Xibei daxue chubanshe, 1988), 456.

28. Peter Schran used the phrase "institutional households." See Schran, *Guerrilla Economy*, 96, 102.

29. In late 1947, when the Communist authorities decided to request that all commercial-related collective assets be turned over to the "big public" (sic), one of the largest reported assets of most of the units was "feizao" (soap). From its value and other indicators, I suspect that this was a synonym for opium. Notably, a report about this centralization of unit commercial assets showed that all units under the auspices of the border region government both maintained opium in stock and had it commissioned for sale by trading companies which legally monopolized the trading of "soap." In the latter arrangement, the "soap" sold by the trading companies counted as revenues of units. See Xing Guang and Zhang Yang, *Jiefang zhanzheng shiqi Shaan-Gan-Ning bianqu caizheng jingji shi ziliao xuanbian* (cited as JFSGN) [Historical materials on finance and economy in the Shaan-Gan-Ning border region during the liberation war] (Xi'an: Sanqin chubanshe, 1989), 445–48. Chen Yung-fa has a detailed study of the opium trade in Yan'an. See Chen Yung-fa, "The Blooming Poppy Under the Red Sun," in *New Perspectives on the Chinese Communist Revolution*, ed. Tony Saich and Hans van de Ven (Armonk, NY: M.E. Sharpe, 1995).

30. Mao also pointed out the problem of giving too much attention to commercial business. See Mao, *Jingji yu caizheng wenti*, 160. According to the Rules on the Supply Work of the Eighth Route Army (1940), only army units above the regimental level could run shops or co-ops and engage in commercial activities. See Beijing junqu houqinbu, *Houqin gongzuo shiliao*, 51–52.

31. Mao Zedong, *Jingji yu caizheng wenti*, 176.

32. Chen Junqi, *Yan'an shiqi caikuai gongzuo*, 112–13; Shangyebu shangye jingji yanjiusuo, ed., *Geming genjudi shangye huiyilu* [Recollections of commerce in the revolutionary base areas] (Beijing: Zhongguo shangye chubanshe, 1984), 18.

33. The two companies, set up in 1942 in the form of limited liability incorporated firms (with shares only by units, not private individuals), were very important in the economic activities of the Communists in the Shaan-Gan-Ning border region for their role in external trade outside the base areas. In the beginning, not only did various units invest in the companies, but they also sent cadres to work for them. These two companies, with the mandate to "sell in large quantity" salts and "local products," especially "soap," grew to have some 400 personnel and dozens of branches by 1945. See *KZSGN*, vol. 4, 226–40; 416–19.

34. On the economic achievements of the production campaign, see Schran, *Guerrilla Economy*, chap. 6. Mark Selden also emphasized the purpose of cadre participation in manual labor as a way of organizational integration.

35. Caizhengbu, *Zhongguo geming genjudi gongshang shuishoushi changbian* [A comprehensive chronology of the history of industrial and commercial taxation in Chinese revolutionary base areas] (Beijing: Zhongguo caizheng jingji chubanshe, 1989), 68.

36. Ibid., 69–70.

37. These two principles were initially advanced, respectively, by Mao and Li Fuchun, who was the CCP's highest official in charge of financial and economic affairs at the time. See *KZJLY*, vol. 1, 1344.

38. See the directive on the production campaign from the CCP committee of the Taihang region and the political affairs department of the Taihang garrison, April 13, 1944, in *KZJLY*, vol. 1, 1355.

39. This was the "Plan for Production and Austerity by Mess Units," named after Teng Daiyuan, then chief of staff of the Front Command of the Eighth Route Army, and Yang Lizhi, deputy chief of staff.

40. *KZJLY*, vol. 1, 1344.

41. Ibid., 1345.

42. *Taihang geming genjudi shigao 1937–49* (cited as *THGSL*) [Historical materials on the Taihang base area] (Taiyuan: Shanxi renmin chubanshe, 1987), 212.

43. Mao Zedong, *Jingji yu caizheng wenti*, 128.

44. *THGSL*, 213–14.

45. The terms "greater public family" (*dagongjia*) and "minor public family" (*xiaogongjia*) and "greater public" (*dagong*) and "minor public" (*xiaogong*) were used during this period.

46. Mao indicated that as early as during the Jiangxi Soviet (1927–34) period, there were some manufacturing and retail businesses run by government agencies. Because the supply of grain and other basic necessities was abundant in Jiangxi, the need for self-production was less significant, however. See Mao Zedong, *Jingji yu caizheng wenti*, 98.

47. See *Ren Bishi xuanji* [Selected works of Ren Bishi] (Beijing: Renmin chubanshe, 1987), 328.

48. Ibid.

49. Xing and Zhang, "Kang Ri zhanzheng."

50. Note here that even during the guerrilla war period there were already instances of

impoundment of fines by agencies. See the discussion below on a similar phenomenon in the reform era.

51. Ibid.

52. *KZJLY*, vol. 1, 1475.

53. Ibid.

54. Mao Zedong, *Mao Zedong xuanji* [Selected works of Mao Zedong] (Beijing: Renmin chubanshe, 1953), 914.

55. Xing and Zhang, "Kang Ri zhansheng," 296–97.

56. *JFSGN*, vol. 3, 442–43.

57. *Balujun junzheng zazhi* [Journal of military and political affairs of the eighth route army] (November 1939). Emphasis added.

58. Mao used the word *danwei* here.

59. Mao Zedong, *Jingji yu caizheng wenti*, 160–61.

60. See Zhu Jianhua, *Dongbei jiefangqu caizheng jingji shigao* [A history of finance and economy of the northeast liberated region] (Harbin: Heilongjiang renmin chubanshe, 1987).

61. Ibid., 218.

62. Zhonggong zhongyang wenxian yanjiushi, ed., *Jianguo yilai zhongyao wenxian xuanbian* (*JNSH*) [Important documents since the founding of the nation] (Beijing: Zhongyang wenxian chubanshe, 1992), vol. 1, 67–69.

63. See the Council of Administrative Affairs directive on prohibiting commercial business by agencies and army units in ibid., 201–2.

64. Xu Guangyi, ed., *Dangdai Zhongguo jundui de houqin gongzuo* [The logistical work of the contemporary Chinese armed forces] (Beijing: Zhongguo shehui kexue chubanshe, 1990), 46–77. See also Qu Yizhi, "Lun zhonggong junban qiye wenti" (The problem of enterprises among the Chinese Communist military), *Zhonggong yanjiu*, 26, no. 12 (1992): 49–57. It is interesting to note that Mao became more fond of the tradition of military communism than in the Yan'an period when he regarded the self-sufficient mode of economy by units as a necessity of special circumstances. After the Great Leap Forward in 1958, Mao seemed to have regarded it as *the* mode of production that best suited the socialist ideology.

65. *Renmin shouce* [People's handbook] (Beijing: Da gong bao chubanshe, 1952), 57; emphasis added.

66. Ibid.

67. Guofang daxue, *Zhonggong dangshi jiaoxue cankao ziliao* (cited as *ZDJCZ*) [Reference materials for teaching and study of CCP history] (Beijing: Guofang daxue chubanshe, 1986), vol. 24, 193–94.

68. Zhou Jizhong, *Zhongguo xingzheng jiancha* [Administrative supervision in China] (Nanchang: Jiangxi renmin chubanshe, 1989), 615.

69. Zhang Xiangling, *Heilongjiang sishinian* [Forty years in Heilongjiang province] (Harbin: Heilongjiang renmin chubanshe, 1986), 334–35.

70. Zhao Ru'en, "Zhan gongjia pianyi zhifeng heyi bianji quanguo?" [Why did the trend of taking advantage of public funds spread nationwide?], *Zhongbao*, January 26, 1987.

71. *Zhongguo tongji xinxi bao* [Chinese journal of statistical information], August 1, 1991.

72. Jia Lusheng and Su Ya, *Heimao baimao: Zhongguo gaige xianzhuang toushi* [Black cat, white cat: Perspectives on current reforms in China] (Changsha: Hunan wenyi chubanshe, 1992), 280.

73. This is revealed in a self-criticism report by the Gansu Provincial CCP Committee to the CCP Central Committee. See *ZDJCZ*, vol. 23, 409.

74. Bo Yibo, *Ruogan zhongda juece yu shijian de huigu* [Recollections of some major decision making and events] (Beijing: Zhonggong zhongyang dangxiao chubanshe, 1993), vol. 2, 763–64.

75. As part of an effort to rectify illicit leveling, the government twice issued directives (in November 1960 and June 1961) requiring that all land and assets obtained from rural communes by government units be returned to the villages. See *ZDJCZ*, vol. 23, 373–74, 475–78. Deng Zihui, who was in charge of agricultural work for the Central Committee, revealed that some units failed to follow that order in a major policy statement about the communes on May 24, 1962. See *JNSH*, 707.

This also helps solve the puzzle Susan Shirk raised when she discussed the "mysterious" "creation of unitism" in the early 1960s. See Shirk, *Politics of Economic Reform of China* (Berkeley: University of California Press, 1993), 31 n 11. As my study shows, "unitism" was created long before then. Two factors may have facilitated its reemergence: the economic crisis and Mao's rekindled reverence for the "revolutionary traditions" of wartime in the late 1950s.

76. Author's interviews in Shijiazhuang, December 1993.

2

From Native Place to Workplace: Labor Origins and Outcomes of China's *Danwei* System

Elizabeth J. Perry

Identities based upon place have long been central to urban Chinese society and politics.[1] Unlike the European or American city-dweller, who meets a person for the first time with the questions "What's your name?" or "What do you do?" the more common query of a Chinese urbanite is "Where are you from?" (*Ni nali laide?*). The combination of a Confucian concern for social position with a rich tradition of urban sojourning[2] gave geographical location a special significance in the construction of Chinese urban identity. In imperial and Republican days, the answer to the question "Where are you from?" was usually a regional loca- tion: "I'm from Anhui province" (*Wo Anhuiren*) or "I'm from Shanghai" (*Wo Shanghairen*).[3] In Communist China, the same question remains the central one for identifying a stranger, but the answer has changed from a regional location to a work unit: "I'm from the Number 17 cotton mill" (*Wo di-17 shachang*) or "I'm from the Bank of China" (*Wo Zhongguo yinhang*).

How did this fundamental transformation in the basis of identity, from native place to workplace, occur and what are its implications for contemporary Chi- nese society and politics? Most social science interpretations of the work unit (*danwei*) in contemporary China highlight the role of the Communist party-state in imposing this new system and suggest that the *danwei* helped to create a quiescent, compliant populace—too dependent upon workplace handouts to un- dertake serious protest.

For some, workplace relations under communism are reminiscent of a much older feature of Chinese political culture: dependency in the face of authority.

An earlier dependence on fellow provincials (through the institution of native-place associations or guilds) gave way to a new reliance on workplace authorities. In Richard Solomon's infamous yet influential formulation, this dependency was linked to the essential "orality" of Chinese tradition.[4] In Andrew Walder's very different model of *neo*traditionalism, it is the new Communist system that renders workers economically and socially dependent on their enterprise, politically dependent on factory management, and personally dependent on their workplace supervisors.[5] Gail Henderson and Myron Cohen summarize the prevailing wisdom in their book, *Chinese Hospital: A Socialist Work Unit*: "Overall, it appears that the structural characteristics of the unit system reinforce the traditional dependent modes of interaction."[6]

But the political culture of so-called traditional China was, of course, extremely diverse and full of contradictions. If one strain emphasized dependence on authority, other strains encouraged resistance to domination.[7] Here I propose that the *danwei* system may be better understood as the outcome of a heritage of protest—specifically labor conflict—rather than as the product of a simple Leninist imposition from above or, still less, as the reflection of any alleged cultural propensity toward an unquestioning obedience to authority. I further suggest that the implementation of the *danwei* system itself, instead of signaling the end of the Chinese labor movement, has helped to generate an impressive record of labor unrest under the People's Republic. The politics of place remain important in China—and just as native-place identities structured much of the labor strife of the pre-Communist era, so workplace identities have shaped much of the unrest of the post-1949 period.

Studies of labor, not only in China but throughout the world, have been dominated by the search for "class." It is generally assumed (à la Marx and Engels) that workers become politically significant only when they shed "feudal" identities based upon ethnic origin, guilds, or patron–client relations in favor of a "modern" class consciousness. This obsession with class has led us to overlook or dismiss the importance of other forms of organization and identity. Yet there is little doubt that the most influential strikes in Chinese history—the May Fourth and May Thirtieth movements, for example—were not generated by class consciousness. Organized by regional gangs, guilds, and native-place associations, workers joined other urbanites to protest as "citizens" or "consumers" rather than as members of a working "class."[8] Native-place origin was a principal basis of labor recruitment and labor activism in Republican China, but it did not foreclose the possibility of participating in large-scale collective actions that altered the course of modern Chinese history.

The imposition of the household registration (*hukou*) system in the 1950s severely curtailed geographic mobility and reduced accordingly the salience of native-place identity in urban China.[9] Yet, Maoist rhetoric notwithstanding, class did not suddenly become the unrivaled basis of identity and action. Place-based divisions of rural and urban residence (*nongcun hukou* versus *chengzhen hukou*)

or collective sector employment versus a job in a state-owned work unit constituted equally significant socioeconomic distinctions in Maoist China.[10] To be
labeled a "class" enemy often meant in practice to lose one's place on the state
payroll and to be forced to relocate, with one's family, to a poor rural area.[11]

The *danwei* system did not incorporate all Chinese, or even all Chinese urbanites or all Chinese industrial workers; instead, it privileged a minority of the
urban industrial work force (those employed at large state-owned enterprises) at
the expense of the majority.[12] It created a gulf between the haves and have-nots
of Chinese socialism that has fueled major strike waves in every decade of
China's history since 1949. It is hardly the case that *danwei*-induced dependency stifled labor protest in Communist China. Alongside each of the famous
movements by dissident intellectuals that have punctuated the history of the
People's Republic of China (PRC) have occurred strike waves by workers in
which the issue of the *danwei* has figured prominently.[13] This was true for the
Hundred Flowers campaign, the Cultural Revolution, Democracy Wall, and the
Tiananmen uprising.[14] In the Maoist era, contract and temporary workers, apprentices, and others shut out of the privileges bestowed by *danwei* membership
protested to demand access. In the post-Mao era, permanent workers at state-
owned enterprises have struggled to hold on to their prerogatives in the face of
new market reforms that threaten the integrity of the *danwei* system itself.

The Labor Origins of the *Danwei*

I have argued elsewhere that the backbone of Shanghai's Communist labor
movement from the 1920s through the 1940s was composed of skilled workers.[15]
Coming out of an artisan guild tradition based on native-place associations, these
skilled workers put a high premium on security and welfare. When the PRC
developed its new system of industrial relations in the early 1950s, the officials
in charge of labor policy (of which the *danwei* became the centerpiece) were
virtually all former leaders of the Communist labor movement in Shanghai: Liu
Shaoqi, Chen Yun, and Li Lisan being the most prominent among them. It was
these individuals who formulated policies that turned state enterprises into institutions remarkably reminiscent of the artisan's native-place guild: One needed an
introduction to join these exclusive organizations, which offered lifetime benefits
to their privileged members.[16]

By way of historical background, it is important to note that a quarter of a
century before the founding of the PRC, Chen Yun, Li Lisan, and Liu Shaoqi had
worked closely together in the Shanghai labor movement. During the May Thirtieth movement of 1925, Li Lisan chaired the Shanghai General Labor Union of
which Liu Shaoqi was general manager; Chen Yun, a skilled worker at
Shanghai's Commercial Press, played a key role in the printers' union—the first
to enlist under the banner of Li and Liu's general union. (These leaders were
joined the following year by Zhou Enlai, sent to Shanghai to help direct the

historic three armed uprisings of 1926–27.)[17] The experience of collaborating on labor issues thus predated the establishment of the PRC by some twenty-five years.

The labor policies that institutionalized the *danwei* system in the early 1950s were authored largely by Li Lisan. On one level, this is not terribly surprising inasmuch as the securities provided to workers at state-owned *danwei* in the 1950s are remarkably similar to those promised to workers who joined the Shanghai General Labor Union under Li's chairmanship back in the 1920s. But Li Lisan, of course, endured a rather checkered career in the Chinese Communist movement. Endowed with a fiery temperament and flamboyant personality, Li often found himself in trouble with the party hierarchy. A tall, heavy-set man, he traveled around Shanghai in the mid-1920s by limousine, surrounded by body-guards of similarly imposing stature. Among those impressed by Li's proletarian prowess was a bathhouse owner and Green Gang master who convinced Li to become his disciple. These ties to the world of organized crime were important in gaining allies for the fledgling labor movement, but they also aroused suspicion about Li Lisan's character. Later, in 1930 Li Lisan was severely criticized for a policy of political strikes and worker insurrections that came to be known in official party historiography as the "leftist error in line of Li Lisan."[18] For fifteen years thereafter, Li took refuge in the Soviet Union. But in 1946 he returned to China to meet in Manchuria with his old colleague Chen Yun, who briefed him on what he had missed and invited him to resume a leading role in the labor movement.[19]

With the establishment in 1949 of the PRC, Li Lisan was charged with primary responsibility for formulating labor policy. As both acting head of the All-China Federation of Trade Unions and minister of labor in the new People's Republic, Li—after consulting with his old comrades Liu Shaoqi, Chen Yun, and Zhou Enlai—wrote the new labor union law (promulgated in June 1950), which gave critical welfare functions to the unions.[20] More important, he penned labor insurance regulations (passed in February 1951) stipulating that these new welfare provisions were to include generous medical care, disability pay, retirement pensions, and the like.[21] These labor insurance regulations (*laodong baoxian tiaoli*; known colloquially as *laobao*) were a defining element of the emerging *danwei*. As Joyce Kallgren argued in her early studies on industrial welfare, these regulations were key to the development of the state enterprise as a welfare institution—an entity that replaced the family or native-place association in providing basic securities to workers.[22] Initially, banks were explicitly excluded from these new regulations (on grounds that their employees were already quite well off), but banks were added five years later, when the insurance regulations were broadened to cover commercial as well as industrial work units.[23]

Li Lisan was also responsible for some sixty-eight other sets of laws and regulations concerning enterprise management.[24] But it was not long before his independent style got him into political trouble again; at the end of 1951, Li was forced out of union work—charged with economism and syndicalism (*jingjizhuyi* and *gongtuanzhuyi*) and accused of having favored allocation (*fenpei*) over production (*shengchan*). Still Li continued his work as minister of labor and, along with Chen Yun, took charge of establishing the wage system in 1954 and the system of party committee management in factories (to replace the Soviet model of one-man management) in 1956.[25] The Cultural Revolution was not a happy time for Li Lisan. The Red Guards delighted in uncovering incriminating evidence of his past exploits; finally, in June 1967, Li committed suicide with an overdose of sleeping pills.[26]

The other principal architect of China's industrial policy, former Commercial Press activist Chen Yun, outlived the Cultural Revolution. As is well known, Chen was an adamant proponent for maintaining aspects of the socialist industrial structure (his famous "bird in the cage" metaphor) in the process of the post-Mao market reforms.[27] True to his own background as a skilled worker, Chen Yun remained loyal to the interests of factory artisans. His concern for providing special welfare benefits to a subset of the industrial work force was made manifest in December 1949, when Chen delivered an important speech entitled "Skilled Personnel Are an Indispensable Force in Implementing National Industrialization." Noting that China's skilled workers numbered only 300,000 people, out of an industrial work force of some 3 million, Chen referred to them as a "national treasure" (*guobao*) deserving special material benefits that would guarantee freedom from financial worries.[28] Development of state enterprises, which offered generous cradle-to-grave welfare provisions to their privileged employees, figured prominently in his plan for battling rampant unemployment and inflation in the early years of the PRC.[29]

That the Chinese Communist system of industrial relations was not simply a wholesale importation from the Soviet Union is further suggested by the role that even former Guomindang (GMD) labor leaders played in its development.[30] Zhu Xuefan, a lieutenant of Green Gang chieftain Du Yuesheng who assumed major responsibilities for labor organizing under the GMD, became an important policy adviser to the Communists as well. In October 1948, Zhu's views on urban industry were solicited. In March and April 1949, he offered his ideas on industrial policy and labor–capital relations at high-level meetings in Beijing. That October, Zhu Xuefan was named first minister of post and communications under the PRC. From the founding of the People's Republic until the onset of the Cultural Revolution, the former postal unionist divided his time between running the Ministry of Post and Communications and helping to manage the All-China Federation of Trade Unions.[31]

The links between the pre-1949 labor movement and the Communist *danwei* system are not only personal but also institutional. In each province and city, the special prerogatives of workers at state factories were overseen by the local federation of labor unions, an arm of the state charged with responsibility for workers' welfare. These unions have been dominated by former activists in the

Communist labor movement.[32] (In the case of Shanghai, the municipal trade union was initially chaired by Liu Changsheng—leader of the Communist underground labor movement in Shanghai from the autumn of 1937; he was later succeeded by Zhang Qi, a former silk weaver who had been active in the Communist movement in the city since the early 1930s.) Although the welfare measures supplied by the *danwei* are financed by the enterprise itself, they are administered through the unions.[33]

The history of the labor movement was far from irrelevant to the consolidation of this new system of trade unions. A memoir concerning union organizing in Shanghai just after the establishment of the PRC makes this clear:

> In newly liberated Shanghai, union-work personnel were dispatched to all the factories to organize unions. Historically, all sorts of people had brandished union signboards to agitate among the workers, so when our cadres went to mobilize them some of the older workers asked frankly: "What sort of union are you organizing, anyway?" The union cadres replied that they were organizing a union of the working class itself. The older workers insisted, "We've seen many that claimed to be the workers' own unions, but they didn't let the workers run things. Only Li Lisan's union was truly our own union, but that was more than twenty years ago." The cadres told them, "Li Lisan is currently vice-chair of the All-China Federation of Trade Unions. Our union is under his leadership." When the workers heard this, they happily joined the union organization.[34]

Hagiographic though this account may be, it suggests how the new regime worked actively to keep alive memories of the pre-1949 labor movement. Just four days after the Communist takeover of Shanghai in May 1949, a workers' congress to commemorate the twenty-fourth anniversary of the May Thirtieth movement was convened. Longtime labor movement activist Liu Changsheng presided over the convocation of more than 2,300 representatives from all industries and trades in the city. He was joined by other former leaders of the underground Communist labor movement who now returned in glory from their exile in the countryside. It was at this meeting that a provisional committee for the new Shanghai Federation of Trade Unions was formed and major efforts to establish a new system of union organizations were undertaken. Some 103 work teams were dispatched to factories throughout the city to help establish unions. In enterprises where the Communist-led labor movement had a firm foundation from the 1940s, pre-existing underground organizations (e.g., *renmin bao'andui* or *huchangdui*—people's security teams or factory protection teams) served as the nuclei of the new unions. In other cases, workers' representative congresses were convened to recruit union leaders.[35] Four months later, the city of Shanghai boasted more than 980 new unions with an enrolled membership of some 667,900 workers.[36]

In preparing to launch the Three Anti and Five Anti campaigns and other elements of the so-called democratic reform movement of the early 1950s, union leaders encouraged workers to "speak bitterness" about past labor struggles. For example, at Shanghai's Shenxin Number 9 factory, where a bloody strike had occurred on February 2, 1948, the union called together the workers in 1952 to remember their earlier battle and convert their anger over the disappointing strike settlement into a firm commitment to the new socialist reforms.[37] Soon thereafter the factory was renamed the Shanghai Number 22 cotton mill in commemoration of this February 2 strike.[38] Similarly, at the Huasheng electronics plant the first step in converting to joint ownership in 1953 was a mass meeting to recall a failed strike of twenty years before. In contrast to the 1933 strike, which had been brutally suppressed by hired thugs, the new union counterposed its own success in implementing the labor insurance regulations that provided retirement pensions, clinic, nursery, bathhouse, and cafeteria to all permanent employees at the enterprise.[39] Memories of the labor movement thus remained important and were consciously fostered—albeit within prescribed limits—by the new Communist regime.

Unionization proceeded rapidly in the early years of the PRC. By February 1950, 70 percent of the permanent industrial work force (the figure was 90 percent for Shanghai) had been unionized.[40] But it is important to remember that permanent workers were a minority of the industrial labor force; a substantial segment of the work force was being systematically excluded from these favorable arrangements. Throughout the transition period, reports and regulations proliferated with respect to the plight of temporary and contract workers and the unemployed. In June 1949, for example, a work report of the Shanghai Light Industry Department noted, "There is no definite time schedule by which temporary workers can become permanent workers; as a result, workers are raising many complaints."[41]

Labor Protest in the PRC

The complaints of those barred from the benefits of workplace socialism grew especially vociferous whenever political circumstances permitted. In 1956–57, as the institutionalization of the *danwei* system was completed in the socialist transformation of industry, a strike wave of monumental proportions swept Chinese cities. When Chairman Mao called upon the masses to criticize "bureaucratism" as part of the Hundred Flowers campaign, workers responded with unexpected zeal. In the six months from the fall of 1956 to the spring of 1957, party Central acknowledged that more than 10,000 strikes had occurred nationwide.[42] And over the next three months, China's industrial capital of Shanghai was engulfed in an outpouring of strikes, slowdowns, and public demonstrations. Labor disturbances erupted at 587 Shanghai enterprises in the spring of 1957, involving nearly 30,000 workers.[43] These figures are extraordinary, even by comparison with the Republican period. (In 1919, Shanghai experienced only 56 strikes, 33 of which were in conjunction with the May Fourth movement. In 1925, Shanghai

saw 175 strikes, 100 of which were connected to the May Thirtieth movement.[44])
The strike wave of 1956–57 was spearheaded by those left out of the new
danwei system: temporary and contract workers, workers at small joint-owner-
ship firms, apprentices, and displaced workers. Stripped of many of the welfare
measures they had enjoyed under private ownership, yet denied the privileges
that came with permanent employment at large state enterprises, such workers
felt particularly disadvantaged by the industrial reforms of the mid-1950s. They
formed autonomous associations ("united command posts," "redress grievances
societies") to demand—unsuccessfully as it turned out—the same securities of
employment and welfare guaranteed to permanent workers at state-owned enterprises in the regulations penned by Li Lisan. When Li's successor as head of the
All-China Federation of Trade Unions, Lai Ruoyu, pointed out that divisions
created by socialism were at the heart of the labor unrest in 1956–57, he too was
accused of the error of "syndicalism" and was quickly removed from office.[45]

Still worker dissatisfaction continued—and erupted a decade later at the outset of the Cultural Revolution. When Chairman Mao called upon the masses to
combat "revisionism," tensions within the work force again burst into flames.
Thousands of contract and temporary workers took to the streets to demand a
redress of grievances,[46] creating a so-called wind of economism (*jingjizhuyi
feng*) that was soon denounced by the regime. The cries of these downtrodden
members of the Chinese work force introduced a socioeconomic note to the
otherwise relentlessly political discourse of the Cultural Revolution. As an eye-
witness to the inaugural ceremonies of Wang Hongwen's Workers' General
Headquarters remembered the distinctive contribution of the temporary workers
to the convocation:

> Those up on the platform were criticizing the capitalist reactionary line of
> the SPC [State Planning Commission], but down below the platform were a
> group of women workers between thirty and forty years of age wearing tat-
> tered work clothes and hats. These women didn't look like factory workers,
> but like temporary workers who pulled carts. They weren't paying any atten-
> tion to the speeches on the platform, but periodically shouted out, "We want to
> become permanent workers!" "We want a pay raise!"[47]

Although Jiang Qing initially took the side of these underprivileged workers,
she quickly recanted—convinced that it would be impractical for the Chinese
state to guarantee equal treatment for those who had been shut out of the benefits
of socialism. The independent organizations set up by these workers to further
their own interests (e.g., the League of Red Rebels for temporary and contract
workers in Shanghai) were now declared illegal and repressive police force was
brought to bear against them.[48]

The wind of economism pointed the finger of blame at the many flagrant injustices inherent in the operations of China's command economy. In this respect, it
represented a much more fundamental criticism of the socialist system than did

Wang Hongwen's rebel movement. But after Chairman Mao personally intervened to declare Wang's rebels the exemplary mass organization, it was clear that the Cultural Revolution would not bring about a serious restructuring of industrial relations in China.[49]

Still labor unrest continued to erupt in the 1970s, 1980s, and the 1990s. On all these occasions, the *danwei* figured as a central issue. Given the opportunity to voice their complaints about being denied *danwei* entitlements, disadvantaged workers did so with vehemence. But even permanent state workers were not immune to protest, as the unfolding of the Cultural Revolution demonstrated. Aware of their privileged position at the apex of the labor pecking order in Maoist China, such workers were admittedly less inclined to raise *economic* demands. Yet *political* protest was well within the bounds of possibility, and, in their case, socialist work units themselves provided a ready organizational resource. For example, in the April Fifth movement of 1976—when more than a million mourners streamed to Tiananmen Square to pay homage to recently deceased Premier Zhou Enlai and vent dissatisfaction with the radical excesses of the Cultural Revolution—it was work units that structured the mass action. Sebastian Heilmann reports:

> In Beijing, up to two thousand danwei laid wreaths on Tiananmen Square. In Nanjing, more than a thousand work units are said to have been involved. . . . *danwei* delegations were the characteristic form of marches in all regional incidents of the April Fifth Movement. In big factories, the actions were planned primarily on the workshop or department level and then made known in the entire factory.[50]

The spectacle of workers marching toward Tiananmen Square behind banners emblazoned with the names of their work units was thus not an unprecedented phenomenon in 1989. Nevertheless, the context changed dramatically as a result of the post-Mao reforms. In 1989, state enterprise employees—who apparently comprised the bulk of the worker protesters at Tiananmen—sought to cling to securities that were being challenged by the new industrial policies. The Beijing Workers' Autonomous Federation (Gongzilian), whose members were required "to show proof of employment at a Beijing work unit," saw Deng Xiaoping's reform era as replete with "economic mismanagement and official duplicity, during which workers gained little. . . ."[51] As beneficiaries of the *danwei* system, these protesters hoped to halt the demolition of the industrial order put in place under the socialist transformation of the mid-1950s.

Despite the draconian repression of the Tiananmen incident in 1989 and its aftermath, labor unrest has continued apace. A confidential report of the All-China Federation of Trade Unions estimated that more than 50,000 Chinese workers engaged in strikes or other protests in the two years following June 1989 "to air grievances over the socialist system's failure to meet their basic needs."

No sector of the industrial economy was spared, but state enterprises were the hardest hit, according to the report.[52]

A new bankruptcy law allowing for the dissolution of unprofitable state enterprises struck at the very heart of the *danwei* system and generated considerable resistance from China's formerly protected state employees. For example, the Chongqing Knitting Factory, which employed nearly 3,000 workers, announced in November 1992 that it was declaring bankruptcy and that its workers would have to seek alternative employment on their own. Moreover, retired workers were to be reduced to monthly stipends of only 50 yuan—in contrast to their original levels of 150 to 250 yuan. To protest these injustices, a petition movement was launched. In taking to the streets, workers manifested a fascinating blend of "old" and "new" styles of protest:

> The retired workers who led the demonstration procession knelt down before the armed policemen, pleading tearfully that they only wanted to lodge a petition to be able to receive their original pensions and only hoped for the right of subsistence. . . .
> The retired workers said that the pensions represented the work accumulation they had made in the past decades and belonged to part of the surplus value they had created. . . . Workers on the job said: We just worked according to orders, and business losses were caused by mistakes in the economic plan for guiding production; the blame should not be placed on the workers.[53]

While claims based on production of "surplus value" and "mistakes in the economic plan" reflected obvious Communist influence, the act of kneeling to present one's petition to the government authorities drew from a much older protest repertoire.[54] The combination of "politically correct" rhetoric with a deferential style of behavior dating back to imperial days proved remarkably effective:

> The workers' reasonable requirements and their rational actions have aroused extensive sympathy. . . . Finally, the authorities in Chongqing were forced to revise the original decision: Pensions for retired workers will remain unchanged; workers at and above 35 years of age will be assigned to new jobs; and workers below 35 years of age will receive vocational training and will receive wages and allowances during the period of retraining.[55]

As state employees lose the securities once guaranteed by their *danwei*, their resistance increasingly takes on overtones of a "moral economy" rebellion to protest the breach of state patronage and to demand family subsistence.[56] The recent unrest has captured the attention of the international business community. *Business Week* records that:

> In March, there were 270 strikes in Liaoning, Shaanxi, and Sichuan provinces, several lasting as long as 40 days and involving 10,000 workers. In Tianjin last fall, laid-off workers marched on a state-run factory, carrying signs asking: "How can we feed our children?"[57]

Similarly, the Hong Kong press reports that:

> Not long ago there was a major disturbance in Heilongjiang province involving 100,000 employees of state-owned enterprises taking to the streets in protest. They demanded subsistence and food to eat; one group of workers committed collective suicide in protest to the authorities. . . . The difficulties of China's workers mean the possibility of the emergence of independent trade unions. According to internal CCP [Chinese Communist Party] sources, underground unions have appeared in some areas where state-owned enterprises are concentrated.[58]

If state workers are turning to autonomous unions to replace the increasingly ineffective official trade unions, among nonstate workers more "traditional" forms of place-based organization are emerging. The mobility of the work force under the post-Mao reforms has apparently stimulated a return of patterns of labor mobilization that long predate the Communist era. In the special economic zone of Shenzhen, for example:

> The number of people coming to Shenzhen from other places has been growing daily in recent years. At the moment, temporary workers number more than 1.2 million, more than twice the permanent population of Shenzhen.
> It was learned that workers from outside have formed *"regional gangs"* which often create disturbances and could become a factor of social instability in the long run. For instance, 15 strikes took place in Longgang Town in Shenzhen, with eight of them instigated by Sichuan workers, three by Guangxi workers, two by workers south of the Chang Jiang and two by Hunan workers [emphasis added].[59]

The recent upsurge in urban sojourning has seen a commensurate resurgence of labor protest based upon native-place identity and organization.

It is sometimes suggested that migrant workers in China, like their counterparts in Latin America, are unlikely to engage in collective protest. As Lynn White puts it, "New arrivals to big cities from rural areas tend to reproduce their conservative form of community within, but politically separate from, their metropolitan environments."[60] However, China is not Mexico. The fact that contemporary China is heir to a rich tradition of urban sojourning imbues its migrant workers with organizational know-how (in the form of regional gangs, native-place associations, and the like) that may render them more likely to undertake collective action than would otherwise be the case. The further fact that temporary and contract labor is not a new feature of the post-Mao era, but was an integral part of the industrial structure instituted in the 1950s, also contributes to the political savvy of China's migrant workers. Their activism during the Hundred Flowers campaign and the Cultural Revolution is ample testimony to the protest potential of this downtrodden segment of the work force.

Although the Maoist era created certain divisions within the labor force that may have inhibited working-class cohesion, this fragmentation did not preclude the possibility of worker protest. Moreover, the intense class-struggle rhetoric of the Cultural Revolution gave all workers, even those most disadvantaged by the *danwei* system, a powerful vocabulary for articulating their grievances. The lingering impact of the Cultural Revolution experience on styles of collective action in China has yet to be fully understood or appreciated, but it is undoubtedly significant. The language of class exploitation and class conflict that permeated the political battles of that period[61] remains a potent weapon in the contemporary initiatives of state and nonstate workers alike.

The founding manifesto issued by the Beijing Workers' Autonomous Federation in the spring of 1989 shows that state workers were well schooled in the art of class rhetoric:

> We have carefully considered the exploitation of the workers. Marx's *Das Kapital* provided us with a method for understanding the character of our oppression. We deducted from the total value of output the workers' wages, welfare, medical welfare, the necessary social fund, equipment depreciation and reinvestment expenses. Surprisingly, we discovered that the "civil servants" swallow all the remaining value produced by the people's blood and sweat! The total taken by them is really vast! How cruel! How typically Chinese! These bureaucrats use the people's hard earned money to build luxury villas all over the country (guarded by soldiers in so-called military areas), to buy luxury cars, to travel to foreign countries on so-called study tours (with their families and even baby sitters)! Their immoral and shameful deeds and crimes are too numerous to mention here.[62]

But privileged *danwei* employees, such as those who comprised the membership of the Gongzilian, were not the only claimants to the Cultural Revolution legacy. In the summer of 1992 an informal group of Beijing street sweepers put up big-character posters calling for a general strike, which showed that even the humblest of China's workers had absorbed some lessons from decades of Communist discourse on exploitation and class struggle:

> We are the masters of society. The honchos depend on our hard work to stay alive, but all they show us is their butt ugly scowling faces. They take all the credit and the rewards and the biggest pay envelopes, while we workers get paid less. We are the ones sweeping the streets and cleaning up the city. Where do the honchos get off acting like lords?
> We say to our fellow workers, comrades-in-arms, brothers and sisters throughout the city: We cannot put up with this any longer. We are people, too. We cannot be mistreated by these honchos. All of the workers and staff at Eastern District Sanitation Team No. 1 are uniting to recover the money that those *blood suckers and parasites* have taken from us workers. We are taking back whatever has been embezzled from us. We are going to show those honchos that the working class is not to be trifled with, that *the working class is the master of society*, that it is a class with lofty ideals. We are going to make every social class and every prominent person sit up and take notice of

the ones with the lowest social position, the ones everyone looks down upon, the ones everyone regards as smelly; the sanitation workers who sweep the streets!

Officials are so cocky and proud. They go everywhere in cars, and bark out what they want to eat, like chicken, duck, fish, squid rolls, swallow's nest soup. . . . The gnawed bones they throw out are the compensation that we, the working class, get. In today's socialist society, can we the working class allow them to treat us this way? [emphasis added][63]

Sarcastic as the tone of these documents may be, they nonetheless demonstrate that workers have acquired a considerable stockpile of analytical ammunition from their Communist educators. Thus, although the form of recently emergent labor organizations (regional gangs and the like) may seem remarkably reminiscent of pre-1949 exemplars, it is entirely possible that the mentality of Chinese workers has been substantially transformed by the Communist experience. Whether this will mean the supersession of a politics of place by a politics of class remains to be seen.

Conclusion

The Communist labor movement of the 1920s–40s, which helped to give rise to the *danwei* system imposed in the 1950s, was largely a movement of skilled artisans—the aristocracy of labor, if you will. Little wonder, then, that the new system they helped to create in the People's Republic looked a good deal like the artisan guilds of earlier days. In both cases, the construction of an identity of place involved the exclusion of a large segment of the working class. Just as membership in a guild of Wuxi boilermakers marked one as privileged vis-à-vis the excluded "other" worker from Subei, so regular employment at the Shanghai diesel engine plant separates one from the unlucky "other" temporary and contract laborer who enjoys none of the perquisites of *laobao* protection.

Of course China is not alone in privileging some members of its urban industrial work force at the expense of others. As Andrew Gordon describes the development of Japan's famous "enterprise society," it too involved the exclusion within the large factories of "millions of women (and some men) designated 'temporary employees' in the 1950s and 1960s and 'part-time' workers since the 1970s."[64] Yet much of our scholarship on industrial relations has taken institutions such as the Maoist *danwei* or the postwar Japanese "enterprise society" as representative of these countries as a whole, with little more than a passing glance toward the excluded majority of the work force. This is a limited vantage point from which to analyze either the origins or the outcomes of East Asian labor relations.

Anathema as the politics of place may seem to adherents of a class-based model of industrial development, it nonetheless helps explain the recent history of Chinese labor. Whether organized by native place or workplace, labor has not been condemned to political passivity. In neither case has the alleged Chinese culture of dependency proved powerful enough to act as an effective deterrent to popular resistance. China's politics of place has also been a politics of protest.

Notes

1. This chapter was first delivered as an oral presentation at a symposium on the Chinese work unit, sponsored by the Center for Chinese Studies of the University of California at Berkeley (April 30, 1994). Participants in that symposium offered many helpful comments. Subsequently it was presented as a written paper at a conference at Harvard University in the fall of 1994. I would like to thank participants at that conference for their suggestions; Andrew Walder's astute critique (albeit delivered in absentia) was especially helpful. Even more critical to the completion of this chapter was the invaluable research assistance of Douglas Stiffler and Robyn Eckhardt.

2. On the tradition of urban sojourning in China, see G. William Skinner, ed., *The City in Late Imperial China* (Stanford: Stanford University Press, 1977), 538–46; and Frederic Wakeman, Jr., and Yeh Wen-hsin, eds., *Shanghai Sojourners* (Berkeley: University of California, Institute of East Asian Studies, 1992), introduction.

3. As William Rowe notes in his study of Hankou, "Geographically determined subethnic distinctions . . . constituted the most important distinguishing feature between individual Chinese in the late imperial period" (*Hankow: Commerce and Society in a Chinese City, 1796–1889* [Stanford: Stanford University Press, 1984], 213).

4. Richard H. Solomon, *Mao's Revolution and Chinese Political Culture* (Berkeley: University of California Press, 1971).

5. Andrew G. Walder, *Communist Neo-Traditionalism: Work and Authority in Chinese Industry* (Berkeley: University of California Press, 1986). For a critique of Walder's work that proposes the term "work unit socialism" as a substitute for the "neotraditionalism" of Walder (following Ken Jowitt), see Brantly Womack, "Transfigured Community: Neo-Traditionalism and Work Unit Socialism in China," *China Quarterly*, no. 126 (July 1991): 324–32.

6. Gail E. Henderson and Myron S. Cohen, *The Chinese Hospital: A Socialist Work Unit* (New Haven: Yale University Press, 1984), 140. An additional study of a *danwei* is Marc Blecher and Gordon White, *Micropolitics in Contemporary China: A Technical Unit During and After the Cultural Revolution* (Armonk, NY: M.E. Sharpe, 1979).

7. David Johnson, Andrew J. Nathan, and Evelyn S. Rawski, eds., *Popular Culture in Late Imperial China* (Berkeley: University of California Press, 1985); and Jeffrey N. Wasserstrom and Elizabeth J. Perry, eds., *Popular Protest and Political Culture in Modern China* (Boulder: Westview Press, 1994).

8. Elizabeth J. Perry, *Shanghai on Strike: The Politics of Chinese Labor* (Stanford: Stanford University Press, 1993), conclusion.

9. A comprehensive study of the household registration system is Cheng Tiejun, "Population Registration and State Control in the People's Republic of China" (Ph.D. dissertation, State University of New York-Binghamton, 1991).

10. Mark Selden, *The Political Economy of Chinese Development* (Armonk, NY: M.E. Sharpe, 1993), chapter 1.

11. Cheng, "Population Registration and State Control," 258.

12. Walder, writing in the mid-1980s, estimated permanent workers as comprising "only 42 percent of the industrial labor force." See *Communist Neo-Traditionalism*, 40. Cheng Tiejun found as late as 1989 that "the fully qualified urban population with non-agricultural hukou is only 46.3 percent (146 million) of the urban population, and a

mere 13.2 percent of the total national population" ("Population Registration and State Control," 293).

13. This point is also made by Anita Chan, "Revolution or Corporatism? Workers and Trade Unions in Post-Mao China," *Australian Journal of Chinese Affairs*, No. 29 (January 1993): 31–62.

14. Further elaboration can be found in Elizabeth J. Perry, "Shanghai's Strike Wave of 1957," *China Quarterly*, No. 137 (March 1994): 1–27.

15. Perry, *Shanghai on Strike.*

16. In this respect, the legacy of the labor movement was very different from that of the peasant movement. As Andrew Walder pointed out in commenting on this chapter, the presence of former peasant movement leaders in the Communist government did nothing to save peasants from the disastrous collectivization and production drive of the 1950s that ended in the starvation of millions. The difference, I would submit, lies in the role of Mao Zedong. Whereas the chairman felt sufficiently familiar with rural matters to intervene at will in agricultural policy, he was much more restrained when it came to industrial policy—leaving it largely in the hands of Liu Shaoqi, Chen Yun, Li Lisan, and others whose revolutionary experience had been centered in the cities rather than the countryside.

17. See Perry, *Shanghai on Strike,* chap. 4.

18. See ibid., 81–84, 103–5.

19. Tang Chunliang, *Li Lisan zhuan* [Biography of Li Lisan] (Harbin: Heilongjiang People's Press, 1984), 128.

20. Ibid., 148. On the welfare functions invested in the unions by the Trade Union Law, see Merton Don Fletcher, *Workers and Commissars: Trade Union Policy in the People's Republic* (Bellingham: Western Washington State College, Program in East Asian Studies Occasional Paper no. 6, 1974), 7.

21. Ibid., 150; Fletcher, *Workers and Commissars*, 18.

22. Joyce K. Kallgren, "Social Welfare and China's Industrial Workers," in *Chinese Communist Politics in Action,* ed. A. Doak Barnett (Seattle: University of Washington Press, 1969), 540–73.

23. Ibid., 546–50.

24. Tang Chunliang, *Li Lisan zhuan,*151.

25. Ibid., 153–56.

26. Ibid., 169.

27. David M. Bachman, *Chen Yun and the Chinese Political System* (Berkeley: University of California, Institute of East Asian Studies, 1985); Nicholas R. Lardy and Kenneth Lieberthal, eds., *Chen Yun's Strategy for China's Economic Development* (Armonk, NY: M.E. Sharpe, 1983).

28. Wang Yu et al., eds., *Dangdai Zhongguo gongren jieji he gonghui yundong jishi* [Annals of contemporary China's working class and labor movement] (Shenyang: Liaoning University Press, 1989), 7.

29. *Chen Yun yu xin Zhongguo jingji jianshe* [Chen Yun and the economic construction of new China] (Beijing: Zhongyang wenxian chubanshe, 1991), 14–16, 223, 417–18, 498–500.

30. For an argument that the Chinese borrowed heavily from the Soviet Union, see Deborah A. Kaple, *Dream of a Red Factory: The Legacy of High Stalinism in China* (New York: Oxford University Press, 1994). Kaple proposes that the PRC industrial model was based upon the "high Stalinist" exemplar of the Soviet fourth five-year plan of 1946–50.

31. Zhu Xuefan, *Wo yu minge sishinian* [My forty years with the democratic revolution] (Beijing: Tuanjie Publishing House, 1990), 197, 229–30, 337.

32. Paul F. Harper, "Trade Union Cultivation of Workers for Leadership," in *The City in Communist China,* ed. John Wilson Lewis (Stanford: Stanford University Press, 1971), 125; Lee Lai To, *Trade Unions in China* (Singapore: Singapore University Press, 1986). In addition to the unions, other state agencies responsible for labor issues have also been dominated by former labor movement activists. The first head of the Shanghai Labor Bureau under the PRC, Ma Chungu, had been secretary of the underground Communist labor movement committee in the city and became labor section chief of the military control commission that took over Shanghai in May 1949. He led a team of more than ten former party underground activists in taking charge of the defeated KMT's Bureau of Social Affairs and preparing for the establishment of a new Labor Bureau. Other members of the party underground took control of the agencies responsible for finance, trade, and commerce. Factory cadres were also recruited from among those who had been active in the labor movement of the revolutionary era. See Li Fang et al., eds., *Jieguan Shanghai* [Taking over Shanghai] (Beijing: China Broadcast and Television Publishing Company, 1993), vol. 2, 132, 163.

33. Kallgren, "Social Welfare and China's Industrial Workers"; Fletcher, *Workers and Commissars.* From the earliest years of the PRC to the present, rationing of scarce commodities has been a key element of the state's social welfare program. In the immediate post-liberation period, the Communist Party took responsibility for supplying urbanites with the "two whites and one black" (*liangbai, yihei*) of rice, cotton, and coal—all of which were in critically short supply. See *Shanghai jiefang sishi zhounian jinian wenji* [Documents commemorating the fortieth anniversary of the liberation of Shanghai] (Shanghai: Xuelin Publishing House, 1989), 109. Subsequently the unions established cooperative stores at state enterprises to offer scarce commodities to workers at low prices. Unions also took the lead in setting up clinics and hospitals to provide medical services exclusively to state workers. See Shanghai Federation of Trade Unions, "Liangnianlai de Shanghai gongren yundong" [The Shanghai labor movement in the past two years], *Shanghai gongyunshi ziliao* [Materials on the history of the Shanghai labor movement], no. 13 (February 28, 1951): 20–22.

34. Tang, *Li Lisan zhuan,* 147.

35. Li, *Jieguan Shanghai,* vol. 2, 133; *Shanghai jiefang yinian* [Shanghai's one year of liberation] (Shanghai: Liberation Daily Publishing House, 1950), 74.

36. Li, *Jieguan Shanghai,* vol. 2, 131.

37. Li Qing et al., eds., *Zhongguo zibenzhuyi gongshangye de shehuizhuyi gaizao* [The socialist transformation of China's capitalist industry and commerce] (Beijing: Chinese Communist Party History Publishing House, 1993), vol. 2, 1200–1201. Emily Honig, *Sisters and Strangers: Women in the Shanghai Cotton Mills, 1919–1949* (Stanford: Stanford University Press, 1986), 234–43, provides an account of the February 2 strike. See also Perry, *Shanghai on Strike,* 213–14.

38. Interview at the Shanghai No. 22 cotton mill, spring 1987.

39. Li Qing et al., *Zhongguo zibenzhuyi gongshangye,* vol. 2, 1304.

40. Tang, *Li Lisan zhuan,* 146; Jiang Yi et al., eds., *Zhongguo gongchandang zai Shanghai* [The Chinese Communist Party in Shanghai] (Shanghai: Shanghai People's Press, 1991), 365.

41. Li, *Jieguan Shanghai,* vol. 1, 277. In February 1950, the Shanghai Military Control Commission promulgated regulations concerning temporary workers at private enterprises, suggesting that their numbers should not exceed 20 percent of the total permanent employees. But employers were permitted to apply to the Labor Bureau for an exception to the regulation. In December 1951, the Shanghai municipal government stipulated that the hiring of both temporary and permanent workers must be handled by the Labor

Introduction Office and issued a prohibition against raiding of another unit's workers. Li et al., *Zhongguo zibenzhuyi gongshangye,* vol. 1, 61, 121.

42. *Zhongguo gongyun* [The Chinese labor movement], no. 7 (1957). Reprinted in Yan Jiadong and Zhang Liangzhi, eds., *Shehuizhuyi gonghui xuexi wenjian xuanbian* [Compilation of study documents on socialist unions] (Beijing: 1992), 176–83.

43. Jiang et al., *Zhongguo gongchandang zai Shanghai,* 472.

44. Shanghai Bureau of Social Affairs, ed., *Strikes and Lockouts in Shanghai* (Shanghai: Shanghai Bureau of Social Affairs, 1932).

45. Perry, "Shanghai's Strike Wave."

46. On January 6, 1967, Shanghai's *Wenhui bao* reported that the day before more than 100,000 temporary and contract workers had assembled at People's Plaza to demand that the party abolish the system of temporary and contract labor and create a new labor system true to the essence of Mao Zedong Thought. Similar protests erupted in Shaanxi, Hunan, and Liaoning provinces.

47. Author interview, Shen Jingbo (Shanghai Federation of Trade Unions staff member), August 1989.

48. "Sources of Labor Discontent in China: The Worker-Peasant System," *Current Scene,* 6, No. 5 (March 15, 1968): 1–26.

49. For detailed discussion of the rebel movement and its impact, see Elizabeth J. Perry and Li Xun, *Proletarian Power: Shanghai in the Cultural Revolution* (Boulder: Westview, 1997).

50. Sebastian Heilmann, "The Social Context of Mobilization in China: Factions, Work Units and Activists during the April Fifth Movement in 1976," *China Information,* 8, No. 3 (winter 1993–94).

51. Andrew G. Walder and Gong Xiaoxia, "Workers in the Tiananmen Protests: The Politics of the Beijing Workers' Autonomous Federation," *Australian Journal of Chinese Affairs,* No. 29 (January 1993), 15, 18.

52. FBIS *(China Daily Report),* August 29, 1991, 31–32.

53. FBIS *(China Daily Report),* April 6, 1993, 67.

54. For a precursor in the pre-Communist period, see Perry, *Shanghai on Strike,* 44.

55. FBIS *(China Daily Report),* April 6, 1993, 67.

56. James C. Scott, *The Moral Economy of the Peasant: Rebellion and Subsistence in Southeast Asia* (New Haven: Yale University Press, 1976). Scott applies E.P. Thompson's concept to peasants suffering the effects of state and market intrusion under colonialism, but it would seem to apply at least as well to state workers in contemporary China facing the erosion of socialist securities.

57. *Business Week,* June 6, 1994, 97.

58. *Kaifang* [Open monthly] (May 1994): 10–12.

59. FBIS *(China Daily Report),* January 30, 1991, 67.

60. Lynn T. White, III, "Migrations and Politics on the Shanghai Delta," paper presented at the twenty-third Sino-American Conference on Contemporary China (Taipei, June 1994), 41; Dorothy J. Solinger, "The Floating Population in the Cities: Chances for Assimilation?" in *Urban Spaces in Contemporary China: The Potential for Autonomy and Community in Post-Mao China,* ed. Deborah Davis, Richard Kraus, Barry Naughton, and Elizabeth J. Perry (Cambridge: Cambridge University Press, 1995). The relevant comparative literature includes Wayne Cornelius, "Urbanization and Political Demand Making: Political Participation Among the Migrant Poor in Latin American Cities," *American Political Science Review,* No. 68 (1974): 1125–46.

61. Elizabeth J. Perry and Li Xun, "Revolutionary Rudeness: The Language of Red Guards and Rebel Workers in China's Cultural Revolution," *Indiana East Asian Working*

Paper Series on Language and Politics in Modern China, No. 2 (July 1993): 1–18.

62. Mok Chiu Yu and J. Frank Harrison, eds., *Voices from Tiananmen Square* (Montreal: Black Rose Books, 1990), 109.

63. FBIS (*China Daily Report*), September 29, 1993, 36–37. More details on strikes in foreign-owned and joint-venture enterprises can be found in FBIS (*China Daily Report*), May 13, 1992, 32–33; and May 19, 1993, 42.

64. Andrew Gordon, "Contests for the Workplace," in *Postwar Japan as History,* ed. Andrew Gordon (Berkeley: University of California Press, 1993), 391.

3

Republican Origins of the *Danwei*: The Case of Shanghai's Bank of China

Wen-hsin Yeh

When the first groups of Western social scientists arrived in China in the late 1970s, they were immediately impressed with a system of social organization called the *danwei* or work unit, and its total envelopment of the individuals within it. They found that just as banks and factories were organized into *danwei,* so were schools, hospitals, research institutes, publishing houses, bookstores, newspapers, universities, theaters, film companies, drama troupes, utilities, power plants, government and party offices, and even state-owned shops, restaurants, and department stores.[1] A *danwei* was, first of all, an organization for work. Although some variations existed, the distinguishing feature of a *danwei* was a lifetime social welfare system virtually from cradle to grave, and a network of relationships encompassing work, home, neighborhood, social existence, and political membership.

Typically, a person would arrive at his or her assigned *danwei* upon graduation from high school or college. The affiliation was likely to be for life. As Andrew Walder's research shows, the unit functioned thereafter not only as the

Research support for this chapter was provided, in part, by the Committee on Scholarly Communication with China; the Luce Foundation; the Hoover Institution; and the Townsend Center for Humanities, the Chancellor's Humanities Fellowship, and the Center for Chinese Studies of the University of California at Berkeley. Earlier versions of various parts of this chapter have been presented at the Townsend Center and the Center for Chinese Studies, University of California at Berkeley; Cornell University; University of California at San Diego; Hoover Institution; Davis Center, Princeton University; Fairbank Center, Harvard University. I am grateful for all the comments and suggestions received on those occasions.

employer for the employee but also as the conduit for the distribution of social services.[2] These services ranged from housing, health care, pension provision, and retirement benefits to nursery school and kindergarten care. By dint of their control over such vital services, figures of authority in the *danwei* became influential presences in an individual's significant personal decisions such as those concerning marriage, education, and career moves.

The *danwei*, furthermore, was an instrument of political mobilization. Party cell organizations and political learning sessions were typically organized within the work unit. The workplace was often where mass political campaigns began. It was, at the reverse side of the same coin, also where state security control took place. When an entire *danwei* became suspect, the party-state sent in work teams consisting of party cadres from faraway places—individuals presumably detached from the personal connections that embroiled the *danwei*—to carry out its inquiries according to the wishes of the state.

For each individual within the unit, the *danwei* maintained a dossier, or *dang'an*, on personnel matters. The *dang'an* personified the individual in the state bureaucratic system. Where the *dang'an* was lodged was also where the person legally belonged. The work unit in that sense owned the individual through its possession of and control over the dossier. Even in the relatively open environment of the 1980s, a person was merely "on loan" from one unit to the next if his or her personnel dossier failed to get transferred along with the move.[3] The *dang'an* in this sense acquired its own persona that sometimes superseded the existence of the physical person in the *danwei*.

Scholars generally agree that the *danwei* system, in its mature form, was characterized by two distinct features: limited mobility or virtual immobility in the labor market and a high degree of dependence in a hierarchy of personal relationships at the workplace. Both conditions contributed to the development of patronage networks and the practice of favoritism. Because of the functioning of the work unit system, informal interactions came to play a much more prominent role in decision-making processes than formal procedures. Some scholars infer that these vertical links of dependency and control in Chinese society impeded the formation of horizontal alliances between professional peers and fellow workers. Urban politics in China, unlike in other modern societies, was thus notable not so much for its politics of protest and collective action as for the personal dynamics of networking, dependence, coercion, and collusion.

By tracing the development of the *danwei* to models of organization formed in Communist base areas during the Sino–Japanese war, Xiaobo Lü (see chapter 1) views the sort of social relationships fostered in Chinese work units as primarily rural and Communist in origin. The system, which was gradually put in place in Chinese cities in the 1950s, is widely seen not as an outgrowth of urban social relationships that had been developing before the Communist takeover but as a later imposition on the cities by the socialist state.

Logically, then, we should expect two related developments in the foreseeable future. With the growth of a market economy and the gradual privatization of ownership, we may anticipate, first, the end of the *danwei* as a primary form of organization. With the increase in horizontal job mobility, the relaxation of vertical chains of control, and the rise of associational organizations formed by workers, students, and others, furthermore, we may expect increasing incidence of collective actions in a variety of forms that range from economic strikes to political protests. Many observers have been hopeful that there lie, in the appearance of student and worker associations in the 1980s, promise for the emergence of a civil society and thus for a gradual transition to a more democratic system of political participation in socialist China.

Most of the research done on the *danwei* system in socialist China has been built on data collected from state-owned industries. In the course of my research on urban life in Shanghai during the Republican period, I came upon sources that shed light on corporate life and personnel practices in Shanghai's financial institutions during the 1930s and 1940s. These sources reveal that life in Shanghai's banks contained certain features bearing a striking resemblance to what we later regard as unique to an authoritarian Chinese socialism after 1949.[4] These developments, furthermore, were directly related to the politicization of the urban workplace during the civil war period (1946–49), which eased the city's transition to the Communist era.

This chapter, which contains my preliminary findings in this search for an urban origin of the Communist *danwei*, is based largely upon the case of Shanghai's Bank of China in the Republican period. The Bank of China was the premier financial institution on the Bund that was also fully owned by Chinese capital. Precisely because life at the bank exemplified life at the top in a hierarchy of urban middle-class professions, what the bank did was not altogether typical of what a majority of urban institutions accomplished. The system that it developed represented, instead, what many other institutions aspired to create. Because the bank's corporate practices led to the creation of a new style of existence with its own ideas of respectability, the Bank of China in that sense occupied a strategically critical position in our study of the emergence of a new middle-class corporate life in Shanghai. In the context of the 1930s it served as an example for others to emulate. As the decades wore on, more and more Shanghai institutions adopted similar arrangements that closely resembled the case of the bank.

This chapter first describes the nature of corporate life at Shanghai's Bank of China in the early 1930s. Then it reviews the transformation of that life after the War of Resistance (1937–45) broke out. At the conclusion of the war, the bank, which came under charges of collaboration by those returning from Chongqing, moved into yet another phase that involved significant changes in the composition of its senior leadership. Junior employees of the bank, who were active in self-help organizations during the war, emerged in the late 1940s to become leaders of in-house protests against the corporate management in disputes over salaries and benefits. These activists, quite often supporters or members of the Communist Party, earned themselves enough distinction to become, after the Communists took power, the new authorities who steered the bank through its socialist reorganization in the early 1950s.

There were thus continuities both in terms of personnel and organizational practices that bridged the bank's experiences across the 1949 divide. By drawing attention to the nonrural and pre-Communist origins of institutional features that prefigured the *danwei*, this chapter offers new perspectives on the mid-century transition embodied in 1949.

Corporate Life in Shanghai's Bank of China in the 1930s

Corporate life in Shanghai's Bank of China in the early 1930s was a product of purposeful construction. To understand the timing and the goals of this construction, it is necessary to begin with a brief review of the bank's history and a sketch of Zhang Gongquan (Zhang Jia'ao) (1889–1979), the man whose leadership shaped the project.

The year 1928 was a turning point in the history of the Bank of China.[5] That year a new Nationalist government was established in Nanjing after several months of fighting. It brought into the new capital the Central Bank, a state institution fully under the new Ministry of Finance. The Bank of China, which until then had functioned as one of the official banks under the toppled government in Beijing, was cut off from its sources of state revenue and granted a new charter by the ministry to become a "special institution" to handle foreign exchange.[6] To adjust to this new situation, the bank relocated its headquarters to Shanghai, where foreign banks were concentrated, and began reorganizing itself from a predominantly state-owned institution into a principally private one accountable to its shareholders.[7]

Before 1928, the bank, headquartered in Beijing, processed tax funds, paid official salaries, transported legal specie, and issued paper currency. Created by an imperial decree in 1897, it was China's first Western-style bank with central government backing.[8] It drew upon government as well as private sources of capital and operated as a modernizing arm of the Board of Revenue. It was staffed, meanwhile, mainly by former tax officials and fiscal clerks who took care to maintain their well-established connections with Tianjin salt merchants, Shanxi money brokers, and various regional warlords.[9] Much of what went on at the senior level involved negotiating with contending factions of politicians and militarists over state funds and war loans. Banking was conducted in political clubs and on social occasions. Part of the job was to strike deals behind the scene.[10]

After 1928, with a reconstitution of its board and investors, the bank redefined its businesses in the areas of private deposits, factory loans, and foreign exchange.[11] The removal of its headquarters to Shanghai signified the decline of the fiscal bureaucrats of the former imperial and warlord governments in the bank and the rise of a new breed of moneymen based in Shanghai. It also marked the bank's entry into a much more market-sensitive environment, where at a place like the Eight Immortals Bridge district alone there were over a dozen rival private banks and scores of old-fashioned *qianzhuang* (native banks).[12] To adjust to the new circumstances, the leadership of the bank turned to new corporate practices. It hired recent graduates trained in business, economics, English, and law from Western-style colleges and universities, and concentrated upon the creation of a disciplined work force responsive to both instructions from above and demands arising in the larger environment.

The man who presided over the bank's reconstitution was Zhang Gongquan, who became a vice president of the bank at the age of twenty-eight in 1917 and was elected to serve as its top officer, bearing the title general manager of the head office, at the age of thirty-nine in 1928.[13] Zhang, a native of Shanghai, came from an eminent gentry-official family of progressive leaning. He received his early training in classics and neo-Confucian moral philosophy from leading contemporary masters such as Tang Wenzhi and Yuan Guanlan, who taught him such Mencian doctrines as "sincerity," "integrity," and "generosity."[14] He then (1906–9) went on to study monetary theory and banking at the private Keio University in Tokyo, where he showed a preference for theories of liberal political economy over those of state capitalism.[15] Zhang used his spare time to master the formal practices of Japanese banking institutions in Tokyo. Thanks to an introduction of his brother Zhang Jiasen, the finance expert and political philosopher, he also became a member of the well-connected gentry-reformer group of constitutionalists led by Liang Qichao. Both activities turned out to be crucial in launching Zhang's career. In 1913, back in Beijing, Zhang became one of the executive secretaries of Liang's Progressive Party, which after the 1911 Revolution came to enjoy extensive connections with the new government.[16] In late 1913, he was named the deputy head of the Shanghai branch of the Bank of China. In Shanghai, he quickly formed several strong friendships in its banking circles, which included not only founders, shareholders, and managers of the city's Chinese-owned Western-style banks, but also heads of the largely British foreign financial institutions.[17] The lunch group that Zhang helped form with "friends with common interests in promoting modern banking" quickly developed into the Shanghai Banking Association—a formal organization with its own charter, regulations, and journals, and an ability to apply concerted political pressure. It was one of the earliest "modern institutions" to appear in Shanghai, and its appearance marked the transition of Chinese urban society "from an archaic and particularistic stage toward a more open *société civile*."[18]

The Bank of China of the late 1920s, reconstituted under Zhang's tutelage, experienced a period of healthy growth as a business enterprise. It was well regarded by the wealthy and attracted a good share of private deposits. It presented a conservative image of high security, and it commanded, by 1933, a national network of 2,000 employees in more than 140 branches. It charged significantly lower fees in the long-distance remittance business than its archrivals, the traditional-style native banks of provincial towns, which appeared to be too embedded in local environments to move nimbly over the map.[19] With the assistance of English and German advisers from the Midland and Darmstadt Banks, the Bank of China modernized its accounting system; improved branch communications networks; set up offices in London, New York, and Osaka; opened up foreign exchange, trust, and deposits departments, and staffed them with new graduates bearing professional degrees from abroad. It also created a research unit to collect economic data and invited specialists to publish journals on finance and the national economy.[20] In Shanghai, it soon replaced the Hong-kong and Shanghai Banking Corporation as the central clearinghouse to which all financial institutions brought their bills of exchange at the end of each business day.[21] Under Zhang's leadership, the bank also acquired the image of a modern, public-minded institution that consistently placed national economic interests above corporate profits.

At the heart of this impressively modernizing banking organization was, meanwhile, a profoundly moralistic managing philosophy, which was in full accordance with the senior leadership's neo-Confucian outlook. This philosophy placed heavy emphasis on the character and behavior of individual employees instead of on the overall division of labor and structure of incentives. The "personnel handbook" (*hangyuan shouce*), a copy of which every employee was required to carry, contained detailed discussions of the "proper spirit and attitudes" that a good company man was expected to possess. The fortunes of the bank, according to the handbook, rested ultimately upon competent men of integrity who devoted themselves to corporate goals. It was vital to the collective strength of the institution that each employee give his unreserved dedication and absolute obedience to his superiors—the way "one would obey a parent." Each employee, furthermore, was also to seek professional self-improvement by participating in activities such as evening classes, lectures, reading clubs, and study societies, so as to better equip himself with up-to-date expertise for service. These individual efforts were critical, because white-collar workers of Republican Shanghai lived in an age of "relentlessly forward-pressing trends." To avoid becoming obsolete on the job, one had to "seize every moment to gain broad exposure" to various branches of new knowledge and "adapt to the trends of the time."[22]

The most striking aspect of the bank's corporate culture, however, was the belief that top leaders were not merely executive administrators with the full power of their offices, but also moral leaders and professional teachers whose conduct and standards were to set an example for the average employee. Much as in the corporate culture developed in Japan and in South Korea and Taiwan later in the century, it was inappropriate for a subordinate ever to question openly the judgment and integrity of a superior, since the latter's very superiority in the corporate hierarchy was a sufficient certification of his superior vision and ability.[23] From an opposite perspective, it was insufficient for the purpose of earning a promotion for members of the rank and file merely to concentrate on one's assigned tasks and not pay attention to overall self-cultivation. A promotion was a recognition not of fulfillment of duties alone but of superiority in general standing. Because of this moralistic philosophy, life in the bank entailed a heavy dose of neo-Confucian self-cultivation.

It was part of one's job at the bank to be constantly involved in learning and teaching: either in the role of the less informed and accomplished subordinate learning from one's manager-superior, or in the role of the better educated and morally exemplary superior instructing his juniors. Several forms of this process took place daily in the reconstituted Bank of China. There was the training of lower-level new recruits, the majority of whom were secondary-school graduates, by designated mentors. There were evening courses in accounting, economics, English, and Japanese for the midlevel clerks. There was the inculcation of values through corporate rituals in group gatherings. Few social occasions were free from didactic implications, and participation was imperative if one wished to become part of the collective whole.

Training

One such training session took place, for instance, after the daily closing of the bank on September 6, 1933. More than a hundred members of the Shanghai branch gathered in the fifth floor dining hall to attend a dinner lecture entitled "Important Dates in the History of the Bank of China." This was part of a series of scheduled evening lectures conducted by the bank's managers and senior experts for the purpose of teaching their lower-level employees about the norms of the bank. Junior clerks were required to take notes during the presentation as if they were attending a class. Three days later, after they had put them in order, the clerks would submit their notes to the associate manager for review. He, in turn, like the head instructor in a school, would grade the notes and select the superior ones for circulation.

On this particular September evening, the speaker, a senior accountant, spoke about the bank's rise and attributed this development to the enlightened leadership of Zhang Gongquan. Some time after Zhang assumed the associate directorship of the Shanghai branch in 1916, according to the speaker, he defied a government attempt to interfere with banking practices and upheld the bank's credibility. Zhang took extraordinary measures to uphold the credibility of the bank's paper notes and retained the public's confidence in the bank's trustworthy business practices. Although Zhang took considerable personal risks charting this course of action, these images and reputation of integrity proved to be major business assets in themselves in the long run. The speaker concluded with an observation about Zhang's exceptional qualities and his courageous defiance of state authority.[24]

Different topics were presented on other evenings. Altogether, the talks helped with the creation and circulation of a narrative about the bank among its own members. This narrative located its points of reference within the institution, as opposed to major events external to it. It showed the thought and action of the bank's senior leadership, rather than impersonal economic conditions, to be the major factor behind the institution's growth. It projected the image of a bank that was uniquely capable of preserving its integrity in moments of crises, hence more deserving than any other financial institution of the full confidence of its shareholders and depositors.

In this climate of business and under this style of leadership, junior employees were urged to acquire the same broad vision and moral courage as their seniors had presumably displayed in the past. To train the employees for public-mindedness and business integrity, the training began in-house with the creation of vertical bonds between managers and employees. Junior employees were grouped into classes according to the year of their entrance and then assigned a "class mentor" from among the managers. There were teachers and pupils as well as supervisors and employees in the bank. Twice a year, the "disciples" would formally present themselves to their mentors in a choreographed public ceremony analogous to the rituals traditionally followed by an apprentice to his master.[25]

Loyalty, integrity, reverence for one's superiors, and dedication to one's work were the main emphasis of the training. It was the duty of the manager-teacher to guide and discipline the trainees firmly so that they could attain these qualities.[26] A unit of properly trained employees would obey their manager the way "a company of soldiers of sons and younger brothers [defers] to their commanding father and uncle." They would "feel for each other as members of the same family" and regard their interests as shared. Eventually junior employees would develop such a profound attachment to the corporate home that they "would be reluctant ever to leave."[27]

A trainee's day was fully scheduled from dawn to dusk. He was to rise at a certain hour, to take classes using an abacus or a calculator, English, and Chinese composition. He was to practice calligraphy, read "beneficial journals, books, and newspapers," and—as was the habit in old Confucian academies as well as in contemporary Japanese banks—keep a diary.[28] In this diary he was required to put down personal reflections and prepare a statement evaluating his own conduct. This record was daily submitted to the mentor for review. Thereafter the diary became the basis of the manager's annual personnel evaluation of a trainee in categories such as "competence," "diligence," "responsiveness," and "willingness to cooperate." The diary gave the corporate mentor a chance to "raise questions and make comments" so as to "offer guidance on personal conduct" and to prevent his charge from "going astray."[29] Trainees were rated by their managers by these yardsticks so that awards and punishments, shame and honor could be openly distributed. One came to be known in the corporate hierarchy precisely for where one stood vis-à-vis others on this moralistic scale.

While the initial molding of a trainee took place in the seclusion of the corporate offices, the further conditioning of the average employee, typically married and with children, required the construction of a larger, more encompassing corporate space. In the late 1920s the bank, like many other Chinese-owned modern enterprises at the time, began building housing compounds for its employees in city after city. These projects were not met with much enthusiasm when the time came for the rank and file to give up their established living arrangements and move in. It did not escape attention that the spatial deployment of the residential units bespoke a certain corporate imposition of values. Many employees nonetheless overcame their initial resistance and moved into the new living units.[30]

Living

The bank believed that there were many advantages in having employees living next to one another: "order," "convenience in management," "friendship," "unity as a group," and "uniformity in thinking." These advantages were even important to have "during an emergency," such as a military coup or bandit raid.[31] Whatever the justifications, dormitory compounds were expressions of the corporation's extensive reach into the everyday life of its employees.

The Bank of China's Tianjin compound was a fully fenced area prominently marked by main gates with the name and logo of the bank on them. Back to back with the logo was a giant mechanical clock, visible to all who passed under it as a daily reminder of the central place of time in the occupants' corporate life.[32]

Leading straight from the gates into the center of the landscaped compound was a long footpath that ended at the steps of a large two-story Western-style building, which was the residence of the branch manager. Flanking the manager's residence, two to a side, were four more two-story buildings for the four associate managers, smaller in size to reflect the occupants' comparative status. Behind these five buildings were eight units of three stories facing each other in two rows. Uniformly constructed in concrete, each apartment house was partitioned into six standardized units with separate entrances, private kitchens, and bathrooms.[33] These regular employee residences were limited to two bedrooms, so that each unit was only large enough for a couple with small children. Although space was allowed in every residence for a maid, no room was made for the multigenerational extended family, the norm for households in the Republican period.[34]

While the bank excluded the extended lineages of its employees from the compound, it sought to make the enclosed space a world unto itself.[35] Interconnected by a web of shaded footpaths were gardens, pavilions, athletic fields, tennis and basketball courts, an auditorium, and classrooms. The latter were used for an elementary and secondary school, which in the early 1930s had a staff of three professional teachers and an enrollment of more than thirty students whose mothers worked as voluntary teachers' aides. These same classrooms were used in the evenings for residents to study English, economics, accounting, and the local dialect. The auditorium was used for meetings and special occasions, such as the birth of a baby, the marriage of a young clerk, the anniversary of a manager—all joyous occasions celebrated in the corporate home. Three times a week a physician, paid by the bank, visited the compound to see patients. Every morning early risers could play tennis or study martial arts with an instructor on the athletic field. While children played in the gardens, their mothers socialized in the pavilions. Household chores were borne by the domestic servants. With the exception of shopping, the genteel wives of the Bank of China's employees saw little need to venture outside the gates of their comfortably designed urban compound.[36]

Similar conditions prevailed in other cities. The Shanghai branch dormitories were located across town from the business office, west of the International Settlement. Shanghai branch employees thus had the additional routine of taking the bank's bus to work, eating lunch in the company dining hall, and riding back to their residences in the late afternoon. Shortly after the bank moved its head office to Shanghai in 1928, it bought a spacious English-style country estate at 94 Jessfield Road. A carefully landscaped estate with gardens, lawns, tennis courts, fish ponds, and multiple guest suites, No. 94 was supposed to be the official residence of General Manager Zhang. Zhang chose, however, to occupy only a portion of the house and turned the rest of the mansion into a regular meeting place as well as a guesthouse for visiting branch managers. Every Friday about sixty members of the bank gathered there for an informal dinner meeting. Zhang set a chatty and confiding tone for the conversation, encouraging those present to speak their minds. The importance of these dinners in smoothing the internal operation of the bank can hardly be exaggerated. Colleagues traded information, heard about developments outside their own departments, and read the collective company mood. Important business plans were often formulated in the dining room at No. 94, which functioned as a high-level policy center rather than a mere residential appendage to the corporate office down along the Bund.[37]

Sports and physical exercise constituted another category of activities considerably emphasized in the corporate compound. Tennis on Sunday mornings was a favorite pastime for many at the head office and the Shanghai branch. At the Harbin branch, ice hockey took the place of tennis for a good part of the year. At Yichang in Hubei, horseback riding was favored over other sports. All these outdoor activities were associated with a Western lifestyle available only to the well-to-do—those who could readily muster the spare time, the economic capital, and the cultural capital of such pursuits.[38] They helped form a public image of bank employees as dashing, innovative, and affluent youth with cosmopolitan tastes and enhanced the impression that employment with the bank was like membership in an exclusive club.

Team sports strengthened the Shanghai group's sense of its solidarity. At least fifty people joined the soccer club of the bank, which also organized basketball teams in 1931. These teams officially represented the Bank of China at annual sports meets held by the Young Men's Christian Association, which linked the bank's players to counterparts from other financial institutions and missionary colleges. These colleges were where many young employees had first acquired their skills in soccer and basketball.[39] In this respect the popularity of team sports among Bank of China employees in the 1930s signaled the ascendance within the corporation of a new cohort of financial workers with college degrees, as opposed to an older generation of experienced moneymen who had done their apprenticeship in the old-style *qianzhuang*.

By 1933, several genres of activities had become firmly established in the daily routines of the Bank of China. There were the organized lectures and classes that permitted the senior experts to appear as instructors and role models for their junior subordinates. The dinner talks and club meetings made possible the free exchange of ideas and the forging of social networks. Sports events, meanwhile, sharpened the bank's youthful image and advertised its modern, Westernized outlook. To the outside world, the bank represented a company of individuals of old-fashioned integrity and new-style expertise—a powerful combination that inspired much customer confidence. To members of its own community, on the other hand, so much of an employee's daily life fell under the orchestration of the corporate leadership that most boundaries between the private and the public, the personal and the professional, were erased in this pervasive moralism.

Paternalism

The descriptions above suggest that corporate life in the early 1930s at Shanghai's Bank of China was largely an expression of a patriarchal conception of the appropriate relationships between employers and employees. This conception led to the rise of a strongly didactic approach in a heavily moralistic tone. Bank leaders often urged their employees to engage in certain kinds of activities not so much for their professional relevance as for their assumed moral and intellectual worth. This moralistic concern was considered appropriate and even necessary, meanwhile, precisely because middle-class culture in Republican Shanghai was often tinged, at a deeper level, by a profound sense of insecurity, which found expression sometimes in a strong concern about the city's moral impurities.

Corporate life in the style of Shanghai's Bank of China, in this connection, was also the product of a middle-class project to construct a secure sense of community in a bewildering urban setting. While bank employees regarded themselves as "fortunate" and "privileged" for occupying offices in multistory buildings equipped with heating and cooling facilities, they were at the same time acutely aware of the multitude of the displaced and destitute who had come in from the countryside and were roaming the streets of Shanghai in search of subsistence. In the words of Xia Yan, Shanghai was where the rich and comfortable built "forty-eight-story skyscrapers upon twenty-four layers of hell"—a metropolis rising on the backs of countless suffering men and women.[40] As the employees heard lectures about moral cultivation, they could not help sensing at the same time signs of the city's chaos and corruption, which were everywhere evident not only in its gambling casinos, brothels, and opium dens but also at the security exchanges and commodity markets.

To safeguard itself from this uncertain environment and to enhance its own image of integrity, the bank created corporate compounds and erected walls, which, by enclosing the banks' members, separated them from their surroundings. The moral order that supposedly was obtained within the communal walls, meanwhile, helped to reassure those who found themselves otherwise threatened by the rapidly evolving social landscapes outside them.

Compared with the socialist *danwei* of the 1950s, corporate communities of the 1930s were created not so much to distribute social services and goods in a planned economy of experienced scarcity as to build a distinct lifestyle that complemented the business needs of a modern workplace. Bank employees were not recipients of social benefits, but consumers with discriminating tastes. Residential compounds built by the Bank of China and other financial institutions were aimed not so much at the provision of basic needs for the employees as at the creation of corporate domains with their own purposes. The construction of these compounds enhanced the bank's image as Shanghai's premier Western-style corporation blessed with old-style moral accountability. This image helped to inspire public confidence in the bank. It also created pride in membership in these financial communities, limited as it was to employees and their immediate families. It was precisely this association with comfort, security, discipline, and purpose that turned the corporate compound into such an attractive idea in the eyes of Shanghai's middle-class employers and employees—so much so that even the victorious Communists made it their top priority to have similar arrangements set up for their prized skilled industrial workers in the state enterprises of the early 1950s.

Bank employees in the 1930s, as noted above, had to sit through numerous sessions during which they heard lectures delivered by their superiors on such topics as "How to Be a Good Employee of the Bank of the China." The ritual and practice readily calls to mind later lectures on topics such as "How to Be a Good Communist" delivered on countless occasions under the People's Republic. The notion of a "good Communist," of course, was an all-encompassing concept that supposedly subsumed all of the attributes associated with being a "good worker" or a "good clerk." However, corporate leaders in the 1930s, compared with their socialist counterparts of the 1950s, were in no position to suggest the equation from an opposite direction: They could not offer superior professional performance as a sufficient condition for solid political citizenship. Unlike the danwei leadership of the 1950s, Shanghai's employers in the 1930s were not part of a larger party-state system. What they had built were expressions of corporate aspirations rather than state instruments of political mobilization.

Quite apart from what their corporate superiors had wanted them to learn, then, Shanghai's bank employees came readily under the influence of forces that emanated from outside the corporate walls—forces such as those generated by the era's urban political campaigns. As military conflicts intensified between China and Japan in the mid-1930s, Shanghai's financial employees, like many other educated members of the city's middle class, found themselves drawn increasingly into the city's public campaigns of patriotic mobilization. These activities, which often involved the organization of song festivals, drama societies, and the reading and publishing of progressive journals, took place typically after working hours. Corporate leaders, who regarded themselves as patriots as well as patriarchs, supported their employees in these pursuits, especially when the Nationalist government, steering a middle course between the aggressive Japanese and an outraged Chinese public, sought to suppress these agitations for immediate armed resistance against the outside aggressor.[41]

Urban mobilization for patriotic goals, however, followed its own principles of organization. The prolonged crisis in the mid-1930s over North China created a groundswell of public support for resistance. In December 1935, Zou Taofen, the former editor of the highly popular weekly *Shenghuo* (Life), organized a group of pro-resistance Shanghai intellectuals, including the banker Zhang Naiqi, to announce the creation of the Shanghai Cultural Circles' National Salvation Association (Shanghai wenhuajie jiuguo hui).[42] The association issued a manifesto calling for a complete withdrawal of all foreign or Japanese troops and foreign-backed puppet political entities from Eastern Hebei and Manchuria. It also demanded that the Nationalist government, instead of making further concessions to appease the Japanese, enlist the support of the nation to oppose them.[43] Shanghai's workers, women, and white-collar employees followed the lead of the city's luminaries to form horizontal alliances of their own, joining the students and intellectuals in political rallies, petition drives, and the issuing of manifestos.[44] They also threw themselves into cultural activities designed to drum up patriotism.

Bank employees, many of whom were readers of Zou Taofen's journals, actively engaged themselves in this mobilization. The National Salvation Association of Shanghai's Banks and Money Guild (Shanghai yinqian ye jiuguo hui), which was the best funded and most active component under the National Salvation Association of Shanghai Employees (Shanghai zhiye jie jiuguo hui), brought together bank workers and *qianzhuang* clerks from both parts of the city. A new form of organization was created on the basis of a shared sense of citizenship and national identity. These horizontal associations cut across corporate boundaries and addressed the political rather than the professional concerns on the minds of young employees.

After the outbreak of the War of Resistance these associations found themselves playing a more and more active role in the lives of Shanghai's bank employees. Corporate leaders, who had to cope with the threat posed by the Japanese military authorities, were forced, meanwhile, to adopt a low public profile. As discussed in the next section, wartime conditions cemented the horizontal bonds among the employees. These alliances brought into Shanghai's corporate environment values and concerns that politicized the workplace. They also contributed eventually to the decline of the corporate leadership's patriarchal authority.

Employee Life in Shanghai During the War of Resistance, 1937–1945

The War of Resistance broke out in Shanghai on August 13, 1937. Shanghai's financial workers had their first encounter with blood and death the following day, when several bombs dropped from a damaged aircraft exploded on Nanjing Road, Shanghai's busiest commercial thoroughfare, during the peak traffic hour, bringing down hotels and department stores and causing hundreds of deaths and injuries. By late November, despite heroic resistance on the ground with casualties exceeding a quarter of a million, Chinese troops, including some of the Nationalists' crack units, were forced to abandon Shanghai. The Chinese sectors of the municipality thereafter fell under the direct control of the Japanese military authorities.

Until the outbreak of the Pacific War on December 7–8, 1941, Shanghai's foreign concessions, which had declared their neutrality in the Sino–Japanese conflict, maintained a precarious state of peace under mounting Japanese pressure.[45] The formation of this "lone islet" (*gudao*), or an oasis of unoccupied territory against the backdrop of rapid Japanese military expansion across the East Asian continent, created the conditions for an extraordinary influx of wealth and people into the concessions, which were widely regarded as a haven and "paradise" for wealthy refugees. The bars, restaurants, theaters, hotels, dancehalls, gambling casinos, movie theaters, amusement halls, and stock and commodities exchanges that catered to the rich kept the city awake and ablaze around the clock, and pushed the concessions to a new height of glamor and prosperity. The salaried employees of the city, for their part, however, saw their living standards eroded by soaring prices. News of deprivation in the countryside and sights of destitute refugees crowding the city's back alleys, furthermore, relentlessly tested their sense of security. They found the war closing in upon them, turning their haven into, at best, a "paradise on sand."[46]

In the summer of 1938, after the fall of Wuhan, the Nationalist government relocated its wartime capital to Chongqing. Despite much diplomatic maneuvering behind the scenes, Tokyo and Chongqing were unable to bring themselves to sit down at the negotiating table, and the war entered a protracted period of stalemate. The Japanese, in an attempt to pressure the Nationalists to capitulate, opened secret negotiations with Wang Jingwei, the number two person to Chiang Kai-shek (Jiang Jieshi) in the Nationalist organizations in Chongqing. Wang managed to leave Chongqing for Hanoi in December 1938. Chiang Kai-shek's secret service, the Military Bureau of Statistics and Investigation (Juntong), sent a death squad in pursuit of him and made an attempt on Wang's life in his Hanoi guesthouse. Although Wang escaped the bullets of the assassins, his longtime personal aide and friend Zeng Zhongming was shot to death in Wang's bedroom during the night. Wang, shaken and enraged, made his way to Shanghai.

In Shanghai, Wang Jingwei collected a team of collaborators including Li Shiqun, a Communist renegade, a former member of the Guomindang Central Committee's Bureau of Statistics and Investigation (Zhongtong) and a man with extensive Green Gang connections in Shanghai.[47] Before Wang's arrival, Li Shiqun, with the support of the Japanese secret service, had already created a terrorist organization at 76 Jessfield Road charged with neutralizing the operation of Chiang Kai-shek's Juntong in the city. After Wang departed the following spring for Nanjing, where he declared the "return" of the Nationalists to cooperate in peace with the Japanese, he named Li Shiqun minister of police of his regime. Li's gang of thugs and assassins, in collaboration with the Japanese military police, thereafter terrorized the city virtually unopposed. His hit squads were particularly active in and out of the neutral zone of the foreign concessions, where numerous pro-Chongqing Nationalist organizations—banks, newspapers, publishing houses, as well as private industries—had converged to seek refuge after the fall of coastal China to the Japanese.

Part of the larger history of the War of Resistance in Shanghai was the financial war of banks fighting banks, especially the furious competition between the Nationalists and Wang Jingwei's regime to have their respective currencies displace their rival's.[48] To dominate local finance and banking circles, both the Nanjing government and the Wang regime disrupted the normal functioning of the financial market through organized speculation, hoarding of commodities, a "tax" of bank officials, the mass murder of bank employees, and the bombing of their premises. The goal was to wrest financial control from each other and to intimidate the bankers into political submission.

Because a majority of Shanghai banks remained pro-Chongqing, they became targets of terrorist attacks, urban guerrilla-fashion, by the hired hands from 76 Jessfield Road, the secret police that served the Wang interest. On the night of March 21, 1941, while puppet terrorists were throwing grenades and bombs into three pro-Chongqing bank buildings, a gang of six gunmen pushed its way past the night watchman guarding the dormitory of the Jiangsu Farmers Bank. The gunmen flipped on the lights and began shooting at random into the beds, killing five bank clerks and badly wounding six more who were left comatose in blood-soaked blankets.[49] Later that night police cars descended upon Centro Terrace, the residence compound of the Bank of China at 96 Jessfield Road, which lay outside the boundaries of the International Settlement. The plainclothes puppet police dragged bank clerks and other employees out of their beds while a small group of Japanese military police watched, and at 3:00

A.M. took 128 of them to the dreaded cellars at 76 Jessfield Road, where they were confined.

The next day, March 23, Minister of Police Li Shiqun admitted the detention of 128 employees of the Bank of China. He complained that "Chongqing terrorists" had attacked Wang regime personnel on previous occasions and demanded that Chiang Kai-shek's government show repentance for these attacks. Li threatened to take "similar measures" against "the entire staff members of all the financial establishments operated by the Chungking [Chongqing] regime in Shanghai."[50]

With these Bank of China hostages in hand, the following day Nanjing terrorists unleashed their bomb squads on pro-Chongqing banks. That afternoon, a frantic employee of the Farmers Bank of China on Avenue Road called the Shanghai Municipal Police and reported that a messenger had left a ticking package. A detective subinspector rushed to the bank and gingerly dismantled the bomb, which was wired for both time and contact explosion. At about the same time, shortly before 4 P.M., the Burkill Road branch of the Central Bank of China erupted. The TNT blast destroyed most of the second story, killing one person and wounding thirty-eight others. Another explosion thundered across the boundary in the French Concession, where the Canidrome branch of the Central Bank of China was also blown apart by TNT. Seven were killed and twenty-one others wounded, most of them clerks and accountants.[51]

Meanwhile, as of April 5, there was no indication of how soon the 128 Bank of China employees would be released from their detention at 76 Jessfield Road. They were told by the puppet police that they were being held hostage to the good behavior of the Chongqing authorities. If Chongqing agents killed any of the Wang regime's bank staff members, Wang police would kill three of the Bank of China members selected by lot from the 128 employees then under guard.

On April 16, Chongqing terrorists, perhaps Juntong agents, shot and hacked to death an assistant chief of accounting of the Wang regime's Central Reserve Bank.[52] Half an hour later Nanjing agents shot the chief cashier of the Bank of China's main office in Shanghai to death.

In a scenario repeatedly recounted with many variations in the years to come,[53] that same day, April 16, 1941, the police authorities at 76 Jessfield Road invited nine senior accountants from among the Bank of China hostages to come to their quarters, where they were cordially entertained for some time. Finally, six of the nine were ordered to leave. The other three—the head of the Sinza (Xinzha) Road subbranch, the chief cashier of the main office, and a third man— were escorted back to the staff quarters of the bank by armed police, lined up, and shot dead in the presence of their families. The police then departed Centro Terrace, leaving the three corpses behind. The seventy-seven families living in the bank compound moved away that same evening. Thereafter the deserted premises of the much-coveted compound were taken over by Nanjing's Central

Reserve Bank.[54] It was widely believed in Shanghai that the motive behind the killing of the three bankers was not just retribution but determination to force acceptance of worthless Central Reserve Bank currency in the foreign concessions.

With the currency war raging on, Shanghai's bank employees sought refuge by turning to one another. The fear, rage, anguish, and anxiety of these men powered the development of the Shanghai Banking and *Qianzhuang* Employees' After-Work Friendship Association (Shanghai shi yinqian ye yeyu lianyi hui, hereafter called the Banking Employees Association), which grew from an initial membership of about two hundred people in November 1936 to an organization of nearly seven thousand men and women by late 1939. This organization represented over half the city's financial workers, particularly the younger ones, who sought in this fraternal alliance a sense of solidarity and camaraderie.[55]

The Banking Employees Association, which had its origin in the national salvation movement of the mid-1930s, was run in the late 1930s by an elected board of directors. Headed by an honorary board of senior corporate leaders and actively run by a handful from over a dozen second-tier institutions, it was an organization that brought together middle- and lower-middle-level employees from nearly four hundred financial institutions in the city.[56] Members of the association spent their after-work hours engaging, as they did before the war, in cultural and educational pursuits such as the study of accounting, foreign languages (English, Japanese, Russian), vocal music, Peking opera, drawing, and publishing. The spoken drama division, with more than 350 active members, was by far the most popular group in the association.

Members also organized a consumer co-op "to facilitate the distribution of national goods *(guohuo)*" and "to counter the effects of hoarding and inflation."[57] The co-op eventually succeeded in supplying the membership at a discounted rate goods procured from more than a hundred retailers of clocks, cosmetics, candy, Western drugs, writing instruments, sports equipment, fabric, shoes, hats, books, tea, cameras, electrical appliances, and coal, plus services from scores of barbers, cleaners, and restaurants.[58] In addition, members launched a "benefits reserve fund" *(fuli chujin)* for themselves through monthly individual subscriptions. Income from this fund was to be used for charities, employee benefits, and unemployment subsidies.[59]

The spoken drama division, which routinely staged performances in connection with fund-raising endeavors on behalf of worthy causes such as refugee relief, propelled the Banking Employees Association to a position of high social visibility, despite frequent threats to their safety and interference by the French Concession authorities. The dramatists were active mainly in the late 1930s. After the Japanese took direct control of the International Settlement in December 1941, the association was forced to suspend all its public activities. The consumer co-op, at the same time, shifted its focus to the supply of basic needs. Because the association, as an industrywide organization, was no longer active, its former members turned to the creation of similar reserve funds and organizations within individual corporate units, such as the Bank of China, which were designed to meet conditions in a new environment of rampant inflation, on the one hand, and harsh economic control, on the other.

In all these activities, the Banking Employees Association functioned, first, as an organization that redirected the energy and attention of Shanghai's bank employees toward their peers and counterparts in other parts of the city, instead of to their superiors within the corporate hierarchy. "Friendship"(*lianyi*) and "collectivity" (*jiti*) became important words in the lives of bank employees, and much of their after-work hours were spent fraternizing—singing, chatting, sharing tea and food, rehearsing, shopping, visiting—with fellow members of the association. The association, in this connection, became instrumental in the creation of a different sort of corporate milieu that, with its constant reference to wartime emergencies and its emphasis on citizenship and patriotism, eclipsed the corporate world's prewar orientation toward individual self-improvement and modern professionalism.

Drama as Corporate Dialogue

As mentioned earlier, the most important form of interaction between corporate superiors and subordinates in the early 1930s involved the use of training sessions during which senior leaders delivered lectures on subjects ranging from company history, personal cultivation, and accounting to bookkeeping. In the late 1930s, with the Banking Employees Association playing an active role scheduling the after-work hours in corporate life, members of the corporation frequently met, instead, in the evenings and during weekends on occasions planned by the Employees Association. These gatherings, called for purposes ranging from fund-raising and membership drives to pure consolidation of "friendship," typically contained a long program of entertainment featuring bank employees as amateur vocalists, guitar players, Peking opera singers, *tanci* (story-telling) performers, and dramatists under the direction of professionals.

The spoken drama performance, often the main program of such gatherings, featured bank employees enacting roles in plays that carried overt social messages. Some of these, with titles like "A Glass of Milk" (*Yi bei niunai*), "The Will to Live" (*Sheng de yizhi*), and "White Tea" (*Bai cha*), were one- or two-act vernacular plays composed locally to present reflections on current conditions. Most of these amateur plays, whether comic or tragic, shared the goal of depicting "how people solve the bread-and-butter issues of daily existence" in wartime Shanghai.[60]

Some of these plays sought to make light of desperate young men's hunger and confusion. A recurring theme in most plays, however, was about how honest employees had been forced into difficult choices between their economic interests and their integrity. In "The Will to Live," for example, a hard-working young bank employee faced the tough question of whether to give up his job or his fiancée, who happened to be an object of romantic fantasy in the eyes of the only son of the bank's senior manager. Those who wielded power and wealth, including the corporate leaders, were shown in these plays to be selfish characters who used their influence for personal gain. Status, wealth, and seniority were treated with suspicion rather than admiration. This contrasted sharply with the pious assumptions that informed the construction of the corporate community in the early 1930s.

Few of these plays made direct reference to the Japanese.[61] The war and the Japanese occupation, however, were never far beneath the surface. By drawing attention to the extraordinary circumstances under which Shanghai's urbanites had been subsisting on the "lone islet," these plays made normalcy suspect and cast stylish comfort and success as inherently unpatriotic. Economic hardship of the sort endured by young employees, on the other hand, became a point of pride—it gave proof of a person's refusal to go back on his principles. To the extent that senior executives continued to hold positions of influence in occupied Shanghai, they were never fully above the suspicion that they, conversely, had compromised on their principles and collaborated with the enemy.

With these evening performances as the main forum of interaction within the expanded corporate community, bank employees seized the initiative in the construction of a new form of dialogue between superiors and subordinates. Upon learning that the association planned to stage a theatrical production, Wu Yunzhai, the head of the Bank of China in Shanghai, presented to its directors a plaque in his own calligraphy, with messages encouraging its members to "mutually assure each other's integrity" (*di li lian yu*).[62] (At the conclusion of the War of Resistance, Wu Yunzhai, incidentally, was jailed by the Nationalist government as a collaborator.) On the nights of the performances senior corporate leaders, honored guests for the occasion, sat and watched passively in the audience, while the employees took to the stage and acted out their messages.

In late November 1938 on the occasion of the fourth membership meeting of the Banking Employees Association, for example, the drama teams of the association, after spending four months rehearsing, staged Cao Yu's play *Sunrise*. *Sunrise* was selected for the occasion because it "exposed the dark side of society . . . as seen through the degenerate and indulgent style of existence prevalent in yesterday's banking circles." That previous state of moral corruption "contrasted sharply with the simple and frugal style that prevailed in today's banking circles." The goal of the performance was patently didactic: it was meant to underscore those contrasts and "deliver a warning."[63] The play, directed by Xia Feng, a member of the Shanghai Arts Theater, and featuring bank employees as actors, meanwhile concentrated on the exposure of the evil design of the powerful financier Jin Ba and on how those who were drawn into his orbit soon lost their integrity.[64]

To the attendant audience, the "evil financier" depicted in *Sunrise*, of course, was not a character of yesterday but very much one of today—a time of vicious betrayal and criminal collaboration with a ruthless and vengeful enemy regime. The contrasts between wanton debauchery and purposeful discipline, furthermore, were not contrasts between past and present, but between the top leadership and the bank's average employees. Lao Yan, an association reporter, wrote after viewing the play: "It may seem superfluous to some that we stage *Sunrise* at this time and expose evil characters such as Jin Ba. I happen to believe, however, that many in the audience were able to read into the play another level of meaning. Just take a look around our lone islet! There are, indeed, sinister characters tens of thousands of times more powerful than Jin Ba in the play, who have taken our destinies firmly into their evil hands! How should we, indeed, try to face up to this cruel reality?"[65] The suicides and deaths in *Sunrise* in that sense were warnings delivered to "all of those who sold their soul to the devil" and "all of those who had capitulated without resistance." These hostages to fate should learn that "there would be no room for [their] existence on this planet" unless they fought to redeem their right to a place.[66]

The most significant aspect about the production of *Sunrise*, however, was not what it sought to convey in this dramatization, but how this was, in the words of Lao Yan, "a play about banking . . . produced by those employed in the banks for the consumption of their fellow members in the banking circle."[67] Because the actors were playing themselves, there was an element of authenticity that allowed many "to capture down to the last detail the darkness and wickedness of banking circles in an earlier time."[68] And because they were, after all, acting, the production of the play was also a reflexive act by bank employees, who sought to catch a glimpse of each of their own lives through a dramatic construction of its meaning. The presentation of the play on stage, furthermore, gave these men and women not only a chance to find a voice for themselves but also a social occasion to act out these thoughts. At least for the evening, they controlled the stage and presided over an audience of their colleagues and superiors. This open production turned their private thoughts into public statements. Whatever the content of their individual thinking, it was amplified and collected into one voice.

The power of this collective articulation was apparently lost on no one. Xu Jiqing, a senior banker in the audience and a member of the association's honorary board, readily acknowledged it after viewing the performance: "The cast was well selected. The emotions were profound and stirring. For bank workers to enact the world of banking, their messages grabbed the attention of those of us in this business the way a hard blow over the head does!"[69] Xu Jiqing's reflections, jotted down and handed over to members of the Employees Association before he left the theater, came close to an admission that it was the middle- and lower-level employees rather than their superiors who pronounced on matters of value in Shanghai's banking world.

With the production of plays such as *Sunrise*, members of the Banking Employees Association saw themselves as having seized the high ground in the articulation of moral authority in the corporate world. In the words of Pei Wei, a member of the association, *Sunrise* and its denunciation of top financiers showed everyone that "the sun has risen over the battlefield in this War of Resistance. All the darkness that enveloped banking circles in the past will soon disappear."[70] If we were to use that same hyperbolic vocabulary, then we would have to say that it was the employees rather than their superiors who had let in the sunlight. They were able to do so because in wartime Shanghai wealth had been tinged by collaboration, and class ambivalence gained justification in nationalistic terms. To the extent that corporate patriarchs were no longer able to present themselves as patriots of impeccable integrity, the hierarchical order that they had sought to build in an earlier time was effectively compromised, during the late 1930s, by the horizontal alliances formed among younger members of the employees in a process of patriotic mobilization.

Sometime after 4:00 A.M. on December 8, 1941, Shanghai residents were jolted out of their sleep by the noises of aircraft in the sky and the furor of artillery fire across the Huangpu River. By dawn word had spread that the Japanese military had opened fire on the International Settlement's two gunboats, one British and the other American, sinking the former and forcing the latter to raise a white flag. At about 10:00 A.M., Japanese troops filed across the bridges over Suzhou Creek in a light drizzle and entered the settlement. Once there, the soldiers took up positions at street intersections and spread themselves out all the way from the Bund to the western end of the Extra-Boundary Road. "Some of these soldiers wore glasses. Others wore a short mustache. A few were smoking cigarettes. All held their guns right across their laps and none made a sound."[71] After the widening of the war in the Pacific, Shanghai's urbanites found themselves entering a new phase of military occupation.

While senior bank officials like Wu Yunzhai and Xu Jiqing found their autonomy seriously compromised by the demands placed upon them by their Japanese overseers, junior employees continued to be active in the organization of welfare associations. Because the Japanese and the Wang Jingwei government in Nanjing now imposed their own currency and adopted a policy of economic control, it became all the more important for banking employees to form their own collectives to fight the full impact of inflation and to guarantee the procurement of basic necessities, such as supplies of rice, cooking oil, coal, and clothing material. The following spring, with Japanese military police posted all around the city, the once bustling metropolis of Shanghai found its transportation arteries cut and its neighborhoods reduced to isolated areas of silence and inactivity. The busy flow of people slowed as tramway services were suspended and barbed wire barricades went up. Shanghai's famed night life came to an end and its neon lights dimmed, as the Japanese cut the electrical power supply. The cultural and educational activities at the Banking Employees Association came to an end. The creation and administration of employees' benefits associations within individual corporate units, however, went on. These associations helped consolidate the junior employees' basis of influence within their home institutions.

After the war ended in 1945, the bank's senior leaders, charged by the Chongqing government with being collaborators, found themselves seriously hampered in their ability to exercise authority within the corporation. The Employees Association, which now commanded considerable influence in the bank, moved into a position to challenge the corporate hierarchy. In the late 1940s, with inflation once again on the rise, numerous incidents broke out in Shanghai's banking world, typically involving protests by organized employees who demanded improvements in their living conditions. Corporate employees rebelled against their superiors, however, not by arguing that hierarchy should be done away with, but by suggesting that a new collective leadership, fit to lead, should take the place of the old one. This new leadership should be able to address all their concerns—moral, political, economic, as well as professional. It was to make life wholesome again, at work as well as at home. The Communist Party, meanwhile, began building up its influence through the employees associations. Even before the People's Liberation Army marched into the city in May 1949, the door was left open for the entry of the Communist Party into Shanghai's corporate world.

Preliminary Conclusions

The foregoing shows that in the early 1930s, Shanghai's leading financial institutions built a communal style of corporate life containing features that call to mind the socialist *danwei* of the 1950s. This community was the expression of a patriarchal conception of authority. Membership in it was often described in kinship terms. The corporation was a large family.

From the mid-1930s onward, however, forces of nationalism swept across Shanghai's middle-class society, and popular campaigns for patriotic mobilization thoroughly transformed employee life in Shanghai's corporate circles. Company culture became politicized in this process. To the extent that corporate patriarchs were no longer able to present themselves as patriots, they found their authority within their own organizational hierarchy significantly compromised.

Bank employees thereafter formed horizontal associations of their own. These organizations, primarily social in nature, nonetheless competed with the formal structure of the corporation for influence over its employees. But although these associations were created by the employees themselves, they were not inspired by visions of a civil society. They were, instead, products of war and nationalism, when individuals were called upon to join efforts with the collectivity. Most significantly, although corporate leaders of the old sort were rejected, no concerted attacks were carried out against the moralistic conception of authority. The ground was thus laid for the rise of a depersonalized form of patriarchal authority, which eased the transition into a sort of personalized Chinese communism that combined collective leadership with institutionalized familism.

Many of the features that characterized the socialist *danwei* were prefigured in a pre-Communist urban setting. The main point here is not to suggest that there were *danwei* before there were Chinese Communists, but to draw attention, instead, to the structure of authority that informed and inspired the construction of communal or collective forms of social existence on either side of the 1949 divide. Although personal dependence and job immobility did not feature very largely in Republican accounts of corporate life, the patriarchal nature of the authority did not, in itself, preclude such possibilities. Even though there seemed to be little room for autonomy under the socialist *danwei*, on the other hand, the ubiquity of the work unit system did not prevent the formation of horizontal alliances among workers and students in Chinese cities in the 1980s.

To return to the questions posed at the beginning of this chapter: Is there a future for the *danwei*? Will the development of a market economy lead to the rise of a civil society? These are large questions involving multiple dimensions. Issues surrounding a moralistic conception of authority, as this chapter tries to show, sometimes transcend divisions between a "capitalist" and a "socialist" system of economic life. Although the construction of the corporate compound took place in Shanghai in the 1930s under specific circumstances and could be seen as a product of the bank's business needs at the time, it is nonetheless worthwhile to note how such needs gravitated toward the rise of patriarchal and moralistic solutions. Until the rise of cultural critiques directed specifically at these underlying assumptions in the organization of social relationships in the Chinese world, then, we may expect to see the basic demands of the *danwei* system reconstituting themselves in one fashion or another, permitting a broad range of dependency in a variety of economic forms.

Notes

1. Gail E. Henderson and Myron S. Cohen, *The Chinese Hospital: A Socialist Work Unit* (New Haven: Yale University Press, 1984); Martin K. Whyte and William L. Parish, *Urban Life in Contemporary China* (Chicago: University of Chicago Press, 1984); Andrew G. Walder, *Communist Neo-Traditionalism: Work and Authority in Chinese Industry* (Berkeley: University of California Press, 1986).

2. Walder, *Communist Neo-Traditionalism*. For a critique of Walder and for further explication on "work unit," see Brantly Womack, "Transfigured Community: Neo-Traditionalism and Work Unit Socialism in China," *China Quarterly*, no. 126 (July 1991): 313–32, and Walder's reply, 333–39.

3. Deborah Davis and Ezra Vogel, eds., *Chinese Society on the Eve of Tiananmen: The Impact of Reform* (Cambridge: Council on East Asian Studies Publications, Harvard University, 1990).

4. Wen-hsin Yeh, "Corporate Space, Communal Time: The Structure of Everyday Life in Shanghai's Bank of China," *American Historical Review* 100, no. 1 (February 1995): 97–122.

5. Although the economy of the Nanjing decade (1927–37) has received a considerable amount of scholarly attention in the West, much of that has focused on the agrarian sector. For insightful accounts about banking and money in this period, see relevant

sections in Frank H.H. King, *A Concise Economic History of Modern China (1840–1961)* (New York: Praeger and London: Pall Mall, 1968); Arthur N. Young, *China's Nation-building Effort, 1927–1937: The Financial and Economic Record* (Stanford: Hoover Institution, 1971); Frank M. Tamagna, *Banking and Finance in China* (New York: Institute of Pacific Relations, 1942); and Ramon H. Myers, ed., *Selected Essays in Chinese Economic Development* (New York & London: Garland, 1980). The most significant recent publication in this area is Frank H.H. King, *The History of the Hongkong and Shanghai Banking Corporation* (Cambridge: Cambridge University Press, 1987–1991), 4 vols.

6. On the reorganization of the Bank of China in May 1912, see Zhongguo yinhang zonghang and Zhongguo dier lishi dang'an guan, eds., *Zhongguo yinhang hangshi ziliao huibian, shang bian,* 1912–1949 [Collected materials on the history of the Bank of China, first edition, 1912–1949] (Beijing: Dang'an chubanshe, 1991), 6–17.

7. The reorganization of the Bank of China was announced by the Nationalist government on October 26, 1928. The bank was incorporated with a total of 250,000 shares valued at 100 yuan each. Of these, 50,000 shares were held by the government. A twenty-member board of directors was created. Four members of the board were Ministry of Finance appointees; the remaining sixteen were elected by shareholders. For details, see ibid., 380–82; Tan Yuzuo, *Zhongguo zhongyao yinhang fazhan shi* [History of the development of major Chinese banks] (Taipei: Zhengzhou chubanshe, 1961), 173, 219–26; Hong Jiaguan, *Zai jinrongshi yuandi li manbu* [A stroll in the field of the history of finance] (Beijing: Chinese Financial Publications, 1990), 261–64; Zhongguo renmin yinhang zonghang jinrong yanjiusuo jinrong lishi yanjiushi (Research Unit, History of Finance, Institute of Financial Research, Head Office, People's Bank of China), ed., *Jindai Zhongguo jinrong ye guanli* [Management practices in modern China's financial industry] (Beijing: Renmin chubanshe, 1990), 354–56.

8. Numerous proposals were drafted in the second half of the nineteenth century for the creation of a Chinese-owned Western-style bank. The first such bank was the Zhongguo tongshang yinhang (Commercial Bank of China), formally inaugurated on May 27, 1897, in Shanghai, under the auspices of Sheng Xuanhuai, minister of railroad affairs. The bank was neither a central bank nor a central government bank, though its creation required the approval of the imperial court. Its founding "capital" included one million taels in silver from the Board of Revenue, in the form of a five-year deposit that required interest payments. But the bank was neither an official nor a private bank. It was governed by a board of merchants appointed by Sheng Xuanhuai in his ministerial capacity, and the bank drew its capital primarily from investments made by late Qing Western-style enterprises formed under the formula of "official supervision, merchant management" (*guan du shang ban*). The Commercial Bank of China created ten branches nationwide in the next three years, appointing to positions of regional heads provincial bureaucrats and holders of civil service examination degrees. The bank sustained heavy losses in subsequent years, especially during the Boxer Uprising in 1900, when its Beijing and Tianjin branches were burned and looted by Western soldiers. By 1905, the bank was reduced to three branches. In August 1905, the imperial court approved the creation of the Board of Revenue Bank. In 1908, this bank, with a national network of twenty-one branches, was renamed Da Qing Bank. Like the Commercial Bank of China before it, the Board of Revenue Bank (Da Qing Bank after 1908) was not a central bank, although it was sponsored by a branch of the central government. Its capital came from the Board of Revenue (funneled through a limited liability corporation) as well as from private merchants. It was neither official nor private, and had a board of directors dominated by official appointees. This bank was entrusted, among other things, with the management of "all state funds and funds of the government treasury," including the issuance of government bonds and securities. After the outbreak of the 1911 Revolution, all operations of the

Da Qing Bank were suspended. The creation of the Bank of China in May 1912 through a "reorganization" of previously existing semiofficial banks was a reorganization that incorporated assets and personnel of the former Da Qing Bank as well as the Commercial Bank of China. For a detailed discussion of this history based on late Qing archival documents, see Hong Jiaguan et al., *Zhongguo jinrong shi* [History of Chinese finance] (Chengdu: Xi'nan caijing chubanshe, 1993), 171–77.

9. Editorial remark, *Zhonghang shenghuo* [Life in the Bank of China] (cited as *ZS*) 1, no. 3 (July 15, 1932): 48; Cao Erlong, "Wo suo yujian de guke" [My experience with customers], *ZS*, no. 16 (August 1, 1933): 319.

10. Zhang Gongquan, "Women de chulu" [Our way out], *ZS*, no. 21 (December 1, 1933): 429. Zhang Gongquan was also known by his courtesy name Zhang Jia'ao. He lived in New York for many years after 1949 and published in English under the name Kia-ngau Chang.

11. This is not to say that Bank of China thereafter ceased to hold assets in the form of government bonds, but rather that as the result of a redefinition of its primary functions, the bank was no longer in the business of handling state funds for government treasury. Government bonds as an item for either investment or speculation, of course, were held by private individuals as well as by financial institutions in the Republican period. It is clearly beyond the scope as well as the objective of this chapter to present a history of China's financial institutions and monetary systems in the Republican period. Interested readers may wish to consult Kia-ngau Chang, *The Inflationary Spiral* (Cambridge: Technology Press of the Massachusetts Institute of Technology; New York: Wiley; and London: Chapman and Hall, 1958), and Arthur Young, *China's Wartime Finance and Inflation, 1937–1945* (Cambridge: Harvard University Press, 1965).

12. Zhang, "Women de chulu," 430. On the history and operation of the *qianzhuang* or native banks, see Andrea McElderry, *Shanghai Old-Style Banks (*ch'ien-chuang*), 1800–1935: A Traditional Institution in a Changing Society* (Ann Arbor: Center for Chinese Studies Publications, University of Michigan, 1976).

13. Zhang Gongquan compiled an unpublished autobiography under the Oral History Project of Columbia University around 1960. On Zhang Gongquan's leadership position in Shanghai's banking circles in the early Republican years, see Marie-Claire Bergère, "The Shanghai Bankers' Association, 1915–1927: Modernization and the Institutionalization of Local Solidarities," in *Shanghai Sojourners,* ed. Frederic Wakeman and Wen-hsin Yeh (Berkeley: Institute of East Asian Studies Publications, 1992), 15–33.

14. Yao Songling, *Zhang Gongquan xiansheng nianpu chugao* [Draft chronological biography of Mr. Zhang Gongquan] (Taibei: Zhuanji wenxue chubanshe, 1982), vol. 1, 10. Tang Wenzhi was one of the most important neo-Confucian moral philosophers of the Zhu Xi school of his time, who served as president of Liaotong University until 1919. See Wen-hsin Yeh, *The Alienated Academy: Culture and Politics in Republican China* (Cambridge: Council on East Asian Studies Publications, Harvard University, 1990), 97–102.

15. Yao, *Zhang Gongquan,* 11–12. Zhang Gongquan first studied at the Institute of Modern Languages in Shanghai and then went to Tokyo.

16. On politics in the warlord period, see Andrew Nathan, *Peking Politics: Factionalism and the Failure of Constitutionalism, 1918–1923* (Berkeley and Los Angeles: University of California Press, 1976).

17. Yao, *Zhang Gongquan,* 21–28. On the Anglo–Chinese patronage network in Shanghai's financial circles at this time, see especially Zhang Zhongli and Chen Zengnian, *Shaxun jituan zai jiu Zhongguo* [The Sassoons in old China] (Shanghai: Renmin chubanshe, 1983), 127–44.

18. Bergère, "The Shanghai Bankers' Association, 1915–1927," 16 and 20.

19. Tang Yusun, "Ruhe chengwei benhang de jinglu" [How to become crack units of our bank], *ZS*, no. 22 (January 15, 1934): 459. Branch number was increased to 203 by the end of 1934. See Zhongguo renmin yinhang zonghang jinrong yanjiusuo jinrong lishi yangjiushi, *Jindai Zhongguo jinrong ye guanli*, 359.

20. *Zhongguo yinhang Shanghai fenhang shi* [History of the Shanghai Branch of the Bank of China] (Shanghai: Economic Science Publications, 1991), 84–85; Tan, *Zhongguo zhongyao yinhang fazhan shi*, 174, 193; Zhongguo renmin yinhang zonghang jinrong yanjiusuo jinrong lishi yangjiushi, *Jindai Zhongguo jinrong ye guanli*, 358, 362–63.

21. Tan, *Zhongguo zhongyao yinhang fazhan shi*, 209–11; *Zhongguo yinhang Shanghai fenhang shi*, 77–79.

22. Bank of China, *Zhongguo yinhang hangyuan shouce* [Bank of China employee handbook], 3–9. Copy in Shanghai Municipal Archives.

23. In the case of Japanese corporations of the mid-twentieth century, Ezra Vogel offers the following observation: "Superiors do not promote someone who cannot win the liking and cooperation of his peers, for an individual's value to his unit is determined by his capacity to work effectively with his peers, his superiors, and his subordinates" (*Japan as Number One* [Cambridge, Mass.: Harvard University Press, 1979], 56).

24. "News Brief," in *ZS*, no. 17 (September 1, 1933): 379; Zhang Gongquan, "Zhongguo yinhang zhi jichu anzai" [Where does the Bank of China lay its foundation?], *ZS*, no. 14 (June 15, 1933): 271–72.

25. At the Shanghai branch, the first such ceremony was held on August 2, 1931. See *ZS*, 1, no. 6 (October 15, 1932): 89, 95.

26. It is instructive in this connection to consider Alfred Chandler's presentation of the development of managerial hierarchy in the United States, which he saw primarily as a result of division of labor by function and specialty in response to a major expansion of market and significant advancement in modern technology (*The Visible Hand: The Managerial Revolution in American Business* [Cambridge: Harvard University Press, 1977], 381–414, passim).

27. *ZS*, 1: no. 6, 89, 95.

28. *ZS*, no. 15 (July 1, 1933): 304. Diary-keeping as part of an employee's moral training was apparently a common practice in those days. See Zhang Jia'ao (Zhang Gongquan), *Yinhang hangyuan de xin shenghuo* [New life for a bank employee] (Nanjing: Zhengzhong shuju, 1934), 36–38; Dai Ailu (Dai Zhiqian), *Yinhang jia, yinhangyuan zuoyouming* [Rules of thumb for bankers and bank employees] (Shanghai: 1932), 178–79. Dai's account took note of diary-keeping as a corporate practice in contemporary Japanese banks. Barry Keenan's research shows that diary-keeping was practiced by Tongcheng School academists including the mid-Qing statesman Zeng Guofan.

29. *ZS*, no. 11 (March 15, 1933): 197.

30. Former employees with the Jiaotong Bank in Shanghai spoke of similar experiences (interview with Lu Shengzu in the dormitory of Jiaotong Bank, Shanghai, January 12, 1991).

31. Yihou, "Gongtong shenghuo zhi yiban—Jinzhongli" [Communal life in the Jinzhongli], *ZS*, 1, no. 4 (August 15, 1932): 60; Xiaoyi, "Gongtong shenghuo zhi yiban, jiushisi hao" [Communal life at the no. 94], *ZS*, no. 13 (May 15, 1933): 259; Li Jin, "Wuren yingdang xingcha ziji de bingtai" [We ought to examine our own shortcomings], *ZS*, no. 12 (April 15, 1933): 233.

32. Yeh, "Corporate Space, Communal Time," 99–102.

33. These units in the style of a multistory communal townhouse were apparently new to the Chinese urban landscape, with first appearances dating to the late nineteenth-century in Shanghai and Tianjin. In the Republican period they tended to be built in blocks with scores of units and taken up as residences by petty urbanite families on a rental basis.

Large-scale construction of these dwellings signified the commodification of urban space in modern Chinese cities. See Luo Suwen, *Da Shanghai: Shikumen, xunchang renjia* [Greater Shanghai: Gates of carved ornament, homes to ordinary households] (Shanghai: Renmin chubanshe, 1991), 3–38.

34. Yihou, "Gongtong shenghuo," 58–60.

35. On the rise of the *xiao jiating* (nuclear family) in Republican cities and its signifi-cance, defined in opposition to the *da jiazu* or extended lineages that continued to be the norm in the hinterland, see Wen-hsin Yeh, "Progressive Journalism and Shanghai's Petty Urbanites: Zou Taofen and the Shenghuo Enterprise, 1926–1945," in *Shanghai Sojourn-ers,* ed. Wakeman and Yeh, 205–214, and Susan Glosser, "The Business of Family" (paper presented at the annual meeting of the Association for Asian Studies, Boston, March 25–27, 1994). Past scholarship on the twentieth-century Chinese "family revolu-tion" has placed much emphasis on the influence of Western liberal ideology and roman-tic individualism. Recent studies approach the issue from the angle of the political economy of the city and place the discussion in the context of the rise of the Chinese nation-state. These studies have shown the conservative dimension of the nuclear family and its embeddedness in urban commercial culture. The rise of the nuclear family in Republican Chinese cities, of course, is a totally separate issue from the question of the role of families and kinship networks in Chinese business organizations. With the rapid industrialization of East and Southeast Asian economies in recent decades, this topic has attracted a considerable amount of scholarly interest. For a conference volume that con-tains a rich collection of empirical information, see Gary Hamilton, ed., *Business Net-works and Economic Development in East and Southeast Asia* (Hong Kong: Center for Asian Studies, University of Hong Kong, 1991).

36. Ibid. The dinner party was apparently the most common form of socializing among these families (interview with Li Wenquan, Shanghai, January 12, 1991).

37. Ibid.

38. Pierre Bourdieu, "Sport and Social Class," in *Rethinking Popular Culture: Con-temporary Perspectives in Cultural Studies,* ed. Chandra Mukerji and Michael Schudson (Berkeley, Los Angeles, Oxford: University of California Press, 1991), 368.

39. Shen Shuyu, "Huhang qiuyi bu zhi guoqu ji qi jinkuang" [Past and present of the team sports department of the Shanghai Branch], *ZS,* no. 17 (September 1, 1933): 386–88; Peiguan, "Huhang tongren gongyu shenghuo xiezhen" [A realistic depiction of after-work life at the Shanghai branch], *ZS,* no. 16 (August 1933): 327–29. Although it is a common practice worldwide these days for business firms to engage their employees in team sports, in Republican China such activities were regarded as quite "modern" and "West-ern." Western-style sports were practiced mainly in urban areas by members of the middle class, who acquired the skills while attending missionary schools or joining the YMCA. See Yeh, *The Alienated Academy,* 72–74, 101.

40. Xia Yan, *Baoshen gong* [Contract laborer] (reprinted Beijing: 1978), 26.

41. On the Sino–Japanese relationship in the years leading up to the War of Resis-tance, see Parks M. Coble, *Facing Japan: Chinese Politics and Japanese Imperialism, 1931–1937* (Cambridge: Council on East Asian Studies Publications, Harvard University, 1991), passim. On the National Salvation Association of the mid-1930s, see especially 283–333. On the tension between the Nationalist government and the Shanghai capitalists during the Nanjing Decade (1927–37), see Parks M. Coble, *The Shanghai Capitalists and the Nationalist Government, 1927–1937* (Cambridge: Council on East Asian Studies Pub-lications, Harvard University, 1980), passim.

42. On Zou Taofen and *Shenghuo,* see Yeh, "Progressive Journalism and Shanghai's Petty Urbanites," 186–238.

43. Parks Coble, *Facing Japan,* 292–93. Zou Taofen, Zhang Naiqi, and five others

were eventually arrested by the Nationalist government as leaders of the national salvation movement in 1935–36. These men were known as the "Seven Gentlemen."

44. On student nationalism during this period, see John Israel's ground-breaking work, *Student Nationalism in China, 1927–1937* (Stanford: Stanford University Press, 1966), and, with Donald W. Klein, *Rebels and Bureaucrats: China's December 9ers* (Berkeley: University of California Press, 1976).

45. Frederic Wakeman, "The Shanghai Badlands: Wartime Occupation and Urban Crime" (paper presented at the International Conference on Urban Progress, Entrepreneurial Development, and China's Modernization, 1840–1949, at the Shanghai Academy of Social Sciences, August 17–20, 1993).

46. Tao Juyin, *Gudao jianwen: Kangzhan shiqi de Shanghai* [Sights and sounds from the lone islet: Shanghai during the War of Resistance] (Shanghai: Renmin chubanshe, 1979), 27.

47. Wen-hsin Yeh, "Dai Li and the Liu Geqing Affair: Heroism in the Chinese Secret Service During the War of Resistance," *Journal of Asian Studies*, 48, no. 3 (August 1989): 552–53.

48. The following discussion of bank wars is based largely upon chapter 10 of Frederic Wakeman, *Shanghai Badlands* (London and New York: Cambridge University Press, 1996).

49. *North China Herald*, March 26, 1941, 483; cited in Wakeman, *Shanghai Badlands*.

50. Confidential U.S. State Department Central Files. China: Internal Affairs, 1940–1944. See 893.108, March 24, 1941, 296. Cited in Wakeman, *Shanghai Badlands*.

51. This account is based on Wakeman's reconstruction in *Shanghai Badlands*, chap. 10.

52. *China Weekly Review*, April 26, 1941, 267; *North China Herald*, April 23, 1941. Cited in Wakeman, *Shanghai Badlands*.

53. See, for instance, Cheng Naishan, *The Banker*, translated with an introduction by Britten Dean (San Francisco: China Books and Periodicals, 1992), chap. 22, especially 337–41.

54. Anonymous letter signed "A Banker," dated April 22, 1941, in *China Weekly Review*, April 26, 1941, 242 and 267. Cited in Wakeman, *Shanghai Badlands*.

55. Pei Yunqing, "Di san jie huiyuan dahui de shiming he fazhan" [The mission and future of the third annual membership meeting], *Yinqianjie* [Banking circles], 2, no. 1 (June 12, 1938): 1; "Shanghai shi yinqianye yeyu lianyihui chengli sanzhounian jian ji di wu jie huiyuan dahui tekan" [Special issue on the third anniversary of the Shanghai banking and *qianzhuang* after-work friendship association and the fifth membership meeting], published on October 29, 1939, 35.

56. Statistical figures compiled in October 1938 showed that the association's 7,000 members were drawn from 97 banks, 101 *qianzhuang*, 164 insurance and trust companies, and 34 other women's organizations. See "Shanghai shi yinqianye," 38.

57. Wu Yaqin, "Fa qi yinqian ye xiaofei hezuo she de yiyi" [The significance of launching a consumer co-op in banking and money circles], *Yinqianjie*, 2, no. 8 (October 1, 1938): 155.

58. Ibid., 41.

59. Huang Dinghui, "Jianyi tongren fuli chujin" [Fellow-worker benefits reserve fund —a proposal], *Yinqianjie*, 2, no. 4 (August 1, 1938): 69.

60. Pingzi, "Sanshi yu danwei huiyuan jiaoyi dahui texie" [Special report on the friendship gathering of members of thirty-some *danwei*], *Yinqianjie*, 2, no. 10 (November 1, 1938): 195.

61. Urban popular fiction in this period, like spoken drama, also made little explicit

reference to the Japanese. See Edward Gunn, *Unwelcome Muse: Chinese Literature in Shanghai and Peking, 1937–1945* (New York: Columbia University Press, 1980). Whether there was a literary resistance movement in wartime Chinese writings is the subject of Po-shek Fu's new book, *Passivity, Resistance, and Collaboration: Intellectual Choices in Occupied Shanghai, 1937–1945* (Stanford: Stanford University Press, 1993).

62. Photographic reprint of Wu Yunzhai's calligraphy, in *Yinqianjie*, 2, no. 11 (November 20, 1938): 206.

63. "Yule xinwen" [Entertainment news], *Yinqianjie*, 2, no. 4 (August 1938): 71.

64. There are obviously many other ways to read the meaning of *Sunrise*. Cao Yu himself would have preferred a different interpretation than Xia Feng's. See Cao Yu (Wan Jiabao), *Richu* [Sunrise] (Shanghai: Wenhua shenghuo chubanshe, 1936), "Postscript,"i–xxxii; Tian Benxiang, *Cao Yu zhuan* [A biography of Cao Yu] (Beijing: Shiyue wenyi chubanshe, 1988), 174–87; Sichuan daxue zhongwen xi, ed., *Cao Yu zhuanji* [Special selections on Cao Yu] (Chengdu: Sichuan renmin chubanshe, 1979), vol. 1, 410–14; vol. 2, 415–95.

65. Lao Yan, "Kan *Richu*" [Watching *Sunrise*], *Yinqianjie*, 2, no. 12 (December 1, 1938): 245.

66. Ibid.

67. Ibid.

68. Huang Yingzi, " 'Richu' chongxian yu wutai" ['Sunrise' reappearing on stage], *Yinqianjie*, 2, no. 12 (December 1, 1938): 242.

69. Photographic copy of Xu Jiqing's calligraphy, in *Yinqianjie*, 2, no. 12 (December 1938): 244.

70. Pei Wei, "Kan le *Richu* yi hou" [After viewing *Sunrise*], *Yinqianjie*, 2, no. 12 (December 1, 1938): 247.

71. Tao, *Gudao jianwen*, 99.

Part II

Danwei in
Comparative Perspective

4

Chinese *Danwei* Reforms: Convergence with the Japanese Model?

Anita Chan

Some Chinese academics and policymakers have made a conscious effort to examine Japanese management philosophy and Japanese enterprise culture, with reforms to the industrial *danwei* firmly in mind. This is reflected in a vast literature on Japanese management published in Chinese management journals.[1] Most of these writings do not explicitly advocate that China should directly emulate Japan; for obvious historical reasons, Chinese feelings toward Japan are sensitive on this particular point. But, notably, about twice as many articles have been devoted to introducing the nature of the Japanese model of industrial management than to American management schemes.[2] Behind closed doors, moreover, heated debates have gone on in the government's think tanks and academic circles on whether China should shift in the direction of one model or the other.[3]

As shown in the following pages, even though this debate has not been settled, certain legacies of Maoist socialism augment the potential for China's core state enterprises to shift somewhat farther toward the Japanese model. This chapter is devoted mainly to teasing out and analyzing these features.

State-, Market-, and Organization-Oriented Employment Systems

The reform of China's state industrial sector is subject to the pulls of two fundamentally different capitalist models.[4] They are, as defined in R. P. Dore's

Two earlier, considerably different versions of this chapter have appeared in Barrett McCormick and Jonathan Unger (eds.), *China After Socialism: In the Footsteps of Eastern Europe or Asia?* (Armonk, NY: M.E. Sharpe, 1995) and *Industrial and Corporate Change* 4 no. 2 (1995).

conception, the organization-oriented system, of which Japan approximates the ideal type, and the market-oriented system that pervades most Western capitalist economies (specifically the British variant).[5] In recent years, interestingly, this latter model has also been gradually adopting, either in large measure or piecemeal, elements of the Japanese model.[6] Dore traces the formation of these two systems to different attitudes toward labor and skill. Under the Western-style market paradigm, "skill is a kind of capital owned by, and embodied in, individuals, and . . . labor services, utilizing those skills, are bought and sold by those individuals in the market . . . that is to say, the forces of demand and supply determine the price (wage, salary) which different kinds of service will fetch."[7] The result is that labor is mobile; the individual theoretically decides regularly whether to be on the move, seeking the highest price for his or her skill; and management always cautiously weighs the returns from its training costs, for the loss of trained skills is a constant threat to the production process. The system is marked by a high sense of insecurity and lack of commitment from both parties. Neither side feels obliged to the other beyond the labor contract, as their relationship is only bound temporarily by market exigencies. Employees therefore do not develop a sense of loyalty to the enterprise. Personal interests and enterprise interests are not perceived as closely linked; in fact, they are often perceived as in conflict. The quintessential example of this ideal type is found in the export-oriented industries of some developing countries, modern equivalents of the hard-nosed industrial-revolution capitalism practiced by the industrialized nations of yesteryear. Marketization of the entire Chinese economy is threatening to force the state sector into this market-oriented mode.

The organization-oriented system, exemplified by the Japanese model, holds a different attitude toward labor. Training and retraining are provided by the firm, which, having footed the bill, is keen to conserve the trained skills. In consequence, high expectations are held by both parties of a sense of permanency in the labor contract, with a reciprocal willingness of labor to enter into a paternalistic relationship.[8] Consequently, payment for labor is person-related rather than skill-related: That is, labor is not paid strictly commensurate with skill levels, but also in accord with other criteria such as age, years of service, even family size. In return, management demands a high level of committed loyalty from the employees, and individual, management, and enterprise interests are perceived ideally as congruent.

The Chinese state-sector *danwei* system does not fall into either of these two categories. It operates by its own internal logic. This we shall call the "state-oriented system" in that the socialist economy was centrally planned, with centrally planned employment and remuneration systems. (This was not always the case in the European socialist economies, which faced labor shortages, but was strictly the case with China.) Neither the market nor the enterprise but the state, represented by different levels of bureaucratic administrative agents, became the ultimate mediator between the production process and labor, as well as in the allocation of resources and the redistribution of wealth. As in Japan, it was a paternalistic provider, and, in the name of the Chinese state, great demands could in turn be placed on the individual to surrender personal interests. This system, too, was characterized by a high degree of security, low job mobility, and a person-related wage system. The state-oriented *danwei* system and the organization-oriented system overlap in these particular aspects, including denial of individual interests; but the objects of identification are different: the former involved submission to the state and its agents, and the latter to the enterprise organization.

The distinction is an important one. In post–World War II Japan the collective welfare of the enterprise takes precedence over those of the state and the individual. (This is not "culturally" bound: In the pre–World War II period, the interest of the state, personified in the Japanese emperor, prevailed over all other interests.) Under Mao, although slogans had supported a balance between the tripartite interests of the state (an abstraction of "the people"), the collective (industrial *danwei* or agricultural collective), and the individual, in practice the highest levels of the polity repeatedly sought to have all interests bow to the overriding will of the party-state and, at the height of Mao's personality cult, the will of the deified leader. The political system manufactured pejorative labels such as "individualism," "economism" (when the *danwei* took any initiative to grant workers higher pay and greater benefits), and "syndicalism" (when trade unions tried to be more independent of the Communist Party) to pre-empt any signs of non-subservience to the state. At the height of political campaigns, these labels could be criminalized to invite sanctions, purges, and imprisonment.

Politically, as of the 1990s, the state-oriented system as described above no longer aptly describes, in any respect, the Chinese government's relationship with the state-owned industrial sector. The state enterprises have come under increasingly severe financial pressures. The Chinese industrial structure is now quite evenly bifurcated: the state sector with socialist characteristics employing about 40 percent of the nonagricultural work force and accounting for 45 percent of industrial output; and a rapidly expanding nonstate sector with all the trappings of capitalism. This nonstate economic sector is now taking over the most labor-intensive industries of the "Four Asian Dragons" as the latter move up-market in their production.[9] Whether the state sector—the industrial *danweis*—can continue to survive will depend on whether they can compete under intense competitive pressures from the nonstate sector. And whether they can hold on to their "socialist characteristics" will depend on their ability to provide decent wages and social benefits to their work force in a climate where the nonstate sector's workers are bereft of job security and enjoy almost no social benefits.

Since the beginning of Deng Xiaoping's reform program, the state-oriented *danwei*-style system of employment has been under incessant attack as dysfunctional and as obstructing economic reforms. It is argued by China's economic reformers that only with the introduction of a labor market will workers' incentives and enterprise efficiency be raised. Through the conscious efforts of advocates of the market-oriented system, marketization has made inroads into the *danwei* system, even if it has not yet completely triumphed. The introduction into the *danwei* of the contract labor system in place of the life-tenure system; the introduction of an award system that is related to the quantity and quality of work done, rather than seniority or other factors; the recruitment of an increasing number of casual laborers into the *danwei* to enhance labor flexibility to changing market demands and in order to drive down labor costs; and the shrinking of fringe benefits, the privatization of housing, the possibility of dismissals or partial layoffs at a reduced wage are all measures that would utterly transform the state-oriented system. Thus far, these policies have been carried out only piecemeal, here and there, now and then, depending on local situations, but the pressures are there.

Two major obstacles have prevented the state-oriented *danwei* system from being dismantled in one fell swoop. First, since the 1980s the state-sector workers in their *danwei* have been resisting the reform measures to take away their "iron rice bowl." Resistance usually has not been manifested in head-on confrontations such as strikes (which are illegal and on which accurate figures are impossible to come by) but, rather, in workers resorting to "weapons of the weak"—absenteeism, go-slows, passivity, lax work ethics, pilfering, even sabotage.[10] The state has been alert to these manifestations of discontent. When workers participated in the upheavals of 1989, which were marked by the emergence of an autonomous trade union,[11] the government responded not only with repression but also by slowing down the industrial reforms in the latter part of 1989 and by resorting to the Maoist tactic of heaping eulogies on the "working class."[12] The political and social collapse of the Soviet Union not long thereafter only served to hammer home to both rulers and ruled in China the importance of maintaining social stability. When the government tried once again in 1992 to lay off surplus labor in money-losing industrial *danwei* by carrying out a "breaking the three irons campaign" (breaking the iron rice bowl, iron wages, and the iron chair of tenured employment), state workers again resisted, and pro-market policymakers cautiously had to retreat once more,[13] though they stopped short of announcing that their policy was inappropriate and should be discarded. In early 1993, new efforts commenced, and again met a rise in worker dissatisfaction.[14] In 1994 this labor unrest escalated. When the government's budget could no longer subsidize money-losing enterprises, 200,000 workers in the Northeast and China's interior reportedly went on strike or publicly demonstrated.[15]

Despite this resistance, for much of the money-losing "rust-belt" sector of state industry the lifetime employment commitment to the work force is being discarded. This is part of a transitional phase of economic and industrial restructuring. But once the downsizing has reached an as-yet unknown level and the country's economic structure stabilizes, the *danwei* system may yet survive. What appears to be happening now is a gradual readjustment of the ratio of core-versus-peripheral labor force within state industry so as to attain nationwide labor flexibility. After all, even in Japan only about a third of the work force, the unionized core workers in large firms, actually enjoy lifetime employment.[16] For the majority of the Japanese work force not in the core sector, the rate of job mobility is about the same as in other industrialized countries.[17] In China, the low-skill end of state industry such as textile manufacture is moving rapidly in this direction and is also introducing the work pressures and piece-rate systems of China's low-skill industry in the private and foreign-funded sectors.[18] But the high-skilled sectors of state industry can be expected, as in Japan, to try to retain the highly trained services of core workers through job-security mechanisms and nonwage perquisites. The extant *danwei* system provides the convenient model.

In some cases, the retention of essential parts of the *danwei* system is not a conscious policy choice but the unintended consequence of some reform policies. These reform measures have caused part of the state sector to drift in the direction of the organization-oriented system as opposed to the market-oriented system, even though the latter is generally the preferred model of high-level decision makers. To comprehend this drift we need first to examine the features of the existing system, both positive and negative, that are legacies of the Maoist system.

The Maoist State-oriented *Danwei* System as a Prototype of the Organization-Oriented System

Many cross-national studies identify shared "Confucian" cultural roots as an ingredient in the economic success of the Four Dragons and Japan.[19] The cultural norms shared by China and Japan (obvious ones like social conformity, deference to authority, attitude toward learning, emphasis on morality, and the like) will be taken, for our purposes, as having provided the two countries with certain similar predispositions on the eve of their respective phases of industrialization and modernization. This chapter, however, relies principally upon an institutional rather than cultural approach; in the discussion that follows, cultural elements are invoked only in reference to their influence on institutional arrangements without the imputation that they hold fundamental explanatory power.

As argued by Dore, the differences between post–World War II British and Japanese employment systems can be historically traced to institutional roots.[20] What are the legacies that are playing and will continue to play a part in molding Chinese industrial relations and employment practices in the direction of the organization-oriented model?

The most tenacious of these Maoist legacies are lifetime employment and promotion based on seniority within the *danwei*. These two practices, as already noted, are being targeted by Chinese reformers as detrimental to the economic reform efforts. Yet they are features seen widely by scholars (including some Chinese scholars) as important to Japan's economic success.[21] The question that needs addressing, then, is why similar practices have engendered such different results. The Japanese lifetime employment system has been successful in cultivating among its employees a sense of security and in turn their strong identification with the enterprise. In fact, some large Western corporations today also recognize the positive side of lifetime employment and have begun instituting it.[22] Why then is it so negatively perceived by Chinese reformers as the root cause of Chinese workers' laziness and low productivity? Could it be possible that, driven by a utilitarian free-marketeer determination to break the "iron rice bowl," they are actually dismantling something that ought to be retained, throwing away the baby with the bathwater? Is it an overreaction to the state-oriented system? Lifetime employment and seniority promotion systems are not the root of the problem. The key issue pertains to the contradiction between individual, collective, and state interests.

Subjugation to the interests of the party-state meant that industrial enterprises under Mao were run by party fiat, often at the expense of economic efficiency. The enterprise *danwei* had to surrender all profits to the state and, as far as the employees were concerned, the enterprise was only the state's surrogate administrative unit in charge of housing and welfare provisions. Income was paid in accordance with a nationwide wage scale, with little relationship to the financial situation of the enterprise. Employees and workers were not able to develop a strong economic identity with their *danwei* since the economic performance of the enterprise had little effect on the individual's economic gains or losses. And their identification with the party-state was only an abstraction. This was one of the reasons for the general lack of work incentive in Chinese industrial *danwei* under Mao and remains the case to a large extent today. The crux of the issue of workers' incentives lay with the state-oriented ethos rather than the practice of lifetime employment.

Beyond lifetime employment, a Maoist feature of the *danwei* that finds close parallels in Japan is that the workplace doubles as a community.[23] In Japan, this is referred to as the "workplace family." In both countries, work colleagues are also neighbors, and work lives and after-hours lives are closely intertwined. The sense of community is reinforced by the workplace being a mini–welfare state that takes care not only of the employees' welfare in work but also their medical needs, their retirement funds, their choice of marriage partners, the education of their children, and so on. In Japan, the large enterprise provides for the bulk of an individual's welfare needs, with the state providing a small portion. In China, a state enterprise, as the agent of the state, similarly takes care of its employees' welfare.

In both countries, an individual's place in urban society is identified by one's workplace. In Japan, one is a Hitachi person or a Sanyo person. In China, the first question asked of someone is: "*Nali?*," literally meaning "where," short for "which work unit are you from?" Without the backing of a work unit, an individual in China would need to overcome great hurdles to get anything done. A person without an official relationship with any work unit becomes a nonperson.[24] However, whereas the workplace as a community in Japan serves economic and social functions, in China the Maoist *danwei* system had held an additional function—political control. The workplace became an efficient agent in the party-state's penetration of society since the boundary between control over one's work life and one's private life was blurred. Political control was omnipresent. With people constantly instructed to be vigilant against class enemies, any colleague/neighbor was a potential informant.[25] The Maoist work unit/community was not blessed with harmonious human relationships; it was a place that bred mutual suspicion and mistrust. By instilling fear, it atomized human relationships.[26] Under such circumstances the Maoist *danwei* squandered opportunities to play a cohesive social role similar to the Japanese work unit.

On the shop floor, the Japanese utilize greater nonmaterial incentives than Western enterprises to raise work force incentives: organizing competitions between work groups, running emulation campaigns, utilizing peer group pressures and visibly displayed score boards. Japanese firms also promote democratic participation to help raise worker morale. Institutional arrangements have been established to solicit workers' opinions on innovative means to increase efficiency, and the Japanese quality control (QC) circle has become widely recognized in the Western world as a highly successful management technique to raise incentives.[27] The Maoist *danwei* system professed very similar practices. For example, workers formally were asked to "raise rational suggestions" (*ti helihua jianyi*) to enhance production, resulting in enormous pressure being placed on enterprises to prove their democratic management style by chalking up the numbers of "rational suggestions" raised by workers, to the tune of a few thousand per enterprise each year.[28] There was also much talk of workers' participation in management, small group competitions, model emulations, granting of honorary awards to model workers, and so on. In fact, these incentive-raising measures, which inundated the Chinese shop floor in the form of campaigns, were given much greater play than in the Japanese system. Yet these Chinese practices became formalistic rituals and never achieved the results intended. The core of the problem was that the nonmaterial incentives were appraised on grounds of political conformity, which only served further to alienate workers from their labor, their colleagues, and the enterprise.[29]

Compared with Western factories, Japanese factories make great efforts to narrow the social gap between management and workers: Well-known practices include using a similar monthly salary system for both white-collar and blue-collar workers, mandatory wearing of the company uniform for all, and establishing single-status eating and toilet facilities.[30] Maoism too espoused egalitarianism. With frugality and conformity imposed, everyone wore basically the same ubiquitous dull-colored garb. Facilities tended to be single-status, the pay system was monthly for all, and the sloganeering was that the "workers are the masters of the state." The distinction between staff and workers in a factory was not visibly marked. In government statistics, staff and workers were always referred to as *zhigong,* as if they were one single category of "working people," in an exercise to fudge the boundary between social groups.[31] In reality, management, staff, and workers did not enjoy equal fringe benefits and social and political status, but the ideology of egalitarianism has had a lasting influence, to the extent that today's economic reformers, who believe that inegalitarianism provides the panacea for national economic and enterprise reforms, consider egalitarian attitudes one of the most tenacious obstructions.[32]

Similarities are also present in recruitment of the work forces of large corporations in Japan and China. To be sure, under Mao job allocations were centrally planned by the state. There was no labor market, no freedom to take or quit any job, and little geographical mobility once in a job, except in cases where one was banished to take up lesser jobs in the countryside. A great drawback was that job assignment was often based on political rather than on meritocratic principles, causing enormous waste of human resources for several decades. The problem was compounded by an oversupply of labor in China's cities during the 1970s. To avoid having their children be sent to the countryside to become peasants, the urban populace had sought to popularize a new system called "*dingti,*" in which children were provided with a job at their parents' *danwei* when they retired.[33] In labor recruitment the Maoist system was the antithesis of Japan's highly organized meritocratic recruitment practices: of top Japanese corporations recruiting graduates from top universities, and so forth down the hierarchy. The *dingti* system infested Chinese enterprises with particularistic blood relationships that compounded the parallel problem of recruitment based on political criteria.

Today, even though a market ideology is supplanting one of political party *diktat,* particularistic and clientelistic relationships continue to play a very influential role in the enterprise *danwei*'s recruitment of new staff and workers. In a country with a massive oversupply of labor, this legacy will not so readily disappear. Thus despite the government's repeated attempts in the 1980s and early 1990s to institute a meritocratic-based labor market, with the erosion of central job allocations parents have been able to continue to pressure their *danwei*'s management to recruit their children.[34] Moreover, cadres have begun to take advantage of their power to place their relatives in coveted positions. According to some surveys, the phenomenon of "familism" (*jiazu xianxiang* or *jiazuzhuyi*) in Chinese state enterprises has worsened rather than improved with the market reforms. This kind of "familism" should not be confused with the "familism" of Japanese enterprises, a term used to describe a paternalistic, harmonious, and cooperative workplace.[35] The nepotistic Chinese practice adversely affects the reforms in state enterprises: It lowers the quality of new recruits into the enterprises; it creates factions and cliques in the workplace; and it further inflates the number of surplus laborers in the enterprises, running diametrically contrary to reform policies. Above all, it provides enterprise cadres opportunities to utilize their own relations to empire-build, inviting charges of favoritism, power struggle, and abuse of power, seriously eroding worker and staff morale and incentives.[36]

In some other respects, though, the recruitment system in these *danwei* has been similar to the Japanese system. In Japan, since most people have been recruited into a work unit not based on specific skills but on level of academic attainment, with the understanding that training for any specific position would be provided upon entry to the enterprise, there is a good deal of flexibility in job assignments on the shop floor, facilitating adjustments to new technologies and enterprise restructuring, in contradistinction to the rigidly defined jobs performed by British workers.[37] The Chinese system of job allocations, despite the adverse effects listed above, avoids this rigid British-style compartmentalization by trade skills and may yet be turned into an asset if only more attention is paid to the general suitability of recruits.

Because the Maoist industrial *danwei* system had always been hostile to the bonus system (used by the Japanese), and more so to the piece-rate system (traditionally used by the British), a flat pay scale based on seniority prevailed.[38] During the less ideologically charged periods of Mao's rule, though, a bonus system was grafted onto the seniority system. Under Deng's economic reforms, bonus systems have been widely adopted to raise incentives, although such bonuses still comprise a small percentage of the total wage income.[39] The types of components in the package, however, are similar to those in the Japanese system. Both countries' monthly wage systems contain a base-wage component tied to seniority, guaranteed to meet basic needs. Both also provide subsidies, reflecting the two systems' paternalistic character. In the Japanese system during the 1970s the bonus in large firms made up 26 percent of the year's income,[40] reaching an average for all firms of 35 percent in 1990.[41] Monthly bonuses in China similarly were increasing yearly in the 1980s, comprising 20 percent of the entire wage package by 1991.[42] It should be noted, too, that under the Chinese reforms the base-wage portion has been shrinking (from 85 percent to 49 percent of total wage income between 1978 and 1991), and constant pressure is being applied to introduce a job/skill-related remuneration component ("*jineng gongzi zhi*"),[43] a component that parallels the job-level supplement in the Japanese system, which even in Japan was a more recent innovation of the 1960s. Before then, for the two decades after the war, the Japanese wage structure was very strongly work-age related, which is to say similar to the Mao-era *danwei* wage system.[44]

In sum, the carryover of the Maoist wage structure and the Dengist transitional structure seem to be leading the Chinese *danwei* wage system in the core state industries in the direction of Japan's system, rather than toward a more market-driven system. The piecework system, for instance, is not widely used in the higher-skill part of the state sector. Among other things, introduction of piece rates in such industries requires sophisticated management know-how in planning and norm-setting techniques, which the Chinese lacked under Mao,[45] and which even today continue to be extremely undeveloped. Though Chinese reformers aspire to introduce "scientific management"[46] in this part of the state sector, in reality Chinese management has no expertise in this respect—a common phenomenon of socialist shop floors.[47]

Management–labor relations also bear the marks of the Maoist institutional legacy, which similarly is now pulling China in the direction of the organization-oriented system. Much as under Stalin, labor under Mao in practice had no representation. A system of politically geared paternalism in the *danwei* had sought to reinforce the ideological notion that under socialism harmony prevails between the workers' state and the long-term interests of the working class. By this logic, contradictions between labor and management could not possibly arise. In reality, there were, of course, repeated conflicts of interest between management and labor, but the ideology of a "workers' state" did successfully hinder the development of a class-based workers' consciousness vis-à-vis the party-state. In contrast, such a consciousness has sunk much deeper roots in capitalist states like Britain, resulting in an adversarial management–labor relationship, whereas in Japan the enterprise union structure and firm-focused ethos have been more conducive to a relatively consensual relationship.

In brief, the Maoist state-oriented employment system in the core industries possesses many of the prerequisites for transformation to a Japanese-style organization-oriented system rather than to a market-oriented one. But these were elements that existed only in a formalistic structure deprived of operational opportunities.

The basis of the state-oriented model could be traced to a highly politicized ethos, and by the 1970s this had become patently dysfunctional.[48] Morale was low; the economy stagnating; and interpersonal and class relationships were strained.

Dengist *Danwei* Reforms and Organization-Oriented Tendencies

Deng's urban industrial reforms commenced in earnest in the mid-1980s. The economic system was decentralized; social controls were relaxed; and the "socialist man" ethos was abandoned in favor of notions of "economic man." In the industrial sector, decentralization meant the gradual release of state enterprises from the control of the party-state and the command economy. Though patron-client relationships could not easily be ended abruptly, increasing numbers of state enterprises saw the apron strings to higher levels formally cut. In July 1992 a new law with sharper teeth was passed to grant enterprises further power to resist bureaucratic intervention.[49] Government departments that violate the new regulation will bear criminal responsibility.[50]

Even more important, the rapid erosion of vertical party linkages, combined with a policy of separating party and administration (*dang zheng fenkai*), alongside the establishment of a management responsibility system, has meant that the party secretary and the party committee, which had hitherto enjoyed near-absolute power, have been marginalized at the expense of the expanded power of the manager.[51] In the eyes of factory employees, the party committee has become irrelevant. In a survey of one hundred staff and workers from several state enterprises, only 1 percent replied that they would initially seek out the party committee to resolve problems; 47.7 percent would first go to the administrative leadership; 8.8 percent to the trade union; and 5.5 percent to the administration and trade union simultaneously.[52] This reflects a situation where the party secretaries not only have little say in management affairs but also do not even carry enough weight to influence decisions.

At the same time, enterprise links with the central state are being greatly weakened. To promote this, the State Commission for Reform of the Economic System (Tigaiwei), a powerful body under the State Council, proposed in 1992 that the industrial ministries be abolished, with their responsibilities and leading personnel shifted to an association for each industry. The enterprises would no longer be subject to the minutiae of government decrees but, rather, to indirect guidance plans emanating from a government agency similar to Japan's Ministry for International Trade and Industry (MITI) (arguably the Tigaiwei itself) and mediated by each of the industrial associations. At the fourteenth party congress in October 1992, Deputy Premier Zhu Rongji, who holds special responsibility for economic reform, accordingly proposed that "government bureaus be abolished and replaced by commissions" (*san bu she wei*), most specifically an economic planning commission and trade commission, and the deputy premier observed that he had MITI explicitly in mind.[53] In March 1993, in furtherance of this plan, it was announced that seven of China's industrial ministries were to be abolished, and at least two of these—the Ministry of Light Industries and the Ministry of Textiles—were transformed directly into federations of associations.[54]

A visit to the main office of the Chinese Leather Industry Association in Beijing in 1995, which was formerly a department of the Ministry of Light Industries before its dissolution, revealed a peak-level association in a sorry state. Now that it has to be financially self-sufficient, its staff size has been cut to less than ten. Its activities are reduced to selling the "genuine leather" insignia to leather factories. The association can only maintain weak links with its former charges (mostly state-run leather factories) and has no links at all with the thousands of new leather-goods factories that have sprung up over the past decade. It does not even possess any up-to-date nationwide statistical data on the industry, not even basic information like the total number of leather-goods factories in the country. Less still can it coordinate any industrial policy.

In short, Chinese state enterprises progressively are being freed from the grip of both the centralized command economy and the party's control systems, with the state-oriented system rapidly giving way to greater enterprise/*danwei* autonomy. In 1993 the proportion of total industrial output value covered by mandatory planning stood at only 4 percent.[55] The factory manager has been given a mission to generate profits and is increasingly able to perform as an economic man, unfettered by the authority of the party secretary or ministry bureaucrats. He is being invested with new discretionary powers to decide on hiring and firing, on wage scales, bonuses, and penalties. Although the state enterprise managers are not capitalists, their role is becoming increasingly similar to that of the factory managers of large corporations in capitalist systems. The reformers among the political elite have placed great expectations on the factory managers to help raise production efficiency through market-oriented employment practices.

The upshot of these new efforts, as noted, has been a rapid climb in industrial conflict between management and workers as the reforms' adverse effects on job security and perquisites prompt workers to fight to preserve the proto–organizational-oriented *danwei* features of the Maoist system.

Worried by the growing worker dissatisfaction and unrest, the government has promulgated a new Enterprise Law that seeks to restore harmony in the factory. Under it, workers are supposed to select representatives to a staff-and-workers council,[56] and the law specifies the council's right to investigate management and also its power to *veto* all regulations vital to workers' welfare: on wages, bonuses, labor safety, penalties and awards, and so forth. It also formally holds the right to decide on how workers' welfare funds should be spent and on the distribution of housing (a vitally important issue to Chinese workers). And the council is supposed to designate at least one-third of the membership of an "enterprise management committee."[57] The enterprise trade union, which is to be the council's "administrative organ," is supposed to play a stronger role within the firm. The idea behind these various measures is to shape a greater sense of identification with, and consensus within, the enterprise. This notion is, again, in line with that of the Japanese model.

In the great bulk of China's state firms, the councils have not yet even been given a chance to function. For a start, the Enterprise Law has not been rigorously enforced to date, and in some regions it is not enforced at all. Some cities have gone so far as to enact local laws to counteract the national law.[58] Moreover, as one of the municipal trade unions has noted in frustration, even the national statute does not provide any mechanisms for penalizing managers who violate it.[59] Yet, on paper, if not in reality, the workers and unions enjoy powers within the enterprise that are at odds with the market-oriented system but in keeping with the organizational-oriented system.

Whether in the future a Chinese enterprise/*danwei* union, in line with its role in the council, will be able to assume an enhanced position in the firm is impossible to predict, but whatever the outcome it is unlikely that the unions will become adversarial trade unions in the Western tradition. For one thing, a tradition of management/union "antagonism" is missing, and this institutional legacy is apt to draw Chinese management–labor relations, if mediated by the unions, closer to the Japanese model. After all, the union federation is still an arm of the state, and its personnel come from the same stock as the state officialdom.

Although the bureaucracies in different sectors of the economy and society increasingly are asserting their own bureaucratic interests and those of their constituencies, it is unlikely that the unions will develop a confrontational stance vis-à-vis the state. The union federation has always abided by the principle of working *with,* not *against,* state or management interests. Its guiding principle is still the time-honored one of balancing individual, collective, and state interests. As of the mid-1990s, the unions subscribe to a concept known as "the enterprise as a body of mutual interests" (*qiye liyi gongtongti*). It recognizes that a *danwei*'s management and workers hold different interests, but stresses that if both parties compromise and cooperate, with income distributed fairly, they work harmoniously toward the collective good of the enterprise.[60]

In addition, the Chinese trade union structure has never been organized along the line of trades or professions as in the British tradition; rather, all staff and workers in a Chinese enterprise automatically become members of a single enterprise union. In this respect, the structure of Chinese unions resembles that of the Japanese enterprise union. Given current trends in China, there exists a good chance that the Chinese labor union structure will converge toward that of the Japanese enterprise-union model.

Adopting the Japanese Model

In the heated debate within think tanks and academic circles as to whether China should learn from the West or from Japan, some advocates for the latter position have argued that the existing structural framework of Chinese enterprises presents preconditions that favor taking the Japanese route. More than this, a popular assumption among these advocates involves a presumed close affinity between Chinese and Japanese cultural roots. Japan's culture of "familism" is seen as the fountainhead of the strong "enterprise identity," harmonious Japanese management–worker relations, and an emphasis on human relationships among Japanese workers. They promote too idealistic a picture of Japanese enterprise culture, but this positive image widely pervades Chinese perceptions of Japan's industrial success.

Some Chinese academics point out that the slogans used by Chinese state-run enterprises are still too centered on national goals to sufficiently inspire workers' identification with their *danwei*.[61] It is believed that if only Chinese "collectivism" could be activated by instilling a Japanese-style "enterprise culture" (*qiye wenhua*)—for example, introducing company songs, wearing company badges and uniforms, daily recitals of a company motto—then Chinese workers' identity and solidarity with their enterprises would be enhanced and in time this would help to raise Chinese workers' incentives.[62] Some enterprises in the past few years have imported such practices in an effort to nourish an "enterprise culture," the codeword for adopting the Japanese enterprise model.[63] Enthusiasts for the model have established "enterprise culture associations" in several major cities, to realize the mission of transforming Chinese enterprises into efficient, modern, civilized, harmonious, people-centered workplaces along the lines of their image of Japan.[64]

An in-depth comparative survey conducted by Japanese academics into Chinese and Japanese workers' attitudes provides additional interesting evidence on the potential for a convergence toward the Japanese model. The study, conducted in 1987, a few years after Chinese state enterprises had switched over to the management responsibility system, measured Chinese workers' attitudes toward their own work and management, and their self-perceptions and identification with their workplace *danwei*. The thrust of this Japanese study was to demonstrate the differences between Japanese and Chinese workers, rather than to seek out similarities in attitude.[65] It was claimed that a "laziness disease" worse than the "British disease" had become entrenched among Chinese workers.[66] However, the survey data revealed that both Japanese and Chinese workers had more in common with each other than either does with American workers. They perceived themselves as organically linked to their workplaces above all other social institutions. In contrast, the Americans identified their social relationships primarily with their residential neighborhood. Unlike the Japanese, though, Chinese workers did not see their self-interest as closely linked to their enterprise.

Surprisingly, when asked to choose between competition or egalitarianism, a higher percentage of the Chinese workers (69 percent) compared with Japanese workers (57 percent) opted for competition. But the Chinese workers also exhibited a high propensity for dependency, and their incentive to work was highly correlated with whether the manager exhibited paternalistic behavior and a human touch and showed personal concern for the workers outside the workplace. Harmonious management–worker relations, a symbolic visit to the shop floor by the manager, and the leader's own personal character (whether he was fair, morally upright, and hardworking) were all factors that seemed crucial in inspiring Chinese workers' enthusiasm for work. Similar to Japanese workers, the Chinese workers' morale and their sense of personal worth were highly correlated with external appreciation and respect rather than the nature of the work itself, such as whether the job itself was interesting, considered important, or creative. (Again, in contrast, the nature of the work was much more important to the American worker.) Remuneration, for both Chinese and Japanese workers, was a comparatively lower priority. Somewhat different from the Japanese workers sampled, the Chinese workers wanted to have the right to speak up when an important decision was to be made.

Interestingly, even some joint ventures and high-tech private firms have recently been seeking to play upon the work attitudes and paternalistic proclivities of Chinese workers by adopting features common to the Japanese-style enterprise-oriented system. For a variety of reasons—the legacy of the *danwei* enterprise cultural norm; the need to poach skilled employees from state enterprises;

to be able to retain them once further training is provided, and to provide the work force with a stable work environment and well-defined career structure so as to raise morale and incentives—these enterprises provide welfare benefits, including new housing and job security, that rival and even surpass those of state enterprise *danwei*s. During field research in 1994, I came across joint ventures, usually involving large Western corporations and Chinese state enterprises, in which the foreign partner provides for the employees much like the *danwei*s of old, even when the Chinese parent company is losing money and is cutting back on the benefits of its own state-enterprise employees.[67] A separate Chinese study of 140 joint ventures discovered that 72 percent of the sample provide housing subsidies, 88 percent provide medical insurance, and 92 percent provide retirement/unemployment insurance.[68]

A further reason for this is that even through a party branch cannot function as an official organ in a joint venture, the trade union chair in these firms usually is filled by either the party secretary or vice secretary. That is to say, the joint venture's party branch has basically incorporated the functions normally performed by the trade unions. A foreign manager who understands how the power structure of the Chinese side works tends to take the union seriously. The trade union/party together with the Chinese manager form a united front and serve as the mediators between foreign management and the Chinese work force. The foreign partner can be assured that the Chinese management will not be too demanding and unreasonable, for it too has a vested interest in making the joint venture a financial success. But, in exchange, the trade union/party secretary presses for provision of a wide range of *danwei*-like benefits.

So, too, much as in state corporations, the Chinese managers, relieved from production and quality-control responsibilities, channel their main energies into redistribution and personnel management. This latter area, where the personnel department in the Maoist tradition functions as a political and social control organ that relies upon particularistic patronage-building, helps to perpetuate the *danwei*-like character of interrelationships in the large joint-venture firms that have state enterprises as their Chinese partners.

At the same time, the Western-invested joint ventures have been influenced, too, by the general trend in Western management schools to adopt the "human resource management" (HRM) technique. The idea is that nurturing people as a resource and maintaining a consensual manager–worker relationship are preconditions to corporate success. After years of contending with adversarial labor representation, some Western managers have become converts to the Japanese consensual management style.[69] As in the Japanese model, on the Chinese shop floor they seek to solicit workers' opinions on the work process and to encourage an enterprise-oriented work ethic among the workers. Thus, Western management–worker relations in these joint ventures are gravitating toward the Japanese model.

In a study of the new private and collective high-tech firms that have mushroomed in the Haidian district in Beijing, Corinna-Barbara Francis discovered that they, too, possess many of the features that we identify with both the *danwei* system and the Japanese organization-oriented model.[70] In terms of welfare, the profitable Haidian firms provide generous benefits including company housing, health insurance, social security, unemployment benefits, retirement pensions, child care, nearly free lunches, magazine subscriptions, recreational outings, and free cultural events. In addition, according to Francis, many of the controls associated with a *danwei* continue to exist, including the companies' manipulative control over personnel dossiers and a willingness to serve as surrogates of the state in non–work-related areas, such as overseeing employees' compliance with public security and birth control functions.

To cite an illustration from my own field research, the biggest of these firms, the Stone Group, has carried over a large range of practices and perquisites from the *danwei* system, the details of which are laid out in a 200–page handbook for its employees. One example from this involves family-visit holidays: Married staff and workers are allowed a thirty-day paid visit to spouses not living in the same city and, if unmarried, a twenty-day paid visit to parents not living in the same city. Not only does the staff enjoy normal pay during such visits, but even the train tickets are paid for by the company.[71] The company is also anxious to improve its "enterprise culture." In 1994, when I was in Beijing, the Stone Company management had just invited a group of academics to carry out a questionnaire survey of its thousand-odd staff to find out their needs in order to establish an even better enterprise environment.

In short, not only are many of the core state-owned industrial enterprises retaining many of the attributes of the *danwei* while giving these a new spin. So, too, have even the Western–Chinese joint-venture firms and the high-tech private sector adopted many of the characteristics of the *danwei,* adapting these to suit the enterprise's organization-oriented goals much as in the Japanese model.

Conclusion

What judgments can we make of the present trends in the "core" firms of the state sector? At present, the *danwei* system in these firms is in transition and has already shifted considerably away from the state-oriented system. The likelihood of a reversal is small. But, in the face of the challenge of the market-oriented practices of the nonstate sector, what are the chances that China's state-owned industrial danweis will continue to converge toward the organization-oriented Japanese model?

Pre-existing attitudes carried over from the Maoist state-oriented danwei system indicate that Chinese workers could become "company men," that like the Japanese they prefer paternalistic managers, that they would work much harder if others were to show appreciation for their work, and that, unlike the British and Americans, they do not regard management–worker interests as zero-sum and contradictory. With state enterprises being granted greater autonomy and with the enactment of the new Enterprise Law, the preconditions are there for a new type of organization-oriented danwei system to develop in Chinese state enterprises. Contrary to the prognostications of some Western economists, the state sector's shift to a market economy does not have to be accompanied by a market-oriented employment system (this is true, as seen, even of the joint ventures and high-tech private firms). "Socialism with Chinese characteristics" (and even core-sector "capitalism with Chinese characteristics") may well end up meaning an organization-oriented, danwei-like system.

Notes

1. Glen Lewis and Sun Wanning, "Discourse about 'Learning from Japan' in Post-1979 Mainland Chinese Management Journals," *Issues and Studies* 30, no. 5 (May 1994): 63–76.

2. People's University in Beijing publishes a reprint series of worthwhile articles from the national and regional journals, entitled *Renmin daxue baokan fuyin ziliao* [People's University newspaper and magazine reprints]. Between 1980 and 1990 its reprint journal on "Industrial Enterprise Management" contained 202 articles on Japanese enterprises, compared to only 122 articles regarding American enterprises. Other good sources for papers on the Japanese model include the journals *Shehuixue yanjiu* [Sociological research], *Shenzhen tequ bao* [Shenzhen special economic zone paper], and *Shehui* [Society].

3. As just one example, in April 1989, at a symposium organized by *Keji ribao* [Science and technology daily], which was attended by some twenty of China's most high-powered academics as well as staff from Zhao Ziyang's think tanks, the director of the Chinese Credit Investment Corporation, who had been a former secretary of Zhao Ziyang in the mid-1980s, criticized those who wanted "to cross the river in one leap," that is, to adopt the Western model wholesale. He suggested identifying the existing organizational arrangements that could help China to develop like Japan. (My thanks to Zhu Xiaoyang, who attended this symposium, for sharing this information with me.)

4. I ought to caution readers who might confuse my usage of Dore's organization-oriented system with Susan Shirk's adaptation of the concept. (Susan L. Shirk, "Recent Chinese Labour Policies and the Transformation of Industrial Organization in China," *China Quarterly*, no. 88 (December 1981): 575–93.) Shirk poses the organization-oriented system against an "efficiency-oriented" system, which implies that an "organization-oriented" system is less efficient than a more market-oriented system. My usage of the term, however, is borrowed strictly from Dore's without adaptation.

5. Dore's conception of the difference between the two models first appeared in *British Factory—Japanese Factory: The Origins of National Diversity in Industrial Relations* (London: George Allen and Unwin, 1973). He systematically developed the concept in *Taking Japanese Seriously: A Confucian Perspective on Leading Economic Issues* (London: Athlone Press, 1987); refer specifically to the table summarizing the characteristics of the two systems on 29–31. The outline of the two employment systems described here is a summary of Dore's ideas. Except for erosion at the fringes, the essential features of the Japanese system have basically remained unchanged (Ronald Dore, "Where We Are Now: Musings of an Evolutionist," *Work, Employment and Society* 3, no. 4 [December 1989]: 425–66).

6. For a recent comparative study of Japanese and American industrial organization based largely on Dore's conception of "welfare corporatism" (a term used by Dore in his 1973 study), see James R. Lincoln and Arne L. Lalleberg, *Culture, Control, and Commit-*

ment: A Study of Work Organization and Work Attitudes in the United States and Japan (Cambridge: Cambridge University Press, 1990). The authors concluded that the American system is gradually shifting toward the Japanese model. For the success of Japanese transplants in the United States, see Paul S. Adler,"Time and Motion Regained," *Harvard Business Review* (January–February 1993): 97–108; and Richard Florida and Martin Kenney, "Transplanted Organizations: The Transfer of Japanese Industrial Organization to the U.S.," *American Sociological Review* 56 (June 1991): 381–98. On the other hand, in Britain such a transfer was less successful because of worker resistance; see Barry Wilkinson and Nick Oliver, "Japanese Influences on British Industrial Culture," in *Capitalism in Contrasting Cultures*, ed. Steward R. Clegg et al. (New York: Walter de Gruyter, 1990), 333–54.

7. Dore, *Taking the Japanese Seriously*, 25.

8. Akira Takanashi, "Japan's High Economic Growth and Industrial Relations," in *Industrial Relations, Wages and Employment in the Japanese Labor Market*, ed. Bert Edstrom (Stockholm: Center for Pacific Asian Studies, Stockholm University, 1994), 12.

9. Michael Minor and B. Curtis Hamm, "The 'Little Dragons' as Role Models," in *Organization and Management in China, 1979–90*, ed. Oded Shenkar (Armonk, NY: M.E. Sharpe, 1991), 85–99.

10. For discussions of workers' dissatisfaction and resistance, see, e.g., *Shijie jingji daobao* [World economic herald], January 25, 1989; *Zhongguo xinwen* [China news], January 4, 1989; and Cao Xiaofeng and Zhao Zixiang, "Duoxing xintai: Qiye zhigong laodong jijixing diluo de yuanyin qianxi" [The Psychology of Laziness: A Brief Analysis of the Reason for the Low Incentives of Enterprise Staff and Workers], *Shehui* [Society], no. 4 (1991): 40–42.

11. Andrew G. Walder and Gong Xiaoxia, "Workers in the Tiananmen Protests: The Politics of the Beijing Workers' Autonomous Federation," *Australian Journal of Chinese Affairs*, no. 29 (January 1993): 1–30.

12. Anita Chan, "The Social Origins and Consequences of the Tiananmen Crisis," in *China in the Nineties: Crisis Management and Beyond*, ed. David Goodman and Gerald Segal (Oxford: Clarendon Press, 1991), 105–30.

13. For reports of these industrial protests see *The New York Times*, June 12, 1992. In August 1992 China's labor minister openly admitted there had been strikes when efforts had been made to lay off one million state workers that year (Reuters News Service, August 3, 1992). For the government's placatory reaction, see, e.g., the special editorial in the *People's Daily* of May 5, 1992.

14. *China News Digest*, August 17, 1993.

15. *Chinese Labour Bulletin* [Hong Kong], no. 3 (May 1994): 8–9.

16. Akira Takanashi, "Japan's High Growth and Industrial Relations," 7–16. The percentage of the unionized work force, which is concentrated in the large firms, actually has been declining, totaling about 25 percent in 1992, down from 33–35 percent in 1956. Also see Kazutoshi Koshiro, "Collective Wage Determination in Japan: Interaction between the Private and Public Sectors with Consideration for Its Macroeconomic Implications," in *Industrial Relations, Wages and Employment*, ed. Edstrom, 17–55.

17. Solomon B. Levine, "Careers and Mobility in Japan's Labor Markets," in *Work and Lifecourse in Japan*, ed. David W. Plath (Albany: State University of New York Press, 1983), 15–33.

18. An extraordinary shop-floor account of this shift in the low-skill "women's work" side of state industry is Minghua Zhao and Theo Nichols, "Management Control of Labour in State-owned Enterprises: Cases from the Textile Industry," *China Journal*, no. 36 (July 1996): 1–21.

19. See, for example, Michael Harris and Geert Hofstede, "The Cash Value of Confucian Values," in *Capitalism in Contrasting Cultures,* eds. Stewart R. Clegg et al (Berlin: Walter de Gruyter, 1990), 383–90. For a comprehensive review of the literature that deals with East Asian culture and economic development, see J.A.C. Mackie, "Overseas Chinese Entrepreneurship," *Asian-Pacific Economic Literature* 6, no. 1 (May 1992): 41–64.

20. Dore, *British Factory—Japanese Factory,* chap. 14; also Malcolm Warner, "Japanese Culture, Western Management: Taylorism and Human Resources in Japan," *Organization Studies* 14, no. 1 (1994): 509–33.

21. Most Chinese advocates of the Japanese model, as noted earlier, do not draw any explicit comparison between Japan and China, still less openly argue that China should seriously learn from Japan. At least one article, though, gingerly suggests that the reforms should not rashly dismantle the lifetime employment system because it has been recognized as a practice essential to the successful Japanese model. See Zheng Haihang, "Zhong–Ri qiye jingying guanli gaige—jianlun Zhongguo qiye gaige" [Comparing Chinese and Japanese Enterprise Management Reforms—Including a Discussion on Chinese Enterprise Reforms], *Gaige* [Reform], no. 6 (1990): 168–75.

22. R.P. Dore, *International Markets and National Traditions: Japanese Capitalism in the 21st Century* (Hong Kong: University of Hong Kong, Social Science Centre, Occasional Paper no. 5, 1992), 16.

23. For a discussion on the Japanese enterprise as a community, see Dore, *British Factory—Japanese Factory,* chap. 8. Also see Thomas P. Rohlen, *For Harmony and Strength: Japanese White-Collar Organization in Anthropological Perspective* (Berkeley: University of California Press, 1974). For the Chinese enterprise as a community, an excellent account of the historical origin and the sequencing of events that culminated in the ossification of the *danwei* system can be found in Lu Feng, "The Origins and Formation of the Unit (*Danwei*) System," *Chinese Sociology and Anthropology* 25, no. 3 (spring 1992). A description of the Chinese *danwei* as a community can also be found in Gail E. Henderson and Myron S. Cohen, *The Chinese Hospital: A Socialist Work Unit* (New Haven: Yale University Press, 1984).

24. For a detailed analysis of the serious social and political consequences of someone not belonging to a work unit in China even today, see Zhu Xiaoyang and Anita Chan, *Xiangzheng yu anliu—1989 de shehui yundong* [Symbolism and Undercurrents—the 1989 Social Movement] (Taipei: Daohe chubanshe, 1994), chap. 5.

25. State penetration into the private lives of individuals through the *danwei* was deeper under Maoism than Stalinism. A good description of the political control mechanisms in the work unit and a discussion of Maoism as a variant of Stalinism can be found in Constance Squires Meaney, *Stability and the Industrial Elite in China and the Soviet Union* (Berkeley: University of California, China Research Monograph no. 34, 1988), chap. 3.

26. For a graphic description of the dangers of being exposed by neighbors, see three short stories written by Chen Jo-hsi, "Residency Check," "Jen Hsiu-lan," and "Chairman Mao Is a Rotten Egg," in *The Execution of Mayor Yin and Other Stories from the Great Proletarian Cultural Revolution* (Bloomington: Indiana University Press, 1978). For a scholarly study of interpersonal isolation in workplaces and neighborhoods, see Ezra Vogel, "From Friendship to Comradeship: The Change in Personal Relations in Communist China," *China Quarterly,* no. 21 (January 1965): 46–60.

27. On the efforts of Western firms to introduce QC circles to China, see John Bank, "Teaching the Chinese about Quality Circles—A Personal Account," in Malcolm Warner (ed.), *Management Reforms in China* (New York: St. Martin's Press, 1987), 99–110.

28. A general description of some of the Maoist practices to motivate workers is contained in Charles Hoffman, *The Chinese Worker* (New York: State University of New York Press, 1974), chap. 4.

29. The failure of the Maoist management practices on the shop floor is well documented by Andrew G. Walder, *Communist Neo-Traditionalism: Work and Authority in Chinese Industry* (Berkeley: University of California Press, 1986), chaps. 4, 5, and 6.

30. This kind of egalitarian work culture is not always easily acceptable to Western management staff. See Barry Wilkinson and Nick Oliver, "Japanese Influences on British Industrial Culture," in Clegg et al., *Capitalism in Contrasting Cultures,* 333–54.

31. This presents researchers with an irritating problem because Chinese statistics do not separate out white-collar and blue-collar staff, and thus it is difficult, for example, to discuss differences in their incomes.

32. On discussions of "egalitarianism" as a problem, see "New Problems in Income Distribution," *Inside China Mainland* (July 1991): 15–17; speech (or document written) by Jiang Zemin, "Renzhen xiaochu shehui fenpei bugong xianxiang" [Seriously eliminate the phenomenon of unfair distribution in society], *Renshi zhengce fagui zhuankan* [Special journal on personnel policies and rules], no. 10 (1989): 2–7.

33. See the "Provisional regulations regarding recruitment of workers in state enterprises" issued by the Labor Bureau on December 8 1990 (*Laodong zhengce zhuankan* [Special journal on labor policy], no. 2 (1991): 13.

34. Shao Lei and Chen Xiangdong, *Zhongguo shehui baozhang zhidu gaige* [Reform of China's social security system] (Beijing: Jingji guanli chubanshe, 1991), 66–68. Also see *Laodong zhengce zhuankan,* 13.

35. Rodney Clark, "The Company as Family: Historical Background," in *Inside the Japanese System: Readings on Contemporary Society and Political Economy,* ed. Daniel Okimoto and Thomas Rohlen (Stanford: Stanford University Press, 1988), 103–5.

36. *Shehui* [Society], no. 4 (1991): 42–45. A survey of fourteen state enterprises revealed that from 1983 to 1989, the total number of employees increased by 86 percent. The percentage of employees who have blood relations in the same work unit increased from 11.65 percent to 33 percent, and of these, 92.2 percent are related as parents/children, husbands/wives, or siblings.

37. For a comparative discussion of the British system, see Wilkinson and Oliver, "Japanese Influences on British Industrial Culture"; for the Australian system, which is patterned on the British system, see Peter Ewer et al., *Politics and the Accord* (Leichhardt: Pluto Press, 1991), chap. 7.

38. A very detailed analysis of the British and Japanese wage systems is found in Dore, *British Factory,* chap. 3.

39. For details of the evolutionary development of China's wage system under the economic reforms, see Akio Takahara, *The Politics of Wage Policy in Post-Revolutionary China* (London: Macmillan, 1992).

40. For medium and small firms, the bonus percentages were 22 percent and 16 percent respectively. Kazutoshi Koshiro, "Development of Collective Bargaining in Post-War Japan," in *Contemporary Industrial Relations in Japan,* ed. T. Shirai (Madison: University of Wisconsin Press, 1983), 205–57. For a detailed discussion of the Japanese wage structure, also see Dore, *British Factory,* 98.

41. Japanese Ministry of Labor, *Basic Survey on Wages Structures* (Tokyo, 1990); cited in Richard Curtain, "Recent Developments in Human Resource Management Practices in Japanese Enterprises" (unpublished manuscript, 1993).

42. The changing proportions of the various components of the Chinese state sector wage structure from 1978 to 1991 can be found in *1992 Zhongguo laodong gongzi tongji nianjian* [1992 Chinese labor wage statistical yearbook] (Beijing: Zhongguo tongji chubanshe, 1992), 125. In 1978 above-quota wages and various kinds of bonuses only made up 2.4 percent of the total wage bill of the country's state workers. By 1988 it had gone up to 19.5 percent, and has remained basically at the same level since. For the

Chinese wage component in 1992, see "Long Live the Working Class," *China News Analysis*, no. 1465 (August 1, 1992): 6.

43. Although the base wage has been shrinking, subsidies in kind have increased, thus canceling out some of the incentive-raising effects of the skill-related and bonus wage components. However, there are constant pressures from the reformers to cut back on subsidies: feasible only if wages keep up with inflation. In times of high inflation, the work force will continue to press for maintaining and increasing subsidies.

44. Bernard Karsh and Robert E. Cole, "Industrialization and the Convergence Hypothesis: Some Aspects of Contemporary Japan," *Journal of Social Issues* 24, no. 4 (1968): 45–63. Also see Dore, *British Factory*, 104.

45. See Barry M. Richman's pathbreaking work on Chinese enterprises in the 1960s. Armed with a comparative perspective drawn from his expertise on the Soviet Union, Richman pointed out the appalling lack of management know-how in Chinese state enterprises (*Industrial Society in Communist China* [New York: Random House, 1969], 819–21).

46. Pat and Roger Howard, "China's Enterprise Management Reforms in the Eighties: Technocratic Versus Democratic Tendencies," in *Advances in Chinese Industrial Studies, Vol. 3: Changes in the Iron Rice Bowl: The Reformation of Chinese Management*, ed. William Wedley (Greenwich, CT: JAI Press, 1992), 37–58. "Scientific management" seems to have spread to the labor-intensive state enterprises, but whether this kind of management practice is truly "scientific" is debatable. They appear most often to be merely coercive and exploitative techniques, as in several textile factories in Henan province that have been examined. For an excellent description of this pseudo-"scientific" management in Henan, see Zhao and Nichols, "Management Control."

47. Paul Thompson, "Disorganized Socialism: State and Enterprise in Modern China," in *Labour in Transition: The Labour Process in East Europe and China*, ed. Chris Smith and Paul Thompson (London: Routledge, 1992), 247–48.

48. The degeneration of the Maoist system in the industrial enterprises is discussed in Walder, *Communist Neo-Traditionalism*, chap. 7.

49. *Beijing Review* 35, no. 46 (November 16–22, 1992): 13–17.

50. *Beijing Review* 35, no. 32 (August 10–16, 1992): 4.

51. That this shift has been deliberate is evident in comments by Yuan Baohua, the chairman of China's Enterprise Management Association (Zhongguo qiye guanli xiehui): "The enterprise is not a political organization. The party's function within the enterprise is not the same as that of the party committees at the central and local levels. . . . The enterprise is an economic organization. All its activities should be centered on the manager. The enterprise is a legally incorporated body, and the manager is the legal representative of this legal body who occupies the central position and is the chief initiator of activities" (Bao Guangqian and Guo Qing, *Yuan Baohua fangtanlu* [Interview records with Yuan Baohua] [Beijing: Renmin chubanshe, 1991], 403.) (I am grateful to Dr. You Ji of the University of Canterbury, New Zealand, for bringing this book to my attention.) As chair of the Enterprise Management Association, Yuan Baohua played a key mediating role in the drafting of the laws and regulations relating to the enterprise reforms.

52. *Liaowang* [Outlook], no. 17 (1988): 11–15. My own observations, gained from visiting three state enterprises in 1991 and 1992, also point to similar developments. In an electronics factory that I visited in 1994, the party secretary's role, to my surprise, was reduced to serving tea to visitors. It should be emphasized, though, that authority now flows through a government bureaucracy, not through higher-ranking party channels.

53. *Jiushi niandai* [The nineties] (February 1993): 46. Zhu noted in an address to the Shanghai delegation at the congress that MITI's relationship with Japanese industry formed the explicit model. (This information derives from an interview in Beijing conducted by Dr. You Ji, to whom I am indebted.)

54. *Jingji ribao* [Economic daily], March 17, 1993, 2. The Ministry of Light Industries has become the Light Industry Federation of Associations (Qinggong zonghui).

55. *Beijing Review* 37, no. 3 (January 17–23, 1994): 4.

56. As early as 1980, staff and workers' congresses that had functioned only in name in the 1950s had been revived in some factories to provide a facade of democratic management. But insofar as the state-oriented structure and ethos were basically left intact throughout the first half of the 1980s, few of the congresses had carried out their purported functions.

57. Bao and Guo, *Yuan Baohua fangtanlu*, 385 and 413. This no-less-than-one-third representation is not spelled out in the law, but was cited by Yuan Baohua, who is an authority on this matter. The rest of the members of the management board, which is to be chaired by the manager, include: the deputy manager, the senior engineer, the senior accountant, the party secretary, and the Youth League secretary (385).

58. Chongqing Municipal Trade Union Research Department, "Countermeasures to Deal with Problems in Implementing the Guiding Principle of 'Whole-heartedly Relying on the Working Class' " (in Chinese). This is an internal document that was presented at a conference in 1991.

59. Ibid.

60. A collection of the essays written by various provincial-level unions is published in the volume *Qiye liyi gongtongti chutan* [Preliminary investigations into the enterprise as a body of mutual interests] (Beijing: Zhongguo gongren chubanshe, 1990). For an example of such a collective contract, see 206–9. The most interesting essays in the collection were compiled by the unions of Jiangsu and Hebei provinces. These recount the history of collective contracting in the two provinces; how the "mutual interest" idea was seen as a solution to the problems that had emerged with the management responsibility system; and the alleged success of the program in reducing management–worker tensions, which in turn was effective in increasing production.

61. See, e.g., Dong Xijian and Guo Dan, "Zhong–Ri qiye: Peiyang he fayang qiye jingshen yitongdian chutan" [Chinese and Japanese enterprises: A preliminary investigation into the similarities and differences in the cultivation and development of enterprise spirit], *Shehui*, no. 10 (1988): 32–36. Also Lu Siulan, "Riben qiye shi zenmeyang diaodong zhigong jijixingde" [How Japanese enterprises instigate staff and workers' incentives], *Shanghai qiye* [Shanghai enterprises], no. 11 (1989): 37–38.

62. This kind of argument can be found in a large number of short articles published in China in general, academic, or management magazines. They all tend to be cliché-ridden, with conclusions arrived at without any empirical studies. For a sampling of such articles, see *Shehui*, no. 11 (1988): 32–36; *Shehui*, no. 5 (1988): 20–21; and *Waiguo jingji guanli* [Foreign economic management], reprinted in *Zhongguo renmin daxue shubao ziliao zhongxin, gongye qiye guanli* [Chinese People's University Reprint Center, Industrial enterprise management journal], no. 6 (1987): 132–34.

63. This information was provided by a researcher at the Workers' Movement Institute (Gongyun xueyuan) in Beijing. There seems to be a consensus among some academics and trade unionists in Beijing that Capital Steel, a national model of a successful state enterprise, has cultivated a commendable "enterprise culture."

64. I know of the existence of such associations, made up of academics, government officials, and factory directors, in Beijing, Shenzhen, and Guangzhou. There is also an umbrella organization located in Beijing.

65. For another effort to refute the notion that the Japanese and Chinese have a lot in common, see Shigeto Sonoda, " 'Same Culture, Same Species' Is an Illusion—Case Studies of Chinese–Japanese Joint Ventures," *Chuo Koron* (July 1994) (Special issue on "Business in China"): 215–23.

66. The research team set up in 1987 was headed by Professor Sengoku Tamatsu of the Japanese Youth Research Institute. The original findings, published in Japanese, were translated into Chinese in a slightly revised version entitled *Zhongguo de laodong lilun—zi Ri–Zhong qingnian gongren yishi diaocha* [Chinese work ethics—From a survey of consciousness among Japanese and Chinese youths], *Dangdai qingnian yanjiu* [Contemporary youth research], no. 6 (1988): 22–30, and no. 7 [1988]: 24–31. The survey covered four Japanese factories and one Japanese department store and eight Chinese factories and one Chinese department store. The questionnaire was designed to be cross-nationally comparative for Chinese, Japanese, and American workers' attitudes. This appears to be the most rigorous study of Chinese workers' attitudes to appear in Chinese publications.

67. For example, three joint ventures that I visited in 1994 in Beijing can be classed in this category: the Beijing International Switching System Corporation (German Siemens), Pacific Dunlop (Australia), and Beijing Jingao Wool Co. Ltd. (Australia). For a more detailed discussion, see Anita Chan, "The Emerging Patterns of Industrial Relations in China—and the Rise of Two New Labor Movements," *China Information* 1, no. 4 (spring 1995): 36–59.

68. Li Zhaoxi and Xu Zhaohong, *Fazhan hezi qiye de chenggong qishi—gongxi tizhi he guanli xingwei* [The successful experiences on the development of joint ventures: Corporate structure and management behavior) (Beijing: Qiye guanli chubanshe, 1994), 249.

69. Greg J. Bamber and Russell D. Lansbury, ed., *International and Comparative Relations,* 2d ed. (Sydney: Allen and Unwin, 1993), 6; Dennis MacShane, "Unions at Home and Abroad," *Dialogue,* no. 104 (February 1994): 52–55. In Beijing, I had the opportunity to listen to an Australian former motor-factory manager doing some soul-searching on how he became a convert to the Japanese management model.

70. Corinna-Barbara Francis, "The Reproduction of *Danwei* Institutional Features in the Context of China's Market Economy: The Case of Haidian District's High-tech Sector" (paper presented at the annual meeting of the Association for Asian Studies, Boston, March 23–27, 1994).

71. Zhang Wanzhong, "Beijing sitong bangong shebei youxian gongsi zhidu huibian (di yi ban)" [A compendium of regulations—Beijing Stone Office Supply Co. Ltd., 1st ed.], 1992, 13.

5

The Russian "Village in the City" and the Stalinist System of Enterprise Management: The Origins of Worker Alienation in Soviet State Socialism

Rudra Sil

Given the common tasks confronting late industrializers, it is not surprising that many of the characteristics of the Chinese *danwei* are essentially the same as those of large-scale industrial enterprises in other late-industrializing societies. In all late industrializers, the state has taken a leading role in accumulating capital and developing the industrial infrastructure, and, for all states, the performance and stability of large-scale enterprises—whether in the private or state sector—has been crucial for both economic development and the maintenance of social order. In all cases, managers have had to institutionalize a complex division of labor linked to mechanization, specialization, and bureaucratization, and they have had to devise a system of material and ideal incentives linked at least partially to industrial output. In addition, the characterization of the Chinese *danwei* as a "village in the city" is applicable to large-scale factories in other late-industrializing societies as well.[1] The process of rapid industrialization in all late industrializers has been typically accompanied by the "social mobilization" of millions of peasants-turned-workers who proceeded to reconstruct traditional, particularistic associations and networks within the context of urban, industrial social settings.[2] Also, in China as well as in other late industrializers, economic elites and managers themselves have frequently attempted to turn the large-scale industrial enterprise into a cohesive entity that is simultaneously a production unit, a moral community, a system of paternalistic authority, and a center for the distribution of goods and privileges.

Unlike large-scale enterprises in most other late industrializers, however, the

Chinese *danwei* is embedded in a Communist or "state-socialist" system. As such, it shares a distinctive subset of characteristics with industrial enterprises in the Soviet Union and in other Communist regimes. The Chinese *danwei* and the Soviet state enterprises were both workplace institutions devised by Communist elites to cope simultaneously with the problems of "catching up" to the advanced industrial powers and "building socialism." In both cases, economic development was to be achieved through an explicitly anticapitalist or antibourgeois route, and the methods for evaluating and rewarding the performance of workers were linked to the question of their moral qualities or "proletarian" class credentials. Subsequently, in both, the large industrial enterprise served a "political–statist function," designed simultaneously to mobilize the population for political participation, control employee mobility, and monitor the political loyalty of employees; it also served a "social–communal function," with the enterprise providing employment guarantees and a host of welfare services, including access to basic necessities, insurance for sickness, old age pensions, as well as educational and recreational activities revolving around the enterprise community.[3] Thus, in both cases, there emerged a situation of "organized dependence," with workers economically dependent on the enterprise, politically dependent on the party's factory committee, and personally dependent on their immediate supervisors.[4]

In some important respects, however, the large-scale Soviet enterprise differed markedly from the Chinese *danwei*. Certain distinctive features emerged in the Soviet model of factory organization, partly as a result of the Bolsheviks' experiences with revolution and civil war and partly as a result of the influence of Western models or management concepts as early as 1918. Subsequently, the ideological and organizational devices employed by Soviet managers increasingly deviated from the initial Bolshevik work ethic as well as from the social legacies inherited by the Soviet proletariat from prerevolutionary institutions. These deviations ultimately paved the way for the increasing "alienation" of the typical Soviet worker from the formal system of enterprise production. Soviet workers may not have been "atomized," but they were certainly not committed to or incorporated within the Soviet enterprise system.[5] This is evident in the levels of labor discipline, absenteeism, turnover, job satisfaction, and black market activity.

This chapter focuses on one important set of reasons why the Soviet industrial enterprise, despite the tremendous concentration of power and resources in the hands of enterprise directors, produced a work force that became increasingly unproductive, undisciplined, apathetic, and ultimately, alienated from the workplace.

The Legacy: The Prerevolutionary Russian Peasantry and the Agrarian *Mir*

All modernizers are faced with the task of reshaping a deeply entrenched set of values, attitudes, and behavioral norms embedded in concrete institutions inherited from preindustrial communities. Modernization theorists in the 1950s and 1960s considered these preindustrial values and norms to be uniform, typical characteristics across all "traditional" societies, and they assumed that such values and norms were inherently incompatible with modern industrial society. However, the concept of "tradition" not only obscured important differences across various preindustrial societies, but also precluded any serious consideration of the specific mechanisms employed by preindustrial communities to maintain social order.[6] In contrast, this chapter employs the notion of a preindustrial historical "legacy," including three assumptions that are at odds with the theoretical framework of classical modernization theory: (1) historical legacies inherited by modernizers are products of gradual change over time, and they vary across different regions and societies; (2) certain aspects of a historical legacy (i.e., a particular subset of values, norms, or organizational patterns) are more likely to persist over the course of modernization than others; and (3) those aspects are neither destined to fade away nor inherently inimical to the goals of building a stable, technologically advanced industrial society.

This examination of the legacy inherited from prerevolutionary Russia focuses particularly on those values and social structures that are most deeply embedded and least likely to be transformed by changing social environments: values and structures that support collective (not individual) definitions of identity and interest in agrarian communities. Beliefs and norms related to identity and interest formation are inherently the most difficult to transform because they are so deeply entrenched and internalized, yet the redefinition of identity and interest is a crucial aspect in the process of creating new "modern" institutions. Although preindustrial values and norms may be embedded in a whole range of social institutions, village communities in a particular region or society are concentrated on here because it is the village that formed the social horizon of most individual peasants, and it is the village where specific mechanisms emerged for regulating social relations among peasants, defining group boundaries and identities, and identifying the shared interests of separate households in the course of everyday life and work.

In the case of prerevolutionary Russia, the dominant social institution among the peasantry was the agrarian commune (*obshchina,* or *mir,* as the peasants referred to it).[7] For the purposes of this analysis, two important points emerge when we place the Russian *mir* in a comparative-historical context: (1) the *mir* emphasized *collectivist values and norms* and frequently subordinated the individual's interests and identity to those of the corporate village; and (2) compared to village communities in many other preindustrial societies, the Russian *mir* was markedly *more egalitarian* both in terms of the predominant values shared among the peasant households constituting the village community and in terms of its actual social structure.

Russian peasants shared a common understanding that the peasant was rarely in a position to act on his own will, and that (s)he was better off acting *po vole mira,* in accordance with the will of the commune.[8] The communes were total corporate entities in which interpersonal ties and social interactions were shaped by the common contexts of everyday life and work, and membership derived from participation in group life, rather than any shared attributes or mythical kinship ties among villagers (as was the case in India, for example). Village life was generally characterized by a dense network of intensely personal relations among members of various joint households who worked everyday on several small strips of land scattered throughout the village. Most peasants encountered their neighbors on a daily basis, and peasant social relations were marked by a great camaraderie (despite occasional drunken brawls).[9] Members of the commune also displayed a shared distrust of outsiders and a disinterest in the affairs of outsiders, and to the extent that they had to deal with outside authorities, they regarded these dealings as strictly functional and even impersonal.[10] As in other village communities, the separate interests and identities of individual households did not disappear, but they were clearly subordinated whenever they conflicted with the goals of regulating collective labor, managing collective resources, or maintaining village harmony.

These collectivist values and norms were institutionalized in the form of specific and regular practices seen throughout the prerevolutionary Russian countryside. As far back as the sixteenth century, the *mir* introduced concrete measures to manage common property, resolve internal conflicts, and promote collective endeavors and mutual assistance. Even under serfdom during the seventeenth and eighteenth centuries, the *mir* continued to regulate collective village life by distributing common tasks and resources among households, determining the tax burdens of households, and providing for the welfare of less fortunate members.[11] After the 1861 emancipation of serfs, the *mir* became even more firmly entrenched and more active; in addition to regulating common land, it also maintained local roads, provided new educational facilities and welfare services, and helped households do their best to pay state taxes and redemption payments owed to the former gentry landowners.[12]

The egalitarian aspects of the Russian commune render it more distinctive. Past discussions of traditional Russian "political culture" have tended to highlight the hierarchical aspects of tsarist Russia—the supreme authority of the tsar, the seigniorial authority of the gentry over serfs, and even the tendency of peasants to regard the tsar as *tsar batiushka* ("little father") in Russia.[13] Moreover, steep hierarchies based on age and gender prevailed in the Russian countryside at the level of the family or household (*dvor*).[14] However, it is the *village* that formed the social world within which the average peasant interacted with other peasants, and it was the *mir* that regulated day-to-day cooperative endeavors in the village. The values and social structure of the Russian *mir* were far more egalitarian than one might expect if one focused solely on households or the institution of serfdom under tsarist rule.

Within the typical Russian commune there was a diffuse sense of hostility toward hierarchical authority structures, both inside and outside the village community.[15] Russian peasants placed a common emphasis on social leveling among households as a crucial component of village harmony. The idea of leveling does not necessarily suggest the absence of any notion of self-interest; but, within the context of a peasant economy, self-interest was actually served by ensuring that no one individual or family could advance too rapidly lest the rest of the village community suffer sharp declines in its collective fortunes.[16] They also upheld the "right to labor" principle, which suggested that every family in the village, no matter how poor, had the right to a land allotment so that it could work the fields as a means of subsistence.[17]

These egalitarian norms were translated into institutionalized practices that had definite consequences for the structure of the commune. In contrast to the sharp concentration of wealth in Indian or Japanese villages, the Russian *mir* engaged in a periodic redistribution of land designed to prevent sharp stratification. According to the system of land repartition, each peasant household could keep a small plot around the house on a hereditary basis, but the bulk of arable land was distributed by the commune as allotments of strips (*nadel*). Repartitions took place according to a complex system for dividing communal arable land into strips and allocating them to different households so that peasants would have equal access to both good and poor soils. Furthermore, a larger number of strips would be apportioned to some while diminishing the holdings of others in order to take into account changes in household composition, labor strength, and tax burdens. Certainly, there were occasional conflicts when the wealthiest households attempted to leave the commune and establish their own farmsteads, but these were exceptions to the rule, and, for the most part, households voluntarily acceded to the periodic repartition process.[18] On the whole, the repartitional commune reflected a genuine and shared concern for social leveling, and economic historians and anthropologists have found that the level of socioeconomic differentiation among the peasantry was markedly lower in comparison to most other agrarian social structures.[19]

Similarly, in contrast to many other societies where decision-making authority was concentrated in the hands of the few of the most wealthy, highest-ranked household heads, the process of collective decision-making in the Russian countryside was far more inclusive. Representation in the Russian village assembly (*skhod*) was extended to the heads of *all* households, not just to the wealthiest or highest-ranked household heads. Nonrepresentatives frequently attended village meetings and addressed important issues. The village headman was an elder (*starosta*) who was required to seek consensus among assembly members before acting on major issues. The *skhod*, even during serfdom, remained autonomous from the jurisdiction of the manorial authorities, and the decisions it reached were often unanimously supported by the representatives and their households. The position of the *starosta* never became hereditary as the position of the village headman did in Japan and elsewhere, and the *skhod* periodically re-elected the *starosta* as well as other officers charged with land-use management, tax collection, welfare, and so forth.[20] Thus, in terms of both socioeconomic redistribution and decision-making authority, the *mir* proved to be a highly popular and relatively homogeneous institution that embraced norms of collectivism, consensual decision-making, and social leveling well into the 1920s.[21]

Workers, Factories, and the Peasant Legacy in Prerevolutionary Russia

The importance of the peasant background of the first Russian workers is seen in nineteenth-century discussions on how to maintain social order and factory discipline in the growing urban industrial centers of prerevolutionary Russia. Most factory "workers" before the 1861 abolition of serfdom were *otkhodniki,* seasonal workers contracted out by their manorial lords to urban factories, and they were still bound by legal, financial, and familial obligations to the villages. As temporary workers, they stubbornly resisted socialization into the system of disciplined labor and factory time in favor of returning to their villages for the annual harvests.[22] From the point of view of tsarist officials and industrialists in the nineteenth century, the very fact that most workers remained bound to the land suggested that patriarchal authority structures would suffice to maintain social order and that Russia would avoid the widespread social unrest plaguing the industrial cities of Western Europe.[23] To the extent that important measures were taken in the nineteenth century to protect the health and welfare of the workers, they were primarily initiatives from above intended mainly to institutionalize the "paternalistic principle" in employment relations and to forestall radical protest among the peasant-workers flooding into urban areas.[24]

By the late nineteenth century (i.e., after serfdom had been abolished), workers were becoming a more permanent urban class, less inclined to return regularly for seasonal agricultural work, and increasingly concerned with wages, shop-floor activities, and working and living conditions.[25] Under these conditions, they took measures to organize themselves to deal with exigencies of long-term factory work and city life. The measures they took, however, reflected some of the core values and practices they had been accustomed to in village life.

The egalitarian norms of the Russian *mir* re-emerged in the urban industrial centers in the form of workers' *artels* spontaneously formed by the first generation of workers who had migrated from the same village (*zemliaki*). In this respect, the first Russian factory workers were very much like the first Chinese workers for whom native-place identity was a crucial basis for mutual assistance and collective action.[26] The Russian *artels* elected an "elder" to manage their affairs, equally distributed wages earned for tasks performed collectively, employed their own sanctions to maintain group discipline, and took care of the welfare of the newer members.[27] In an environment of uncertainty and flux, "the *artel* was the only institution capable of mitigating the isolation of the peasant *otkhodnik* in a strange city and allowing him to share the burden of his employment and subsistence problems with fellow villagers."[28]

The social trust shared by the members of *artels* did not, however, extend to Russian factories. In fact, the continued importance of preindustrial identities and the distrust of outsiders meant that workers neither trusted nor regularly obeyed their supervisors, managers, or employers. To the extent that managers and officials in the late tsarist period believed that some sort of appeal to tradition would suffice to preserve order, they focused mostly on the patriarchal familial authority rather than the commune or the *artel*.[29] However, for most workers, familial patriarchal authority did not translate into factory discipline or blind obedience to orders from superiors. And, given the fact that most *artels* and other workers' associations were shaped primarily by regional ties, the typical large enterprise in tsarist Russia tended to have a "balkanized" work force.[30] The legacy of the *mir* thus remained limited to egalitarian values, social trust, and collective labor, and it was evident only in *informal* social relations among the members of spontaneously created *artels*. If this legacy was to be reconstructed so as to support social order throughout large-scale factory establishments, a more elaborate approach was required by managerial elites.

However, the real drama was yet to unfold. By the turn of the century, only a fraction of the Russian population had migrated to the urban industrial centers, and more than 80 percent of the population remained rural. It was only after the Bolshevik revolution that millions of peasants entered the industrial work force, either having migrated in search of factory work or having been forced off their communes during Stalin's collectivization campaign beginning in 1928. It was the Bolsheviks who would face the real challenge of managing preindustrial legacies while finding a workable formula for workplace organization in the course of building socialism.

The Shift in Bolshevik Ideology: The Decline of Collective Egalitarianism

In the months leading up to and immediately following the October 1917 Revolution, the pronouncements of Lenin and other Bolshevik leaders emphasized both collectivism and egalitarianism, ideals that appealed to, or at least resonated with, workers who had formed production *artels* as well as peasants still living in the *mir*. As Siegelbaum has noted: "For a short period, it appeared that this organic relationship between the Soviet state and the 'toiling masses' might be able to sustain itself and serve as the basis for building the new socialist order. Factory committees, soviets, and the collectivist ethos with which they were suffused seemed to herald the kind of commune-state about which Lenin wrote in *The State and Revolution*."[31] Even though it was the party that was to be the "vanguard of the masses," Lenin publicly emphasized the importance of spontaneous action by the proletariat, praised the "creative energy" of the masses, and criticized administrative controls from above. Although Lenin had emphasized unity, conformity, and centralization of decision-making power when it came to party discipline and the revolutionary seizure of power, in matters of day-to-day administration and decision-making, the official formulas emphasized "democratic centralism" and kollegial'nost', leadership through collegial decision-making and consensus-building among the participants.32

In the context of the enterprise, this idea translated into the notion of "workers' control," suggesting some sort of elected committee-type administration collectively making critical production decisions with the concurrence of factory personnel of all ranks and skill levels. Thus, the Commissariat of Labor established direct workers' control councils in all industrial enterprises. The individual factory councils would be unified under the All-Russian Council of Workers' Control, which would supervise production, monitor costs of production, and even settle budgetary accounts. Workers themselves began implementing these councils, setting up conferences, organizing procedures for making decisions, and drawing up detailed instructions on the methods and scope of workers' control.33 Moreover, in keeping with the egalitarian ideals of a "classless" Communist society, Lenin and the Bolsheviks initially upheld the ideals of "equal wages for equal labor" in factories with little acknowledgment of variations in skill levels and performance. Similarly, while labor discipline was important to the Bolsheviks, it was seen as something attainable through collective self-discipline among workers; thus the Bolsheviks initially rejected harsh labor codes of the tsarist era in favor of a "voluntary and conscientious cooperation" in the factories.34

Such principles as "workers' control" and "equal wages for equal labor" emphasized both collectivism and egalitarianism, and were consistent with the social legacies inherited from the prerevolutionary countryside. This initial congruence did not survive beyond the first few months of Bolshevik rule, however, as the ideological assertions made by the Bolshevik leaders themselves became increasingly ambiguous, and even contradictory. By 1918, the Bolsheviks were engaged in a bloody civil war, industrial production was in shambles, and Lenin was predicting economic catastrophe in Russia unless there was "iron discipline" in the factories.

In this period of "war communism" (1918–21), Lenin and Trotsky reaffirmed the authority of the "bourgeois specialists" to make day-to-day technical decisions in factory management, and the ideological locus as well as the political and economic institutions took on a different look from those suggested in the earlier writings of major Bolsheviks. Lenin now announced that kollegial'nost' was a leadership style only suited for a later stage when full-blown socialism could be realized; in the meantime, it was important to draw upon the expertise of bourgeois specialists while workers acquired the necessary knowledge and experience. By 1919, official Bolshevik policy switched from kollegial'nost' to "one-man management" (edinonachalie) with full authority and responsibility vested in a single administrative leader, the enterprise director.35 The Bolsheviks took measures to ensure that workers, while being schooled in certain administrative tasks, were kept from direct management functions. By 1920, the factory trade union committees and the workers' control councils in nationalized enterprises became little more than "a facade behind which the workers employed at the individual enterprises could be deprived of an effective voice in the management of those enterprises."[36]

Although the period of the "New Economic Policy" (NEP) from 1921 to about 1925 is regarded variously as a "retreat" or a "reversal" of the war communism period, little changed in the large-scale factories engaged in heavy industrial production.[37] These factories represented the "commanding heights" of the Soviet economy and remained firmly under state control even as market-based exchange emerged in the light industrial and agricultural sectors. Also, since industrial production remained in disastrous straits until well after the end of the civil war, and since factory workers had become increasingly restive, the hierarchical control and "iron discipline" of war communism was steadfastly maintained in state enterprises and the idea of "workers' control" remained at best a distant goal.[38]

Beginning with Stalin's famous "left turn" in 1928, a clear program emerged for dealing decisively with the question of the preindustrial "legacy" and establishing a systematic set of management practices at the enterprise level.[39] The result was a two-pronged strategy based on two different kinds of theories about culture and social change. The first was an all-out "cultural revolution" consisting of a violent attack on "class enemies," including the total destruction of the stubbornly resilient peasant *mir*, whom Stalin viewed as the most significant threat to the Communist Party of the Soviet Union (CPSU). This program was spearheaded by the collectivization campaign that began in 1928. The collectivization drives proved to be much more than an attempt to replace traditional peasant agriculture with mechanized collective farms; they were more than an economic strategy to weaken wealthy peasants and extract resources from the countryside to finance rapid industrialization. They also represented a massive campaign to root out attitudes, values, and habits embedded in precapitalist social institutions that Stalin viewed as inherently opposed to the building of socialism under a vanguard party.[40] That the ideals of the commune were not in every respect opposed to the ideals of Bolshevism was irrelevant for Stalin, for whom the chief issue became control and consolidation of the new regime along with the urgent construction of heavy industry.[41]

The second part of the Stalinist strategy was less radical; it relied primarily on the experience of factory socialization. Stalin still insisted that new attitudes and values must be inculcated among the work force. However, "[t]o attain such goals, much faith was placed in the transformative powers of the factory system. With the socialist revolution, the factory, far from being a place of exploitation . . . was to become a palace of labor manned by politically conscious, literate, and skilled workers filled with pride in their work."[42] Once the peasant had been uprooted and transformed into a member of the urban, industrial proletariat, Stalin assumed that he would easily be molded into the "new Soviet man" simply by virtue of the experience of socialist labor. This expectation—that the experience and tenor of life and work in Soviet factories would produce a uniformly committed socialist work force—in effect, reflected Stalin's own theory of social change. One Soviet author, representing the dominant ideological thrust during the first five-year plan, wrote in retrospect: "Socialist industrialization . . . made possible the socialization of the toilers in the spirit of socialism, the development of new forms of life and culture, the intensification of the influence of industrial centers on the village, the strengthening of the union of working class and peasantry."[43]

However, the massive urban migration during the late 1920s and 1930s led not to the emergence of an easily malleable "new Soviet person" but to increasing difficulties in integrating the peasant-worker into the new environment of the large-scale, mechanized industrial enterprise. Persistent problems with factory discipline, strikes, and labor turnover led the party to focus less and less on egalitarianism and collectivism and more on hierarchical control, loyalty to the party leadership, and individual achievements in "socialist labor." Within the specific context of large-scale enterprises, Stalin put an end to any thoughts of reviving the original ideals of "workers' control" and "equal pay for equal work." The formal management practices under Stalin became increasingly inconsistent with the original ethic of collectivist egalitarianism that appeared in the peasant *mir,* the workers' *artel,* and the original Bolshevik ideals. This is evident not only in the extent of hierarchical managerial control institutionalized within the factory but also in the organization of work, the system of material and ideal incentives, and the informal social relations of the workplace.

The Evolution of Management Practices in the Stalinist Enterprise

First, the shift away from collectivism and egalitarianism during the 1918–28 period is evident in the institutionalization of *hierarchical control* through *edinonachalie,* defined as the "complete subordination of all the employees in the productive process to the will of one person—the leader—and his personal responsibility for the assigned work."[44] Even during the period of war communism, Lenin still left in place some constraints to keep the old "bourgeois" managers in check from "below" by setting up the People's Commissariat for Workers' and Peasants' Inspection, a governmental agency supposedly representing "workers' control." During the period of NEP in the early 1920s, Lenin also endorsed a sort of "managerial parallelism" with the enterprise director, the party cell secretary, and the factory trade union committee chairman all playing key roles. Although the director had the formal authority to make technical decisions, he was still unreliable as a "bourgeois specialist," and both the party secretary and the factory trade union committee chairman sought to influence key decisions affecting factory administration.[45] But throughout the 1920s, the trade unions as well as the People's Commissariat proved less a tool in establishing industrial democracy or workers' participation than a means of applying pressure on enterprise directors and keeping them under the control of party elites.[46]

Under Stalin, the turn from workers' control to *edinonachalie* became more explicit and definitive. Beginning in 1928, Stalin began to purge the old managerial elite from their positions to make room for a new class of managers (the "Red Directors") that had risen from among the ranks of the working class and been trained during the period of Bolshevik rule. During this period, the movement for workers' control briefly resurfaced, but mainly for the purpose of enabling Stalin and his aides to identify and purge the "wreckers," "saboteurs," and other petty-bourgeois "class enemies" who had allegedly emerged among the ranks of the old specialists. Between the late 1920s and mid-1930s, the old managers and specialists had been replaced en masse by "Red Directors" who were loyal to Stalin and officially committed to meeting the targets of the five-year plans.[47]

Now it was no longer necessary to keep the enterprise managers under check, and one-man management came to suggest for Stalin "not only sole managerial command but strictly individual managerial responsibility for the wielding of power and the results of its use, in particular the fulfillment of plan targets."[48] Thus, Lenin's "managerial parallelism" gave way to an all-powerful enterprise director who not only bore full responsibility for the factory but now had the power to make decisions entirely on his own. While the "control commissions" and trade union committees remained in place, real power became totally concentrated in the hands of the enterprise directors. In the early 1930s, Stalin ended independent workers' participation in factory management by directly attacking the "destructive criticism" that was interfering with effective factory administration, and he turned the trade unions into "transmission belts," concerned more with the cultural activities and political training of the workers than with the independent representation of workers' control or working-class interests.[49] By the time of World War II, the power of factory managers had become virtually unassailable from the viewpoint of workers, and the operational autonomy of the new directors had reached new heights.[50]

In addition to the disappearance of "workers' control" and participation from "below," the two decades following the Bolshevik revolution also witnessed the fading of the idea of "collective labor" and the emergence of a Taylorist system of work organization that stressed competitive *individual* performance as in the firms of the more advanced industrial countries. Before 1918, Lenin had joined the socialist parties of Europe in condemning Taylorism and "scientific management" as a ruthless form of capitalist exploitation that resulted in the "enslavement of humankind to the machine."[51] However, by the time war communism was in full swing, Lenin had come to believe that Taylor's "scientific management" could benefit socialist accumulation as long as some minor modifications were made to reduce the exhaustion and exploitation of the individual worker. He now praised the "rational, logical distribution of labor within the factory"

along with the elimination of superfluous motion, and he called for the establishment of an efficient system of centralized management, specialization, and a
rigid system of accountability and control.[52]

Alexei Gastev, the "Russian Taylor," set up the Central Institute of Labor in
1920 with Lenin's blessing and called for new training methods based on inten-
sive drilling in the "biomechanics of the stroke." "Throughout the 1920s, large
groups of trainees would be brought to the Institute to perform rhythmic drills
paced by metronomes at varying rates in order to train the workers' mind and
muscles to work in a certain posture at an automatic pace with economical,
regular motions."[53] The "scientific management" movement led to the creation
of labor institutes throughout Russia with half a million workers and specialists
engaged in the science of labor, studying methods to improve the rationalization
of production through further subdividing mechanical tasks. Although Gastev
was criticized for ignoring individual initiative and overemphasizing automation
and biomechanics, most Bolsheviks agreed that industrial work had to be based
on individually specialized tasks with the individual as the sole unit of performance.[54]

As a logical component of the Taylor system of work organization, a system
of individual piece rates had been introduced as early as the period of war
communism, tying the wages of workers to their output in various spheres of
production. In response to trade union leaders' suggestions that piece work
would lead to the workers' physical exhaustion and premature death, a maximum
level was established in order to prevent the breakdown of workers who had
overexerted themselves.[55] By 1920, the Bolsheviks had established bureaus of
"normalization" in the factory committees in order to set individual productivity
norms and to record and register the productivity of each worker in an enterprise.
Implicitly, Lenin was acknowledging that unequal work would also mean differences in earnings and that these differences would not disappear anytime soon.
He was also recognizing that there were indeed individual variations in the aims
and capabilities of the proletarian masses.[56] After the civil war ended in 1921,
the government officially rejected the equalization of wages. While certain minimum rations were guaranteed through the state enterprises, basic wages for each
worker required that a certain quota be filled. By 1926, more than 60 percent of
the work force was being paid by piece work.[57]

However, full-fledged competition among individual workers was still not
officially sanctioned, and it is worth noting that the Bolsheviks continued to
stress the anonymity of individual workers coupled with the glorification of the
proletariat as a collective whole. The Bolshevik "labor ethic" suggested that the
performance of individual duty and self-sacrifice was meaningful primarily because it furthered the collective achievement of labor for the Soviet state. Thus,
through the early 1920s, the original Bolshevik ethic of labor, not unlike the
Maoist system of rewarding workers for proper moral and political behavior
(*biaoxian*), still ignored the significance of individual achievement and rewarded

the spirit of collectivism and loyalty to the new regime.[58] The Bolsheviks also encouraged movements and campaigns designed to exhort workers collectively and voluntarily to raise productivity and "Communist consciousness."[59]

Stalin intensified the focus on the individual worker's competitive performance by linking both material and ideal rewards to the overfulfillment of individual productivity norms for each minute aspect of the production process. In 1928, Stalin set up a new system of wages for each industry, specifically denoting the output-related wage rates for each grade of worker in each department of each industry. New collective agreements were adopted formally to establish the new, highly systematized wage scales differentially rewarding workers with different skills and different levels of productivity.[60] In 1931, Stalin launched his famous critique of "petty-bourgeois egalitarianism" in the wage system, and set up a new wage scale that went much further than the wage-scale revisions of 1927–28 in employing higher pay and privileges to reward highly productive workers and Red Directors who had come to power in the place of the old "bourgeois specialists."[61] By the mid-1930s, antiegalitarian wage scales were in full effect. In marked contrast to the work-group system institutionalized in Chinese factories in 1957, the new class of Stalinist managers worked hard to ensure that material rewards would be tailored to the performance of the individual, not the work group.[62]

A new series of campaigns further intensified the focus on individual performance. The idea of "socialist competition" had been introduced while Lenin was still alive. At the time it was meant to encourage competition not among individual workers but among factories and work brigades in the spirit of overfulfilling production quotas. However, under Stalin, new campaigns for "shock workers" and "socialist competition" sought to single out and reward exceptional individual effort through a combination of material bonuses, special privileges, and honorary awards. The stakes were further raised with the introduction of the Stakhanovite movement, named for Alexei Stakhanov, a Donbass coal miner who allegedly cut 102 tons of coal in a single shift by not only working intensively but also creatively finding new techniques and rationalizing the production process.[63] Shock workers and Stakhanovites gained access not only to higher wages but to scarce consumer goods and special privileges such as free medical service at home, free holidays in resthomes, free tuition, and a standard of living considerably higher than the majority. Moreover, individual shock workers or Stakhanovites received social recognition, mostly in the form of medals such as the coveted "Order of Lenin."

The Stakhanovite and shock-work movements paved the way for privileges and promotions for a few diligent and fortunate employees, with the main beneficiaries being young workers who had been raised in the cities and educated in new Soviet schools. However, these movements also increased resentment among the majority of workers, who suddenly found themselves faced with rapidly rising productivity norms and declining wages.[64] Older, skilled workers as well as less experienced peasant-workers unaccustomed to factory work resisted Stalin's socialist competitions. As an alternative to shock brigades, they attempted to form "production communes" modeled after the old *artels,* and skilled workers began to leave factories where socialist competition was in full swing for factories where managers promoted the production communes. However, the purges and campaigns against "wreckers" and "saboteurs" prompted most managers and workers to abandon the production communes and to join the socialist competitions.[65] In the end, while it is questionable whether the differentiated wage policies and socialist competitions had positive effects on worker productivity, what is clear is that the Stalinist enterprise system, "for all its collectivism, typically left each worker as a single producing 'unit' with a quota to fulfill and a wage to earn."[66]

Finally, it should be noted that social mobility and party membership did not translate into status or social recognition for most workers within the context of the social hierarchies in the factory as a whole. As a result of the increasingly hierarchical system of administrative control and a highly inegalitarian distribution of material rewards to a new privileged stratum, social relations at the Soviet factory became steeply hierarchical and stratified, with very little social contact across different status groups. In the factories of tsarist Russia, older, more skilled workers received higher wages and recognition, and they would treat the new *otkhodniki* as unproven underlings, but the latter were expected to work their way up through the ranks of skilled labor. Not only did these status distinctions persist after the Bolshevik revolution but, after Stalin's rise to power, there were now different grounds for stratification at the workplace, and the divisions among different strata of workers became sharper and more irreconcilable. The most successful "shock workers" or "Stakhanovites" turned out to be young, semiskilled urbanites who had grown up in the cities and were thus more accustomed to factory life, better educated, and, at the same time, prepared to handle new roles and tasks within the increasingly mechanized production process. These workers eventually became a Soviet "labor aristocracy" despised by the older skilled workers, who considered themselves the original "proletariat."[67] The new stratum of individual "heroes of socialist labor," together with the new class of "Red Directors" promoted under Stalin, rose to the top of a sharply stratified social structure in Soviet industry.

Whether or not it is appropriate to refer to these privileged groups as a Soviet "middle class," as Vera Dunham has, it is clear that the system of authority, the wage structure, and the campaigns of socialist competition produced a fairly exclusive elite social stratum. In exchange for their loyalty and conformism, the regime-sponsored public values came to equate heroic service to the socialist state with their private goals of wealth, stability, social status, and some degree of social mobility.[68] The social distance between this "new class" and the various strata of the industrial work force is seen in surveys of former Soviet citizens, which show how little social contact occurred and how little trust there was between most factory workers, on the one hand, and white-collar employees and managers, on the other.[69]

In addition, social relations and the day-to-day interactions between superiors and subordinates in the Stalin era were characterized by a level of harshness and "rudeness" (*grubost*) not seen in the past. The term *borzovshchina* came to suggest for most Russians a crude and sometimes brutal quality of social relations between members of the upper strata and their subordinates in virtually every sphere of social life.[70] This does not mean that the majority of workers came to value hierarchy or stratified social relations; in fact, within their particular categories, workers continued to exhibit inclusiveness and equality in the conduct of informal social relations.[71] However, when it came to relations between different status groups or categories of workers, there was no question that control at the work place remained in the hands of a distinct new class that was very much aware of its status and power.

The "Stalinist system" of enterprise management remained more or less intact through the 1980s. With Nikita Khrushchev's ascension to power in 1956, the severe labor laws of the Stalin era were immediately overturned and replaced by a new set of rules and regulations to guide labor–management relations within the framework of "socialist legalism." However, his most important initiatives—the attempts during the late 1950s to reduce the differentials in wages, benefits, and educational opportunities among different social groups—were resisted by the Central Committee and were never implemented at the enterprise level. Similarly, his efforts to "democratize" the workplace went nowhere since managers either ignored criticisms or retained the power to launch reprisals against their critics.[72]

Under Leonid Brezhnev, there was less emphasis on ideology, "storming" (concentrated attack on certain problems in production), and campaigns for socialist competition, and greater emphasis on regularity, rational planning, and social stability.[73] In addition, a 1979 policy shift attempted to make the work brigade, rather than the individual worker, collectively responsible for carrying out a set of tasks, internally dividing up these tasks without the intervention of management, and distributing material incentives collectively earned by the brigade. Although on paper the reforms appeared to be a success, ultimately, the problems of high targets, uncertain supplies, and sudden transfers of personnel prompted most managers to continue past practices of assigning separate individual tasks, setting individual norms, and rewarding individual workers.[74] Similarly, whatever egalitarianism Soviet officials claimed to have achieved in the wage structure was achieved mainly by boosting the wages and basic supplies received by workers at the lower end of the wage scale and by tolerating the proliferation of the "second economy." Differentials remained high after bonus payments and privileged access to goods were figured into the real earnings of managers, white-collar employees, and blue-collar workers.[75] The Brezhnev leadership did not bring about any far-reaching changes in the system of enterprise organization set up in the Stalinist period.

Throughout the 1956–85 period, the wage system continued to be in effect a piece-rate system.[76] Individual specialization as a principle of complex bureaucratic organization also became more thoroughly entrenched, with a more clearly defined system of responsibilities and spheres of jurisdiction at all levels of the Soviet economy.[77] Managers in the post-Stalin era became an ever more distinct "new class" that wanted to retain bureaucratic ranks, income differentials, and status markers as part of a "deal" with the regime. Workers did not gain any concessions in the form of new wage scales or control over the workplace, but they were allowed to pursue quietly new avenues for earning income through moonlighting or trading on the black market.[78] On the whole, the post-Stalin era did not produce a fundamental transformation of the Soviet enterprise. Instead, with the decline of coercion in the post-Stalinist era, the problems with worker commitment that began in the 1920s intensified, producing an increasingly apathetic, undisciplined, and alienated work force.

Soviet Management and the Alienation of Workers

In the 1920s, Bolshevik cadres and managerial elites had treated the problems of low labor discipline, absenteeism, and turnover as evidence of low proletarian consciousness and the survival of petty-bourgeois attitudes.[79] Stalin's cultural revolution and industrialization drives were supposed to pave the way for the creation of a loyal, committed socialist work force. However, with the exception of the sharp reduction in strikes from the late 1920s onward, little evidence of a committed work force emerged in the 1930s. Industrial production did grow impressively, and large-scale industrial enterprises became important units of production. Much of the boost, however, came not from a motivated labor force or the efficient organization of labor, but from the massive investment of capital, the rapid development of an industrial infrastructure, and the huge influx of labor after the collectivization campaign.[80]

During the period of the NEP, strikes increased. During Stalin's era, although strikes became dangerous, a high rate of labor turnover essentially served as a substitute for organized labor protest.[81] From the late 1920s to the early 1930s, the average annual rate of discharge climbed from 100 percent to 150 percent, meaning that every worker changed jobs at least once a year and sometimes twice a year. These rates are particularly stunning in view of the fact that a worker who changed jobs more than once was labeled a "disorganizer of production" and that the worker's access to basic rations and services depended on having labor books that attested to his diligence and work discipline.[82]

Also worth noting is the opposition to individual piece rates and the survival of the *artel* well into the 1930s. It was expected that new management practices, socialist competition, and the actual experience of factory work would transform the *artel* into a socialist workers' brigade. But, for most workers, the distinction between the two was not very clear. Even at the height of the Stakhanovite and shock workers' campaigns, many managers continued to treat their brigades as collective labor units, paying the collective earnings of brigade members to the leader who would proceed to divide up the earnings equally regardless of the output recorded for each worker.[83]

General problems with factory discipline also persisted as technological change and the emphasis on specialization undermined the existing "work culture" of the skilled workers.[84] Although managers hoped to use workers' brigades to enforce discipline from above, the brigades actually helped workers to form their own "circles of protection" (*krugovaia poruka*) to circumvent factory regulations and evade the harsh penalties established under Stalin to punish violators. The Stalinist period also witnessed the emergence of *blat,* as workers of various ranks as well as supervisors learned to make use of personal connections and informal networks to help each other circumvent regulations and help less efficient workers report higher outputs and qualify for bonuses.[85] All these informal aspects of factory social relations show that workers were far from "atomized" in the Stalinist era, but they also show that workers were not committed to the official goals or formal system of production and distribution.

In the post-Stalin era, all these problems not only continued but intensified. Material conditions for the Soviet population improved, but the "real" incomes of workers were not rising, especially given the rising expectations of an increasingly educated working class. Even if some of the older workers became more content in seeing their wages and standards of living increase relative to conditions during the Stalinist era, most of the better-educated and more ambitious younger workers found their efforts inadequately compensated for by a combination of wages and benefits.[86] Dissatisfaction over material conditions, however, is not by itself a sufficient condition for worker alienation. It is possible to forestall alienation and sustain commitment among workers with only marginal improvements in wages or benefits as long as there remains some expectation of future rewards or the future realization of some ideals or goals. However, given the persisting tensions between Soviet management practices, on the one hand, and the ideals espoused by pre-1917 social institutions and the first Bolsheviks, on the other, there was little chance of recapturing the commitment of workers in the post-Stalin era.

First, there is evidence of growing potential for industrial conflict in the post-Stalin era. Although reliable statistics are not available for industrial disputes in the Soviet period, there is evidence that the number of strikes increased in the early 1960s and again during the 1970s. Sometimes, striking workers had to be dispersed through a show of force, as in the case of the Dnepropetrovsk and Dneproderzhinsk strikes in 1972. In addition, there were frequent work stoppages and walkouts along with the deliberate production slowdown by workers, which was probably the most widespread form of industrial protest in the post-Stalin era.[87] There is also the evidence of a general decline in labor discipline and productivity as reported by Soviet scholars themselves. For example, one

Soviet study conducted in the Brezhnev era showed that, between 1962 and 1976, the violations of labor discipline doubled while the number of workers who surpassed their quotas (as reported by managers themselves) fell from 63 percent to 43 percent.[88]

Problems with labor turnover also continued unabated in the post-Stalin era. Although turnover rates declined from the late 1930s onward because of the harsh penalties written into the 1938 and 1940 labor codes, in the post-Stalin era the rate climbed steadily once again. In the 1970s and early 1980s, 20 percent of the industrial work force at the typical large-scale enterprise switched jobs annually, meaning that one worker in five left his place of employment *every year.* Again, younger workers were especially prone to switching jobs, and their rate of turnover was twice the national average.[89] Having one-fifth of the work force switch jobs in a given year may not be too unusual in the context of a free labor market, but it is extremely high in a situation where the regime made every effort to prevent workers from switching jobs and where the enterprise was the main provider of most basic necessities in life, from housing and schooling to health care and recreational or cultural activities.

The alienation of Soviet workers from their workplaces is further evident in the dissatisfaction of workers with the nature of work organization and the content of their jobs. One major Soviet study, conducted by noted Soviet sociologists in the 1960s, examined how occupational structures shaped the attitudes of young workers in Leningrad. Their major finding was that the "content of labor" (i.e., the opportunities for creative work, the challenges posed by tasks, and the responsibilities built into those tasks) had a stronger positive correlation with the workers' attitudes toward labor than did wage increases or participation in campaigns or Communist labor competitions. In fact, they found that dissatisfaction with the content of work was often a more important factor than higher wages in spurring labor turnover.[90] Other studies show that most workers in the post-Stalin era did not believe that they could influence decisions concerning the production process or their own assignments and that they seldom participated in the movements for greater rationalization or suggested improvements in the organization of labor.[91] Attempts by both Brezhnev and Mikhail Gorbachev to stimulate a greater sense of participation and membership only resulted in "*pro forma* activism" by cynical workers who displayed little genuine concern for either their enterprises or the official system of production as a whole.[92]

Finally, one can point to the increase in corruption, theft, and the diversion of resources into the "second economy" during the 1970s. The informal "circles of protection" and *blat* networks based on reciprocal exchange that emerged in the Stalin era became widespread in the Brezhnev era and even tacitly accepted by the regime. By the early 1980s, the Soviet enterprise was beginning to resemble the Chinese *danwei*: In both, there emerged an elaborate system of clientelism and vertical networks of loyalty, linked to "a vigorous subculture of private exchange and mutual support, which sometimes includes petty corruption."[93]

The rise in corruption, along with theft at the workplace, and the diversion of energy and resources in the "second economy" during the 1970s–80s clearly demonstrated that the collectivist values and social relations that survived among the Soviet work force were very different from the collectivism that the Soviet regime had hoped to foster in the "new Soviet person."[94]

Conclusion: Lessons for Post-Soviet and Chinese Reformers?

In their classic study of the "Soviet citizen," Alex Inkeles and Raymond Bauer note: "Even a totalitarian system cannot operate effectively unless there is considerable congruence between its institutions and objectives and the prevailing ideological orientations of the people."[95] Within the institutional context of the Stalinist enterprise system, no such congruence existed. The regime that had initially espoused "workers' control," collective labor, and social egalitarianism ended up promoting a set of managerial ideals and practices that directly challenged both the original Bolshevik ideological pronouncements as well as the attitudes, values, and habits of the majority of workers flooding into the factories from the countryside. Citizens who were once accustomed to collectivism, egalitarianism, harmony, and paternalism gradually came to be confronted with a highly centralized system of administrative control, individual task assignments, a system of material and ideal rewards based on individual performance, and a degree of hierarchy and stratification not seen in earlier Bolshevik doctrines or in preindustrial peasant communes. This lack of congruence between official managerial practices and the inherited legacies was one important reason for the progressive decline in labor discipline, productivity, and commitment in Soviet enterprises.

Post-Soviet reformers should take note of the fact that when workers protested against Gorbachev's *perestroika* in the late 1980s, they did not criticize the brigade reforms emphasizing collective labor or the general call to improve productivity and product quality; what they objected to most vehemently was the increased de-leveling of incomes that would accompany further efforts to reward the discipline and productivity of individual workers.[96] Similarly, when the coal miners struck in 1989, they were not leading a working-class revolt against every aspect of the Soviet enterprise system; they were mainly protesting the failure of the regime to deliver basic goods and supplies promised to workers by paternalistic enterprises. Moreover, workers in the steel industry resisted the pressures to join in the strikes, and, in fact, some wrote letters urging the coal miners to return to work.[97] These are extremely telling facts for anyone generally concerned with reforming the economic institutions in any state-socialist system. They suggest that the legacy of past patterns of enterprise organization and industrial relations are likely to influence workers in post-Soviet Russia; they also suggest that workers may not be terribly receptive to incentive systems based on competitive evaluations of individual performance in the enterprise even if sweeping market reforms are carried out at the level of macroeconomic institutions. Before rushing to imitate the organizational patterns of firms in the advanced industrial West, Russian reformers should consider the extent to which the values and social relations that evolved during seven decades of Soviet rule are consistent with the fundamental assumptions that undergird industrial relations and enterprise organization in the West.

Similarly, before replacing the entire *danwei* system with firms modeled after those in the West, Chinese reformers should pay careful attention to the legacies they have inherited, that is, to the attitudes, values, and behavioral norms exhibited by workers and their supervisors. These attitudes were a product of both a socialist regime that actively sought to prevent the emergence of bourgeois individualism and a Confucian system of values and norms inherited from pre-industrial Chinese villages. It is highly unlikely that the typical worker in the present-day *danwei* will prove to be a cooperative, motivated, and disciplined one in a social environment that resembles the "market-oriented" bureaucratic firms of the West. Rather, Chinese reformers might be better off creating within the *danwei* a structure of authority, a system of work organization, and a framework for material and ideal incentives organized around Chinese work groups rather than excessively specialized individual tasks and skills. While rewards linked to *biaoxian* may be a thing of the past, there is no reason for incentives to focus solely on material rewards linked to individual performance. If the enterprise is seen as the provider of basic goods and services, then there is no reason to abolish the system of company paternalism that emerged in the post–Cultural Revolution era even if *danwei* managers want to streamline the services provided. As for social relations on the shop floor, there may be something to be gained from attempts to *capture* the networks of trust that emerged through the "hidden bargaining" among workers and supervisors so that these networks may be turned into a foundation for cooperative and harmonious labor relations in the *danwei*.[98]

The market-based models sponsored by international financial institutions may help to jump-start economies mired in bureaucratism and inefficiency. But Chan is correct that "the state sector's shift to a market economy does not have to be accompanied by a market-oriented employment system" (see chapter 4).[99] Instead, an "organization-oriented" model approximating the Japanese firm may be more applicable given the emphases on employment stability, predictable wage increases, and group-based work organization. The Japanese firm is not the only alternative model of management for all societies, but the contrast between the Japanese and Soviet experiences suggests that a committed work force is difficult to sustain when management practices are institutionalized without regard for the values and attitudes of the workers themselves. In the case of the Chinese *danwei*, it is necessary to understand the pre-existing attitudes carried over by Chinese workers and managers from their experiences in the *danwei* system because these attitudes are likely to play an important role in determining the fate of whatever management ideologies and practices reformers put in place.

Notes

1. See the introductory chapter in this volume by Lü and Perry.

2. The concept of "social mobilization" was first employed by Karl Deutsch to capture the typical experiences of millions of people worldwide who would be physically, socially, culturally, psychologically, and politically uprooted from their traditional communities and turned into individuated citizens available for recommitment to new roles, identities, tasks, and institutions. See Deutsch, "Social Mobilization and Political Development," *American Political Science Review* 55 (September 1961): 493–511.

3. On the "political–statist" and "social–communal" functions of the *danwei*, see Lü and Perry's chapter in this volume.

4. See Andrew Walder, *Communist Neo-Traditionalism: Work and Authority in Chinese Industry* (Berkeley: University of California Press, 1986). In the labor-short Soviet economy, there was more "mutual dependence" given the managers' need to maintain a surplus labor supply; see Stephen Crowley, "Barriers to Collective Action: Steelworkers and Mutual Dependence in the Former Soviet Union," *World Politics* 46, no. 4 (July 1994): 589–615.

5. An older literature on Soviet "totalitarianism" employed the term *alienation* to refer to the atomization and anomie supposedly experienced by workers living in an atmosphere of terror and hierarchical control. I use the term *alienation* here in the sense that the *formal* system of production and exchange established by Soviet planners, despite the concentration of power in the hands of management, failed to produce a committed, loyal work force. That is, most industrial workers were not so much suffering from anomie as they were unable to identify with the formal organization of work and authority in the factory.

6. As Dankwart Rustow pointed out long ago, the traditional/modern dichotomy is based on a residual understanding of "traditional" societies: "The tribes of camel herders in the Arabian desert; the villages of Tropical Africa; and the imperial civilizations once governed by the Manchus in China and the Ottomans in Turkey—all become similar only as they are confronted in fact or contrasted in concept with modern civilization. Traditional societies are non-modern societies" (Rustow, *A World of Nations* [Washington: Brookings Institution, 1967], 12). On modernization theory in general, see Talcott Parsons and Edward Shils, *Toward a General Theory of Action* (New York: Harper and Row, 1951), 76–88; and Alex Inkeles and David Smith, *Becoming Modern: Individual Change in Six Countries* (Cambridge: Harvard University Press, 1974).

7. Despite variations in rural culture and social structure throughout the vast Russian countryside, several historians and anthropologists have pointed to the existence of a relatively high degree of homogeneity throughout most of European and Central Russia (the regions where industrialization first took off), not only in terms of basic household operations, property customs, and agricultural practices, but also in terms of cultural orientations. See Theodor Shanin, *Russia as a "Developing Society"* (London: Macmillan, 1985), 77–78.

8. Ibid., 83–84. See also Edward Keenan's discussion of "village political culture" in Russia in his "Muscovite Political Folkways," *Russian Review* 45, no. 2 (April 1986): 128.

9. The emphasis on social order and camaraderie did not necessarily preclude conflicts among peasants, but the contenders rarely challenged the importance of maintaining collective harmony and joint responsibilities. See Christine Worobec, *Peasant Russia: Family and Community in the Post-Emancipation Period* (Princeton: Princeton University Press, 1991), 7; and Victor Magagna, *Communities of Grain: Rural Rebellion in Comparative Perspective* (Ithaca: Cornell University Press, 1991), 206–12.

10. Richard Pipes, *Russia Under the Old Regime* (New York: Scribner's, 1974), 159–60.

11. On the role of the *mir* during the period of serfdom, see ibid., 109; and Magagna, *Communities of Grain,* 195.

12. In the early twentieth century, the *mir* even survived the Stolypin reform plan that had been designed in 1906 to dissolve communal agriculture and set up individual farmsteads and capitalist agriculture. As late as 1916, according to even the most favorable estimates, more than two-thirds of all allotment land held by the peasantry remained under the control of communes. According to some estimates, within European Russia, only 10.5 percent of the households lived in noncommunal individual farmsteads. See Shanin, *Russia as a "Developing Society,"* 73–75; Pipes, *Russia Under the Old Regime,* 19; and Donald Male, *Russian Peasant Organization Before Collectivization: A Study of Commune and Gathering, 1925–1930* (Cambridge: Cambridge University Press, 1971), 18–19.

13. For example, the arguments by Richard Pipes and Zbigniew Brzezinski suggest that the "totalitarian" system erected under Soviet communism was essentially a product of the hierarchical, authoritarian political culture of tsarist Russia. See Pipes, "Did the Russian Revolution Have to Happen?" *American Scholar* (spring 1994): 215–38; and Brzezinski, "Soviet Politics: From the Future to the Past?" in *The Dynamics of Soviet Politics,* ed. Paul Cocks et al. (Cambridge: Harvard University Press, 1976).

14. See Worobec's excellent analysis of patriarchy in prerevolutionary Russian households.

15. Pipes, *Russia Under the Old Regime,* 155.

16. See ibid., 110; and Andrei Amalrik, *Will the Soviet Union Survive Until 1984?* (New York: Harper and Row, 1970), 33.

17. Moshe Lewin, *The Making of the Soviet System* (New York: Pantheon, 1985), 76.

18. See Worobec, *Peasant Russia,* 20–24; Magagna, *Communities of Grain,* 200; and Dorothy Atkinson, *The End of the Russian Land Commune, 1905–1930* (Stanford: Stanford University Press, 1983), 26–37.

19. Only some 4 percent of the peasant households regularly hired wage labor, and, even then, only 1 percent hired large enough numbers of peasant laborers to be really called "capitalists." The vast majority (90 percent) basically lived, worked, and participated in subsistence agriculture organized around household farming. See Shanin, *Russia as a "Developing Society,"* 94–102.

20. Ibid., 74–75.

21. Even as late as the 1920s, 222 million hectares were farmed on the basis of repartitional commune holdings and common crop rotations, while individual farmsteads and socialist collective farms accounted for only 10 million hectares. See Male, *Russian Peasant Organization,* 21–22; and E.H. Carr, *Socialism in One Country, 1924–1926* (London: Macmillan, 1964), 214.

22. On the plight of *otkhodniki* before 1861, see Reginald Zelnik, *Labor and Society in Tsarist Russia: The Factory Workers of St. Petersburg, 1855–1870* (Stanford: Stanford University Press, 1971), 16–20; and Charters Wynn, *Workers, Strikes and Pogroms: The Donbass-Dnepr Bend in Late Imperial Russia, 1870–1905* (Princeton: Princeton University Press, 1992), 51–52, 98.

23. Zelnik, *Labor and Society in Tsarist Russia,* 24–35.

24. Even the Great Reforms of Alexander II (1855–81) did not call into question patriarchal authority; many of the reforms were intended to ensure social stability in the course of advancing the state's interest in industrial expansion. And where employers and managers did comply with new labor laws, their compliance only reflected little more than a commitment to patriarchal authority and familialism within the factory context. See Walter Pintner, "Reformability in the Age of Reform and Counter-reform, 1855–94," in

Reform in Russia and the USSR: Past and Prospects, ed. Robert Crummey (Urbana: University of Illinois Press, 1989), 87, 89; and Alfred Rieber, *Merchants and Entrepreneurs in Imperial Russia* (Chapel Hill: University of North Carolina Press, 1982), esp. chaps. 1, 3.

25. Victoria Bonnell, "Introduction," to *The Russian Worker: Life and Labor Under the Tsarist Regime,* ed. Bonnell (Berkeley: University of California Press, 1983), 18–22; Bruno Grancelli, *Soviet Management and Labor Relations* (London: Allen and Unwin, 1988), 11–12.

26. On pre-1949 Chinese workers, see chapter 2 in this volume, Elizabeth Perry, "From Native Place to Workplace: Labor Origins and Outcomes of China's *Danwei* System."

27. David Hoffman, *Peasant Metropolis: Social Identities in Moscow, 1919–1941* (Ithaca: Cornell University Press, 1994), 62. Hierarchical social relations were not absent in the *artel,* as Hoffman as well as Bonnell (8–13) note. There was some stratification based on varying levels of skill and experience. But it is important to note that this hierarchy was based on the common acknowledgment that experience and skills were reasonable prerequisites for the status and authority of elders and senior workers. In time, the young apprentices and newcomers would have the opportunity to join the ranks of skilled workers and gain greater status within the group.

28. Zelnik, *Labor and Society in Tsarist Russia,* 21. By the twentieth century, *artels* had somewhat declined in their importance and village ties had become less direct, but village-based regional identities continued to form the basis for social networks and neighborhood organizations, and the villages continued to serve as a form of social security for workers in the absence of adequate compensation for unemployment, illness, injury, or old age. In addition to Zelnik, see Wynn, *Workers, Strikes and Pogroms,* 38, 50; and Bonnell, *The Russian Worker,* 14–16.

29. There had been a proposal circulated in the late nineteenth century (by the Shtakel'berg Commission) to directly employ the *artel* as a model for promoting cooperation in the factory, but the proposal did not go anywhere as most bureaucrats and managers continued to emphasize coercion and hierarchical authority in the maintenance of factory discipline; see Zelnik, *Labor and Society in Tsarist Russia,* 137–45.

30. Wynn, *Workers, Strikes and Pogroms,* 63.

31. Lewis Siegelbaum, "State and Society in the 1920s," in Crummey, ed., *Reform in Russia and the USSR,* 128–29.

32. On the debates over *kollegial'nost',* see Frederick Kaplan, *Bolshevik Ideology and the Ethics of Soviet Labor, 1917–1920* (New York: Philosophical Library, 1968), 320–32.

33. Margaret Dewar, *Labour Policy in the USSR, 1917–1928* (London: Royal Institute of International Affairs and Oxford University Press, 1956), 18–26.

34. Timothy Luke, *Ideology and Soviet Industrialization* (Westport, CT: Greenwood Press, 1985), 112–18; quotation from Lenin, "How to Organize Competition," in *The Lenin Anthology,* ed. Robert Tucker (New York: Norton, 1975), 428–29. See also Dewar, *Labour Policy in the USSR,* 103–6.

35. The Third All-Russian Congress of Trade Unions agreed to this policy change in 1920, demonstrating that the trade unions were increasingly becoming instruments of central party control rather than independent voices for factory workers. See Jeremy Azrael, *Managerial Power and Soviet Politics* (Cambridge: Harvard University Press, 1966), 13–17; and Kaplan, *Bolshevik Ideology,* 320–32.

36. Kaplan, *Bolshevik Ideology,* 311–19; quotation is on 318.

37. For a detailed discussion of economic policies under war communism and NEP, see Alec Nove, *An Economic History of the USSR,* rev. ed. (Harmondsworth, UK: Penguin Books, 1984), 46–118.

38. In fact, given the extent of control from above and the terms under which workers labored in these large factories, the NEP was frequently referred to not as the "New Economic Policy" but rather the "New Exploitation of the Proletariat." See E.H. Carr, *The Interregnum, 1923–24* (London: Macmillan, 1954), 47; and Siegelbaum, "State and Society," 135.

39. The "left turn" refers to Stalin's attack on the "Rightists" (Bukharin, Tomskii, Rykov, and others) with whom he had allied in ousting Trotsky from contention during the succession struggle after Lenin's death in 1924. With the "left turn," Stalin essentially combined the Rightists' view that, in the absence of an international revolution, socialism would have to be built in one country with the Trotsky–Preobrazhenskii line that "building socialism" meant rapid industrialization based on the extraction of labor, resources, and surplus capital from the agriculture sector. On the debates of the 1920s, see Mary McAuley, *Soviet Politics, 1917–1991* (Oxford: Oxford University Press, 1992), 37–42; and Sheila Fitzpatrick, *The Russian Revolution, 1917–1932* (New York: Oxford University Press, 1982), 98–134.

40. See Sheila Fitzpatrick, "Cultural Revolution as Class War," in *Cultural Revolution in Russia,* ed. Fitzpatrick (Bloomington: Indiana University Press, 1977). All Bolsheviks had been in agreement on the importance of a cultural revolution in producing a "new Soviet person" with socialist attitudes and values. However, after Stalin rose to power, the idea that such a revolution could be achieved gradually and through a patient, pedagogical approach was condemned as "an anti-revolutionary, opportunist conception of cultural standards—a conception which does not distinguish between bourgeois and proletarian elements of culture" (quoted in Fitzpatrick, "Cultural Revolution," 10); see also Luke, *Ideology and Soviet Industrialization,* 189–93.

41. Many scholars have vigorously disputed Stalin's assumption that the peasantry could be analyzed in class terms and that wealthy peasants were "class enemies." See, for example, Shanin, *Russia as a "Developing Society,"* and Moshe Lewin, *Russian Peasants and Soviet Power* (New York: Norton, 1975).

42. Stephen Kotkin, "Coercion and Identity: Workers' Lives in Stalin's Showcase City," in *Making Workers Soviet: Power, Class and Identity,* ed. Lewis Siegelbaum and Ronald Suny (Ithaca: Cornell University Press, 1994), 281.

43. Cited in Walter Connor, *The Accidental Proletariat: Workers, Politics, and Crisis in Gorbachev's Russia* (Princeton: Princeton University Press, 1991), 34; translated and quoted from A.M. Panfilova, *Formirovanie rabochego klassa SSSR v gody pervoi piatiletki* [Formation of the working class in the USSR in the years of the first five-year plan] (Moscow: Moscow State University Press, 1964).

44. G.A. Kozlov and S.P. Pervushin, eds., *Kratkii ekonomicheskiislovar* [Short economic dictionary] (Moscow, 1958), 75; translated and quoted in Jerry Hough, *The Soviet Prefects: The Local Party Organs in Industrial Decision Making* (Cambridge: Harvard University Press, 1969), 80.

45. Hiroaki Kuromiya, *Stalin's Industrial Revolution: Politics and Workers, 1928–1932* (Cambridge: Cambridge University Press, 1988), 63–64.

46. Ibid., xvi, 62; Connor, *The Accidental Proletariat,* 29; and Dewar, *Labour Policy in the USSR,* 72–75.

47. Beginning with the Shakhty trials directed against engineers in the Donbass coal mines, some 2,000–3,000 nonparty managers and technical specialists were purged in 1928–32 on charges of wrecking and sabotage mostly as scapegoats to deflect mass hostility linked to economic conditions and hardships. Most had done little wrong other than to fail to meet extraordinarily high production targets called for in the five-year plans (FYP). After the more widespread purge of the mid-1930s, any remaining bourgeois specialists were purged along with anyone who had criticized the excessively high targets

and tempo of the five-year plans. The new Red Directors who took over control of industry in the late 1930s had only completed elementary education, but they came to form a reasonably competent, loyal class with a solidarity and sense of common purpose revolving around the major industrial projects drawn up in the first and second FYPs. See Azrael, *Managerial Power and Soviet Politics,* 52–77, 99–104.

48. Kuromiya, *Stalin's Industrial Revolution,* 54–55.

49. Grancelli, *Soviet Management and Labor Relations,* 37–41.

50. Azrael, *Managerial Power and Soviet Politics,* 104–5.

51. Quoted in Rainer Traub, "Lenin and Taylor: The Fate of 'Scientific Management' in the Early Soviet Union," *TELOS,* 37 (1978): 82–92; from Lenin, *Works,* vol. 18 (Moscow, 1972), 594.

52. Traub, "Lenin and Taylor," 82–84.

53. Luke, *Ideology and Soviet Industrialization,* 164.

54. Traub, "Lenin and Taylor," 87–91.

55. In addition, the Bolsheviks were also worried that, given the resurgence of the peasant communes after 1917, many employees might have simply tried to earn as much as possible as quickly as possible and then return to their villages; thus the limits on piece rates were designed to make the worker produce more steadily over longer periods of time so that overall productivity would be increased. See Traub, "Lenin and Taylor," 85; and Kaplan, *Bolshevik Ideology,* 335–38.

56. Ibid., 345–46. For a more elaborate discussion on differential wages during the 1920s, see Dewar, *Labour Policy in the USSR,* 36–90.

57. See E.H. Carr, *The Bolshevik Revolution, 1917–23, Vol. 2* (Harmondsworth, UK: Penguin, 1966), 114, 419; and Traub, "Lenin and Taylor," 84, 90.

58. Kaplan, *Bolshevik Ideology,* 390–4; and on *biaoxian* as a basis for Mao's wage system, see Walder, *Communist Neo-Traditionalism,* chap. 6.

59. Most noteworthy was the campaign for "Communist Saturdays"—one of the few initiatives not originally proposed by the central leadership, but enthusiastically promoted by it. This campaign called upon the working class to contribute voluntarily an extra day of labor to the state on Saturdays as an indication of their dedication to building socialism. See Siegelbaum, "State and Society," 129–30.

60. Trade union leaders in 1928 had called for a retreat from piece rates in favor of collective bonuses for the total outputs of work groups and shops, but Stalin brushed aside these attempts; see Dewar, *Labour Policy in the USSR,* 134–37.

61. Nove (*Economic History,* 209) has estimated that, under the new wage scale, the most highly skilled workers earned as much as 3.7 times what the unskilled workers earned on average.

62. Stalin and his lieutenants defended the use of antiegalitarian wage scales by pointing to the simultaneous application of the principle of "socialist emulation." N.M. Shvernik, leader of the trade unions, argued that the new wage scale "not only does not betray socialism but turns wages into a powerful lever for the organization of labor and for the improvement of the material conditions"; quoted in Kuromiya, *Stalin's Industrial Revolution,* 307. On the distribution of wages in the Chinese work-group system see Walder, *Communist Neo-Traditionalism,* 102–12.

63. "Shock workers" were diligent workers who overfulfilled productivity norms; the Stakhanovites were supposed to be not only diligent but active in devising new methods to rationalize production and improve efficiency. For an excellent study of the Stakhanovite movement, see Lewis Siegelbaum, *Stakhanovism and the Politics of Productivity in the USSR, 1935–41* (Cambridge: Cambridge University Press, 1988).

64. Robert Conquest, *Industrial Workers in the USSR* (New York: Praeger, 1967), chap. 2, *passim.*

65. The older workers viewed Stalin's campaigns as new "methods of compulsion," and they managed to get some factory managers to abandon socialist competition. But, by 1931, most managers and workers reluctantly joined in the campaigns to multiply productivity. While at the end of 1929, only 10 percent of the work force were labeled "shock workers," by the middle of 1931, more than 65 percent were officially identified as "shock workers" regardless of their actual output. See Kuromiya, *Stalin's Industrial Revolution,* 130–32, 178–82; the figures are from 320.

66. Connor, *The Accidental Proletariat,* 179. Similarly, Kotkin notes: "[A]lthough the impact of the differentiated wage policy on productivity may have been questionable, its effect on the understanding of workers was plain. Workers were individualized and their performance measured on a percentage basis, which permitted ready comparisons" ("Coercion and Identity," 49).

67. Kuromiya, *Stalin's Industrial Revolution,* 118–31, 236–44.

68. See Vera Dunham, *In Stalin's Time: Middle-Class Values in Soviet Fiction* (Cambridge: Cambridge University Press, 1976), esp. 1–18.

69. One data set reveals that members of the intelligentsia and white-collar groups associated almost exclusively with other members of the professional and white-collar classes, while both skilled and unskilled industrial workers primarily formed friendships with other workers. Moreover, class cleavages coincided with a lack of social trust. Intelligentsia and white-collar employees, for example, found the manual working class to be most likely to be harmful to the well-being of other groups, and vice versa. See Alex Inkeles and Raymond Bauer, *The Soviet Citizen* (Cambridge: Harvard University Press, 1959), 201, 311.

70. Lewin, *The Making of the Soviet System,* 237; and Alec Nove, "Is There a Ruling Class in the Soviet Union?" in his *Political Economy and Soviet Socialism* (London: Allen and Unwin, 1979).

71. While older historical studies of the Stalin period have focused exclusively on hierarchy, social control, and the atomization of the masses under the "totalitarian" system of rule, more recent studies, such as the previously cited works by Hoffman and Kotkin, show that workers themselves remained fairly egalitarian and formed networks on the basis of regional ties or common membership in the same labor brigade. On this point, see also chapter 6 in this volume by Kenneth Straus, which emphasizes the re-creation of communities by factory workers.

72. Donald Filtzer, *Soviet Workers and De-Stalinization: The Consolidation of the Modern System of Production Relations, 1953–64* (Cambridge: Cambridge University Press, 1992), esp. 41–45, 115–17.

73. Hough, *The Soviet Prefects,* 278.

74. See Connor, *The Accidental Proletariat,* 180–1.

75. See Joseph Berliner, *Soviet Industry* (Ithaca: Cornell University Press, 1988), 283–85; and Connor, *The Accidental Proletariat,* 104–5.

76. Berliner, *Soviet Industry,* 26–28.

77. Hough, *The Soviet Prefects,* 279.

78. See Hedrick Smith, *The Russians* (New York: Ballantine, 1976), 30–67; and James Millar, "The Little Deal: Brezhnev's Contribution to Acquisitive Socialism," in *Soviet Society and Culture: Essays in Honor of Vera S. Dunham,* ed. Terry Thompson and Richard Sheldon (Boulder: Westview, 1988).

79. Siegelbaum, "State and Society," 135; and Vladimir Andrle, *Workers in Stalin's Russia: Industrialization and Social Change in a Planned Economy* (New York: St. Martin's Press, 1988), 128–29.

80. Kuromiya, *Stalin's Industrial Revolution,* 220.

81. Lewin, *The Making of the Soviet System,* 255; and Grancelli, *Soviet Management and Labor Relations,* 51–53.

82. On turnover rates in the Stalin era, see Nove, *Economic History*, 198; Kuromiya, *Stalin's Industrial Revolution*, 209; and Grancelli, *Soviet Management and Labor Relations*, 45. Even the official Soviet history of the working class recognized that "[e]xcess labor turnover impeded the training of personnel, had a negative impact on the work of production collectives and disorganized intra-factory planning." See Y.S. Borisova, L.S. Gaponenko, A.I. Kotelents, and V.S. Lelchuk, *Outline History of the Soviet Working Class* (Moscow: Progress, 1970), 201.

83. Andrle, *Workers in Stalin's Russia*, 148; Kuromiya, *Stalin's Industrial Revolution*, 247–48; Donald Filtzer, *Soviet Workers and Stalinist Industrialization: The Formation of Modern Soviet Production Relations, 1928–41* (Armonk, NY: M.E. Sharpe, 1986), 103–4; and Lewis Siegelbaum, "Soviet Norm-Determination in Theory and Practice, 1917–1941," *Soviet Studies* 1 (1985): 45–68.

84. Kuromiya, *Stalin's Industrial Revolution*, 78–107.

85. Filtzer, *Soviet Workers and Stalinist Industrialization*, 236; and Berliner, *Factory and Manager*, 324–25, 182.

86. Connor, *The Accidental Proletariat*, 117–38.

87. Grancelli, *Soviet Management and Labor Relations*, 184–88; and Alex Pravda, "Spontaneous Workers' Activities in the Soviet Union," in *Industrial Labor in the USSR*, ed. Arcadius Kahan and Blaire Ruble (New York: Pergamon Press, 1979), 348–50.

88. See V.A. Iadov, "Motivatsia truda: problemy i putirazvitiia issledovani" [Work motivation: problems and methods for the development of research], in *Sovietskaia sotsiologiia* 2, ed. T. Riabushkin and G. Osipov (Moscow: Nauka, 1982); and E. Kopolv, *Rabochii klass SSSR* [Working class of the USSR] (Moscow: Mysl', 1985), 223–40; both cited in Vladimir Shlapentokh, *Public and Private Life of the Soviet People: Changing Values in Post-Stalin Russia* (New York: Oxford University Press, 1989), 52–53, 58.

89. Basile Kerblay, *Modern Soviet Society* (New York: Pantheon Books, 1977), 190–91. This figure is confirmed by Soviet economists themselves; see Mikhail Sonin, *Sotsialisticheskaia disciplina truda* [Socialist labor discipline] (Moscow: Profizdat, 1986), 77–78; and A. Kotliar and V. Trubin, *Problemy regulirovaniia pereraspredeleniia rabochei sily* [The problem of regulating turnover in the work force] (Moscow: Ekonomika, 1978), 41–42; both also cited in Shlapentokh, *Public and Private Life*, 54.

90. V.A. Iadov, V.P. Rozhin, and A.G. Zdravomyslov, *Man and His Work*, trans. Stephen P. Dunn (White Plains: International Arts and Sciences Press, 1970), 47–48, 103, 286. See also Kerblay, *Modern Soviet Society*, 192, for a comparison between U.S. and Soviet employees' ranking of job-appreciation factors.

91. In a 1977 study of five enterprises in Murmansk, only 12.2 percent said that they felt they "personally participated" in managing the enterprise while 65.7 percent said that they did not. A similar survey in Gorkii in 1980 found that only 16.4 percent of the workers believed that they could "affect decisions on matters concerning the development of their own collectives." And in the aforementioned study by Iadov et al., 88 percent stated that they no longer participated in campaigns for rationalization. See Iadov et al., *Man and His Work*, table C-4a (Appendix); Connor, *The Accidental Proletariat*, 166.

92. Grancelli, *Soviet Management and Labor Relations*, 152–58; Connor, *The Accidental Proletariat*, 167, 180–2.

93. Walder, *Communist Neo-Traditionalism*, 12.

94. Grancelli provides an excellent summary of black market activities, corruption, and the system of mutual complicity, and he cites Soviet sources that pointed to these illegal and quasi-legal activities as far back as 1970; see Grancelli, *Soviet Management and Labor Relations*, 96–104, 168–80.

95. Inkeles and Bauer, *The Soviet Citizen*, 233.

96. Gorbachev attempted to pursue simultaneously brigade reforms emphasizing col-

lective labor and market reforms within the enterprise emphasizing greater material rewards for individual "effort and merit." Gorbachev did not view the two strategies as
based on inherently contradictory principles, although one placed responsibility on the
individual for the performance of tasks, and the other emphasized collectivities that would
jointly determine the division of labor and the distribution of rewards. Workers, however,
seemed to recognize the contradiction and mostly attacked the new incentive system. See
Connor, *The Accidental Proletariat,* 143–45, 180–223.

97. See Crowley, "Barriers to Collective Action," 589–615; and Michael Burawoy,
"The End of Sovietology and the Renaissance of Modernization Theory," *Contemporary
Sociology* 21 (November 1992).

98. On "hidden bargaining" in the *danwei,* see Walder, *Communist Neo-Traditionalism,* 239–40.

99. See chapter 4 in this volume, Anita Chan, "Chinese *Danwei* Reforms: Convergence with the Japanese Model?" On the "organization-oriented" and "market oriented"
models, see Ronald Dore, *British Factory—Japanese Factory* (Berkeley: University of
California Press, 1973).

6

The Soviet Factory as Community Organizer

Kenneth M. Straus

It was once widely accepted among non-Soviet historians that the Soviet industrial labor force was sullen and "captive" after 1930, as the regime's policy of *edinonachalie,* or one-man management, took effect, followed by a series of "draconian" labor laws aimed at "attaching" the Soviet worker to his/her factory, if not directly to the workbench itself.[1] To readers of this volume, this perspective might seem to lend support to the idea that the Soviet enterprise of the 1930s was a precursor to or basis for the Chinese *danwei,* which developed in the 1950s as a factory-based system of population regulation and settlement control for the cities, and of labor control in the factory. This chapter argues, to the contrary, that the Soviet factory was not a prototype for the *danwei;* rather, it suggests that the Soviet factory became an "inclusive" rather than "exclusive" institution, accelerating the growth of Soviet cities even more rapidly than the party's ambitious central plans called for. Furthermore, it suggests that, like the *danwei,* the Soviet factory assumed the basic functions of housing, transporting, and feeding its workers, but that this was necessary to hold onto these workers, who would, otherwise, leave for another factory or city. The Soviet labor market, unlike the Chinese, was a "seller's," or what I call an "inverted," labor market. The result was a strong element of social control by the factory administration over the workers. Significantly, however, the workers, technical and managerial staff, plant trade union officials, and plant party officials, as this case study of the Proletarian district (Proletarskii raion, or PR) of Moscow and the "Hammer and Sickle" steel factory ("Serp Molot," or SiM) shows, became actively engaged in forming a new urban community and, in the process, turned the factory into a "community organizer." The phenomenon of workers and staff making use of the factory they worked in to serve

"The Soviet Factory Worker," is from the forthcoming book *Factory and Community in Stalin's Russia: The Making of an Industrial Working Class,* by Kenneth M. Straus, © 1997 by the University of Pittsburgh Press. Abridged and reprinted by permission of the University of Pittsburgh Press.

their needs and interests in urban society has escaped the analysis of historians operating in terms of "social control" theories.

The "Inverted" Labor Market and Official Stalinist Ideology of the Factory

In accordance with the Stalinist ideology of the first five-year plan (FYP) period, the Soviet factory was supposed to become a "Bolshevik fortress" which meant expelling the "class enemy."[2] By the end of the first FYP, in 1933, however, it looked more like a "sieve," as workers and personnel were coming and going so rapidly that the factory personnel department, the *otdel kadrov* ("cadre department") could not keep track of personnel on the payroll from month to month, let alone separate out "cadre proletariat" from the so-called class enemy. The regime took drastic measures to halt this hemorrhaging of personnel, beginning with what have been called "draconian labor laws" in 1930, firing workers for absenteeism, and culminating with an internal Passport Act in December 1932. By December 1932, labor turnover (*tekuchest'*) had reached a crisis point. Enterprises were instructed to lay off superfluous workers in the first half of 1933, and the Passport Act was rigorously enforced for the next six months to keep new migrants out of the cities. By late 1933, however, the pressure of high enterprise output targets forced the regime to lift wage fund restrictions, allowing firms once again to begin hiring workers, and enforcement of the Passport Act was relaxed.

An "inverted" labor market, different from that in any capitalist economy, but also different from what happened later in the Chinese or Indian "socialist" economies, saw the enterprise's demand for labor power exceeding its ability to recruit new workers, retain them, and train them. This gap appeared during the first FYP as a general feature of the Soviet economy for the first time in Russian or Soviet history. When the gap widened until it reached a crisis level in 1932, it might have been called a new "scissors crisis" since it resembled the famous "scissors crisis" between industrial and agricultural prices that Trotsky diagnosed in 1923. Then, after a brief hiatus with the 1933 layoffs, the "inversion" reappeared, and it remained a consistent albeit less severe feature of the Stalinist industrial system thereafter, into the 1980s. The gap widened again to a crisis level during World War II, and then, like the hiatus of 1933 after the first FYP, there was suddenly and briefly a surplus of labor power in 1946, as postwar demobilization of Red Army troops caused civilian (mostly female) layoffs. The contrast with the *danwei,* which from the 1950s through the 1980s restricted peasant-migrants' and would-be workers' access to factory work and city apartments in the context of a large labor surplus, could not be clearer.

In the context of this crisis, the Stalin regime saw labor turnover during the first FYP as sabotage or as a form of popular resistance, and not as an economic problem of labor markets. It therefore drafted the infamous "draconian labor laws," which were an attempt to "attach" workers to a specific factory and work station and to make quitting very difficult. The regime also adopted the discourse of the factory as "Bolshevik fortress," an ideology of proletarian "purity" in which the so-called class aliens, mostly peasants, were to be expelled. However, they could not be expelled, since the enterprises desperately needed their labor power to meet plan targets. Primarily for that reason, the regime would shift metaphors after 1933, referring to the factory more frequently as a "forge of the new Soviet man"—heroes who were called "shock workers" and then "Stakhanovites." Both official metaphors of factory as "fortress" and "forge" corresponded poorly with the factory's influence with workers. Instead, the factory assimilated millions of new workers of widely differing social backgrounds by providing them with housing, transportation, and food, the prerequisites for survival in the city, and the basis for their participation in organizing a new urban community.

Three other theories of the factory and city during the industrialization drive present themselves, and all are more useful than official Stalinism and have influenced my approach in various ways. First, negative utopias, composed by Soviet dissident writers of the 1930s and since that time, portrayed factory work and urban community life under the Stalinist industrialization drive and urbanization as a kind of living hell, in which neighbors spied on one another under ubiquitous state controls, which negated all individualism. Negative utopias ranged widely, from surrealist to mock socialist realism. Perhaps the most famous was Bulgakov's masterpiece, *Master and Margarita.* For our purposes, a novella by Andrei Platonov from 1930 and the attempt by Alexander Zinoviev to put his ideas in nonfictional form in an essay published in exile in 1981, offer the most promising ideas from a negative utopia perspective on factory work and urban community life or its absence.[3] My theory of a factory community organizer was, in part, a reaction to this.

A second alternative approach was also Soviet but unofficial in origin. This was an ideal for the factory, which took root among the Soviet workers, managers, and local trade union representatives as well as plant party officials. They began, during the 1930s, to think of a factory as the Soviet institution fundamentally responsible for providing "cradle to grave" welfare and job security with guaranteed work, that is as the institutional building block of socialism. This chapter builds on this idea, but also suggests that the factory was to become a central institution in community formation or organization in the city.

A third theory I considered here might be imagined as an attempt to flesh out a new description of the factory as a "total institution," parallel to the "totalitarian" theory of Stalinism. Such an approach might borrow from Foucault's ideas concerning the prison and the poorhouse, or what he called Panopticism in *Discipline and Punish.*[4]

Housing

The construction of housing, grocery stores, public baths and pools, sports clubs, day-care centers, and public transportation for the population of Moscow lagged far behind the expansion of the city's industry, the opening of new factories, and the growth in its working-class population during the first FYP. This obvious fact was never mentioned in speeches at plenums, conferences, or congresses of the Communist Party of the Soviet Union in 1929 and 1930. Finally, with the situation becoming intolerable in Moscow (as in other cities), at the June 1931 Central Committee plenum, a plan was introduced for the reconstruction of Moscow, and party leaders acknowledged what every Muscovite knew: that living standards had plummeted as the city's social facilities, or "infrastructure," had not even remotely kept pace with Moscow's industrial reconstruction or with the total growth of the city's population.[5]

The situation with "infrastructure" was even worse in the Proletarskii raion than in most of the city, as it was destined to become, by plan or by accident, the cutting edge of the Soviet industrialization drive in Moscow during the first FYP. As the foundations for new factories were being laid in every corner of the raion, thousands of peasant migrant construction workers were housed in nearby or distant barracks. Many stayed on to work in the new factories when they were completed and went "on line." Gradually the barracks were replaced by permanent housing, usually during the second and third FYPs. Those two events constituted the most significant change in the history of Moscow. Migrant and itinerant peasant construction workers became permanent factory production workers and, for the first time, together with their families, became permanent city dwellers in communal apartments (the *kommunal'ka*).

The housing fund, in thousands of cubic meters, increased for all of Moscow from 12,598 on January 1, 1929, to 14,415 on January 1, 1933, to 15,012 on January 1, 1934. That was a total increase of only 14.4 percent for the whole of the first FYP, and of 4.1 percent for 1933.[6] Meanwhile, the city gained over a million new inhabitants, its population jumping, in those same years, from 2,319,000 to 3,600,000.[7] The increase in the housing stock in Proletarian district was slightly above average for the city. From 739,000 cubic meters on January 1, 1929, the housing stock increased to 912,000 cubic meters on January 1, 1933, and then to 960,000 cubic meters on January 1, 1934. This was an increase of 23.4 percent for the first FYP, and of 5.3 percent for 1933. Only the Stalin district, with a 37.4 percent increase in housing stock for the first FYP and an 11.2 percent increase for 1933, had a faster rate of growth. However, this was hardly satisfactory since the population of PR more than doubled in the same first FYP period, from 141,600 to 296,600.[8]

The party plenum in June 1931 admitted that new housing and other essential amenities lagged far behind the in-migration of people to Moscow. The plenum resolution stated that:

> the development of the city's facilities is lagging behind the increase in workers and working population of the capital, and lags behind their needs. This lagging is especially heightened by the serious inadequacies in the work of the Moscow utilities. Precisely because of these inadequacies have appeared gaps in our

tram system, housing shortfalls, poor results in road construction and in underground work, extremely unsatisfactory sanitary conditions in the city, etc.[9]

In response to these problems, the plenum adopted a program for massive reconstruction of Moscow, which, in three years, was supposed to provide new housing for 500,000 people. In addition, the plan was to build enough new cafeterias, cafés, laundries, and day-care and nursery centers, to accommodate the new population.[10] Whereas the plenum envisioned housing for a half million new Muscovites during the first FYP, the city's population actually increased by almost a million between January 1, 1931, and January 1, 1933, to reach over 3.6 million. The 1935 General Plan for the Reconstruction of Moscow did much better than the 1931 plan, mainly because population growth was so much slower and steadier during the second and third FYPs. In six years, from January 1, 1933, until January 1, 1939, Moscow's total population increased one half million, to just over 4.1 million.[11] Furthermore, under the 1935 General Plan, considerably more was invested in Moscow's housing, transportation, schools, stores, and other communal facilities than during the first FYP; it envisioned a city of 5 million by 1945 and set that as the permanent limit for the city's population.[12] Most significantly, whereas during the first FYP housing projects were often designed only on paper or as foundation pits, during the second and third FYPs, many of those foundation pits actually became apartment dwellings.

The failure of a citywide plan to resolve the problems of an expanding population during the first FYP invariably forced the enterprises themselves to find solutions for their own workers and their families. The factory was forced into taking an active role in providing housing for its workers, otherwise the factory administration could not hope to successfully recruit workers, halt—or at least reduce—the rampant labor turnover, and train the new recruits. The significance of the enterprise in housing construction can be roughly quantified for the first FYP. For Moscow as a whole, 3,696 new apartment buildings were constructed and 206 existing apartment buildings were considerably enlarged.[13] The municipal government (city and raion soviets) built only 290 of these, Workers' Housing Construction Cooperative (RZhSKT) (trust) built 197, and private construction accounted for 1,105. On the other hand, enterprises and institutions built 2,310. Thus, enterprises and institutions accounted for almost 60 percent of the total new housing construction in Moscow.[14]

In the Proletarskii raion (PR) in the first FYP, 354 new apartment buildings were completed but there is no information on how many of these were constructed by enterprises.[15] Hence, we have to shift to anecdotal evidence from SiM and from AMO (Moscow Automobile Association). The auto plant would initiate massive housing projects in the later 1930s, which would transform the entire PR, which since the 1935 General Plan had been divided into three, with the PR extending to the south along the river, and dominated by the ZiS plant and its workers.

In 1926–27, construction of new four- to six-story apartment buildings began in the Moscow metropolitan area.[16] These new residential districts, in combination with the barracks that were built at the beginning of the first FYP at Sokolinaia hills, Novogireevo, and Reutogo, provided housing primarily for SiM workers. The apartment projects of the 1920s were located between existing factories and toward the eastern edge of the PR, whereas the barracks were located beyond the eastern edge of the city when they were thrown up during the first FYP. (Today, they are all well within the Moscow city limits, except Novogireevo, which is just inside the eastern edge of the Moscow Beltway, which has defined the city limit since it was completed in 1960.) It is not clear what agency was responsible for this housing construction.

According to one historian, who wrote a history of the "Trekhgornaia Manufaktura" plant on the other side of Moscow,[17] the Dubrovka housing project in Proletarskii raion typified the new housing for the workers of Moscow. It was built on the eastern edge of the city, where the new factories were located, and apartments there provided, on average, 5.5–6 cubic meters per person.[18] Dubrovka housing, according to a more recent article, was for SiM, Dinamo, and AMO workers.[19] Again, these sources leave it unclear as to what agency undertook this construction.

The February 26, 1932 edition of the SiM factory newspaper *Martenovka* (Open Hearth Furnace), which devoted all of page four to problems of housing SiM workers, showed clearly that there had been a transfer of authority for providing housing from Moscow's municipal institutions (*Mossovet,* the city soviet, and the *raisovety,* the district soviets) to the enterprises. SiM was supposed to build six new buildings in 1932 to house workers. The factory had already prepared the blueprints, but Mosgorplan (Moscow City Planning) had still not ratified them as of February 26 of that year. This put the factory in a difficult position for procuring the needed construction materials and for gathering the construction work crew, because the construction season would begin in a month. The buildings would be run by a plant co-op, RZhSKT, with workers paying shares, which ranged from 5 rubles to 100 rubles, depending on the number of family members and on the size of the family's wage packet.[20]

The PR *raisovet* began building new communal apartments in 1932 on the Bol′shaia kommunisticheskaia ulitsa. A SiM worker suggested that the *raisovet* should assign 450 new apartment units to SiM workers. He complained that 400 factory vocational training school trainees at SiM were without housing, and the article suggested that the *raisovet* should build a temporary dormitory for them.[21] The same edition of *Martenovka* published a letter to the editor by a woman working at SiM, who complained about three new buildings that were being constructed for SiM workers. Apparently the designers had "forgotten" about building communal showers, kitchens, rooms for day-care and kindergarten, and even bathrooms in these buildings.[22] Obviously, such buildings were virtually uninhabitable, but under the circumstances of the housing crisis, people quickly moved in anyhow.

Thus, the factory was left to improvise, negotiating with the district soviet or the city soviet for permission and space to build new apartments, materials, construction workers, and funds, and more often than not taking over the task of building apartments since these municipal authorities could not meet the demand for housing and were not directly concerned with the situation of the factory workers at each factory. Here, a Red Director, like Stepanov at SiM, used his pull in the higher levels of economic administration (for example, with Ordzhonikidze, the commissar of the All-Union Council of the National Economy [VSNKh]), or by establishing direct personal connections with the head of the Moscow housing construction trust, and bypassing the municipal authorities, succeeded in building new housing, stores, and even schools for their workers' families. The idea of the factory's responsibility for housing its workers became well established, first among the directors and his management team, and then among the salaried staff and production workers. The Stalin regime was last to realize the potential of this devolution of responsibility to the enterprise and then endorsed it after it had become established practice. By 1937, therefore, the regime would use the inadequacies in housing (which remained widespread) as a pretext for arresting many Red Directors.

Transportation

If housing was a disaster during the first FYP, matters were not fundamentally different with respect to transportation for factory workers and other inhabitants of the factory districts of Moscow. As it underwent massive construction and reconstruction, entire sections of the PR were really nothing more than muddy construction pits. There were few paved roads in PR, and a few trams and horse-drawn cabs were still the major means of transportation within the raion.

The inadequacy of transportation within the PR and the SiM settlements, which spread into the Stalinskii district, was graphically illustrated by several incidents in 1934, concerning the Novogireevo housing project, where the SiM factory trade union committee and party committee had recently built nine new apartment buildings, housing 940 people, of whom 700 worked at SiM. The workers were apparently satisfied with these new apartments, which were larger, brighter, and cleaner than what they had lived in before. However, they had to walk two and a half kilometers to the tram stop to meet the tram that would then take them to the plant.

One kilometer of the walk traversed woods, where it was muddy and dark. Hooligans gathered here and robbed the workers. For example, on November 20, 1934, at 9:00 P.M., the best roller in the rolling steel shop and the winner of several premiums for his shock work* records, Comrade Fokin, was robbed of his new coat, suit, and boots while walking through these woods.[23] This was the most egregious case of poor transportation negatively affecting SiM workers, as Novogireevo was beyond the city limit in 1934, technically

---

*Production output records often set in special "socialist competitions" by individual workers or "shock work teams."

within the confines of the expanded eastern zone of the Stalinskii district.

After the Fokin incident, five workers from SiM sent an open letter to the plant director, P.F. Stepanov, calling attention to the problem of transportation at the settlement at Novogireevo. The workers complained in their letter, published in *Martenovka,* that the idea of running a bus line to Novogireevo had already been proposed, but that nothing had happened. They claimed that it would require a directive from Stepanov to get action. They suggested a bus line from the Kuskovo highway to their new settlement, which was on the extreme eastern edge of the city, adjacent to what is today the ring road, not far from the old Sheremetev Kuskovo estate.[24]

The situation had not improved much, according to a letter to *Martenovka* in early 1935, which described living at Novogireevo "like living on an island."[25] Later in 1935, the situation evidently had not improved, because workers always walked through the woods in groups of ten for protection against hooligans.[26] It was not until 1939 that *Martenovka* reported that a tram line had finally been completed that went out to Novogireevo.[27] From peasant barracks to permanent apartments, which were gradually connected by tram to the factory and the rest of the city, such was the pattern of development in the three prewar five-year plans in Moscow. Novogireevo was the last SiM to achieve this urban status.

The situation was similar at Sokolinaia gora in 1932, another housing district for SiM workers in which barracks were thrown up during the first FYP. For a long time, it would remain completely isolated because of a lack of public transportation. As *Martenovka* described it,

> The Sokolinaia gora district is completely removed not only from the factory, but also from cultured and enlightened society, where there are theaters and cinemas. The barracks are far away, and the lack of trams force the workers to stay in their barracks [when they are not at work]. Going to and from work, the workers spend more than an hour on the trip; [many also spend another hour going back] for lunch, leaving no time for relaxation.[28]

Not only was intra-raion transport poorly developed, but inter-raion transport was also very thin. Proletarskii raion as a whole was geographically and physically isolated from the rest of Moscow in unique ways. The Iauza and Moscow rivers, and the factories themselves, blocked access to the city's center. The PR remained unique in Moscow in its degree of isolation from adjoining city districts. The Zamoskvoretskii district to the west of PR, across the Moscow River, and the Baumanskii district to its north and west, the route to the Moscow city center, were inaccessible as bridges across the two rivers for pedestrians and cabs hardly existed. As late as 1934, at the thirteenth Raion party conference, a "Dinamo" worker, Burev, complained that to get into Moscow, the workers had to traverse the ZiS plant and cross by the bridge running from the plant into the city. He called on the party to consider building a new bridge.[29]

The isolation of Proletarskii raion from the rest of the city was nothing new.

A famous incident during the February Revolution was the shooting down of I.T. Astakhov, a steel worker at "Guzhon" (as SiM was called until 1917) who was leading a column of factory workers across the Iauza bridge.[30] The workers had to cross the bridge in order to reach the city center, where the revolution was under way, and cadet units from the nearby army barracks blocked their way momentarily at the bridge. AMO and Dinamo workers faced similar obstacles in trying to reach the city center, as the February Revolution swept away the Moscow state administration.[31]

This geographic isolation did not change at all during the 1920s, and only changed during the later 1930s. During the first FYP, access to the center of the city was still limited to the two bridges crossing the Iauza and connecting Proletarskii raion to the city center (one railroad and one paved highway), and to two others farther south, crossing the Moscow River and connecting Proletarskii raion to the Zamoskvoretskii raion. Only in 1938, with the completion of the two Ustinskii bridges, was the entire southeast quadrant of the city connected directly to central Moscow. By 1938, the PR had been carved into three districts, including a small new Proletarskii raion (with the ZiS and Dinamo plants), the new Taganskii raion, and the new Pervomaiskii raion (or First of May district), which incorporated SiM. These new *raiony* had been carved out of the PR in April 1936, when, following the directives of the General Plan of 1935, the number of city districts increased from ten to twenty-three. The Ustinskii bridges finally guaranteed quick access from SiM by bus or cab from the city's central districts and the Baumanskii and Stalinskii districts to the north. The factory finally became part of Moscow, as did some of the workers' settlements near the factory.[32]

During the first FYP and throughout the decade, some workers commuted to SiM from outside the Proletarskii raion. However, the means for commuting were very limited. It was probably easier for peasant-workers commuting daily from the villages in Moscow oblast to the east of the city on the train line that stopped at a station called SiM, en route to the Kursk railroad station. This was an important modern type of "symbiosis" between village and city, replacing the seasonal migrant worker with the daily "commuter" but seems only to have become widespread after World War II.

At the June 1931 Central Committee plenum, where the idea of the total reconstruction of Moscow was first proposed, the party passed a resolution calling for the construction of an inner-city electric train line that would link the Northern, October, and Kursk lines.[33] This may have helped commuters at SiM in the later 1930s from outside the PR, but more likely it was not until the Moscow metro was itself extended into the southeast quadrant of the city near the ZiS plant during World War II that workers could make the commute to SiM from the western or northern districts of the city. Furthermore, the opening of the "Avtozavodskaia" metro station on January 1, 1943, meant that ZiS and Dinamo workers had rapid and immediate access to the rest of the city, but it was several miles from SiM, and even farther from where the SiM workers lived.

The metro finally came out to SiM in the 1980s, as the station Ploshad il'icha, with direct access to the SiM plant, opened in December 1979. At that time, the communities of SiM workers were also finally linked by metro to the factory and to the rest of Moscow, as the Kalinin Line stations to the east of Ploshchad il'icha, including Aviamotornaia, Shosse Entusiastov, Perovo, and Novogireevo all opened at the same time. They all fed into the Marksistskaia station at the western terminus of the Kalinin Line, which was joined with the Taganskaia station, which was located both on the circle line and on the Zhdanovsko–Krasnopresnenskaia line.[34]

The June 1931 plenum also resolved to build a new circular tram line, thus linking the city's *raiony,* one to the other, along a northern route.[35] This, too, however, would have only limited use for workers traveling to SiM from other areas of the city because it would bring them in a wide arc and would deposit them well beyond the factory, to its east. Until paved roads and bridges were completed in the Proletarskii raion, and until ZiS manufactured some of the first Soviet buses, workers would have to rely on their feet and on the limited tram network to get to work and remained largely cut off from the rest of the city.

Thus, for SiM, Dinamo, and ZiS workers, and also for the construction workers who built more than one dozen new factories in the PR and then stayed to work in these factories, the PR was more like a foundation pit than a city during the first FYP.[36] The influx of a new peasant-migrant population would strain every aspect of the raion's infrastructure. While we might surmise that longtime residents of the PR were deeply bitter about the declining standard of living in this district, and the continuing isolation of the district from the rest of the city, whether or not the new migrant construction workers were dissatisfied about these problems is not clear.

The PR was a new high-tech zone in terms of the designs for its advanced factories, but in terms of urban life-style, it was more like a frontier city springing up in Siberia or the Urals, at least for those who had to live there in barracks amid the construction and the foundation pits. Whether they were living in the permanent housing at Dubrovka, Dangauerova, Vorontsovskai ulitsa, or Rogozhskii poselok, all built during the late 1920s, or in the new barracks that were quickly thrown up during the first FYP at Sokolinaia gora, Novogireevo, and Reutogo, Shosse Entuziastov, and Perovo, farther east and north in the PR and the Stalinskii district, which is where most of the peasant-recruits were housed, SiM workers were living in "outer Moscow."

Chaotic though things were, however, already during the first FYP, this new "outer Moscow," or "industrial Moscow," of the PR did not resemble its predecessor, the semirural Rogozhskii and Simonovskii districts before 1917, when these same areas of the city were only sparsely inhabited primarily by "fourth estate" dwellers (i.e., peasants with permission to reside temporarily in the city) who were factory workers legally defined as peasants whether they worked seasonally in the city, returning to the land for extended periods each year, or lived and worked permanently in Moscow. These early Rogozhskii and Simonovskii districts had also included some third-estate (i.e., permanent urban dwellers) artisans, defined not as peasants but as "urban dwellers" (meschane). The barracks set up during the first FYP seemed to promise the duplication of the same, transitory, peasant-migrant population in Soviet Moscow that had been so typical of imperial Moscow. Instead, however, the barracks would quickly give way to permanent apartment housing during the second and third FYPs, just as seasonal work would yield to permanent work.

To be sure, the new housing was in dismally cramped new communal apartments, the *kommunal 'ka*. Still, the difference between it and barracks was fundamental. The *kommunal 'ka* typically had only one bath and kitchen for up to a hundred residents living on a single floor, and each family had, at best, a single private room. Often even that single room was partitioned by furniture or curtains so that kin, fellow villagers, or even total strangers could live in the same room. Nonetheless, for a family, obtaining a room in such an apartment building was not only an improvement, but meant the realization of the dream of settling permanently in the city. It also signified the shift to having children in the city and raising them there, a fundamental change in Russian/Soviet urban life. Even after the October Revolution and under the New Economic Policy (NEP) from 1921 to 1925, "split" household units, in which a male worker's wife and children lived in the village, were typical in Moscow.

Families, not individuals, typically applied for and received rooms in these new communal apartments. This was important in the changing outlook of the peasant-migrant since it was a fundamental break from earlier patterns of migration and the duplication of peasant village life in the city. It marked an end to the "bird of passage" mentality of the Russian peasant-migrant workers, who, even after the revolution, viewed their urban stint as temporary or seasonal. Like Piore's transcontinental "bird of passage" who anticipated earning a lot of money in America and then returning to his family in the Old World,[37] the Russian peasant-migrant factory worker always lived with one foot in the new urban world, and the other in the village. This change, it would seem, was also an important factor in the rapid decline of fertility in the Soviet Union, as the permanent peasant-migrants now apparently adopted urban norms in this regard.

Mikhail Tomskii, head of All-Union Council of Trade Unions, called the peasant-migrants "guest workers" at the seventh Trade Union Congress in 1926.[38] That reflected very well the perspective of Bolsheviks and Mensheviks since the turn of the century, and it anticipated the terminology widely used in Europe in the second half of the twentieth century to label the Yugoslav, Turk, and other migratory laborers. The Stalin regime perpetuated this traditional Social Democratic outlook, but used far more pejorative labels than Tomskii, describing the peasant-migrants as "self-seekers," "grabbers," "rolling stones," and, worse, as "class aliens."

The regime unleashed the "class struggle" against them with the cry of turning the factory into a "Bolshevik fortress." Ironically, however, the regime was unleashing this "class struggle" against peasants and other "class aliens" just when the peasant-migrant was finally settling in the city and abandoning the idea of returning to the village. The peasant-migrant's vision changed, in part, of course, because collectivization brought such a dramatic decline in living standards in the village, culminating in mass rural starvation during the winter of 1932–33. The change could also be attributed to the sudden and wide availability of full-time new construction and factory jobs. Whatever the reasons, instead of the split family household, and "symbiosis" of seasonal migration between city and village, either husband, wife, and children were all migrating together and settling in Moscow or more and more unmarried young peasant men and women were on the move, migrating to Moscow where they would marry and establish a family in the city.[39]

The shift to full-time factory worker and urban inhabitant was symbolized in two roughly concurrent and central events in the lives of most of these peasant-migrants. First, most of them would shift from working in construction building factories and housing to factory production work. This happened roughly when entire factories or new shops of existing factories went "on line" (*pusk*), typically toward the end of the first FYP. The official celebration of going on line, which became an elaborate new Soviet ritual and holiday, therefore, resonated with the life experience of these new workers. It provided an important landmark for the regime, the factory, and for these new workers. That was the time when these new peasant-workers began to think of and call themselves "workers" (and were, with increasing frequency, called workers by foremen, managers, and in regime discourse, instead of peasant-migrants). At about the same time, many of the peasant workers were shifting from itinerant or migratory work, living in Moscow barracks and migrating seasonally back to the village to permanent or settled lives in apartment housing in the city. When the new apartment dwellings were ready for occupation, and when urban transportation was adequate to bring them to the factory, also merited celebration.

Once these peasant migrants had gained a room in a *kommunal'ka,* they could construct an urban family life. They would, at about that time, begin to think of themselves and to call themselves Muscovites or Moskvichi, and the authorities began to call them that. The social and psychological impact, in those days, of being called and of calling oneself a "worker" and a "Muscovite" should not be underestimated. We might note, however, that the inhabitants of the new "outer," "peripheral," and "industrial Moscow" were unskilled workers. Such districts were still not anything like the capital city within the Garden Ring just on the other side of the Moscow River, but a world apart. As the PR and other outlying districts of Moscow began to take permanent urban shape in the 1930s as mixed residential and factory zones, they would remain distinct from the "inner Moscow" where the new elite lived in pompous neoclassical apartment buildings.

From 1948 to 1952, SiM workers and all inhabitants of the PR and the southeast quadrant of Moscow saw the boundary of "inner administrative Moscow" become symbolically demarcated from "outer industrial Moscow" by one of seven new "Stalin skyscrapers" at the Kotelnicheskaia naberezhnaia, or Embankment, at the conjuncture of the Iauza and Moskva Rivers.[40] Later, the metro would finally connect them to that "inner" Moscow, as "tourists."

Food

After housing and transportation, food was the most important variable limiting the pace of urbanization, success in recruiting and retaining workers, and hence also of industrialization. And as with housing, so too, food supply was a disaster during the first FYP, which caused the enterprises, initially by default, to assume primary responsibility for feeding their workers. As food became increasingly scarce in cities and in the countryside throughout the USSR during the latter part of the first FYP, culminating with the devastating famine of 1932–33, the factory food supply network and the so-called social feeding network became not merely a convenience but a critical necessity for the survival of the workers and their families.[41]

Until July 1930 there was not a single cafeteria or buffet at SiM.[42] While most workers apparently brought their own lunch with them, about 1,500 trekked each day to the cafeteria at the Rogozhskii Market.[43] The Rogozhskii Market cafeteria was labeled Moscow Cafeteria no. 26. To get there, workers had to cross the Kursk railroad tracks and then wait in long lines. Apparently the cafeteria was dirty, and the workers called it the "Obzhorka," the "Gluttony."[44] In July 1930 this market cafeteria was converted into a SiM factory cafeteria and made into a closed facility.[45] This set a new precedent as many community facilities in the PR, mainly cooperatives or municipal stores, were taken over by the factories, excluding the general public and becoming closed facilities for factory staff. It also became the first of six cafeterias that opened at SiM during these next two years.

In that same period, at SiM, each *tsekh* (or shop) was supposed to open up its own buffet.[46] Whereas in 1930, SiM had only one cafeteria for its 10,000 workers, and workers had to wait forty-five minutes in line, and then eat their lunch standing, by 1932, the plant had built a new kitchen that prepared the food for the eight cafeterias and twenty buffets, including one dietetic cafeteria.[47]

One source retrospectively attributes the decision to install factory kitchens, cafeterias, and buffets to the party leadership.[48] It draws attention to the sixteenth party congress in June 1930, which, it claims, already recognized that the distribution of consumer goods and food for workers was seriously inadequate. While it is true that some of these supply problems were mentioned at that congress, the resolutions adopted clearly show that the leadership did not make this issue a party priority. Rather, the congress made food supply issues a priority for the trade unions, which were blamed for these problems.[49] Thus, the party leadership in June 1930 did not, in any real sense, anticipate the methods by which the enterprises would themselves organize factory-kitchens and "closed stores" for consumer goods supply and distribution to workers.

Of course, opening new cafeterias and buffets at SiM was no guarantee that the food was edible or the service efficient. There were frequent complaints about the quality of the food and the chefs who prepared it. In 1932, a *Martenovka* article exposed "fake cooks."[50] In 1934 in the rolling steel shop, workers complained that they were wasting all their lunch time waiting in line, only to receive kasha every day,[51] while in the open hearth shop, workers complained about "black eyes" in their soup.[52] Nonetheless, with famine stalking the countryside in the winter of 1932–33, and with a severe deficit of food supplies in the cities that year, the SiM cafeterias and buffets[53] offered its workers incomparably better access to food than other urban inhabitants had. The cooperative and municipal network of food stores and cafeterias that served the Moscow public at large had longer lines, and much less available selection.

Cafeterias and buffets were not the only food services that the factory provided for its workers. SiM established a special closed grocery store and ensured its own supply of fruits and vegetables by establishing its own vegetable garden and by taking control of collective farms and "attaching them" to the plant to supply its own closed grocery. This was sanctioned, indeed encouraged, again after the fact, from above:

> The party directive that each factory set up its own food shop, with its own food product base [*prodovol'stvennaia baza*] found a response in the worker collective at SiM. In Reutov, twelve kilometers from Moscow, the first SiM vegetable garden was established. SiM workers put in 7,000 work days there. . . . Thus the basis for an independent food product base was established. At the beginning of 1932, SiM was *given the Sovkhoz, Moscow Vegetable Trust* . . . [for its food base]. All of 1932 was dominated by the struggles for widening the food product base, for rabbit breeding, for fishing, for milk firms, for pig breeding, etc.[54]

Factories not only were "given" state farms (*sovkhozy*) in this way, but they were also encouraged to adopt collective farms (*kolkhozy*) under so-called *sheftsvo* (guidance) arrangement, putatively to help them with sowing and harvesting campaigns by providing additional personnel in the peak periods and by supplying them with skilled mechanics who knew how to repair tractors and other machinery. However, the factories, which were supposed to be repaid for their labor services and expertise with food produce, seem to have used this relationship to plunder the farms that were "attached" to them.[55]

For example, the contract establishing SiM *shefstvo* over the Mozhaiskii raion in Moscow oblast obligated the peasants in several *kolkhozy*, according to point 8 of 12 enumerated and contractual obligations, to set aside 30 hectares for gardening for SiM and to provide the factory with 16,500 poods* of fresh cabbage, 3,000 poods of fresh table beets, 7,300 poods of carrots, 3,000 poods of fresh cucumbers, 33,000 poods of potatoes, 100,000 poods of lettuce, 800,000 poods of tomatoes, and so on.[56] The contract even stipulated how many hectares were to be allocated for each crop. The factory was thus expected to become a *kolkhoz* organizer.

While food was the most important commodity, other consumer goods were also falling under the control of the factory distribution network at this time. In October 1930, by decree of Kaganovich, then party first secretary of Moscow, SiM took over the Mostorg Univermag no. 20, the department store serving all of the Proletarskii raion. It became a closed store, serving only SiM workers and their families.[57] The closed distribution system stipulated that: "To receive goods, each worker and white-collar worker of our factory receives from his shop or division a special book, which lists his/her last name, salary, and number of family members."[58] This entitled the family to purchase available goods at the closed stores. For deficit goods, special ration coupons (*talony*) were issued to workers through the workplace. In all, the store served 43,000 people, which meant almost one-quarter of the population of the PR.[59]

A flourishing illegal trade in these booklets and *talony* sprang up at SiM (which was no exception in this respect). *Martenovka,* on September 3, 1930, ran an article indicating that the problem was widespread and, in addition, mentioned that the nephew of the buffets chef was carrying food home illegally and that the person in charge of one of the buffets was cheating on the quantity he served to each worker at lunch and absconding with the rest in order to sell it outside the plant. Finally, the article noted, service at the SiM internal workers' cooperative was poor, because it was supposed to serve 8,000 workers, but it employed only 160 people.[60]

By the end of 1930, the closed distribution network had already become the predominant form of consumer goods distribution in the Proletarskii raion, but it still did not meet the needs of all the workers, let alone of the rest of the community. This was made clear by Gaidul', the raion party secretary, at the fourth party conference at SiM held late in December 1930. Gaidul' noted that in the raion, nineteen closed distribution stores served 93,000 people, while the remaining nine (presumably open distribution stores) served 64,000 people, including many workers who still had no access in their plants to closed distribution stores.[61]

What these figures do not reveal is the fact that inventory was generally much more extensive at the nineteen closed distribution stores than at the nine open stores that remained for the community. The greater the store's inventory, the less time wasted standing in line. In addition, the special advance ordering de-

---

*1 pood = 16.38 kg. or 36 lbs.

partment in the factory (*zakaznyi otdel*) and better service offered by the closed stores greatly reduced time spent waiting in line. This was no small advantage. Thus, what was essentially a two-tiered system of consumer product distribution went into effect, which evolved spontaneously largely by factory initiative, and was then endorsed, after the fact, by the regime.

The endorsement, when it came, attempted to organize the factory food distribution as a new all-union network. A Resolution of the Party Central Committee and the Council of People's Commissars, "On Widening the Rights of Plant Administrations in the Matter of Supplies for the Workers, and on Improving the Card System" was passed December 4, 1932.[62] The resolution stipulated four measures. First, for "group I enterprises," the "internal workers' cooperatives" were to be put directly under the control of the plant administration, which was to incorporate them into a new "Department of Supplies for Workers" (ORS). Second, for other enterprises in large-scale industry, and railroads, the workers' co-op was to remain a consumers' co-op, but the enterprise director was to sit on its board of directors. Third, a high-level commission including Kaganovich (member of the Politburo), Mikoian, Piatakov (members of the Central Committee in Charge of Industry), Shvernik (head of the Trade Union), and three others, was to report to Sovnarkom (the Soviet cabinet) within three months with a plan outlining how to supply those enterprises without any ZRK. Fourth, the procedure for issuing books and ration coupons giving access to the co-ops or the ORS was to be tightened up.[63]

Elaborating on this fourth point, the resolution explained that the books and ration coupons were to be issued only to workers and their families, by name and number, in order to prevent misuse. They were to be issued by the accounting office in charge of wages and distributed by the cashier in each shop. If a worker was dismissed or left an enterprise, the books and ration coupons were to be returned to this cashier. Finally, speculation in books or ration coupons would result in criminal prosecution under article 58, paragraph 7, article 105 of the criminal code of the Russian Socialist Federated Soviet Republic (RSFSR), and corresponding articles of the other union republics. A new type of ration coupon was to be issued on January 1, 1933, to replace the old ones.[64]

Whatever the myriad problems and inefficiencies of the system, by the end of the first FYP, SiM workers ate their lunch at the factory cafeteria, had their morning coffee or tea (if there was any) at the shop buffet, and frequently purchased food from the same buffet to take home for dinner. Furthermore, the worker purchased food for her family at the factory ZRK, and then after 1932 at the factory ORS. Whereas, in America, this type of company store generally had a poorer selection and higher prices than in other communities, in Moscow, they had a greater selection of goods and at the same or lower prices than the state groceries, which were open to the public at large. They had much lower prices than the "peasant markets" legalized in May 1932.[65] Most significantly, with the *zakaznyi otdel* and internal shops, the factory worker did not have to waste hours in line every week to obtain food.

Beyond housing, transportation, and food, the factory also provided its workers with basic health care in its clinics, with vacation and rest homes, with vocational retraining and night school opportunities for literacy classes, with nurseries and day-care centers for infants and toddlers, with secondary schooling along with vocational training in the factory vocational school, and with technical college education. Workers' accident insurance, pensions, and vacations came via the factory trade union committee, and workers' leisure activities ranging from film to soccer also fell under the purview of the factory administration and trade union committee, as did the factory clubs, and the "Palace of Culture." In sum, the factory, through the activity of its managers, its trade union committee, and its party committee, was becoming not only a cradle-to-grave welfare institution and provider of a lifetime of work and job security for its workers but also a center of community life and activity, that is, a "community organizer."

Conclusion: The Factory as "Community Organizer"

That workers looked to the factory and used it as a center for community formation and organization, in the first instance, was a consequence of the ways in which work practices in the factory were evolving and changing. It was also a consequence of the rapid integration of previously excluded social groups on the shop floor, most notably peasant-migrants, women-housewives, and youth-students. The factory was becoming a sort of "social melting pot."[66]

In addition, it was a consequence of the lobbying power that factory Red Directors could exert on behalf of a work collective clamoring for everything from basic necessities to community life. The Red Directors took the initiative for such projects (housing, transportation, food, training, social insurance) that they saw as absolutely essential for successfully recruiting, retaining, and training their work force. Meanwhile, the work collective and their families, from the least skilled worker to engineers and managers, all of whom were suffering from the same problems of chaos in daily life and lack of community, began to see the factory as a means of community organization.

That idea evolved spontaneously as the factory began to alleviate or at least ameliorate the abysmal situation in food supplies, transportation, and housing. In securing these absolute essentials, the work collective began to conceive of the factory as a focal point for community organization in a social and cultural sense as well. The Red Directors were delighted to foster such tendencies, as it provided them with a lobbying constituency, while the regime would belatedly realize that this was an opportunity for establishing social control. The source of community organizing spirit nevertheless came from the work collective. It is from that premise that I find deficient all four theories of the factory I discussed at the beginning of this chapter.

The factory was glorified in the official Stalinist metaphors, first as "Bolshevik fortress," and then more often, after the first FYP, as a "forge of cadres."

Whereas the "Bolshevik fortress" metaphor invoked the first FYP mantra of the class struggle, in which the "core" proletariat was under siege from "class aliens," the "forge of cadres" metaphor marked a shift toward individual self-development and the promotion of exceptional individuals (the promotees, or *vydvizhentsy*). This was an old theme taken from the tradition in revolutionary Russian literature where "new men" and "new women" became leading figures in the revolutionary movement. In the socialist realist novel of the 1930s, the process of personal growth and development had shifted to the factory, where raw recruits were transformed into outstanding workers, even heroes, who were "sprouting like mushrooms before our very eyes," as the saying went. The archetype or heroic ideal was Pavel Korchagin, in N. Ostrovskii's *How the Steel Was Tempered*. Then, after Ostrovskii had created a semiautobiographical fictional archetype for a hero, the regime found or invented a human archetype of a hero, named Stakhanov. These phenomena have been already carefully analyzed and need no further comment here.[67] They had little to do with the experience of the rank-and-file worker, and nothing to do with the emerging urban community.

The negative utopias by Zinoviev and Platonov described a hellish communal existence or a deep individual alienation growing out of meaningless construction work and barrack existence. Alexander Zinoviev, a dissident writer, attempted, after he landed in exile, to summarize and to systematize the ideas from his many novels, in a theory of Soviet communism. In his essay, he described Soviet communism as a recapitulation of all that was most negative in the Russian village and communal tradition. Peasant "communalism," with its intense "nosiness," in which all the important events in the lives of any household were immediately common village knowledge, was, for Zinoviev, the negation of individualism and the foundation for Soviet communism.

Under Soviet communism, he argued, these negative aspects of peasant "communalism" reappeared under the auspices of the state not only in the *kolkhoz* but also in the factories and especially in the city, where people lived in communal apartments, the *kommunal'ka,* the urban equivalent of the village.[68] Furthermore, in the factory order, with the draconian labor laws to "attach" the worker (*zakreplenie*) to the factory workbench by means of passport, and later work book, and through the provision of apartments and of food, and social security, many have noted the rise of something like a second urban serfdom. This, it has been argued, was comparable to the internal passport system under the tsar that controlled migration to the city, and which outlasted serfdom by some fifty years, and also was parallel to what the peasants called the "second serfdom" of the *kolkhoz*.

Platonov's *Kotlovan* presents a different sort of negative utopia, considering oppressive the meaninglessness of work that only laid "foundations" for the means of production and never actually produced anything that people could consume. He shows barrack life from the perspective of a totally alienated individual, Voshchev, his antihero, who seems to escape total and oppressive control only through his total human alienation. Rather than the "superfluous man" of the nineteenth century—who could not escape from emotional misery and human alienation, reflecting a lack of personal purpose among the intelligentsia—the sad figure of Voshchev demonstrated an alienation just as deep for a common person of peasant or worker background, who, it would appear, adopts it as a self-defense mechanism. This was at once a parody of socialist realism and an attempt to show a strange heroism in the anti-hero's alienation.

While I have invoked Platonov's title time and again to describe the muddy condition of the PR during the first FYP, it is another matter to consider his antihero Voshchev as somehow indicative of widespread popular attitudes. As with Zinoviev, Platonov's assumption that private life was devoid of any meaning because of constant public-communal scrutiny or oppressive state mechanisms of propaganda and control would be impossible to prove or disprove, but would seem to be about as relevant as the heroic mythology of Soviet socialist realism.

A third theory of the factory, which I am incorporating in my approach, grew out of the experience of the factory workers and staff, who came to see the factory as a welfare provider, a "cradle-to-grave" welfare institution, and as the institutional foundation for the full-employment economy and welfare state. I have no disagreement with this theory, and neither did the state, which supported the factories and underwrote their welfare functions differentially, according to the priority that it assigned to each factory. Gradually, during the Brezhnev years, virtually all factories could provide for the basic needs of their workers and their families. The state endorsed this idea, as it endorsed the idea of the factory as community organizer, after the fact, following the factory director, the staff, and workers, who quickly came to understand the potential of the factory.

Finally, the fourth theory of the factory institution in Soviet society is hypothetical in that nobody has suggested it. It would be closest to the *danwei* and might be based on Foucault's idea of the prison as a "total institution" of social control. While this might suggest "totalitarianism" penetrating down at the grass roots, it might also suggest a less sinister type of social control emerging from negotiations at the grass roots through forms of "discipline" that were modern, rational, and insidious because they were internalized. Such control, in the context of the Soviet factory, might have been achieved by means of the daily measuring of output performance and assigning a wage value to it, and by the daily structuring of leisure and social activity by the factory organizations (rationalization of daily life, or *byt*) and through the daily packaging of the news in the factory newspaper *Martenovka*. On the other hand, social control in the context of the Stalinist factory was periodically established or reasserted by resort to some exceptional methods, such as the mass movements in production geared to promote sudden new "leaps" in production output and, at the same time, to strengthen discipline in a more conventional sense than in Foucault's usage. The two aspects, mundane daily regulations, observation, and discipline, what

Foucault called Panopticism, on the one hand, and the use of naked coercion in the "draconian labor laws," worker productivist movements such as shock work and Stakhanovite campaigns, and even terror and the widespread use of forced labor in the gulag, on the other hand, might be called a twentieth-century Soviet variant on modern bourgeois mechanisms and systems of discipline.[69] This theory is appealing in many respects and would seem to correspond to many aspects of the *danwei*. However, Foucault's theory, if extended from Panopticon to the Soviet factory and city, does not readily take into account the factors of social solidarity and the active attempt by the workers to create an urban community out of mud foundation pits and dirt roads, and semifinished communal apartment buildings.

Traces of community organization are difficult to discern in the Soviet Union because the regime was not concerned with this question and was unaware of the phenomenon. Rather, the archival records and the newspapers from the 1930s abound with discussions of the crises in housing and food supply, and transportation problems, and evidence for how these problems were resolved in an ad hoc fashion at the level of the enterprise. This chapter has traced how that happened, and, in doing so, I have suggested that workers and others began to conceptualize an urban community organized around the factory, as the factory began to offer some solutions to their problems of daily life.

The role of the factory as a provider of housing and transportation and as a distributor of food and clothing, and even as the organizer of leisure and cultural activity, and creator of information, certainly did not, by itself, lead to the creation of an urban society. What was needed was the active participation of workers, establishing a new coherent and cohesive force of inclusiveness, which could connect neighbors who previously had been strangers. This did not happen overnight. It was learned in the process of resolving the intolerable living conditions of the new city. It paralleled and was based on the integration of new workers on the shop floor, in new occupations and work brigades. The resolution of the ubiquitous social conflict of the first FYP factory shop floor, in the process of integrating the newcomers at work and into a new urban community, was the central drama of Stalinism during the 1930s and again after World War II. It was both working-class and community formation. The *danwei,* while similar, was based on exclusion, creating closed-off island-cities. The Soviet cities, despite internal passports, were basically wide open.

The Chinese leadership, after 1949, faced a chronic labor surplus as peasant-migrants seemed to pose a threat to urban living standards and to urban labor productivity. The Soviet regime, from 1929 until 1991, faced a chronic labor deficit (with the exception of 1933, which saw intentional "downsizing" of enterprise work collectives, and 1946, which saw demobilization and temporary labor surplus), and this fact caused the Stalin regime to abandon its perception of the peasant-migrant as a threat to urban society and the working class, a perception that lasted only through the first FYP. The fundamental difference in labor markets shaped the fundamental differences in regime responses in the USSR and the People's Republic of China. The Soviet factory, instead of becoming a "Bolshevik fortress" to exclude the peasant-migrants, women-housewives, and the student-youth, became a social "melting pot" integrating these newcomers. That held true even through the purges and terror.

In conclusion, however, I would note one important aspect of Soviet industrialization and urbanization that may have anticipated the *danwei* in China. The rise of "closed" shops in Soviet factories during the 1930s, that is, shops devoted strictly to military production and requiring special clearance for hiring workers, was an important phenomenon. Workers in these shops were given privileges, and hiring and quitting was much more tightly controlled than in the civilian sector. Furthermore, such "closed" shops were a prototype for the first of the Soviet "closed cities" and secret cities, where development of nuclear weapons and then other military- and space-related production was conducted. Cities such as "Krasnoyarsk-80," for example, with tens of thousands of inhabitants but no location on Soviet maps, were a well-known phenomenon during the Brezhnev era. One émigré sociologist, Victor Zaslavskii, has suggested that Soviet workers in these "closed" factory shops, closed factories, and closed cities constituted a large privileged stratum, a sort of "labor aristocracy" during the Brezhnev years.[70]

Perhaps so, but during the 1930s, those workers who labored in the "closed shops" at SiM lived together, to the best of my knowledge, with other workers from the "open" shops of their factories and of other factories. Thus, they were not such a distinctive "stratum" in the community even if they were in the workplace. We might conclude, therefore, that the Soviet "closed shops" and the "closed cities" were closer to the *danwei* system in China than were other enterprises and cities. Discerning whether or not they actually served as a "model" for the Chinese leadership, however, would require investigation into other types of archival records.

Notes

1. This interpretation was advanced long ago by Solomon Schwarz, *Labour in the USSR* (New York: Praeger, 1952), and was reiterated by Donald Filtzer, *Soviet Workers and Stalinist Industrialization; The Formation of Modern Soviet Production Relations* (Armonk, NY: M.E. Sharpe, 1986).

2. The first FYP ran from October 1, 1928, through the end of 1932. The second FYP ran from January 1, 1933, through the end of 1937. The third FYP ran from January 1, 1938, through June 22, 1941.

3. Andrei Platonov, "Kotlovan" (Foundation Pit), can be found in a collection of his novellas and short stories published as *Gosudarstvennyi Zhitel'* (Inhabitant of the State) (Moscow, 1988), 108–97. Platonov wrote the novella between December 1929 and April 1930. Aleksandr Zinoviev wrote his nonfictional account of Soviet communism in exile, *Kommunizm kak Real'nost* (The Reality of Communism) (Lausanne: Editions L'Age d'Homme, 1981). In some respects, David Hoffmann's approach in *Peasant Metropolis; Social Identities in Moscow, 1929–1941* (Ithaca: Cornell University Press, 1994) seems to

have incorporated Zinoviev's argument, although for Hoffmann peasant communal culture in the city was, as the regime saw it, a source of cultural if not political opposition.

4. Some aspects of Foucault's theory of discipline have been recently incorporated in Stephen Kotkin's *Magnetic Mountain; Stalinism as a Civilization* (Berkeley: University of California Press, 1995), although Kotkin is careful to dissociate his analysis of how social control worked in the Magnitogorsk Metallurgical Kombinat and in the city of Magnitogorsk from any claims about totalitarian political control or even "total" party control in the city or the Kombinat. Still, Kotkin emphasizes how through both coercive (penal) and noncoercive (measurement, observation, and negotiation) daily practices, Bolshevik rhetoric ("speaking Bolshevik") became widespread in the factory and community.

5. *KPSS v resoliutsiiakh I resheniiakh s'ezdov, konferentsii i plenumov TsK* (Communist Party of the Soviet Union in Resolutions and Decisions of the Congresses, Conferences, and Plenums of the Central Committee), vol. 5 (Moscow, 1984), 317–18.

6. *Moskva v tsifrakh* (Moscow in Figures) (Moscow, 1934), 183.

7. Ibid., 13. On January 1, 1928, the population was 2,167,300; on January 1, 1929, it was at 2,313,900; on January 1, 1930, 2,468,700; on January 1, 1931, 2,724,000; on January 1, 1932, 3,135,000; on January 1, 1933, 3,666,300; and on January 1, 1934, 3,613,600. Thus, the rate of annual increase peaked at 16.9 percent in 1932, and then the population fell by 1.4 percent in 1933. Data for Leningrad show a comparable pattern, with an increase from 1,678,800 on January 1, 1928, to 2,776,400 on January 1, 1933, and a slight decline to 2,711,000 on January 1, 1934. See *Leningrad v tsifrakh* (Leningrad in Figures) (Leningrad, 1935), 5.

8. *Moskva v tsifrakh*, 183 (housing), and 12 (population).

9. *KPSS v resoliutsiiakh*, vol. 5, 317.

10. Ibid., 317–26.

11. *Istoriia Moskvy* (The History of Moscow), vol. 6, book 2 (Moscow, 1959), 87.

12. Ibid., 44. The 1959 census showed a population of over 6 million, and the population increased by roughly 1 million each decade thereafter, almost reaching 9 million in the 1989 census.

13. *Moskva v tsifrakh*, 106.

14. Ibid.

15. Ibid., 107.

16. V.E. Poletaev, "Zhilishchnoe stroitel'stvo v Moskve v 1931–1934gg," (Housing construction in Moscow from 1931 to 1934), *Istoricheskie zapiski* (Historical Notes) 66 (1960): 4.

17. S. Lapitskaia, *Byt rabochikh trekhgornoi manufaktury* (The lifestyle of the workers of the "Trekhgornaia Manufaktura" textile plant) (Moscow, 1935).

18. S. Lapitskaia, "Zhilishchnoe stroitel'stvo novoi Moskvy" (Housing construction in the new Moscow), *Bor'ba klassov* (Class Struggles), nos. 7–8 (1934): 220–21.

19. Poletaev, "Zhilishchnoe stroitel'stvo v Moskve," 10.

20. *Martenovka* (Open Hearth Furnace), February 26, 1932, 4.

21. Parfenych, "We Have the Right to a Building," ibid., 4.

22. Parvenova, "Showers and Baths in the New Homes," ibid.

23. *Martenovka*, November 28, 1934, 1. Crimes of this type were infrequently discussed in *Martenovka*, but this does not prove that they were infrequent events. We know that the Soviet media generally did not report crimes unless they were able to link the prosecution of the criminals to a political point. Thus, for example, a year before in *Martenovka*, March 5, 1933, 2–3, we learn that "hooligans" knifed and killed a SiM sheet metal worker, Kondakov, on March 2, 1933. Kondakov had worked at SiM for eight years and was a shock worker and *master* instructing new workers on the fourth shift at mill no. 7 when he was killed. At the trial of the four young criminals, the procurer, Novikov,

argued that they were "class enemies" because each had left or been fired from his job. Two, Korolev and Efimov were shot; Matveev received a ten-year prison sentence and Leonova a five-year sentence.

24. *Martenovka*, November 28, 1934, 1.

25. *Martenovka*, January 14, 1935, 2.

26. *Martenovka*, May 14, 1935, 1.

27. *Martenovka* August 26, 1939.

28. *Martenovka*, March 30, 1932, 4.

29. *Martenovka*, January 10, 1934, 2–3.

30. *Svet nad zastavoi* (Light above the gateway) (Moscow, 1959), 95–96.

31. *Istoriia Moskovskogo avtozavoda imeni I.A. Likhacheva* (The history of the Likhachev Moscow Auto Plant) (Moscow, 1966), 34.

32. On the bridges, built in 1938, see *Moskva entsiklopediia* (The Moscow encyclopedia) (Moscow, 1980), 435. On the two Ustinskii Bridges, see 615 and 621.

33. *KPSS v resoliutsiiakh,* vol. 5, 320.

34. *Moskva entsiklopediia*, 97, 506. Most of the SiM workers had settled during the late 1920s and especially the 1930s in apartment blocks or complexes situated at Novogireevo, Perovo, Aviamotornaia, or Shosse Entuziastov, or at Sokolinaia gora and beyond near the "Stalin Park of Culture and Rest." Now called the Izmailovo Park, these SiM worker settlements to the north of the Kalinin metro line were served by the Arbatsko–Pokrovskii Line of the metro and by the station "Izmailovskaia," which opened January 18, 1944. See *Moskva entsiklopediia*, 377 and 401.

35. *KPSS v resoliutsiiakh*, vol. 5, 320.

36. Perhaps Andrei Platonovich Platonov's short story *Kotlovan*, (Foundation pit) best captures this sense as a "negative utopia" of a modern or postmodern genre. Soviet socialist realism presented a "positive utopia" of the *Kotlovan* in the 1973 painting with that title, by T.V. Riannel' depicting the Saiano–Shushenskii Electric Station. Platonov's *Kotlovan* was written in 1929–30 and published serially in *Novyi mir* (New world) in 1987. Riannel''s painting is plate number 172 of *Iskusstvo i rabochii klass* (Art and the working class) (Leningrad, 1983). Iu.I. Pimenov's 1962 painting "Wedding on Tomorrow's Streets," plate number 123 of the same collection, is perhaps a better rendition of the "positive utopia" of the *kotlovan*, depicting a happy newlywed couple traversing the muddy streets and heading towards their new flat in one of Moscow's new districts (perhaps Cheremushchinskii) constructed too rapidly under Khrushchev.

37. Michael J. Piore, *Birds of Passage; Migrant Labor and Industrial Societies* (Cambridge: Cambridge University Press, 1979).

38. Margaret Dewar, *Labour Policy in the USSR, 1917–1928* (London: Royal Institute of International Affairs, 1956), 148.

39. The idea of "symbiosis" of peasant-migrants moving between city factory work and village agricultural work, and spanning both worlds, was first suggested by Robert E. Johnson, *Peasant and Proletarian; The Working Class of Moscow at the End of the Nineteenth Century* (New Jersey: Rutgers University Press, 1979). The regime's way of counting *otkhod* (peasant out-migration) during the first FYP, which confused and conflated seasonal and permanent migration, reflected this fundamental transition, as has the confusion in the accounts of Soviet historians since then. I have discussed this issue in chapter 3 of my forthcoming study, *Factory and Community in Stalin's Russia; The Making of an Industrial Working Class* (University of Pittsburgh Press). *Otkhod*, both seasonal and permanent rural–urban migration, was encouraged by the regime under *orgnabor*, the so-called organized recruitment of labor. The regime hoped that the seasonal peasant migration would become permanent out-migration, which was happening as more and more peasants came to the conclusion that their life in the village was over and that survival meant life in the city.

40. It was built at the embankment near the juncture of the Moscow and Iauza Rivers by gulag inmates, according to Timothy Colton, *Moscow; Governing the Socialist Metropolis* (Cambridge, MA: Harvard University Press, 1995), 329 and 335. Colton calls the two Moscows the "monumental city" and the "minimal city" (326–51).

41. The "social feeding network" was the *set obshchestvennogo pitaniia*. Access to the factory food-supply network, for some peasant-migrants, literally meant the difference between life and death. The Passport Law of December 1932, which halted in-migration from the countryside, condemned many would-be migrants from rural areas to starvation, since they could find no food in the destitute *kolkhozy* or in neighboring villages or towns.

42. State Archive of the Russian Federation (GARF), f. 7952, op. 3, d. 326, l. 131. (In Soviet times GARF was called the Central State Archive of the October Revolution [TsGAOR].) This document was labeled "chapter 13" and would have become a chapter of the volume on the history of SiM in the Gorky "History of Factories" project, had that volume ever been published.

43. Ibid.

44. GARF, f. 7952, op. 3, d. 283, l. 182.

45. GARF, f. 7952, op. 3, d. 326, l. 132.

46. Ibid.

47. GARF, f. 7952, op. 3, d. 283, l. 1–2.

48. A document, a collection of manuscripts from 1930 to 1932, begins with a piece entitled "Supplies and Food for the Workers in Service of the Promfinplan" (GARF, f. 7952, op. 3, d. 283, l. 1. Promfinplan is an acronym for "industrial-financial plan."

49. Thus, in the section of the congress resolutions entitled "The Most Important Tasks in the Development of Industry," the list begins with liquidation of the fuel deficit and the deficit in electrical energy in the most important regions (Donbass, Kuzbass, Leningrad, Moscow, Nizhnii Novgorod, and Ural), and providing the tractors that will be needed on the new collective farms, and finally, toward the bottom, calls for expansion of light industry for consumer goods, foodstuffs, and paper and other industries needed for cultural activities of the working population. See *KPSS v resoliutsiiakh . . .* , 151–53. For the resolutions adopted by the congress, see 178–80. These resolutions talk about rising income, rising living standards, and then, in no. 4, note, "The congress considers that the trade unions, in the past period, have devoted completely inadequate attention to the questions of workers supply, to the struggle to lower costs, and to improve the work of the cooperatives . . . . The trade unions must achieve a faster development of the network of factory-kitchens, and improve their quality while reducing the price of "social meals" (*obshchestvennoe pitanie*), 179.

50. *Martenovka*, June 20, 1932, 4.

51. *Martenovka*, January 12, 1934, 3.

52. *Martenovka*, January 14, 1934, 3.

53. Workers were often able to purchase food at the buffets to take home to their families. They functioned as a kind of internal food distribution network.

54. Emphasis added. GARF, f. 7952, op. 3, d. 326, l. 132.

55. Contracts were signed for *shefstvo*, and the factory was obligated to help the *kolkhoz* in a kind of crude barter arrangement that resembled the *orgnabor* contract, under which the factory was also supposed to compensate the *kolkhoz* for each recruit. Such compensation was altogether inadequate, and under *shefstvo*, most of this "help" actually involved bringing the party line on collectivization to the countryside. There were, for example, twenty-two obligations that SiM took upon itself under *shefstvo* to aid the Mozhaiskii raion farms, which included helping them to fulfill the Promfinplan for the farms, helping the *kolkhozy* to consolidate "socialist agriculture," helping with all major

political and economic campaigns (including sowing and harvesting), and helping to set up the machine-tractor station. See S. Filatov, *Partrabota na zavode "serp i molot"* (Party work at the "Hammer and Sickle" Plant) (Moscow, 1931), 131–37.

56. Filatov, *Partrabota na zavode "serp i molot,"* 130.

57. GARF, f. 7952, op. 3, d. 283, l. 2.

58. Ibid., l. 6.

59. Ibid., l. 6. Population of the PR on April 1, 1931, was 198,400. See *Moskva v tsifrakh*, 18.

60. "The Distribution Book Cannot Be in the Hands of the Class Enemy; Strengthen Workers' Control over the Activity of the Cooperative; Repress the Speculators and Wreckers; Liquidate Speculation in Coop-Books and *Talony*," *Martenovka*, September 3, 1930, 4.

61. *Martenovka*, December 23, 1930, 1.

62. *Martenovka*, December 1932, 2–3.

63. Ibid.

64. Ibid.

65. On May 20, 1932, the bazaar or *kolkhoznyi rynok* was legalized, allowing peasants to market some of their surplus at prices considerably above the fixed prices of the state stores. As Moshe Lewin notes in "Taking Grain: Soviet Policies of Agricultural Procurements Before the War," in Chimen Abramsky, ed., *Essays in Honour of E.H. Carr* (London: Macmillan, 1974), 298, the law was amended so that only after the procurement targets had been fulfilled could the peasants market surplus products. These markets quickly became the most abundant source of food in the city. However, not many people could afford bazaar prices, at least not for the bulk of their purchases.

66. I develop these ideas in chapter 7 of my forthcoming study *Factory and Community in Stalin's Russia*.

67. Ostrovskii's novel was published serially from 1932 through 1934. It was, in many ways, modeled on earlier works by Chernyshevskii (*What Is to Be Done?*) and Gorki (*Mother*), which anticipated socialist realism as it evolved in the 1920s and especially after 1934 and the first congress of the Writer's Union. The role of all three works in the evolution of a formulaic socialist realism under Stalin is described in Katerina Clark, *The Soviet Novel; History as Ritual* (Chicago: University of Chicago Press, 1985). The rise of Stakhanovism in September 1935 is thoroughly analyzed in Lewis Siegelbaum's study, *Stakhanovism and the Politics of Productivity in the USSR, 1935–1941* (Cambridge: Cambridge University Press, 1988).

68. Zinoviev, *Kommunizm kak Real'nost*.

69. Michel Foucault, *Discipline and Punish; The Birth of the Prison* (translated by Alan Sheridan, New York: Vintage Book Editions, 1979), 202.

70. Victor Zaslavskii, *The Neo-Stalinist State* (Armonk, NY: M.E. Sharpe, 1992).

Part III
Danwei Under Reform

7

Danwei: The Economic Foundations of a Unique Institution

Barry Naughton

For more than two decades, from the early 1960s well into the 1980s, the Chinese urban work unit, or *danwei,* maintained its unique status as an extreme example of a certain kind of social organization. The *danwei* was not solely a "work unit" or productive enterprise. Rather, the *danwei* had multiple social, political, and economic functions and a permanent "membership" of workers with lifetime employment. This chapter argues that the most distinctive features of the *danwei* are best understood in light of the distinctive characteristics of the economic environment in which Chinese enterprises operated. The evolution of the economic environment thus provides insight into both the emergence of the distinctive *danwei* institution and its subsequent decline. Today, changes in the economic environment induced by economic reforms are causing dramatic changes in the *danwei* system. Since the early 1980s, economic reforms of a progressively more fundamental character have reshaped the urban economy, increasing labor mobility and changing many of the other economic foundations of the *danwei* system. These changes inevitably spell profound change in the *danwei* system, and point to its eventual abolition; yet the *danwei* system also displays remarkable tenacity. In the face of economic changes of unprecedented magnitude, the *danwei* system has survived to the present, although in modified form, and continues to be important in China.

Orientation

In all societies, the employment relationship has a special status that differentiates it from other contractual relationships. In developed market economies, the labor contract carries with it some degree of protection for the worker, such that dismissals cannot be made entirely arbitrarily or without notice. Moreover, the indispensability and relative stability of the employment relationship leads governments both to regulate employment (for health and safety objectives) to use the employment relation to organize eligibility for social benefits, including health care and unemployment insurance. Thus, the workplace in all developed countries ends up serving functions beyond merely organizing productive labor. There is, however, a wide variation in the extent to which the employment relationship is treated like an ordinary economic transaction. Near one extreme is the United States, in which the employment relationship is generally seen as a voluntary contract between two parties, more or less freely entered into and terminated at will by either party. It is illegal for employers to terminate employees for the wrong reasons (discrimination on account of age, race, or sex) but not illegal to terminate employees for no reason at all or simply in pursuit of the company's economic advantage. Despite some government regulation, the relationship is widely regarded as being a specific example of a general category of voluntary economic contracts. In Japan, the relationship is quite different, at least in large firms. Japanese courts have created a body of case law that makes it extremely difficult for companies in Japan to lay off workers for anything less than gross misconduct or dire economic distress. Moreover, companies have internalized these guidelines into a common practice of permanent employment within the large firm sector.

China's *danwei* system, then, is not unique because of the presence of permanent employment or enterprise social services. However, it is unique in the extent to which these functions are performed. Despite its roots in Soviet organizational practice, the Chinese *danwei* developed the tendencies discernible in Soviet institutions to a much more extreme degree. What demands explanation is the extreme nature of the Chinese institution. It makes some sense to discuss the *danwei* as an ideal type. In this ideal type, workers are permanently attached to the enterprise, and the enterprise is multifunctional. Production and revenue earning are primary functions, but all enterprises also have social, cultural, and political functions. They assume full responsibility for other activities, including provision of social services, especially health care, welfare, and housing. Political control is exercised by the *danwei*. Indeed, all enterprises have a similar bundle of responsibilities and, partly as a result, are required to have a similar organizational form. The enterprise is the building block for nearly all the important organizational systems of urban society. The enterprise encompasses a multiplicity of functions and uniformity of organizational form. Employees are not so much contractors with the *danwei* as they are citizens of it. The *danwei* is a microcosm of urban society, into which individuals are born, live, work, and die.

By contrast, a purely market-oriented enterprise may engage in a variety of activities, but all these activities will be directly subordinate to a single function: to earn revenue through the sale of a good or service. The enterprise will contract with individual workers for their productive services, and the contract will be subject to termination by either side or renewal by mutual consent. The enterprise is free to take on any organizational form that it deems appropriate for its purposes. Thus the capitalist enterprise can be characterized as a bundle of contracts, entered into to accomplish revenue-generating activity. It exists in a "sea" of heterogeneous organizations, created for different purposes, as needed, according to different principles. Each organization is specialized, and there is a multiplicity of organizational forms. Employees owe no special allegiance to a work organization, and the enterprise knows no allegiance to them.

This chapter stresses the economic conditions that permitted the emergence of the *danwei* system, which today are reshaping and may eliminate the *danwei* system. Among these economic conditions, by far the most important is the absence of labor mobility that characterized the Chinese economy precisely during the years when the *danwei* system was most highly developed. It is not accidental that the *danwei* in China was unique among the socialist countries or that China was also unique among socialist countries in abolishing urban labor markets and virtually eliminating labor mobility. Other conditions, however, were required for the emergence of the extreme form of the *danwei* system: a sheltered competitive position for the enterprise and the trend toward administrative simplification as China's administrative apparatus slid backward during the Cultural Revolution. Since economic reforms began after 1978, these shaping conditions have diminished in strength. Yet the result has not been a linear transformation toward a familiar market-system enterprise and employment relationship. On the contrary, early reforms, in particular, sometimes had the paradoxical effect of strengthening the *danwei* characteristics. Even today, despite much progress, the *danwei* form persists.

The Emergence of the Danwei in Its Classic Form

The *danwei* system emerged during the mid-1960s, as part of the Chinese administrative adaptation to the new economic circumstances created by the Great Leap Forward disaster. Three factors were most important to the *danwei*'s emergence in its classic form: the curtailment and gradual elimination of labor markets and job mobility; the regularization of an enterprise financial system that created substantial surpluses for most enterprises; and the program of administrative simplification that emerged during the 1960s.

The Absence of Labor Mobility

During the 1950s, in the initial phases of Soviet-style industrialization in China, urban labor markets were quite fluid. Rapid expansion of production was accompanied by large-scale rural-to-urban and interregional migration. New industrial workers enjoyed higher incomes than before, but did not automatically or universally receive coverage under the new social security and health insurance systems.[1] Policymakers expressed concerns about the high cost of providing new urban jobs, continuing unemployment in urban areas, and the difficulties of sustaining continued rapid urbanization. Regulations were adopted between 1956 and 1958 that would have had the effect of restricting migration to cities. However, before these regulations came into effect, the Great Leap Forward (1958–60) intervened. During the Leap, millions left agricultural work and crowded into existing factories as well as hurriedly erected new plants, including the well-known "backyard steel mills." This sudden human flood into the factories was churned up by the bizarre political utopianism of the Leap, but also corresponded with the interests and aspirations of individual migrants. A factory job and urban residence were clearly the keys to a better life. The calculation to move in response to politically generated opportunities was individually rational, but collectively disastrous. The exodus from agriculture was far too great for China's agricultural economy to support. With the shift of millions from agricultural to industrial occupations the food balance swung inevitably into deficit. Food production collapsed, and mass starvation and hunger inevitably resulted.

Out of this immense catastrophe emerged a new set of economic conditions, which created the foundations for the Chinese *danwei* system. Faced with imminent starvation, the urban population, through a combination of voluntary action and a government removal program, shrank by 14 million between 1960 and 1963. Subsequently, tight controls were put in place—ultimately based on the pre-Leap regulations—that essentially halted new migration from rural to urban areas. It is clear that the fundamental motivation for this policy was the fear that if the decision were left to voluntary choice, migration of rural residents to the cities would quickly resume and the burden on food supplies would again become too great to sustain. The gap between rural and urban living standards was becoming wider: more crucially, it was also becoming increasingly evident and showing signs of becoming permanent. The government felt compelled to freeze the existing population in place. When this was done, the status of existing urban residents changed. Increasingly protected from inflows of rural migrants, urban residence became an even more privileged status, possessed by individuals, usually for life, and inherited by their children. Mobility of all kinds, and including job mobility, thus declined sharply.[2] At about this time, the government also assumed direct control over the hiring process, a control that had eluded it throughout the 1950s. From the early 1960s, the government began directly or indirectly to allocate almost 95 percent of first jobs in urban areas, taking away the hiring function from the individual enterprise.[3]

Following these changes, voluntary job mobility *within* urban areas—that is, job changes from one urban job to another—began to disappear. The state still reassigned workers to new enterprises—including those in distant cities—in accordance with state needs, but resignations, dismissals, and job transfers became virtually nonexistent for ordinary workers. A few numbers can flesh out these observations. Our first data on labor mobility come from 1978, but evidence indicates that the situation prevailing in 1978 began in the 1960s. At the end of 1978, there were 63 million long-term, or "permanent" (*guding*) state workers in China, and during that year, slightly over a million workers left the state sector. However, almost half the job leavers were retirees. Only 37,000 workers quit or were fired in 1978, about one-twentieth of one percent of all permanent workers. During the same year, 150,000 state workers died. Thus death was four times as important a cause of job-leaving as were resignations and being fired; and retirements were thirteen times as important. If workers converted to collective status are added, the total leaving the state sector for reasons plausibly relating to individual or managerial choice still falls short of one-tenth of one percent.[4] This measure is not a complete measure of job mobility because it does not capture workers who quit (or are fired from) one state job and accept another within the year. However, it does give a good idea of the order of magnitude of voluntary job mobility: virtually nonexistent.

It is worth stressing how unusual this was in the socialist context. In the Soviet Union and the East European socialist countries, ordinary workers changed jobs frequently. It was common for a worker to leave his or her job and search for a better job in the same city. "The Soviet labor market is very active. Until the end of the 1970s, Soviet state employees could quit a job on two weeks' notice; today [1987] the required notice is two months. In 1978 in the Russian Republic, 16 percent of all industrial manual workers quit their jobs during the year."[5] Voluntary job turnover was about a hundred times more common in the Soviet Union than in China under the *danwei* system. Moreover, in the Soviet Union two-thirds of all hiring was done directly by the enterprise (at the factory gate, in the case of industrial enterprises) and another 10 percent consisted of voluntary matches arranged by municipal labor bureaus. Beginning in the 1960s, urban Chinese were, with rare exceptions, assigned to a work unit upon leaving school and then remained with that single work unit for the remainder of their working lives.

Additional features of the Chinese employment system differentiate it from "permanent employment" in market economies such as Japan. First, the Chinese system applied indiscriminately to all state workers. In market economies, long-term employment relations predominate only in occupations where they are likely to enhance productivity through the creation of work skills that are specific to a given firm: if skills are nonspecific, there is little to be gained by tying workers to a specific employer. Thus, white-collar employees in any country are often effectively "permanent," and in Japanese industry only a portion of the work force (perhaps one-third) are covered by permanent employment arrangements. The presence of permanent employment arrangements among Japanese blue-collar workers is frequently linked to the fact that the work force is relatively highly skilled and to flexible work rules that build firm-specific human capital among a portion of the blue-collar labor force.[6] Similarly, in the Soviet Union, most of the extensive labor turnover occurs among ordinary production workers with skills that are easily transferable between enterprises.

Second, the initial work assignment for the Chinese school graduate was typically his or her final assignment as well. There was little trial employment or "sorting" of workers and employers to find appropriate matches. By contrast, in Japan there is considerable "sorting" of the blue-collar labor force in the first years of work. Two-thirds of new blue-collar employees of large firms have had previous work experience in other firms.[7] Thus the labor market permits enough flexibility at the outset to avoid some of the most unsatisfactory matches between individuals and their work environments. Moreover, permanent employment positions are generally with more desirable enterprises in Japan, so competition between entry-level applicants also provides an effective sorting mechanism. By contrast, virtually all Chinese urban school-leavers were assigned to a work unit that immediately became their permanent employer, with little possibility of adjustment. The likelihood that the employment relationship was resented and impeded productivity must therefore have been far greater in China. So, despite the natural temptation to draw parallels between the Chinese system and those prevailing in the Soviet Union or in Japan, there are clear differences: In both comparisons, the Chinese system is more rigid and extreme.

Profit Stream

During the mid-1960s, the Chinese budgetary system developed into its mature form, which relied heavily on state-owned industry to produce revenues. After the start-up phase of the early 1950s and the disruption of the Great Leap Forward, China's industry entered a phase of ordinary operation in the 1960s. Given the existing price system and the control the government exerted over rural production and marketing, ordinary operations in industry implied that industry was tremendously profitable. Even during the 1950s, industrial workers had created a "surplus" (total profit and tax) for the state greater than their own wage. But, during the 1960s, the surplus created by each worker climbed to a much higher level and in 1965 surpassed four times the value of his total wage for the first time. In that year, state-owned industry produced a total profit and tax of 30.92 billion yuan—virtually all of which was turned over to the government— or slightly over 2,500 yuan per worker. By comparison, the annual industrial worker wage in that year was 633 yuan. Through 1978, state-owned industry more than doubled in size, and more than doubled its labor force, but the basic financial relationship remained unchanged. In 1978, each state industrial worker created total profit and tax of just over 2,500 yuan, and the average industrial wage was 631 yuan.[8] Throughout this period, the typical state-owned enterprise (SOE) was generating a surplus for the government equal to about four times what it paid to the enterprise workers.

These financial relationships are due to the protected competitive position of SOEs. Prices were set by the government, and no serious competition was allowed. Prices were set in a way that discriminated against farmers and benefited urban work units. The result was that most urban work units were profitable, and the government could then tap these surpluses to fund its own activities. The goal of the system was, of course, to provide an easily mobilizable tax base for the government. By transferring financial surpluses from its own enterprises to the government budget, the authorities could be assured of the resources they needed for ambitious programs of economic, military, and political construction.

Yet the volume of the surplus at the enterprise level was also significant because a large surplus was the necessary condition for the creation of a prosperous work unit. Even though the *danwei* was required to turn over virtually all its surplus to the government, the reality was that the *danwei* had at least initial control of a large revenue stream, and the diversion of even a small proportion of that revenue could have a significant impact on the workers' standard of living.[9] Realistically, enterprises were in a position to skim a portion of revenues and use them to finance improvements in living standards. Moreover, the national government was at worse ambivalent about the diversion of a small part of the enterprise revenue stream. After all, the government had as one of its policy objectives to provide benefits to urban workers, and the enterprises had the money to finance those benefits. "Collective" benefits were seen as being ideologically preferable to individual wage increases. Thus while the government attempted to monitor and control the rate at which enterprises tapped into these large revenue streams, it was by no means hostile to the idea that increased profitability would finance some improvement in workers' living standards. Workers in state industry enjoyed benefits not available to those in other sectors as industry emerged as the "cash cow" of the economic system. These financial relationships provided another of the basic preconditions for the *danwei* system. During these years, the system of social insurance and benefits became universal in state-owned enterprises.

Administrative Simplification

As the Chinese economy recovered from the Great Leap Forward debacle, policymakers once again began to face some choices about economic strategy. After a period during which all available resources had to be devoted to survival and recovery, gradually improving economic conditions began to provide some "surplus" resources by the mid-1960s. Policymakers made some crucial calculations about the allocation of this surplus. How much of the increasing surplus would be devoted to improving living standards? How much would go toward building and consolidating the institutions and bureaucratic apparatus that governed the economy and provided the basis for a developed society. Under pressure from Mao Zedong's increasingly utopian conception of socialism, policymakers basically decided to allocate almost nothing to improving living standards and to institution building. Instead, they opted for political mobilization and the development of what we might term "austerity socialism." Under austerity socialism, increased resources were devoted almost entirely to industrial and military development, with the objective of giving Chinese society "survivability" in what was seen as an increasingly hostile world.[10]

This decision had important implications for the evolution of Chinese enterprises. First, it led to the creation of new enterprises in remote rural locations in the Chinese interior. These "Third Front" enterprises were created for national defense purposes and were thus located as far as feasible from existing urban infrastructure.[11] This remoteness meant that these enterprises had to provide and subsequently manage their own physical infrastructure and social services. Third Front enterprises thus became extreme examples of the *danwei* even when compared to the Chinese norm, itself extreme by international standards. Third Front enterprises were often literally "small societies," or firms that incorporated within them all the functions of small cities. There was no urban or social context into which these firms could be embedded.

Even for existing urban enterprises, the trend toward austerity socialism implied changes in social organization. A process of administrative simplification detached the worker from reliance on independent bureaucracies that provided alternative sources of support or assistance, and reinforced the worker's dependence on the work unit as such. China's evolution in this respect was again in contrast to that of the Soviet Union. In the Soviet Union after the Stalinist era, there were always competing and overlapping jurisdictions within urban areas. Different functional bureaucracies oversaw and checked one another, even while each carried out specified core functions. In China, by contrast, the enterprise assumed direct control over diverse functions, making external bureaucracies superfluous.

An important example of this difference is the lesser importance of labor unions in China than in the Soviet Union, and in fact the disappearance of labor unions during the time period under consideration here. In the Soviet Union, labor unions have consistently been a significant part of the distribution of power and benefits in the enterprise. Labor unions administered much of the benefit package and served as a vehicle for the expression of certain of the workers' (nonpolitical) interests.[12] Unions were always less important in China than in the other Soviet-type economies. Because the Chinese Communist Party's revolutionary strategy has been based on peasant mobilization since the late 1920s, union organization played little effective role in the Communist political triumph. Although union organizations were set up on the Soviet model immediately after 1949, those organizations lacked influence both within the enterprise and in national politics. Union leaders were on the losing side of two important political campaigns during the 1950s and were further marginalized by the Maoist radicalization of the Great Leap Forward. As Jeanne Wilson put it:

> A distinguishing feature of Chinese trade unions is their institutional weakness even in comparison with unions in other communist states. . . . The devel-

opment strategy of the Great Leap, with its stress on voluntarism, mobilization, and the heritage of the party's experience in Yenan. . . . relegated the trade unions to the periphery of the enterprise, patently Soviet-style structure in an increasingly anti-Soviet environment.[13]

During the 1960s, the congenitally weak status of Chinese unions sank even lower. Immediately after the beginning of the Cultural Revolution in January 1967, the All-China Federation of Trade Unions (ACFTU) was formally dissolved, and virtually all enterprise unions ceased to function. The abolition of labor unions inevitably meant that the administration of the benefits and social security system was taken over by the enterprise management itself. Conversely, the absence of labor mobility, already becoming institutionalized, meant that enterprises were in a position to assume responsibility for social services administration without serious problems. Initially, responsibility devolved to the "revolutionary committees" that were the newly constituted enterprise executive organs.[14] Subsequently, as normalized management structures began to re-emerge during the 1970s, enterprise management groups assumed control of social welfare functions. In some enterprises, unions were revived and, in some cases, resumed significant welfare functions. But, even in those cases, welfare administration was delegated to the enterprise union by the enterprise management. No national labor union system existed, and the unions ceased to function as a separate delivery system. Naturally, this meant that there was no longer an option of a worker leaving an individual welfare delivery system. Not surprisingly, these developments substantially reinforced the trend toward the *danwei* system. No longer did the individual worker retain the option of leaving his enterprise but maintaining his benefit package through his union membership. Benefits, along with housing, for the first time began to tie workers to specific enterprises.

The evolution of the trade unions was only one part of a broader trend toward direct Communist Party management of the enterprise. Although this trend did not receive any formal endorsement, it was inevitable under the intensely politicized Cultural Revolution environment. Gradually party control and direct management of the enterprise coalesced into direct party management. Competing administrative bodies were sidelined during the initial Cultural Revolution struggle for power. Subsequently, the need to restore order in the factories invariably led to the creation of a single political authority, the revolutionary committee. The revolutionary committee in most cases reflected an uneasy compromise among different factions, but it was given the sole direct management authority within the factory. In no case was any kind of pluralism or balancing of functions within the enterprise tried as an approach to restoring normal functioning. As the Communist Party hierarchy gradually resumed functioning, the revolutionary committees were subsumed within that hierarchy. During the 1970s, unified management under the Communist Party (*dangde yiyuanhua*) became a common slogan. The separate hierarchies of government—in this case, economic administration—and party were progressively united into a single hierarchy. The party secretary was the "boss" (*yiba shou*), who either had the ultimate authority over the factory manager or else took over the factory manager's job.

These changes simplified the enterprise's administrative relationships, in the sense that they took previously separate hierarchies or systems and merged them into one. But, conversely, the "simplification" made the authority relationships within that single remaining hierarchy all the more complex, since they now covered a much broader scope. Decisions about production, politics, and welfare were now channeled through a single chain of command. The *danwei* became all-encompassing in part because many types of important decisions were channeled through the *danwei* leadership. In the 1970s, a new form of social control was added to this mix, as compulsory birth control targets were introduced. Factory managers were charged with monitoring reproductive behavior (through their deputies) along with their other responsibilities.

At the same time, these changes in social service delivery form were essentially predicated on the end of job mobility. It would have made little sense to transfer responsibility for these things to enterprises away from society-wide institutions such as labor unions, unless the worker could be depended on to remain with the firm. And they were greatly facilitated by the strong financial position of most firms. These three elements, then, made up the basic economic preconditions for the *danwei* system. By the mid-1960s, all three were in place in China.

Aspects of the Classic Danwei System

It is worth taking a brief snapshot of the operation of the *danwei* system in its classic form. Doing so brings to light three key aspects of that system: the *danwei*'s important role in social service provision; the internal complexity of the *danwei,* and its lack of autonomy.

Social Service Delivery

Overall, state enterprises have played a substantial role in the provision of social services. Only about two-thirds of the industrial SOE work force consists of actual industrial workers, with perhaps one-fifth of their work force devoted to providing services that would not be similarly provided in a capitalist enterprise. (Table 7.1 provides figures on the labor force of industrial SOEs in 1990.) More than 70 percent of state enterprises ran schools of some kind.[15] About 40 percent of all general hospital beds were in the state-owned industrial system. State enterprises constructed most of the new housing in cities and owned a large share of the total housing stock.

While the *danwei* system existed in virtually all SOEs, it was most developed in the large, heavy industrial SOEs. Large firms were more likely to have abun-

Table 7.1

State Industrial Workers and Staff, 1990

	Million	Percent
Total	43.64	100.0
Production workers	28.93	66.3
Apprentices	1.07	2.5
Engineers and Technicians	2.52	5.8
Managerial	4.74	10.8
Service	4.54	10.4
of which:		
Elementary and Middle	0.57	1.3
College	0.04	0.1
Medical	0.47	1.1
Commercial	0.2	0.5
Other	1.84	4.2

Source: Zhongguo laodong tongji nianjian [China labor statistics yearbook 1991] (Beijing: Zhongguo laodong chubanshe, 1991), 331, 319.

dant revenues to fund benefits, and they were more likely to enjoy government priority during investment, so that they could provide housing and other facilities to their workers. Although few in number, large firms (*dazhongxing*) play a significant role in Chinese industry. According to the 1985 Industrial Census, which offered the first detailed look at Chinese industry, there were 8,285 of these large firms, of which 7,946 were state-owned. These comprised less than 2 percent of all SOEs, but accounted for 45 percent of state light industrial employment and 64 percent of state heavy industrial employment.[16] Moreover, these factories were highly profitable and relatively efficient by Chinese standards. In fact, large enterprises accounted for almost two-thirds (62.3 percent) of the total profit and tax generated by independent accounting industrial enterprises.

These more than 8,000 large industrial enterprises in 1985 employed 21 percent of the total state system health workers. Similarly they have almost exactly half the hospital beds within the industrial system, or 19.4 percent of the total general hospital beds. The housing owned by just these 8,285 enterprises equals 32 percent of the *total* housing stock in the 317 largest cities in China.[17] Within the category of large enterprises, heavy industrial enterprises accounted for three-quarters of the workers and staff, and these heavy industrial SOEs also provided substantially greater levels of services to their workers than did light industrial enterprises. Consider the comparisons shown in Table 7.2: Large heavy industrial enterprises tended to be from 80 percent to 400 percent as well endowed with social services as light industrial enterprises. What accounted for this difference? Three factors were important. First,

Table 7.2

Social Services Provided by Large Industrial Enterprises in 1985

	Light industry	Heavy industry
Enterprise-owned housing (m² per worker)	10.4	18.6
Health-care personnel (per 100 workers)	.84	1.80
Hospital beds (per 100 workers)	.37	1.24
Elementary students (per 100 workers)	4.4	16.2
Secondary students (per 100 workers)	2.8	12.2
Vocational and post-secondary (per 100 workers)	1.0	2.9
Children in nursery school (per 100 workers)	7.1	7.2
Library books (per worker)	2.6	3.6
Recreational facilities (m² per 100 workers)	.26	.45
Workers studying (vocational and post-secondary) (per 100 workers)1.0	2.01	2.62

Source: Industrial Census Leading Group, *Zhonghua renmin gongheguo 1985 nian gongye pucha ziliao* [Materials on the 1985 industrial census of the People's Republic of China] (Beijing: Zhongguo tongji chubanshe, 1987), vol. 1, 202, 608, 624.

heavy industrial enterprises were simply privileged, enjoying higher prestige and receiving higher levels of benefits. Second, 49 percent of the workers in large light industrial enterprises were female, compared to only 28.5 percent in large heavy industrial enterprises. If we suppose that benefits to family members were disproportionately supplied via the father's work unit, the underlying inequality between families may be less than the apparent inequality among work units. In this regard, note that nursery facilities are the only service provided equally to both sectors. Third, more heavy industrial facilities are outside major urban areas, including in remote Third Front areas. These enterprises must bear a disproportionate burden of social services since they must provide virtually all available services, and cannot rely on urban facilities. The picture of the overall *danwei* system is somewhat biased to the extent that it relies on large, heavy industrial work units as the basis for generalization. In fact, these enterprises were considerably better endowed than the average Chinese *danwei*.

Internal Complexity

The fact of permanent employment lay behind the subjective reality of the *danwei*. This subjective reality was that of a dense, sometimes suffocating, network of complex but familiar relations between human beings. Those relations could develop this overgrown lushness only because of their permanence. This reality—taken for granted by most mainland Chinese—is highlighted in the reactions of one mainland cadre after he went to work in Hong Kong in the early 1980s:

I was surprised to discover that nobody paid any attention to my private circumstances. In China, if there's a newcomer in any unit, before long everybody knows his background, history, wage grade, political behavior, whether there are any black marks on his record, what sports he's good at, and with whom he does or doesn't get along. . . . A whole range of matters must go through public evaluation, such as wages, bonuses, designation as a progressive worker, being sent out to study, promotions and punishments, and allocation of housing and other benefits. At a critical moment, just a word in the wrong place can do great harm, so people have to sound out everybody else carefully. Rumors, gossip and nasty remarks are common, too, and this leads to pointless quarrels, making the relationships between people complicated and tense.[18]

People have long histories and long memories.

The complexity of work unit relationships also derives from the fact that the *danwei* was the unit for the delivery of a variety of services and also for the exercise of political control. The Chinese industrial enterprise has multiple functions to fulfill. As a result, managers are under enormous time and information pressure. One study of a small sample of Chinese managers found that they worked long hours (on average nine hours and forty minutes per day) and performed many different tasks. Among these tasks, those related to the welfare functions of the enterprise were particularly demanding.[19] Particularly striking is the comparison between the 26 percent of time spent on personnel and welfare, compared to only 4 percent of time spent on supply and marketing.

Lack of Autonomy

One aspect of this is that although we stress the cellular nature of the *danwei,* it is important to recognize that that cell is embedded in the social body and not an autonomous cell. It has *insularity without autonomy.* Alternatively stated, although the *danwei* may appear to be nearly self-sufficient in terms of the provision of goods and services to its members, it is far from autonomous, even with respect to its own organization. This lack of autonomy is perhaps most striking with respect to political control—a large topic that is discussed below. But the enterprise's inability to shape its own organizational form also extends to various functional departments. In general, the enterprise is required to have an internal department that corresponds to each of the bureaucratic organizations with which the firm must deal. Thus the *danwei* typically was required to have a measurement division, a testing office, an energy section, an equipment management division, a safety section, and a quality section, as well as larger and more fundamental divisions such as finance and accounting, purchasing and sales, and labor.[20] While it is probably essential that any enterprise have personnel who carry out these functions, the point here is that they must be organized in a certain way that is dictated by outside organizations: They must be *duikou* (compatible).

Chinese enterprises resemble branch plants rather than corporations. They have a relatively uniform organizational structure and a restricted product line. This monotonous character is due, on the one hand, to the multiple superior bodies with which the enterprise must coordinate its activities and, on the other hand, to the continuing principle of territorial monopoly over production. The first of these features was well described by Boisot and Xing:

> The organizational structure of the typical firm is standardized to meet external requirements and cannot be easily modified. It is designed to match the organizational structure of the supervising agencies. . . . which seek direct control of organizational departments putatively reporting to the director.[21]

Therefore, the typical firm has a finance department that coordinates with the Ministry of Finance, a planning department that coordinates with the State Planning Commission, and so on. This organizational straitjacket has been greatly resented by managers, even those who are not very entrepreneurially oriented. A 1986 survey conducted of 170 managers of large and medium-size factories in Liaoning revealed that the greatest source of discontent was the lack of authority managers had over wages and personnel and over the organizational structure of their enterprises. Managers believed that they were effectively compelled to replicate within their enterprise every organizational division existing in hierarchical bodies.[22]

This general lack of organizational autonomy was especially pronounced in areas relating directly to political control. The enterprise was permeated by political organizations that owed ultimate allegiance to distant masters. Most sizable firms have a public security office within the firm. (It is a subordinate agency of the local public security bureau, or a *paichu jigou.*). But the most important is the Communist Party. The party has significant influence over the *danwei.* Typically, the party committee had under it four offices: the party secretary's office, the organization department, the propaganda department, and the discipline inspection department.

The Ironic Strengthening of the *Danwei* in the 1980s

Economic reforms begun after 1978 were ultimately to transform every aspect of the Chinese economy, including the *danwei* system. But, ironically, the initial effects of reform often strengthened the *danwei* system. Reforms began tentatively, and without a clear strategy or blueprint. It was inconceivable, under these circumstances, that the fundamental institutions underpinning the *danwei* system would be transformed in the early stages of reform—no serious attempt to create labor markets or transform social security systems could be anticipated at this phase. But early reforms did significantly increase the volume of resources under the control of the enterprise. Decentralization and increased autonomy to the enterprise implied expanded resources for the enterprise. In the short run, increases in enterprise resources naturally increased the importance of *danwei* relations with urban workers. This is evident in two areas.

Early economic reforms unfolded in an environment of intense pressure on employment. Large groups of young people were entering the labor market just as millions of "sent down" urban youth were returning from the countryside.[23] In order to provide employment for young people, older workers for the first time were encouraged to retire (previously retirement had been discouraged on the grounds that everyone should contribute his all to national construction). During the two years 1979–80, 6 percent of state workers retired. In subsequent years, more than 1.5 percent of state workers retired annually. This change had two consequences. First, the number of retired workers and outlays from pension funds grew rapidly. From 3 million in 1978, the number of retirees soared to 15 million in 1984, and then grew steadily to 29 million by 1994. Enterprise outlays climbed in tandem with the number of retirees. Second, many of the retirees were replaced by their own children. Under special provisions in force through 1982, older workers were able to retire in favor of their own children, even before the official age of retirement. The attachment of workers to the *danwei* went from being permanent to being perpetual, as the link now crossed generations.[24]

As reforms broadened and deepened, enterprises were allowed to retain progressively larger shares of the surplus they generated. The primary objective was to provide enterprises with incentives to cut costs and improve productivity. At the same time, the abandonment of austerity socialism meant that enterprises were increasingly encouraged to use these funds to upgrade workers' living standards. One result has been a huge boom in housing construction, financed primarily by enterprise funds. Between 1978 and 1994, the per-capita living space of urban residents in China more than doubled, increasing from 3.6 square meters to 7.8 square meters.[25] Most of this was financed by enterprises, and the share of enterprise-owned housing in total urban housing has grown sharply. Although not all this housing was constructed on the grounds of existing enterprises, there seems little doubt that more workers than ever lived in the physical compound of the enterprise in which they worked. More enterprises than before set up subsidiary retailing operations, often "collectives," in order to provide employment for children of existing workers. Workers were tied more closely to their *danwei* and probably lived in even closer proximity. Relaxation of economic controls in a situation where the enterprise had substantial resources inevitably strengthened the tie between enterprise and worker and thus indirectly the whole *danwei* system.

New Pressures Reshaping the Enterprise

Despite the trends toward providing enterprises with more resources and more autonomy in the use of those resources, the most fundamental forces unleashed by the reform process have begun steadily to push the enterprise away from the *danwei* model.

Steadily Increasing Labor Mobility

Although still low, labor mobility has been creeping up steadily in China throughout the reform period and has become significant during the 1990s. Some of this is the direct result of institutional reforms. Since 1986, new workers have been hired on the basis of five-year contracts, and the evidence is now substantial that those workers are more likely to quit (or be fired) when their contracts expire than are old-style permanent workers. By the end of 1993, contract workers reached one-third of all workers in manufacturing.[26] The 1995 Labor Law decreed that all long-term workers should become contract workers by the end of 1996. Moreover, permanent workers are now considerably more likely than in the past to resign or be fired. Anecdotal evidence suggests that the number of state workers "taking the plunge" into the private sector (*xia hai*) increased substantially during the early 1990's economic boom.

Available statistics reflect these changes, albeit imperfectly. Figure 7.1 displays available information on workers leaving the state sector. The measure shown aggregates workers quitting or being fired, who did not renew their employment contract. This measure, which was only 0.06 percent in 1978 (six-hundredths of one percent) has been increasing steadily since 1983 and reached 1.3 percent of the relevant labor force in 1994.[27] This measure clearly shows the magnitude of the changes in the Chinese labor market. Changing jobs is now at least fifteen or twenty times more frequent than it was in 1978. Yet the measure is imperfect and certainly understates the total amount of job mobility in the early 1990s. First, it does not show how many workers changed jobs between enterprises within the state sector, which by most indications is a fairly large number, probably larger than the number leaving the state sector. Moreover, the data for 1993 include a large "other" category of workers leaving the state sector, representing 1.8 percent of total employees. Some of these factors probably explain an alternative labor mobility figure for 1993 given by the State Statistical Bureau (without explanation). It reports that worker mobility in 1993, explicitly including movements between state-owned units, reached 3.2 percent of the state-employed labor force.[28] A mobility rate of this order of magnitude is still well below that of the relatively restless workers of Russia and the United States, but probably not too far behind that of Japan.

Competitive Pressures

The dominant process driving Chinese economic reforms forward has been the creation of competitive pressures by the entry of new producers.[29] Initially created by the growth of township and village enterprises and locally run SOEs,

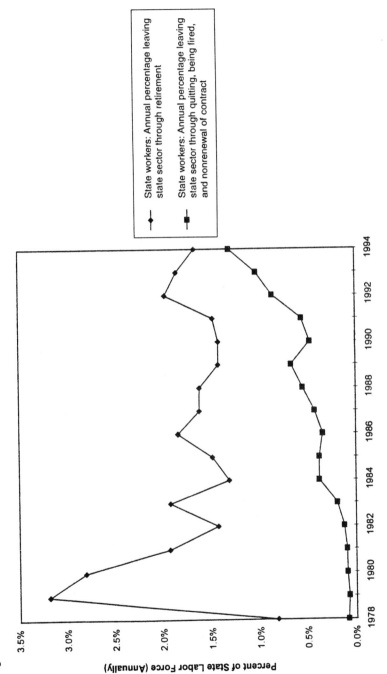

Figure 7.1 **Labor Turnover in State-Owned Units**

- ◆ State workers: Annual percentage leaving state sector through retirement
- ■ State workers: Annual percentage leaving state sector through quitting, being fired, and nonrenewal of contract

Percent of State Labor Force (Annually)

Source: See note 27.

competition in the 1990s has increasingly been fostered by private and foreign-invested firms. Competition has eroded the comfortable profit margin that SOEs once enjoyed and created serious challenges to the management of state firms.

Consider first the erosion of profits. We saw above that from the mid-1960s through the end of the 1970s, state industrial workers produced a total "surplus" (profit and tax) equal to four times their total wage. By contrast, in 1993, state-owned industry produced a total profit and tax of 245.5 billion yuan, of which a significant share was retained by the enterprises. Even leaving aside the enterprise retention, each worker was producing a potential "surplus"—most of which was still going to the state—of 5,455 yuan. But by comparison the annual manufacturing worker wage in that year was 3,562 yuan.[30] The workers' "surplus" had declined, on average, to one and a half times the annual wage. Thus, SOEs simply no longer have the luxury of disposing of substantial surpluses that can be diverted into funding the institutional peculiarities of the *danwei*.

More generally, SOEs face an imperative created by competition: to restructure their activities. In the simplest terms, restructuring means that state firms need to increase efficiency, producing more and better output for a given input of capital and labor. But restructuring actually refers to a much more complex task: SOEs need to reallocate resources within the *danwei* so that they are more effective in responding to market demands. In order to do this, enterprises need to do not only what they have already been doing more efficiently; they need to learn to do different things. The classic *danwei* bundled together production tasks and worker welfare delivery. The contemporary SOE, in order to respond to competition, needs to add a range of activities to its existing repertoire.

One way to look at this is to adapt a paradigm from the business literature, that of the "Value-Added Chain" (see Figure 7.2).[31] This chain comprises the total sequence of activities that create value in the overall production and sales process. It stretches from research and development and product design, through procurement and sourcing, production, marketing and sales, and ends with post-sales service and repair. Any of these activities are potentially productive and profitable: Different firms take up different positions on the value-added chain, depending on the overall business strategy that they pursue. Only the largest firms—a General Motors, for instance—find it reasonable to perform nearly all the activities in the value-added chain themselves, and even they rely on subcontractors for important parts of the production process. Most firms specialize in one or more links on the value-added chain. Companies such as Nike and Apple Computers do very little actual production. Instead, they specialize in research and design, at one end, and distribution and marketing at the other end. Most actual manufacturing is contracted out to other firms, often in Asia. In a market economy, competitive advantage is obtained by specializing in certain areas, while relying on the market to buy goods or services when lower-cost providers are available.

These relationships are applicable not only to consumer goods firms, which

Figure 7.2 **Value-Added Chain**

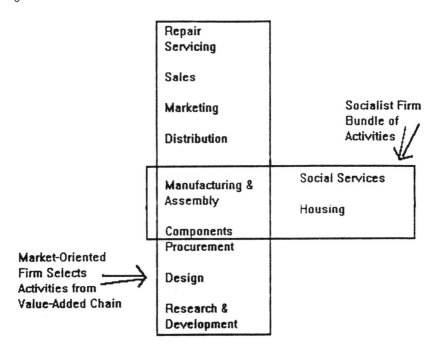

produce diversified products for often-fickle markets. They apply, albeit in somewhat altered form, to the large heavy industrial plants at the heart of the *danwei* system. Consider this account of the development of the American industrial corporation:

> The cost advantage of larger plants cannot be fully realized unless a constant flow of materials through the plant or factory is maintained to assure effective capacity utilization. . . . In the capital-intensive industries the throughput needed to maintain minimum efficient scale requires not only careful coordination of flow through the processes of production, but also the flow of inputs from the suppliers and the flow of outputs to the retailers and final consumers. Such coordination cannot happen automatically. It demands the constant attention of a managerial team, or hierarchy. Thus, scale is not only a technological characteristic. The economies of scale, measured by throughput, require organizational input. Such economies depend on knowledge, skills, and teamwork—on the human organization essential to exploit the potential of technological processes.[32]

In Chandler's account, the need for coordination of inputs, production, and distribution within the firm is the fundamental cause of the rise of the large industrial firm in the United States. Socialist economies have giant firms, of course, and managerial teams as well, but those managers are not accustomed to integrating distribution and production into a single business strategy.

Indeed, in relation to the value-added chain, traditional SOEs are overwhelmingly concentrated on the manufacturing activities in the middle of the chain. The supply and marketing functions traditionally have not been performed by the producing enterprise. Those functions were reserved to planners (drawing up material balance plans) and to specialized commerce and material supply organizations (for consumer and producer goods, respectively). Industrial firms use allocated inputs and sell output to a predesignated purchaser. Thus, firms typically had little or no knowledge of market conditions and little experience developing marketing strategies. Instead, SOEs are predominantly "horizontal" organizations (see Figure 7.2). After production, their next most important activities are likely to be the provision of education, housing, or health care. SOEs were units for the delivery of social services as well as the "cells" of political organization. Their fundamental form is poorly suited to the demands of a market economy.

SOEs need to shed some of these auxiliary activities, but without thereby totally alienating the work forces that depend on them. But that is not enough since they would still be left helpless amputees. They need to learn new activities: grow new limbs, as it were. Perhaps, most important, they need to grow a cerebral cortex, a center of higher intelligence that will create a strategy for the organization as a whole.[33] That is, firms need to develop corporate headquarters that can strategically position the firm where it wants to be and oversee the development of new functions.

These firms need to remake themselves. The task is challenging, time-consuming, complex, and costly, and it causes conflict. One of the remarkable things about the Chinese experience in the 1980s was the finding that government-imposed incentive systems could push managers to adapt to market conditions. Sufficient restructuring of the managerial incentive system in China meant that managers had a certain minimal interest in the performance of their firms. Managerial compensation can be shown to be clearly related to firm profit and sales.[34] Under those circumstances, managers arguably have some incentives to restructure firms, provided that they are allowed to do so by bureaucratic superiors.

New Institutions Are Available to Shoulder Some of the Burden

The reform process has been accompanied by a gradual, indeed painfully slow, process of creating new institutions that will relieve the *danwei* of some of the burdens of providing social services. One of the essential milestones in this process was the adoption of the factory manager responsibility system, whose implementation began in 1984. Factory manager responsibility made the manager the top authority in the factory, concentrating power in his hands, and placing the party secretary in a secondary, although still potentially important, role. Gradually, the party secretary's power began to diminish and that of the manager began to increase. The secretary still had influence, but increasingly the institutionalized, routinized vehicles through which the secretary exerted influence over the enterprise were restricted. Many factories amalgamated the former four party offices into a single party office, or eliminated it, amalgamating it into the manager's office.

Authority over pensions has been gradually separated from the enterprise management. Enterprises were required to begin contributing a portion of the wage bill to a provincial pension fund. In practice, many enterprises (especially wealthy ones) clung to the old ways by first paying their own retirees, and then depositing any additional funds with the provincial authority up to the total amount of the pension fund set-aside required by law. Both enterprises and retirees preferred to maintain the direct link between the enterprise and its pensioners. In spite of this interesting peculiarity, the pension system spread steadily from the late 1980s, and by 1994, more than 95 percent of SOE workers participated in pension fund arrangements. Indeed, the pension funds had accumulated more than 20 billion yuan in reserves, held mostly in treasury bonds.[35] The institutionalization of this process accelerated with the passage of the 1995 Labor Law. That law endorsed a general model for reforming the financial relationship between enterprises and workers' social welfare funds. The law calls for the adoption of five different funds to be managed by local governments rather than enterprises: pension, unemployment compensation, accident and disability, maternity, and medical insurance. Of these, pension funds are now almost universal, while medical insurance funds exist in only a few localities. Unemployment and disability funds, followed by maternity funds, are widespread, but still short of universal.[36]

Similar efforts have been made with respect to housing reform. Housing rent is being raised; some enterprise housing is being sold off; and individuals are being encouraged to invest in their own housing. Although a start has been made, there is universal agreement that housing reforms have not yet begun to succeed and have not changed the fundamental state of affairs under which most urban housing is controlled by *danwei* of various kinds.

Limitations and Future Prospects

The process under which economic conditions are changing is already quite advanced. If the process relied solely on the creation of alternative institutions to relieve the *danwei* of some of its burdens, it would be difficult to be optimistic. But in fact the process of change, as is so often the case in China, is being pushed forward by multiple factors. Workers are increasingly ready to change jobs, and so they create a partial constituency for greater "portability" of benefits and relaxed *danwei* control. Enterprises are struggling to survive, and so they seek ways to relieve themselves of different kinds of burdens and remake their internal institutions. The government seeks to accommodate these demands by creating new institutions. The process of institutional creation lags behind the need, yet it continues to be pulled forward precisely by the magnitude of those needs. The most powerful, most fundamental, and most long-lasting forces are those that undermine the *danwei* system and push the system toward greater marketization.

At the same time, for many reasons it would be naive to think that progress will be quick or linear. First, again ironically, in the current reform environment, it is precisely the large state firms that have survived. Small-scale state firms have practically disappeared, outcompeted by rural collectives and private firms. However, the larger state firms, particularly in heavy industry, have survived, protected by government regulations and the importance of economies of scale. That is, it is precisely in those firms where the institution of the *danwei* was most highly developed that change has been the smallest. Among state firms, the *danwei* institutions are still quite prominent.

Indeed, we should expect that successful SOEs will hold onto as much of the apparatus of social service provision as they can. In part, this is because there will be increasing competition for good employees, and some of this competition will take the form of benefit provision. In part, this is because successful firms will continue to control large revenue streams, most of which they are supposed to give up to the government. Naturally, they will continue to divert as much as possible to their own benefit. Moreover, the comparison with Japan (and even with the United States) shows that there are good reasons to tie workers with special skills to enterprises for long periods. Firm-specific skills can be fostered by continuous investment in workers, and it should be made advantageous to those workers to remain with the firm that invested in them. Precisely those large, capital-intensive and technologically sophisticated firms where the *danwei* system was most developed before reform are those most likely to exhibit these conditions. Some, at least, of these firms will retain *danwei*-like institutions in the competitive market economy because they find them consistent with their competitive advantage.

Second, progress in dismantling the *danwei* system is hindered by ambivalence about giving up political control. After the June 4, 1989 Tiananmen incident, central leaders tried to re-establish party organs in the enterprise. Document no. 9 of 1990, published by the Central Organization Department, decreed certain standards of party representation in the enterprise: the party offices were not to be eliminated or amalgamated with administrative organs; specific quotas for personnel devoted to party tasks were re-established, including a directive that at least 1 percent of total personnel should be in full-time party work (not including the union and the Communist Youth League).[37] There should be both a "center"—the factory manager—and a "core"—the party committee—in each factory. We can see in such attempts a last-ditch attempt to restore some of the functions of the old *danwei* system. By struggling to retain the *danwei* as an instrument of political control, China's current leaders reveal their anxiety about the more open, fluid society that is emerging in the country.

Third, China's continuing administrative weakness will retard attempts to dispense with the *danwei* altogether. This is particularly evident in the implementation of the pension system. Expert advise is in complete agreement that pension programs should be instituted at the national level, with uniform provisions nationwide. As an insurance program, and a key element of social equity, social security ought to be a national policy. China has, however, implemented a social security system in local areas first and intends to build up to a nationally united system gradually. This choice probably reflects a realistic assessment of the national government's administrative capabilities. But it also creates a difficult and paradoxical situation. Local implementation has the benefit that local experimentation can help determine the best form for the emerging social security system. At the same time, local experimentation also means that social security programs are not uniform. Thus pension benefits are still not portable across provincial (or sometimes municipal) boundaries. Perhaps more crucially, as funds accumulate in pension funds, struggles break out to control those funds. Local governments that implement unified pension funds covering state, collective, and foreign-owned enterprises must establish new, locally controlled bodies to manage those funds. This is to the advantage of the local government, and the existence of such a fund then gives the local government an incentive to resist national unification and regularization of the pension system.[38] Under these circumstances, over the next several years the *danwei* will continue to be significant, albeit less so.

Notes

1. The number of workers in state-owned and urban collective units jumped from 16 million in 1952 to 31 million in 1957. Of the 31 million urban workers in 1957, only 11.5 million were covered by labor insurance programs. See John Dixon, *The Chinese Welfare System, 1949–1979* (New York: Praeger, 1981), 38; *Zhongguo tongji nianjian* [China statistical yearbook 1995] (Beijing: Zhongguo tongji chubanshe, 1995), 84.

2. Sulamith Potter and Jack M. Potter, "A Caste-like System of Social Stratification: The Position of Peasants in Modern China's Social Order," chapter 15 of *China's Peasants: The Anthropology of a Revolution* (New York: Cambridge University Press, 1990); Harry Xiaoying Wu, "Rural to Urban Migration in the People's Republic of China," *China Quarterly*, no. 139 (September 1994): 669–98; Cheng Tiejun and Mark Selden, "The Origins and Social Consequences of China's *Hukou* System," *China Quarterly*, no. 139 (September 1994): 644–68.

3. Yanjie Bian, "*Guanxi* and the Allocation of Urban Jobs in China," *China Quarterly*, no. 140 (December 1994): 973; David Granick, "The Industrial Environment in China and the CMEA Countries," in *China's Industrial Reform*, ed. Gene Tidrick and Chen Jiyuan (New York: Oxford University Press, 1987), 109. By contrast, only college graduates were routinely assigned work in the Soviet Union.

4. The numbers, which will be further discussed below, are an incomplete measure of labor mobility because they do not cover workers changing jobs within the state sector, either through voluntary choice or job reassignment. *Zhongguo laodong tongji nianjian 1993* [Yearbook of labor statistics of China] (Beijing: Zhongguo laodong chubanshe, 1993), 318. The categories of tuizhi and tingzhi (resign or discharge and suspension,

respectively) were almost as important as those who quit or were fired in 1978, with 31,000. However, these categories imply administrative action, rather than voluntary worker or management choice. The measure reported here covers all state workers (including administrative and nonprofit workers). State enterprise employees have slightly more job mobility than do state workers as a whole.

5. Granick, "The Industrial Environment," 110.

6. See Kazuo Koike, "Human Resource Development and Labor-Management Relations," in *The Political Economy of Japan. Volume 1: The Domestic Transformation,* ed. Kozo Yamamura and Yasukichi Yasuba (Stanford: Stanford University Press, 1987).

7. Ibid., 296.

8. State Statistical Bureau, *Zhongguo laodong gongzi tongji ziliao 1978–1985* [China labor and wages statistical materials] (Beijing: Zhongguo tongji chubanshe, 1987), 40–41, 153; State Statistical Bureau, *Zhongguo gongye jingji tongji nianjian 1988* [China industrial economic statistics yearbook] (Beijing: Zhongguo tongji chubanshe), 1988),48. Note that the measure of wage used here includes all monetary payments to the worker, thus including bonuses and subsidies.

9. To this day, there is a substantial distinction between a wealthy enterprise and an impoverished enterprise. Even if wage standards are identical between the two, conditions are far better for the worker in the wealthy enterprise because of the access to facilities and fringe benefits that a wealthy enterprise can provide. The argument here is by the mid-1960s the average industrial enterprise had achieved at least middle-income status.

10. Barry Naughton, "Industrial Policy During the Cultural Revolution: Military Preparation, Decentralization, and Leaps Forward," in *New Perspectives on the Cultural Revolution,* ed. William Joseph, Christine Wong, and David Zweig (Cambridge: Harvard University Press, 1991).

11. Ibid., and idem., "The Third Front: Defense Industrialization in the Chinese Interior," *China Quarterly,* no. 115 (September 1988).

12. On labor unions in the Soviet Union and other Soviet-style economies, especially their involvement in social insurance administration and social benefits delivery, see Emily Clark Brown, *Soviet Trade Unions and Labor Relations* (Cambridge: Harvard University Press, 1966), especially 125–28 and 163–68; Blair Ruble, *Soviet Trade Unions: Their Development in the 1970s* (Cambridge: Cambridge University Press, 1981); and Alex Pravda and Blair Ruble, eds., *Trade Unions in Communist States* (Boston: Allen and Unwin, 1986).

13. Jeanne L. Wilson, "The People's Republic of China," in *Trade Unions in Communist States,* ed. Alex Pravda and Blair Ruble (Boston: Allen and Unwin, 1986), 219, 223.

14. John Dixon, *The Chinese Welfare System, 1949–1979* (New York: Praeger, 1981), 121–31, 153–54; Lee Lai To, *Trade Unions in China 1949 to the Present: The Organization and Leadership of the All-China Federation of Trade Unions* (Singapore: Singapore University Press, 1986).

15. State Economic Commission, *Guanghui de chengjiu* [Glorious accomplishment] (Beijing: Renmin chubanshe, 1985), 16.

16. Industrial Census Leadership Small State Council Group, *Zhonghua renmin gongheguo 1985 nian gongye pucha ziliao* [Industrial census materials of the PRC] (Beijing: Zhongguo tongji chubanshe, 1987), vol. 1, 204, 608, 624.

17. *Zhongguo shehui tongji ziliao* [Social statistical materials] *1987* (Beijing: Zhongguo tongji chubanshe, 1987), 91. Not all these enterprises are in large cities.

18. Ding Yang, "A Mainland Cadre's Impressions of Hong Kong after Three Months," *Zheng ming,* no. 3 (1983): 77.

19. Max Boisot, and Xing Guoliang, "The Nature of Managerial Work—Chinese Style" (paper presented at the International Conference on Management in China Today,

Leuven, Belgium, June 19–21, 1988). A similar picture of the daily activities of an industrial manager emerges in the fictional portrayals of Jiang Zilong. See Jiang Zilong, *All the Colors of the Rainbow* (Beijing: Panda, 1985).

20. A Chengdu firm interviewed in 1990 had attempted to consolidate their measurement and testing sections, but had not been permitted to do so (Interview file 90C57).

21. Boisot and Xing, "The Nature of Managerial Work."

22. These opinions were the more remarkable in that this group of managers did not generally favor enhanced autonomy for the enterprise. The vast majority of managers thought that prices should continue to be controlled or allowed to float within narrow margins; only 22 percent wanted a smaller production plan; and 29 percent wanted the right to independently sell a greater proportion of output (Liaoning Statistical Bureau, "The Opinions of Managers of Large and Medium-Size Enterprises on Several Problems of Reform," *Tongji*, no. 3 [1987]: 32–33). Thirty-three percent of respondents thought that the plan was about right, and 37 percent wanted a larger plan; 26 percent thought that independent sales were about right, and 39 percent wanted a smaller sales responsibility.

23. During the Cultural Revolution, urban youths were sent to the countryside to be "re-educated by peasants." After some years, these resettled youths began to return to the cities in the late 1970s. By the mid-1980s, most of them had left the countryside.

24. The cross-generational link was implicitly there before the large-scale retirements of the late 1970s, since the provisions for replacement already existed. However, they did not become real until a significant number of workers actually retired.

25. According to household surveys (*Zhongguo tongji nianjian 1995* [China statistical yearbook] [Beijing: Zhongguo tongji chubanshe, 1995], 257).

26. *Zhongguo tongji nianjian 1994* [China statistical yearbook] (Beijing: Zhongguo tongji chubanshe, 1994), 100. See also Deborah Davis, "Job Mobility in Post-Mao Cities: Increases on the Margin," *China Quarterly*, no. 132 (December 1992): 1062–85.

27. *Zhongguo laodong gongzi tongji ziliao 1978–1987* [China labor and wage statistical materials] (Beijing: Zhongguo tongji chubanshe, 1988), 40, 67; *Zhongguo laodong tongji nianjian 1990* [Yearbook of labor statistics of China] (Beijing: Zhongguo laodong chubanshe), 79, 88–90, 204, 217; *1991: 295–96; 1992: 331–32; 1993: 301, 318; 1994: 352–53; 1995: 400.* Tom Rawski generously lent me some of these yearbooks.

28. State Statistical Bureau, "Woguo jiuye jiegou de zhidu bianhua" [Ten major changes in China's employment structure] (Beijing: mimeo, October 1994). Unfortunately, the report does not provide sufficient detail for us to understand exactly what definitions have been used to compute the mobility rate. Nonetheless, it is consistent with the figures cited above. The report is described in Lu Hongyong, "Booming Economy Reshapes Labor," *China Daily—Business Week*, October 23–29, 1994. The Statistical Bureau also reports that mobility rates are 6.3 percent in "other ownership" (predominantly foreign-invested) firms, and 20 percent in private and individual firms.

29. Barry Naughton, *Growing Out of the Plan: Chinese Economic Reform, 1978–1993* (New York: Cambridge University Press, 1995).

30. *1994 Statistical Yearbook of China* (Beijing: Zhongguo tongji chubanshe, 1994), 126, 374, 381.

31. Bruce Kogut, "Designing Global Strategies: Comparative and Competitive Value-Added Chains," *Sloan Management Review* (summer 1985): 15–28; (fall 1985): 27–28.

32. Alfred D. Chandler, Jr., "The Emergence of Managerial Capitalism" in *The Coming of Managerial Capitalism*, ed. Chandler and Richard Tedlow (Homewood, Illinois: Irwin, 1985).

33. Ryutaro Komiya, "Japanese Firms, Chinese Firms: Problems for Economic Reform in China," *Journal of Japanese and International Economies* 1 (1987): 31–61, 229–47.

34. Theodore Groves, Hong Yongmiao, John McMillan, and Barry Naughton, "Au-

tonomy and Incentives in Chinese State Enterprises," *Quarterly Journal of Economics* 109, no. 1 (February 1994); idem., "China's Evolving Managerial Labor Market," *Journal of Political Economy* 103, no. 4 (August 1995): 873–82; Gary Jefferson, and Thomas Rawski, "Enterprise Reform in Chinese Industry," *Journal of Economic Perspectives* 8, no. 2 (spring 1994): 47–70.

35. Lu Hongyong, "Workers Funding Pension Reserve," *China Daily—Business Week,* October 23–29, 1994. Unfortunately, treasury bonds paid interest at rates below the rate of inflation, so these pension reserves were declining in value. Small wonder that enterprises preferred to pay funds to their workers directly.

36. Anne Stevenson-Yang, "Re-vamping the Welfare State: China Aims to Weaken the Link Between Employers and Benefits," *China Business Review* (January–February 1996): 8–17.

37. Interview file 90C71.

38. Jean-François Huchet, "Retraites et transition en Chine: vers l'établissement d'un système national de protection sociale?" (Tokyo: Maison Franco–Japonaise, 1996).

8

The Impact of the Floating Population on the *Danwei*: Shifts in the Pattern of Labor Mobility Control and Entitlement Provision

Dorothy J. Solinger

The advent of economic reform allowed peasant labor to enter urban industry in large numbers. Unlike the temporary workers in state firms or the rural workers in collective town and village enterprises of the past,[1] this section of today's "floating population" is working full time, and in large numbers, as wage-compensated, individually contracted employees in urban, state-owned factories.[2] Although this hiring of peasants by state firms is not new, the scale today is far larger and the procedures more regularized than before reform began; moreover, one element is altogether novel in the People's Republic of China (PRC): People from the fields are now also finding jobs in the foreign-funded firms (FFFs) that began to appear in China in the 1980s.[3]

Accompanying this arrival of rural workers, one might suppose, would be fundamental alterations in two of the central functions of the former *danwei:* its

An earlier version of this chapter was presented at the annual meeting of the Association for Asian Studies, Boston, March 23–27, 1994. Another version was published in *Modern China,* April 1995. I am grateful to Wang Hui and Zhou Lu of the Tianjin Social Science Academy, Huang Hongyun of the Wuhan Social Science Academy, and Yin Guilan of the Wuhan Foreign Affairs Office for arranging the interviews cited in this chapter. Comments by Elizabeth Perry and Christine Wong are also appreciated. I also wish to thank the Committee on Scholarly Communication with China for research support for my trip to China in 1992 during which I conducted the interviews cited in this chapter.

control over labor mobility and its provision of entitlements for its workers. This chapter examines the extent to which these changes are occurring. It contains two sections: The first will explore the extent to which the entry into urban enterprises of these new employees from the country has meant a shift in the form of job recruitment, edging out the old state-planned style of employment. The second investigates the manner in which urban state-owned firms are actually handling the allocation of their limited package of entitlements in the face of the incursion of peasant migrant labor.

The chapter also offers a contrast between recruitment strategies and the treatment accorded migrants in state-owned firms, on the one hand, and non–state-owned ones (chiefly, collective enterprises in the rural areas and foreign-funded firms), on the other. The behavior typical of many non–state-sector firms may serve as a harbinger of the future, as state firms themselves are in the midst of restructuring their hiring practices and shedding their welfare functions, even for their formal, urban labor force. A larger message of the chapter is that as market reforms gradually alter the former functions of the state-sector *danwei,* reducing both its power over its work force and its paternalism toward it, *danwei*–migrant interactions both illustrate and, over time, may actually exaggerate these effects. Thus these migrants drive a reciprocal process, as, in league with the reforms, they alter the *danwei,* even as, as a means of survival, the *danwei* stretches itself and shrinks its welfare role in order to incorporate them.

But, as of the mid-1990s, the outcome of this process has not yet been any full-scale evisceration of the *danwei.* Instead, what has transpired to date is simply a transitional hybridization of the firm: Certainly where migrant labor is concerned—and increasingly for regular, urban labor as well—the reforms have transposed the average *danwei* into a mix of bureaucratic and marketized practices. If the old state *danwei* lies at one end of the spectrum, and the typical nonstate firm of today at the other, the average current state firm today can be found somewhere in between.[4] In general, it is likely that the closer to the former end of the spectrum the firm employing them lies, the better both migrants and formal labor will fare.

It is clear that market forces are, indeed, having an effect on migrant labor in manufacturing. Several factors, all stemming from the program of economic reforms begun in the late 1970s, account for the expansion and systematization of using farmhands in factories.

Among these are, first, a set of interrelated measures that altered the operations of the state firm, the typical *danwei.* These were the decision to enhance enterprise autonomy[5] and the injection of the profit motive into the calculus of the firm, as firms have been given the right to retain a portion of their profits, all of which have contributed to a new cost-consciousness in the management of state and other firms.[6] These changes, when combined with a more recent movement to reduce state involvement in benefit provision, have steadily transformed the old objectives of the *danwei,* as they diminish management's concerns with its three chief previous preoccupations: full employment, welfare security, and maximum output.[7]

Three other types of policies have affected the amount of recruitment of migrants and the ways in which workers from outside the city are treated. These include granting urban youth far greater leeway than in the past for making their own employment decisions,[8] and the series of decisions permitting peasants to enter the cities to work and even to obtain a kind of household registration there.[9]

The combination of urban young people's rejection of careers in certain sectors,[10] and the availability of peasants to fill their vacancies has inclined many *danwei*, pressed to find hands for their machines, to populate their plants with peasants to a far greater degree than in the past. A last significant influence upon hiring peasants—more disposable and purportedly more pliable than urban labor—has been the invitation to foreigners to invest in enterprises in China.[11] Seemingly, market forces are fueling all these new policies that bear on the employment of peasants in industry.

Given the effect of reform on weakening the *danwei*'s three customary objectives noted above—full employment, welfare security, and maximum output— we should expect both recruitment and provisioning practices pertaining to peasants to diverge sharply from those that affected permanent, urban labor in the typical state socialist firm (the archetypical *danwei*) as it existed before the reform era. There, most recruiting was accomplished by state allocation and so was bureaucratically, not market, driven;[12] and full labor insurance, retirement and copious welfare benefits, and lifetime job tenure were the norm, in terms of benefits.[13] We expect such divergence in the treatment of peasant labor—in any kind of firm today—from the way permanent labor was treated in the old state *danwei*. This is because, unlike in that model firm, whose management was beholden to its urban administration's concerns over achieving full employment in the city, the management in no firm today would have any such regard for ensuring the placement of the outsiders, the peasants.

Moreover, profit-seeking and, as its corollary in the state firms, fund retention,[14] have superseded pure output as goals in today's enterprises. This new-found focus on gathering and holding funds must dispose even the state *danwei* to be far stingier with benefits for outsiders than it has been for decades toward its permanent urban work force, at least until recent reforms that entail state disinvestment from worker entitlements.[15]

And yet, during China's transition from socialism, market reforms do not fully explain the current status of the relationship between the firm and its work force. Instead, as an examination of the floating population in the factories shows, the nature of both the transitional economy and of firms in it are the product not only of new economic influences such as the reforms and the world market but also of political and institutional legacies from the system passing away. When it comes to engaging peasants, these legacies, not surprisingly, particularly affect procedures in the state-owned (as opposed to the non–state-owned) firms, where their influence was once fundamental.

The chapter also implies the following outcome for the future: The peasants in the plants may turn out to be not primarily marginal but rather precursors, subject as they are to processes that may, with time, reshape the lives of a major segment of the Chinese work force, including those now holding permanent status in the state firms. Given the recent onslaught of state disinvestment, the increasing prominence and flourishing of private sectoral firms, and the continuing and growing disdain of urban workers for the restraints and inefficiencies of the state socialist *danwei,* what is happening to the floating population may hold messages for the nature of what may become the typical Chinese *danwei* and for its stance toward its work force in the days ahead.

Recruitment of the Floating Population

The Data

Recruitment of the Floating Population into State Firms

My data, admittedly anecdotal, make it abundantly clear that, as of the early 1990s, the influence of a market rationale, with its universalistic criteria, is still marginal if not nonexistent in selecting among workers from outside the cities to hire in the state firms. Instead, the data show, a combination of ascriptively-based and bureaucratic procedures dominate the process. While my sources cannot be considered a representative sample, it is significant that they all point in the same direction.

These sources include interviews with bureaucrats, scholars, and migrants in several Chinese cities, government documents, research studies by Chinese social scientists, reportage literature published in China, and material from the Hong Kong press. According to a 1994 research report by the head of a population institute at a major university in China, "more than 80 percent of those who leave their rural homes find their way [in the job market] through friends, relatives, and neighbors."[16] As one official informant aptly quipped, "It's hard to get a job if you don't have any relatives or friends in town."[17] Even spokespeople from the labor bureau of a major metropolis explained that firms find their farmers through the friends and relatives of their staff and workers, or else contact the labor departments in places with which they have cooperated in the past.[18]

The labor bureau of another sizable city published a book revealing, similarly, that, "75 percent of the employers go through relatives and friends, or through those introduced by labor hired in the past"; and that "units hire on their own those recommended by their staff and workers from nearby suburbs, counties, or other areas within the province, or the city government designates the peasants of particular places."[19] In Wuhan's No. 1 Cotton Mill, where 18.75 percent of the work force of 8,000 were straight from the countryside in mid-1992, these peasants arrived one by one, their arrival mediated by relationships with their friends and relations.

At the city's No. 2 Mill, on the other hand, the management signed a collective contract with the neighboring Hong'an county government, thus utilizing bureaucratic channels, in the belief that a group from one home place would be "easier to control."[20] Similarly, Tianjin's No. 3 Silk Weaving Mill had 72 outsiders of its total of 779 staff and workers in mid-1992. Seventeen of these came from one county and one *zhen* (township) in Henan, an area with a reputation for poverty; the other 55 hailed from Hebei and were people with relatives among the staff who knew where there were women with nothing to do. The factory hired all these women after receiving approval from the city's textile and labor bureaus, and the rural governments selected the women in line with the mill's demands.[21]

In Zhengzhou, textile plants hired some of their peasants from villages linked to the factories through "support the poor spots" campaigns; some relied on the friends and relatives of the factories' own personnel or those introduced by urban officials.[22] In 1989, when one of these firms, a colored weaving dye factory, announced that it would recruit peasant workers, the staff's friends and relatives quickly transmitted the news and rural women "signed up in swarms," so that in only a few days 200 had put in their names for 40 places.[23] Thus despite railings against private hiring (*sizhao, luangu*),[24] the practice is widespread.

Here it is worth noting a distinction between recruiting on ascriptive grounds (*sizhao*), which is generally tacitly accepted, and hiring in a "chaotic" manner (*luangu*), which is more of an infraction. That is, whereas even official agencies in charge of placing workers openly rely upon nepotistic and other kinds of ascriptive, personal contacts, the *numbers* of "outside labor"—essentially a euphemism for peasant floaters—hired should at the least be governed bureaucratically, that is, limited by quotas and therefore not "chaotic."

These quotas are to be determined by urban labor bureaus in conjunction with the city's planning commission, and the target number is supposedly set on the basis of a city's construction needs and the level of unemployment of its own native population. In Wuhan in 1990, for instance, 90,000 was the maximum allowable figure. Each urban district and each trade are allocated a set number of slots, which they distribute to their subordinate firms, after receiving applications from the firms in demand of such workers.[25]

Thus enterprises deemed in need of such workers are permitted to hire a specific number of outside workers and are given the funds to pay them. The plan for outsiders exists alongside, but separate from, the one for regular, permanent workers for each factory.[26] But the extent to which even this element of the rules is transgressed is readily apparent in the following statistic: In Wuchang district in the late 1980s there could be found 11,000 outside laborers, an amount that surpassed the district's allocation more than threefold. Meanwhile, the area housed 17,000 local persons who were unemployed.[27]

Recruitment into the Nonstate Sector: Foreign-Funded
Firms and Township and Village Enterprises

Recruitment of peasant temporary labor into the non–state-owned sector is surprisingly similar to that into state firms, again a mixture of personalism and bureaucratism.[28] As a general statement, according to journalists writing from Guangzhou, "In enterprises in the Pearl River Delta, processing firms[29] and TVEs [township and village enterprises] hire mostly from Guangdong, Guangxi, Hunan, and Sichuan, and they mainly go through friends and relatives in doing so."[30]

One fascinating example comes from a volume recounting the travels through China in 1989 of two journalists, intent upon capturing the story of the floating population. This is their graphic account of rural hiring by one of these nonstate firms:

> Last year, the director of the labor bureau in Guizhou's Bijie county went to Dongguan twice to try to arrange for export of his county's surplus labor. He paid a visit to Dongguan's labor service company's vice director. . . . Once an urban youth starts to wait for a job, he/she will be waiting for several years. In 1987, Guangdong and Guizhou agreed that Guangdong would accept surplus labor from Guizhou in the form of "using labor recruitment to support poverty." In the first batch, Guizhou decided to take care of Bijie. . . . With reform, following the import of goods from Guangdong, Bijie people's yearnings toward Guangdong increased daily: Shenzhen, Zhuhai, Dongguan, etc., in the imagination of many Bijie girls became the equivalent of Hong Kong or Macau. So when the news spread in Bijie that Dongguan would be hiring labor, city and rural girls all strove to be first to sign up; many household heads, facing fierce competition, sent gifts. The county labor bureau, as if recruiting formal labor, let individuals apply, the household head or the township or village presented certificates, and went through examinations and formal procedures.[31]

In this example, the procedures are bureaucratic, the final selection influenced by personalism. A similar case occurred when Jinggangshan asked the Ministry of Civil Affairs to demand that Shenzhen "support poverty" by accepting its young, enabling them to go to the southeast to earn money by doing coolie labor.[32]

Another report is of a township-owned raincoat factory, formed as a joint venture with a merchant from Hong Kong, which employed rural female primary-school graduates. The girls came, explained the writer, through the introduction of friends, without knowing that they would work fourteen hours a day, eating only two meals.[33] A county-run construction enterprise whose personnel I interviewed had a personnel organ for recruitment, which works entirely on the basis of personal relationships in finding workers.[34]

Analysis

We have seen that recruitment of the floating population, into both state firms and the TVE/FFF firms, is partly bureaucratic and partly, as in informal economies elsewhere (in both the developed and the less-developed world), network-driven, personalistic, and carried out according to ascriptive characteristics.[35] To put it schematically, bureaucratic quotas are set (and exceeded) and then people get jobs because of their personal connections—whether kin-based or native-place–based—or because of special, historical relationships between their area of origin and the hiring agents.

Another variant of this *bureaucratic-cum-personalistic* format occurs when the personnel of the state firm or the recruiting agents for the non–state-owned enterprise engage employees via a contract with officials of the home area of the firm's employees. In these cases, the home area is chosen because the place has been recommended (by word of mouth) as a source of surplus labor.

Thus, at this stage, market-rational criteria are not directly determining firms' recruitment choices when they hire peasant labor; rather, what we have is an amalgam of statist, administrative behavior supplemented, undoubtedly to a greater degree than in the past, by ascriptive connections. Certainly achievement and merit are not at work in the recruitment of rural workers;[36] at best, one could say that the market operates by directing hiring agents toward areas of supply in response to the work unit's demand.

Consequently, legacy factors—namely, the state plan and party rule—still go a long way toward explaining the nature of the recruitment of the floating population. Some twenty-five years of job allocation according to the state plan in the urban industrial sector has had two primary effects. First, it has stymied what would otherwise have been a natural maturation of the labor market with increasing industrialization.[37] As one group of Chinese researchers explained this, the pervasive force of vertical, administrative hierarchies for decades pressed labor allocation into bureaucratic channels; it thereby severed horizontal bonds among city and country, among regions, and between firms and those seeking jobs. As a result, with the loosening of these cords, all people have to fall back upon in searching for work outside their localities are the primary social bonds offered by their friends, relations, and fellow townspeople.[38] Other relevant conditioning factors pointed out by Yanjie Bian are the continuing poverty of employment ads and of formal, marketized hiring procedures; these gaps have elevated the significance of *guanxi* once bureaucracy slackened in the reform era.[39]

Moreover, today, from the point of view of the employers, with the refusal of urban young people to sign up for certain types of manufacturing work, enterprises lack experience in locating appropriate personnel to take their place. Forced to rely upon peasants,[40] people barred even from entering the cities for decades, the *danwei* have no recourse but to resort to composite modes of finding labor that are part bureaucratic and part ascriptive.

A second legacy of the days of domination by state planning is the reaction that the procedures of that regimen sparked against the onerous and copious regulations that attended the plan's bureaucratic arrangements. For instance, "Some enterprises have complained about complicated procedures when trying to employ workers through the labor departments and said they have found it much easier to employ workers from other provinces through private channels."[41]

Presumably the ethos of enterprise autonomy attending the economic reforms is emboldening these managers to circumvent some of the bureaucratism that saddled them so heavily for decades. Such a reaction occurs in industrialized, capitalist contexts;[42] it would be even more likely in the midst of a time of loosening in a socialist state-in-transition—such as China—where the planned, socialist economy was fully laced through with regulations at every step for many years.

Besides the lingering legacy of the state plan and its regulated mode of operation, yet another bequest from the past influencing the recruitment process is decades of party rule. Walder has convincingly shown how the privileged position of the party officials in state firms—and the discretion that accompanied that privilege—corrupted the hiring process even during the days of strict state planning, when the offspring or other relatives of favored employees, or the family members of officials poised to help the enterprise, got preference.[43] Such nepotism and favor-trading must leave a mark on current behavior.

Thus our empirical data all suggest the same thing: economic reform has provided both the need—because of its liberation of urban youth from the old job allocation system while production must yet go on—and the opportunity for peasants to fill in the niches in the state-owned plants left vacant by supercilious city folk and to grab for positions they know little about that will take them out of the villages. As this occurs, the modes of their placement represent an incipient shift in the operation of urban labor markets, away from more predominantly bureaucratic patterns and toward ones more blatantly personalistic—rather than marketized—as compared with the past.

Benefits for the Floating Population

Our second concern is to consider what changes in plants' usual provisioning of labor the presence of peasants may be occasioning; in what ways, that is, firms alter their welfare function in receiving ruralites. The comparative literature suggests that migrants, treated as a labor reserve, would be denied benefits and that they would toil under highly uncertain tenure.[44] Chinese peasants in the *danwei,* residing today in the city nominally just on a "temporary" basis and lacking urban household registration, would appear to serve as a labor reserve army.

Yet the picture is not so straightforward. This will become apparent as contrasts emerge between the treatment of migrants in—at least the best-endowed of—the state firms, and that accorded them in the nonstate sector, where state regulations are weak at best or even ignored altogether. Again, the state-owned enterprise, at least as late as the early 1990s, remained in a transitional position, even though its probable trajectory will ultimately take it much farther along the route predicted in the comparative literature.

Indeed, already in the 1980s, rural workers took jobs mainly in the textile, machine-building, chemical, and building materials trades within the state sector,[45] and in apparel, toy, and plastic manufacturing enterprises in the foreign-invested and township and village firms. Like their fellows elsewhere in the world, they are usually found in manual labor jobs in these sectors, drudging at dirty and tiresome posts that have been disdained by urban workers, whether for their pay, their poor working conditions, their labor intensity, or the lower social status they afford.

Moreover, the provisioning treatment accorded peasants today must be viewed against the backdrop of entitlements extended to the permanent urban labor force before the reform era: Fringe benefits varied from firm to firm, but for the most part the state-owned *danwei* could offer at least some of the following perquisites: extremely cheap housing, free medical care for the worker and partial care for his or her dependents, dining halls, nurseries, very generous pensions, and job security.[46] Estimates differ, but most analysts agree that the monetary value of the fringe benefits—not even counting housing—distributed to workers has been about half the total wage bill.[47] Consequently, if these costly benefits for peasants could be avoided, a firm would stand to save a lot of money. As Castells and Portes point out, "The best known effect of the informalization process is to reduce the costs of labor substantially."[48]

The Data

Treatment of Peasant Workers in State Firms

According to a State Council document of October 1991 on the employment of peasants as contract workers by state-owned enterprises,[49] peasants hired on a temporary basis in such firms are officially to be treated rather similarly to permanent, urban contract workers,[50] with only a few exceptions. They are to receive bonuses, general as well as food subsidies, and paid holidays. If they become ill or injured outside the factory, as for urban contract laborers, the firm is to give peasant-workers sick-leave wages and medical care for three to six months, depending on the specifications of the contract they have signed. The workers' relatives, however, do not enjoy half-price medical treatment.

If they are injured on the job, the firm is to provide them with free medical care and, while they are being treated, to give them their standard wages. For those who have become partially disabled, the firm is to send them back home to the villages, with compensation for the loss. And those who have become completely disabled are to receive 70 percent of their original wages until death. Even those who have only lost some of their ability to work are to be presented with a one-time payment, the amount proportional to the degree of injury. Even the pension system is mentioned, though the concrete details are to be worked out by the provincial and lower levels of government.

A researcher for the World Bank visiting several large cities in late 1991 was informed that in 1990 on the average 25 to 40 percent of those floaters who had entered the labor market were then being covered by various social security schemes and that, in Shenzhen, the majority of the floaters were actually enrolled in pension plans.[51] Why are his percentages variable? According to scholar-interviewees in Guangzhou, the distribution of welfare benefits depends very much on features of the enterprise in question: Variables mentioned included the income or "business success" of the unit or the nature of its management.[52] This discrepancy is alluded to by two Chinese scholars who reported that, "Some enterprises with poor conditions need to hire peasant workers but are not capable of properly solving the various problems of their livelihood." The result is that "peasants have to spend too much for their accommodation and daily needs."[53]

Despite the fact that regulations promulgated in 1991 were meant to apply nationwide, even the official city labor bureaus interpreted them variously; the more specialized management bureaus in more direct contact with the "outsider" workers as well as the firms below them diverged as well. In Tianjin, for instance, officials from the city Labor Bureau's planning office explained, "Their wages are like those of regular labor, but the content differs. Outsiders don't get subsidies or bonuses." Moreover, regular workers are paid by time-rates, most peasants by piecework.[54]

Also, although they alleged that each individual *danwei* may decide on its own on the terms of the welfare it provides, these men at the same time spoke as if there were citywide rules, telling me that sick workers received three months of full pay, like regular workers, but that they would be dismissed, with a one-time subsidy to be paid by their own home governments, if their illness lingered beyond that time limit. There was no insurance of any kind for the outsiders, they claimed. For those workers whom the factory is unable to provide with housing, "the factory wouldn't give any money for rent."

A man in charge of outside labor from that same city's Textile Bureau, however, had a somewhat different story. According to his account, peasant workers are indeed sometimes given subsidies, for high temperatures or for working the night shift. Those falling ill in an "ordinary" way may use factory hospitals, and the factory will pay a percentage of the fee. They emphasized that the hours of labor, the lunch period, and the workweek matched those of the permanent laborers.[55] There is no insurance fee (*baoxianfei*) for any workers in Tianjin textile firms, he reported.

And at one more level lower down, conditions diverged again. Management at the city's No. 3 Silk Weaving Factory said that at their plant wages did not include bonuses, but that workers who performed well had a chance to be granted some, just as any regular worker did. This *danwei* put aside 3 yuan a month for each outside worker to be used in case of sickness, but if the illness entailed higher fees, the fees would have to be covered by the worker herself; for minor illnesses, sick workers got free care but no wages, whereas if they fell seriously ill, they would be sent home with no pay. In addition, the firm pays an insurance company 30 yuan per worker every six months for life insurance and "accident" insurance, which could be drawn upon for accidents occurring off the job. All of the seventy-two outside workers hired here were female, in part to facilitate housing them all together in one collective dorm.[56]

At Wuhan's prosperous No. 1 Textile Mill, management's initial claim was that for the temporaries, wages, work, and welfare were just the same as those of the regular labor. Closer questioning revealed some discrepancies, however. For instance, the factory only managed to find the funding to house half of its 1,500 peasant workers, putting them up six to eight per room. For the others, most of whom were accommodated by relatives and friends, the firm contributed 3 to 5 yuan per month to help out with the rent. Moreover, although an amount of money equal to 19 percent of the wages of each was set apart each month for insurance expenses, to be returned to the worker at the termination of the contract, for the regular workers, the amount was 22.5 percent of their pay, which became part of their pensions. Sick workers were able to get 60 to 70 percent of their pay while they were ill, just like the regulars, and had a full six months to recuperate from a severe illness before being let go. Unlike the permanent employees, however, once they were dismissed, the firm's responsibility would end, whereas a "permanent" worker on sick leave could collect 60 percent of his/her wages until death.[57] We must take into account that all these data come from official interviews and visits to officially selected plants, places doing well financially and so more prone to offer generous benefits.

But even a critical report in a government-sponsored investigation of state-run textile mills in Zhengzhou contains evidence of at least some bonuses and subsidies and tells of no humiliating treatment. In these *danwei,* it took temporaries, who in the late 1980s still earned only 44 yuan in their first year of work, five years to work themselves up to the standard wage of the post they occupied. In the meantime, however, they were eligible for monthly bonuses between 10 and 20 yuan, night subsidies of 18 yuan, food subsidies of 15 yuan, grain subsidies of 5 yuan, and washing subsidies of 6 yuan.

These bits of money were essential: It cost the workers up to 70 yuan per month just to eat in the workers' cafeteria, and those whom the factories could not accommodate sometimes were forced to pay as much as 40 yuan a month to rent a dwelling. And, despite national regulations, they received no paid holiday time to visit families and no time off for attending weddings or funerals. It is striking that two of the women who had entered the mills in 1989 had to ask for 20 to 30 yuan from home each month just to survive.[58] Added to these financial strains, according to this report, these workers are given the inferior machines to work on, they are not informed of factory activities, and they are not permitted to marry or give birth while on contract.

All these things are problems, granted, but they surely pale next to the plight of the peasants in the nonstate sector.[59] Thus, while these various accounts all differ substantially on the particulars, both from each other and from the national regulations as well, a general conclusion can be reached: In the state-owned firms, despite the sizable discrepancies in treatment between their own and that extended to the permanent work force, temporaries as late as the early 1990s were still entitled to at least some benefits, more in some cases than in others, some in one category and some in another.

Treatment of Peasant Workers in the Nonstate Sector

With the exception of the World Bank researcher, literally all of the other reportage I have seen on the nonstate sector decries its execrable treatment of peasant labor.[60] This finding is reinforced by the statement of a reporter who interviewed the ex-executive director of Hong Kong's Occupational Safety and Health Council: "As bad as safety conditions in state-owned factories may be, industry analysts agree that China's private and collective industries represent the most grievous threat to workers' safety."[61]

Indeed, in many ways the management of these firms perched on the edge of state oversight, with their "slave-like conditions,"[62] unpaid overtime, abuse and disrespect, hearkens back to the miseries of imperialist-run factories of the 1930s, whose "bullying and assaulting of workers" Elizabeth Perry has quoted a foreign observer as having attributed to "pervasive racism."[63]

One of the fullest reports on the foreign firms comes from a Chinese scholar who compared capital–labor relations in the "sanzi" firms[64] to those in the factories of the early 1950s.[65] In one representative joint venture, where the partner was from Hong Kong, workers were only given two 10–minute rest periods a day, during which more than two hundred women had to compete for two toilet stalls. Other appalling conditions abound in the firms he surveyed: 16– to 18–hour workdays with no extra pay were often the norm; in some Japanese firms, if a worker was late, he/she would have to stand outside and suffer humiliation for an hour. Cursing, beating up the workers, deductions of their wages and bonuses, and arbitrary firings are not uncommon. And in a Hong Kong–Chinese cooperative enterprise, the "frisk system," thrown out forty years before, had made a reappearance, he found.

Chinese journalists writing in a Guangdong magazine revealed that in the *"sanlai"* firms and TVEs alike in the Pearl River Delta, twelve- to eighteen-hour workdays, seven-day weeks, twenty-minute lunches, and a total absence of labor protection, all flying in the face of state regulations.[66] There are grueling tales of fires, such as one (of many) in a Shenzhen factory in November 1993, in which eighty-four peasant workers, locked in to prevent theft, were suffocated and burned to death.[67]

As for injury compensation, one sobering tale told by our traveling journalists referenced above provides a sense of things:

A half year ago one worker had half his finger crushed by a machine. He wrote a letter to the local labor bureau, asking for help, since he had received no compensation from the factory. He had already worked there for nearly two years, since the factory first opened.

After several months of treatment, the injury had begun to take a good turn, but it's very inconvenient not to have a right index finger.

"I requested compensation from the manager, but he said my treatment period had surpassed the budget; delegating a worker to watch me also cost money, etc. Could my broken finger heal itself without treatment?" the boy bemoaned. . . . "I've suffered a serious spiritual and material loss."

This letter to the Shenzhen Labor Bureau was then sent to the county labor bureau with only three characters: "Please read and handle."

I[the reporter] asked the county labor bureau chief what happened. He signed with feeling and said, "This kind of letter is especially plentiful recently; sometimes we even get a lot in just one day. But the bureau hasn't the energy to investigate and without policy and legal foundation to help solve it, can only take it in and that's it."[68]

In short, the nonstate sector, much celebrated by American business and the U.S. government, in many ways is not really to be admired as a shining example of China's advance to economic practices "just like us." It is, rather, a throwback to the totally unregulated laissez-faire capitalism of the mid-nineteenth century.[69]

Analysis

The prediction from the comparative literature, which suggested that peasant labor would be treated as expendable and denied welfare benefits, has turned out, on the basis of our evidence, to be only partially accurate in the case of transition-era state-owned Chinese firms. Although both state and nonstate firms have fallen victim to the lures of profit-making and foreign investment—the market factors—state firms, still subject in varying degrees to legacy factors, appear to be significantly more benevolent employers than are those in the nonstate sector, as recounted in the press and in reportage literature.

Not surprisingly, market reforms do indeed provide a large measure of the explanation for the behavior of firms of any type in their relationship to their temporary labor force in China today. But, as Castells and Portes predict, this is true especially in the more informal firms, such as the TVEs and FFFs. It is especially the case in the FFFs, where a far larger percentage of the firms' output is exported, and where, consequently, the weight of international capital is particularly heavy. This is in part because of efforts to keep costs down to keep up with the competition;[70] in part it is because these firms' orders are so much more a product of the state of demand in the international market, which can be volatile and more unpredictable than the domestic one.

Castells and Portes, writing of a global effect, see informal firms essaying to save costs not so much by cutting wages as by avoid[ing] the 'indirect wage' formed by social benefits and other employee-related payments to the state. . . . By lowering the cost of labor and reducing state-imposed constraints on its free hiring and dismissal, the informal economy contributes directly to the profitability of capital.[71]

But what about the local state management departments in charge of the places where the more informal, foreign-funded, firms are situated? What happened to the restraining forces on their actions? Apparently when there is a possibility of attracting foreign capital into their domains, they too fall under the sway of the logic of international capitalism, as Hollifield, discussing the weakness of the state in the face of the world market's magnetism, affirms in the case of European business: "The first constraint is economic: the international market for labor in Europe . . . it is extremely difficult for the state to prevent firms and employers from participating in it."[72]

This looming influence of the potential benefits promised from foreign investment appears in the reluctance of local government officials to require that the foreign investors in their cities meet regime-mandated safety and hygiene standards, "for fear of scaring the foreign investors away." In fact, in some scurrilous instances, no inspections at all were carried out before granting permission to the foreigners to set up business.[73] As our journalistic commentators, writing on late 1980s China, depict the scenario:

> An old Guangdong official said in a sneering tone: "The bosses' pockets are awesome, so no one wants to offend them. In labor-capital disputes, we management personnel often stand on the bosses' side, very rarely saying an impartial word on behalf of the *mingong* [migrant labor].[74]

In these instances, where foreign investors have appeared at their door, the chance to earn their money has elevated finances above state managers' usual concerns about order and stability, disgruntled workers, and possible strikes: "Some localities and departments, in their desire to make money, are afraid of offending [foreign] bosses but not concerned about rebellion by workers."[75]

But it is not just with regard to the informal sector, whose operations are far less subject to the surveillance of the state, that market considerations influence the handling of hired help. Still, the significant point is that state firms essay to save money not by altogether eliminating costs, but by hiring more expendable labor.

Certainly the cost-consciousness of state *danwei* and the bureaus managing them has risen since economic reforms began.[76] In the pre-1979 period, according to Emerson, temporaries were paid not from the wage fund, but from general administrative expenses or from petty cash [presumably as the firm in question saw fit] and were simply not eligible for benefits. Indeed, they were not even listed on the books of the enterprises.[77]

Economic reforms, which by 1986 had legitimized the hiring of peasant labor in state firms,[78] and gradually regularized it, made it both possible and even necessary to hire peasant labor in substantial numbers in certain trades. But, along with that, reforms imposed official constraints upon its use, dictating that outsiders' wages would come from the firms' budgets.[79]

The reforms also considerably enhanced the value of peasant labor over what it had been in the past, as urban youths refused to sign up for jobs in several manufacturing sectors. Many citations could be offered asserting that firms in specific sectors of industry would actually have to shut down if they could not draw upon the peasants.[80] Short of coming to a full halt, according to the reckoning of the textile bureau there, the six large cotton mills in Zhengzhou's textile trade in the late 1980s were still sorely dependent upon their outside labor from the countryside. Reportedly, without these women, 30 percent of the weaving and spinning machines would have had to be stopped, and the annual loss would have been 230 million yuan in output value and 63.34 million yuan in taxes and profits. These same firms managed to increase their foreign exchange intake 2.3–fold because of the toil of the 5,800 peasant women they employed in the five years of the second half of the 1980s.[81]

Cognizant of this enhanced value of the outsiders, but also constrained at least somewhat by new regulations on their usage, the management of state firms is careful not to abandon all benefits. It is nonetheless keenly conscious of the savings that can accrue by maintaining peasants as an *under*entitled portion of its work force. Enterprises hiring temporaries have found that they can afford to pay the temporaries regular or even slightly higher wages than the permanent employees receive and still save money by cutting back on, even though not entirely eliminating, benefits.[82]

Several of my interviewees commented explicitly on the cost-saving their *danwei* could enjoy by relying on outsiders to supplement their regular work force. Officials from the Tianjin Bureau of Labor listed some sources of such savings: no insurance had to be paid; the young people engaged were unlikely to become seriously ill (and, with their limited-term contracts, would depart before they got much older); no schools had to be set up for their benefit, since they were required to be unmarried and thus childless; their housing, with half a dozen or more squeezed into one dorm room, was remarkably cheap; and regular workers had to be paid whether they worked or not, which was not the case for the temporaries.[83]

Their subordinate, No. 3 Silk Weaving Factory, all of whose peasants were female, had a few points to add to this tally: The factory saves by not needing a nursery for these women, by not having to pay for any pregnancy or for the standard four months of maternity leave, need not supply any funds to pay for the delivery, need not exempt them from the night shift for a year as it does for the permanent workers, can avoid releasing them for feeding time during the day, and provides them with no pension.[84]

More precise are the calculations performed by the Zhengzhou Textile Industrial Bureau, two of whose staff prepared a report that specified the savings very exactly, as of 1989, as below:

(1) no wage subsidies (labor insurance, 1/2 price medical care for family), for 1 person/1 year saves 216 yuan; (2) no maternity leave (three months), or award of three months' vacation for having just one child, for one person saves 500 yuan; and (3) no family dorm; if the 6,000 peasant workers in the plants lived in factory housing at the rate that regular staff do (60 percent), we would need 20 million yuan to house their families.[85]

These accounts of savings bespeak a different calculus for peasants than for permanents in the state plants. Still, although market reforms and the incursions of foreign funds have affected both the traditional *danwei* and the nonstate firms, the extent and nature of the influence is decidedly different. Benefits may be skimpier for outsiders than for regulars in the state firms, but there are no reports of a total lack of benefits, of assaults on workers' dignity and bodies, of exposures to poisons, excessive overtime, embezzled wages, or frisks and searches, as we find repeatedly in the press about the FFFs.

Given this difference, it makes sense to see the transitional-era *danwei* as a unit undergoing alteration, but not yet having been totally overrun by market influences, as of the early 1990s. Thus, in understanding what goes on in the state firms, we need to consider not just the market factors but legacy factors as well. Most centrally, despite its corruption and inefficiency, the state sector is still the only place where government regulations were honored into the 1990s with at least some measure of seriousness.

In his study of immigration in Western Europe, Hollifield has emphasized the significance of "the accretion of rights" and "legal cultures," which offer "protection from arbitrary powers of the state and employers." Granted, decades of party rule in China vitiated any conception of legality that might otherwise have developed in a nonsocialist, modernizing China. But at least the regulations of the state, a poor substitute, perhaps, have informed the workings of the state-sector *danwei* for four decades. Thus, as with recruitment, certain socialist legacies—in this case, the regulatory environment—have not yet been lost. In the years since the reforms began, both central and provincial governments have issued regulations on the legal rights of temporaries in the *sanzi* and collective enterprises, but to little avail.[86] As our roving journalists characterized the situation, "Some enterprises, especially rural enterprises, private-owned, and foreign processing enterprises, don't seriously implement these regulations and laws of the government. . . . In a lot of rural and private firms, the contracts enterprises sign with the workers are limited only to the factories' restraints on the worker. A lot of enterprises use their own factory rules to replace the contract."[87] The Shanghai scholar Jiang Kelin wrote of a study revealing that barely more than half the *sanzi* firms bother to follow the state's regulations.[88]

All these data reveal that, the State Council ruling of 1991 notwithstanding,[89] peasant contract labor in any sort of firm simply does not have the rights and powers of the permanent, urban workers. But, at least in the state firms, no matter how great the enticement of earnings, in the last instance management has until recently governed, more or less, under the aegis of the state and its operating creed.

This creed, which translates into a kind of institutional culture, privileges worker pacification, popular stability, and the security of the state and its apparatus above all other ends—even economic ones—and cringes, then quickly gears into action, at any sign of adverse worker power. One could cynically make the case that this creed informed, if it did not wholly dictate, two of the three objectives of the old *danwei* listed earlier in this chapter: full urban employment and full security for city workers.

Moreover, in the state firms, the machinery for ensuring this passivity remained rather firmly in place into the mid-1990s. In the nonstate sector (and in the management bureaus of localities where foreign investors have overwhelmed the old ethos of the socialist state), on the other hand, profit considerations have come to dominate over order goals. There it is not the central state apparatus but the foreign investors or local, localistic cadres to whom management responds and is responsible. Besides, here the mechanisms for enforcement of the larger state's policies and regulations are weak or absent. As one researcher told me:

> Some TVEs are totally privately managed and don't follow regulations. They feel it's taking money from their own pockets to give welfare. Government management just can't keep up to check on them. . . . We [presumably referring to the situation within the state sector] have regulations to ensure there are basic guarantees on welfare, and government investigations to check up.[90]

One more indication of the lack of state penetration into most FFFs is this comment of a Chinese scholar: "The majority of foreign owners refuse to establish trade unions."[91]

Another contrast concerns the respective motives for firing workers in state versus nonstate firms. Although peasant labor can be dismissed at will in firms of both sorts, contracts, generally of three to five years, are taken rather seriously in normal times in the state firms. There the primacy of peace and order goals means that rural labor may be let go in times of state-induced recession (again, evidencing statist concerns with control), but this is often to make way for the urban unemployed.[92] And, just as in any place to which migrants go, even when the economy is healthy there is a reluctance to offer jobs to outsiders when local people need jobs.[93]

My own interviews with officials from the Tianjin Textile Bureau, Labor Bureau, and the No. 3 Silk Weaving Factory also raised the issue, exposing a profound contradiction.[94] In contrast to the representatives of textiles and the factory, who wanted to hire more peasants to keep their machines humming, the labor bureaucrats were trying to keep such hiring to the minimum, emphasizing the state's concerns with order: "For city stability it's important to employ local labor."

This conflict illustrates how the reforms have split—and created opposed constituencies behind—what were once the intimately linked *danwei* objectives of full employment and security (for urban labor), on the one hand, and maximum output, on the other. In this case, we see that the statist forces have the upper hand, for now.

But in the Pearl River Delta, dissimilarly, firings follow not statist but economic objectives, in accordance with the priority on profits that predominates there. According to a Chinese periodical, "Most enterprises in the *sanlai* trade rely on outside laborers to 'come when beckoned and leave when dismissed.' "[95] For instance, "In Bao'an county, several enterprises involved in foreign trade fired 2,500 workers because American stocks fell."[96]

Yet another telling quotation from the mouth of a young woman who had already worked in five different factories in three different towns in the delta was recorded by our two itinerant journalists: "We temps labor, aren't we here to earn money; you bosses, aren't you just using us for our labor power? Who doesn't sell to whom, who doesn't owe whom? If satisfied, we go on; if not, change firms—mutually select—everyone's free!"[97]

That it is in the nonstate sector that treatment of peasant labor is markedly inferior is evident, too, in that it is here that all the strikes against actual *present mistreatment of workers on the job* (as opposed to those demonstrations clamoring simply for the retention of privileges and entitlements long in place[98]) have burst forth.[99]

Thus where market forces are strongest, in the FFFs and TVEs, benefits and job tenure are without guarantee. But even here, one could view this unmitigated market as itself a product of earlier times. Where there are no state overseers to intervene, the lack of legality bequeathed by decades of party rule has aggravated the mercilessness of the market, rendering the capitalism practiced in these firms totally unregulated and laissez-faire, far removed from the welfare capitalism to which we are accustomed in the late twentieth-century West. In the state firms, on the other hand, the ethos and the apparatus of the state still manage to ensure a modicum of welfare for peasant workers, shored up by a regulatory regimen not yet fully decimated.

Conclusion

This chapter explores the changes that the availability of reserve, peasant, labor has brought to the *danwei,* in light of data on two broad types of *danwei* that are using peasants in manufacturing: those in particular trades in the state sector; and those in foreign-funded and township and village enterprises, the "nonstate" sector. The first type of change concerns recruitment. Here we found not so much an elimination of bureaucratic modes as an admixture of personalistic connections; market forces, however, have not yet been much in evidence in determining who among the peasants is selected for employment in either the state sector or the nonstate firms. Instead, our data suggest, legacy factors—the influence of the state plan and of party rule—if now diluted, proved more potent at this stage than market forces.[100]

The second shift, in the realm of benefits, entitlements, and treatment, also exhibits this evolutionary flux. Unadulterated market forces do determine how peasants are handled in the most marketized, export-oriented firms, it is true. Laissez-faire capitalist conditions are largely permitted to run wild because decades of party rule, a legacy factor, have not allowed for the development of a nationwide and potent legal climate. But firms in the state sector into the 1990s were still affected by the statist ethos of order and peace in the firm and are still influenced by the regulatory climate and the tradition of benefits and welfare that shaped the *danwei* for some forty years. Therefore, although their treatment of peasants is inferior to that accorded to urban labor—farther along on the evolutionary path toward pure marketization, perhaps—through at least the early 1990s peasants were faring far better in the state firms. This is so except insofar as their presence there clashes—principally in times of state-induced recession—with what in China are considered to be "socialist" goals of full urban employment and a state-controlled economy. At those times, they have been pushed out of town and back to the plow.

This contrast between two types of firms has illustrated the lingering influence of statist management in the handling of migrants in the state-owned firms, even as the *danwei* undergoes gradual, if unmistakable, transformation. This is evident in these firms even after fifteen years of reformist policies, especially given that stark demand for workers to run their machines that the reforms themselves created. It thus demonstrates that, in the transition from socialism, market forces do not take over immediately where the state has been deeply entrenched. This bequest betters the lot of those ruralites who are lucky enough to land a slot in a state-owned *danwei*. But at the same time, the presence of peasants in the cities, along with the reforms that brought them there, is gradually chipping away at the identity and the roles of the previous *danwei*.

The chapter also suggests that, in the immediate postsocialist period, where the state is absent, especially in the firms subject to the vicissitudes of the international market, an instant transition to welfare-state capitalism as we know it does not take place. Instead, because of the socialist legacies of a heavily regulated, administratively arranged labor allocation system, an absence of legality, a lack of opportunity for workers to organize to defend rights, and a tradition of personalism rooted in local party officials' unlimited discretion, what we see is a raw, unabashed, laissez-faire capitalism.

Recently, however, and increasingly as reforms intensify and accelerate, we are witnessing sudden layoffs not just of temporary but of permanent workers from the state-owned firms, with cost-accounting and profit-seeking as the motive. Interestingly, the solution is not to replace fired permanent workers in state firms with members of the floating population.[101] Rather, it is to close the state firms and cast off their employees to the private, nonstate sector, as an early 1993 issue of the *China Daily* made clear. An article there announced that almost 16 percent of the workers in state firms would be moved to other jobs in 1993, 10 million of whom would have to rely upon their own resources to find new jobs. The remedy for this, the writer promised, would be that: "The number of private, collective, and foreign-funded enterprises is expected to increase sharply this year, creating millions of jobs for workers to be laid off from state enterprises."[102]

This statement, and the motivating impulse evident behind it, raise the intriguing question: Do the floating peasants in the nonstate factories of today represent a vanguard, the future of labor (at least in the manufacturing sector) in once-socialist China? Does their situation illuminate the route along which what Manuel Castells and Alejandro Portes have called the "disenfranchisement" of the permanent work force may unfold?[103]

Eerily, in this same piece, these authors offer a possible future that China— driven, like the capitalist countries they consider, by the dynamic of an informal economy quite similar to China's nonstate sector—may come to experience: "A new society based on the relationship between unrestrained capital and primary social networks."[104]

Notes

1. On these workers of the past and their situations, see Andrew G. Walder, *Communist Neo-Traditionalism: Work and Authority in Chinese Industry* (Berkeley: University of California Press, 1986), 48–56.

2. Township and village enterprises had absorbed approximately 110 million rural residents as of the end of 1993. See Foreign Broadcast Information Service [hereafter FBIS], January 31, 1994, 29. Davis reports that, by 1986, recent rural migrants already constituted some 20 percent of the work force in several of the largest cities (Deborah Davis, "Urban Job Mobility," in *Chinese Society on the Eve of Tiananmen: The Impact of Reform,* ed. Deborah Davis and Ezra F. Vogel [Cambridge: Council on East Asian Studies/Harvard University, 1990], 85). Between 1978 and 1987, 10,165,000 people from the rural areas were employed in the cities, averaging an annual increase of 1,270,000 (Chen Yicai, "The Influence of the Floating Population on Social and Economic Development," *Renkou xuekan* [Population studies bulletin] [hereafter *RKXK*], no. 2 [1988]: 41); as of 1989, rural contract labor amounted to approximately 3.47 percent of urban enterprises' staff and workers (Ding Jianhua, "Peasant Contract Labor's Wait," *Shehui* [Society], 11 [1989]: 17). But Shanghai shi tongjiju [Shanghai City Statistics Bureau], ed., *Shanghai liudong renkou* [Shanghai's floating population] (Shanghai: Chinese Statistical Publishing House, 1989), 216, says that more than 200,000 outside laborers were working in state enterprises in Shanghai as of the late 1980s, and that Shanghai Bureau of Labor research on 77 enterprises in 1988 found them to be employing outsiders who accounted for 5.2 percent of the enterprises' staff and workers. Peasant workers in Guangzhou's construc-

tion, sanitation, textile, and chemical trades totaled more than half the staff and workers, according to Beijing City People's Government's Research Office, Social Section, "A Comprehensive Report on the Issue of the Floating Population in Eight Big Cities," *Shehuixue yanjiu* [Sociology research] 3 (1991): 21.

3. According to FBIS, September 21, 1993, 49, at the end of 1992, foreign-funded enterprises employed about 4.8 million mainland staff and workers; again, many of these were peasants. There is no breakdown given as to temporary versus permanent staff in these firms.

4. Where along the spectrum any particular firm may lie is probably a function of such factors as those identified by Andrew Walder in his article, "Property Rights and Stratification in Socialist Redistributive Economies," *American Sociological Review 57 (1992), 524–39. These would include features such as the size of the enterprise, the sector in which it lies, its bureaucratic rank, and its contribution to the economy.*

5. According to the official newspaper, *China Daily* [hereafter *CD*], October 6, 1992, "As enterprises get more power over employment, they are more willing to hire laborers from the countryside because they accept low pay and are easy to manage."

6. For instance, see Wuhan shi laodongju [Wuhan City Labor Bureau], ed., *Chengshi wailai laodongli guanli* [The management of outside urban labor] (Wuhan: Wuhan chubanshe, 1990) [hereafter, Wuhan shi], 6: "Enterprises under the contract system use lots of outside labor to save money"; and ibid., 128: "Units with wages linked to results don't respect the control quota figures" [meant to limit the numbers of floating population hired].

7. See Walder, *Communist Neo-Traditionalism*, 11, on the fact that the employment relationship in the old firm was "not primarily a market relationship"; and on "employment . . . play[ing] a welfare role."

8. Hu Teh-wei and Elizabeth Hon-Ming Li, "Labor Market Reforms in China" (paper presented at Center for Chinese Studies, Spring Regional Seminar, University of California, Berkeley, April 11, 1992), 49; Ye Shengyao, "Inquiry into the Issue of the Temporary Population in Suzhou City," *RKXK*, no. 2 (1989): 57; Liu Dawei and Wang Qiangzhi, "An Investigation Report on the Problem of Labor Being Hard to Find in Beijing City," *Shehui kexue yu shehui diaocha* [Social science and social investigation] 1 (1987): 36; and Li Mengbai and Hu Xin, eds., *Liudong renkou dui da chengshi fazhan de yingxiang ji duice* [The influence of the floating population on the development of big cities and policy response] (Beijing: Jingji ribao chubanshe, 1991), speaks of "the urban young's . . . unwillingness to condescend to take a post offered." Thanks to David Zweig for sending me a copy of this valuable volume.

9. The two most important of these decisions are, first, the "State Council Notification on the Question of Peasants Entering Towns and Settling" of October 1984, which gave peasants the right to residency in market towns with a population under 60,000 and was aimed at those who could raise their own funds, take care of their own grain, and find a place of abode in the market towns. This was published in *Guowuyuan gongbao* [State Council bulletin] [hereafter SCB], no. 26 (447) (November 10, 1984): 919–20. The other, entitled the "Provisional Regulations on the Management of Population Living Temporarily in the Cities," created a category of those whose work (opening stores or factories, engaging in construction and installation work, transport business, or in service trades) would keep them in town for more than three months ("for a relatively long period") and gave them their own special certificate, labeled the "card for residents living with others" (jizhu zheng). This document appeared in Renmin ribao, September 8, 1985, 4, and is translated in FBIS, September 12, 1985, K12–14. Neither of these specifically applied to peasants working in factories, but they laid the groundwork for that. In 1989 the State Council passed its "Provisional Regulations on the Management of Temporary Labor in

Enterprises Owned by the Whole People," *SCB*, no. 19 (1989): 714–16.

10. This resembles the situation in Western Europe. See James F. Hollifield, *Immigrants, Markets and States: The Political Economy of Postwar Europe* (Cambridge: Harvard University Press, 1992), 110; and Jan Vranken, "Industrial Rights," in *The Political Rights of Migrant Workers in Western Europe,* ed. Zig Layton-Henry (London: Sage Publications, 1990), 54. According to these writers, outside workers get jobs in Western Europe not, as is currently the case in China, because of a sudden injection of market forces, but simply because natives, having become more educated, accustomed to rising living standards, and consequently, having higher expectations, reject the low-skill, underpaid, heavy work grabbed up eagerly by migrants.

11. For background on this, see Margaret Pearson, *Joint Ventures in the People's Republic of China* (Princeton: Princeton University Press, 1991).

12 Recently published research by Yanjie Bian, however, emphasizes the extent to which personal relations always supplemented administrative forms of recruitment, even in the days of maximum state planning. He makes the point, nonetheless, that jobs found through *guanxi* (personal relations) increased as bureaucratic controls were reduced with the reforms. See Yanjie Bian, "*Guanxi* and the Allocation of Urban Jobs in China," *China Quarterly* [hereafter, *CQ*], no. 140 (1994): 971–99. The point just cited is on 973.

13. On this type of firm, see Walder, *Communist Neo-Traditionalism,* especially 40–43, and 56–68.

14. On this, see Terry Sicular, "Public Finance and China's Economic Reforms," University of Western Ontario, Papers in Political Economy, n.d.

15. Reforms have been under way since the mid-1980s to reduce the scope of *danwei* benefits for its regular, permanent work force, but such "reforms" have been markedly gaining momentum in the past year or so. Relevant reforms in progress are discussed in Yok-shiu F. Lee, "The Urban Housing Problem in China," *CQ*, no. 115 (1988): 387–407; Elizabeth J. Perry and Ellen V. Fuller, "China's Long March to Democracy," *World Policy Journal* (Fall 1991): 663–85, on reductions in price subsidies; FBIS, January 4, 1993, 52, and April 22, 1993, 22, on the new pension system; FBIS, April 19, 1993, 26, and September 1, 1993, 35, and *CD,* December 20, 1993, 4, on the new unemployment insurance system; FBIS, August 13, 1993, 37, on cuts in state subsidies for grain and edible oil; FBIS, August 26, 1993, 31, on schools run by local people, which are to be "conducive to reducing the state's financial difficulties in allocating educational funds and sharing the burdens relating to employment"; and FBIS, December 1, 1993, 24, on raising rents. Temporary labor in the state firms was never accorded the benefits that permanent labor received. See Walder, *Communist Neo-Traditionalism,* 54.

16. Gu Shengzu, "Where Will Chinese Rural Surplus Labor Go?" *Nongcun gaige* [Rural reform], no. 4 (1994): 87. Gu heads the population institute at Wuhan University.

17. Interview at a residents' committee in Wuhan, May 30, 1992.

18. Interview at the Tianjin Labor Bureau, June 16, 1992.

19. Wuhan shi, 115, 137.

20. Interview at the Wuhan No. 1 Textile Mill, May 23, 1992. Was it thought that the Hong'an county workers would be easier to control because they would have a leader who would mediate problems with the mill's staff? Or because a plant populated by peasants from several places would be plagued by interregional squabbles? In the event all the Hong'an natives joined in complaining when any problems arose, and all took off together for an unapproved fifteen-day break at New Year's.

21. Interview at the mill, June 18, 1992.

22. Li and Hu, *Liudong renkou,* 342.

23. Ibid., 346.

24. Zhang Qingwu, "Thinking about Problems Relating to the Floating Population in

the Cities," *Zhongguo renkou kexue* [Chinese population science], no. 3 (1989): 55, is just one example among many.

25. Interview at the Wuhan Labor Bureau, September 19, 1990.

26. Wuhan shi, 32, 175; and interview with the Wuhan Labor Bureau, May 23, 1992.

27. Wuhan shi, 175.

28. Township and village enterprises are often, technically speaking, owned by a subset of "the state," since they are usually the creation of the local government in the countryside and smaller towns. But I still choose to term them "nonstate," since they operate outside the regimen of the old state plan and the stricter controls for management which the plan placed upon urban firms.

Lora Sabin, "New Bosses in the Workers' State: The Growth of Non-State Sector Employment in China," *CQ*, no. 140 (1994): 944–70, discusses recruitment in the foreign firms via job fairs, personnel exchange centers, and advertisements. But she is talking here of the recruitment of workers who already are employed in the urban state firms.

29. Actually, the statement refers to *"sanlai yibu"* firms. The *"sanlai,"* or "three imports," are the materials, the patterns, and the equipment; the *"yibu,"* or "one compensation," stands for compensatory trade. This term is best translated simply as processing enterprises.

30. Wang Zhiwang and Jiang Zuozhong, "One Million 'Migrants' Go to the Pearl River," *Nanfang chuang* [South window], no. 5 (1988): 29.

31. Ge Xiangxian and Qu Weiying, *Zhongguo mingongchao: "mangliu" zhenxianglu* [China's tide of labor: A record of the true facts about the "blind floaters"] (Beijing: Chinese International Broadcasting, 1990), 139–40. For a story on Bijie as a poverty prefecture, and as part of a special state program to help such places, see FBIS, June 26, 1996, 30.

32. Ge and Qu, *Zhongguo mingongchao*, 145.

33. Jing Yi, "Records from Visits to Family Members of the Victims of the Donghuang Fire Disaster," *Zheng ming* [Contend] [hereafter *ZM*], no. 169 (1991): 22–27.

34. Interview in Wuhan at the worksite, May 25, 1992.

35. Manuel Castells and Alejandro Portes, "World Underneath: The Origins, Dynamics, and Effects of the Informal Economy," in *The Informal Economy: Studies in Advanced and Less Developed Countries*, ed. Alejandro Portes, Manuel Castells, and Lauren A. Benton (Baltimore: Johns Hopkins University Press, 1989), 11–37.

36. As work by William Parish et al. indicates, mature labor markets involve returns to human capital, as opposed to hiring on the basis of administrative procedures or simple interpersonal connections. See William L. Parish, Xiaoye Zhe, and Fang Li, "Nonfarm Work and Marketization of the Chinese Countryside," *CQ*, no. 139 (1995).

37. Walder (1986) notes that in the first decades of the twentieth century in the United States, a "progressive bureaucratization of labor relations resulted in complex regulations and collective agreements governing the compensation and hiring and firing of workers," such that the previous personal discretion of supervisors was much diminished (*Communist Neo-Traditionalism*, 21).

38. Rural Surplus Labor Transformation and Labor Markets Study Group, "An Investigation of the Interregional Mobility of Rural Labor from Twenty-eight Counties," *Zhongguo nongcun jingji* [Chinese rural economy], no. 4 (1995): 22.

39. Bian, *"Guanxi* and the Allocation of Urban Jobs," 979.

40. The desperation of the firms in the textile, machine-building, and chemical trades is mentioned in the following places: Ye, "Inquiry into Temporary Population," 57; Liu and Wang, "Investigation into Labor," 34; *CD*, July 24, 1991, 6; Li and Hu, *Liudong renkou*, 339, contains a detailed, statistically informed account of the difficulties of the textile trade in Zhengzhou in the late 1980s in this regard.

41. FBIS, July 25, 1991, 53.

42. For a comparative perspective on this dynamic, see Castells and Portes, "World Underneath," 28; and Alejandro Portes, Manuel Castells, and Lauren A. Benton, "Conclusion: The Policy Implications of Informality," in Portes, Castells, and Benton, *The Informal Economy,* 299; and Hollifield, *Immigrants, Markets, and States,* 105. Hollifield's remark is especially interesting: "The dual labor market argument suggests the continuing demand for foreign labor can be explained by *the high degree of regulation* of the domestic labor market. . . . Such regulation creates incentives for employers to look outside traditional labor markets for cheaper, more tractable labor" (emphasis added).

43. Walder, *Communist Neo-Traditionalism,* 22 and 58–59.

44. For comparative material on the phenomenon of migrants being taken as a labor reserve and accordingly treated poorly in terms of benefits and tenure, see Michael J. Piore, *Birds of Passage: Migrant Labor and Industrial Societies* (Cambridge: Cambridge University Press, 1979); Alejandro Portes, "Migration and Underdevelopment," *Politics and Society,* 9, no. 1 (1978): 1–48; Saskia Sassen-Koob, "Immigrant and Minority Workers in the Organization of the Labor Process," *Journal of Ethnic Studies,* 8, no. 1 (1980): 1–34; Saskia Sassen, *The Mobility of Labor and Capital: A Study in International Investment and Labor Flow* (New York: Cambridge University Press, 1988); James D. Cockcroft, *Outlaws in the Promised Land: Mexican Immigrant Workers and America's Future* (New York: Grove Press, 1986); Michael Burawoy, "The Functions and Reproduction of Migrant Labor: Comparative Material from Southern Africa and the United States," *American Journal of Sociology,* 81, no. 5 (1976): 1050–87; Stephen Castles and Godula Kosack, *Immigrant Workers and Class Structure in Western Europe,* 2d ed. (New York: Oxford University Press, 1985); Larissa Adler Lomnitz, *Networks and Marginality: Life in a Mexican Shantytown* (New York: Academic Press, 1977); and Gay Willcox Seidman, "Labor Movements in Newly-Industrialized Countries: South Africa and Brazil, 1960–1985" (Ph.D. dissertation, University of California at Berkeley, 1990).

45. Interview with the Wuhan Labor Bureau, September 19, 1990.

46. See Walder, *Communist Neo-Traditionalism,* 59–68.

47. See Pat Howard, "Rice Bowls and Job Security: The Urban Contract Labour System," *Australian Journal of Chinese Affairs,* no. 25 (1991): 100; Hu and Li, "Labor Market Reforms in China," 45, claim that the value of housing subsidies was equivalent to 23.5 percent of a worker's income in the late 1980s; John Philip Emerson, "Urban School-Leavers and Unemployment in China," *CQ,* no. 93 (1983): 8, wrote of the early 1980s, "A job in a state-owned plant offers a variety of subsidized welfare benefits that amount to more than half the basic wage of an urban worker." Also, Perry and Fuller, "China's Long March to Democracy," 673, state that "urban workers enjoy welfare subsidies equivalent to an average of 54 percent of their basic wage." FBIS, February 19, 1993, says, "In a considerable number of enterprises the ratio between the basic wage income and other income is presently one to one, with the latter sometimes far surpassing the former." Christine Wong, however, has alerted me to the fact that, if the value of the rents workers living in rent-subsidized housing were calculated in, the *overall* value of benefits would far surpass 50 percent of salaries.

48. Castells and Portes, "World Underneath," 30.

49. *SCB,* no. 28 (667) (October 18, 1991): 1001–6.

50. Michael Korzec, "Contract Labor, the 'Right to Work' and New Labor Laws in the People's Republic of China," *Chinese Economic Studies,* 30, no. 2 (1988): 117–49. See also Gordon White, "The Politics of Economic Reform in Chinese Industry: The Introduction of the Labour Contract System," *CQ,* no. 111 (1987): 365–89. On page 367 he lists the main elements of the labor contract system. As these pertain to our concerns, they are: "The enterprise's previous responsibility for providing welfare benefits should be shifted

to labour insurance companies and state welfare agencies outside the firm"; and "renewal of the contract would depend upon the performance of the worker and the labour requirements of the enterprise"; and Deborah Davis, "Unequal Chances, Unequal Outcomes: Pension Reform and Urban Inequality," *CQ,* no. 114 (1988): 239.

51. Michal Rutkowski, "The China's Floating Population and the Labor Market Reforms [sic]," preliminary draft (Washington, DC: World Bank, December 1991), iii, 20. On page 18, Rutkowski notes that, in Shanghai, 20 to 30 percent of the temporary migrants in the labor market were covered entirely or partially by the bonus system; on page 19, he states that some received subsidies as for commuting and winter heating, and on page 20, that 15 to 25 percent were being accorded some pension coverage. Housing, however, was usually not free, unlike for the permanent work force, although he was informed that 15 to 20 percent did have it; on page 21, he records that medical benefits were "sparser."

52. Informants included two scholars at the Population Research Institute of the Guangdong Social Science Academy on May 10 and May 11, 1992, respectively, and scholars at the Population Research Institute at Zhongshan University, on May 12, 1992. This variability applies whether the firm is state-owned, private, or foreign-funded, although its content depends on type of firm.

53. Feng Lanrui and Jiang Weiyu, "A Comparative Study of the Modes of Transference of Surplus Labor in China's Countryside," *Social Sciences in China,* 9, no. 3 (1988): 74.

54. Interview, June 16, 1992.

55. An eight-hour day, a half-hour lunch, and a five-day workweek.

56. Interview at the factory, June 18, 1992.

57. Interview with management, May 23, 1992.

58. Li and Hu, *Liudong renkou,* 343–44.

59. These facts are reported in ibid., 344–45.

60. Sabin, "New Bosses in the Workers' State," 955–56, notes the permissiveness of regulations on labor management in foreign-funded firms, dating back to 1980, in particular in laying off unnecessary employees. On pages 25–26 she explains that highly skilled labor in these firms does receive benefits, but this is because the firms are anxious to attract and hold onto this prized commodity in a competitive market. For those wanting to hire peasant labor, on the other hand, there is a buyer's market.

61. Carl Goldstein, "Safety Indicator: Shenzhen Blast Raises Doubts about China's Workplaces," *Far Eastern Economic Review,* August 19, 1993, 55.

62. This term was used in an Agence France-Presse [hereafter AFP] article translated in FBIS, September 28, 1993, 36.

63. Elizabeth J. Perry, *Shanghai on Strike* (Stanford: Stanford University Press, 1993), 62. Of course, today many of these "foreign" employers are also Chinese, from Hong Kong or Taiwan; in the TVEs they are Chinese as well. But in all these cases there is still almost an ethnic sense of superiority over what the employers consider crude and ignorant bumpkins from the benighted inland. Anita Chan, Richard Madsen, and Jonathan Unger, *Chen Village Under Mao and Deng* (Berkeley: University of California Press, 1992), 304, discuss what they call a "caste system of sorts based on immigrants' place of origin," which determines the job placement and the wages of transient peasants in rural factories in the Guangdong countryside.

64. "*Sanzi* firms" are those financed by three forms of capital: Chinese–foreign joint ventures; wholly foreign-owned firms; and Chinese–foreign cooperative enterprises, including those with capital from Hong Kong, Taiwan, and Macau.

65. Jiang Kelin, "The Prominent Role of Unions—Shanghai's Foreign Enterprises in the 1950s: A Historical Examination and Illumination of the Relation Between Labor and

Capital" (prepared for presentation at the Luce Seminar on Shanghai Labor, May 8, 1993, Center for Chinese Studies, Berkeley), 16–17.

66. Wang and Jiang, "One Million 'Migrants,' " 30. There are myriad similar reports. See Beijing Domestic Service, August 1988, translated in FBIS, August 23, 1988, 40; *Ming bao* [hereafter *MB*], translated in FBIS, March 30, 1991, 67; and *Zhongguo tongxunshe,* translated in FBIS, July 25, 1991, 53. One article in Guangzhou's *Nanfang ribao* [Southern daily] [hereafter *NFRB*], July 16, 1990, 1, reviewed its readers' letters, which complained that the "*sanzi*" enterprises were delaying wages for up to half a year, forcing workers to borrow money just to eat, and were compelling the workers to labor for more than eighty hours a week with no overtime pay.

67. *Liaowang* [Outlook], no. 4 (1994): 40, translated in FBIS, February 4, 1994, 17–18.

68. Ge and Qu, *Zhongguo mingongchao,* 154–55.

69. For a comparative perspective, see Castells and Portes, "World Underneath," 15, where they refer to "the resilience or growth of informal arrangements in contexts in which they were believed to be extinct or in which they were expected to disappear with the advance of industrialization."

70. Vranken, "Industrial Rights," 55, makes this point in speaking of Western European capital: "Employers urgently need[ed] cheap labor for these [low-paid, dirty, heavy, low-status jobs in mining, cleaning, catering] . . . to cope with international competition."

71. Castells and Portes, "World Underneath," 30.

72. Hollifield, *Immigrants, Markets, and States,* 94.

73. From Zhongguo tongxunshe, translated in FBIS, November 9, 1992, 47, a report on occupational hazards in foreign-funded enterprises. This report claims that in an investigation of 657 foreign enterprises in Guangdong's special economic zones, only 26 percent of the firms had been examined for hygiene before operations had begun, and only 28.4 percent were using imported equipment with dustproof and poison protection devices.

74. Ge and Qu, *Zhongguo mingongchao,* 155–56. A similar, if less graphic account appears in *MB,* January 30, 1991, 7, translated in FBIS, March 30, 1991, 67. Also, the Chinese scholar Jiang, in "The Prominent Role of Unions," 17, says the same thing: "To avoid influencing the environment for foreign investment, concerned departments shield the foreign side."

75. FBIS, March 30, 1991, 67, a translation of the *MB* article cited in note 74.

76. Walder, *Communist Neo-Traditionalism,* 11, thus describes the nature of the pre-reform calculation on the use of labor: "The system of planning and budgeting provides weak incentives to economize on costs of production, including labor."

77. John Philip Emerson, "The Labor Force of China, 1957–80," in Joint Economic Committee of the U.S. Congress, *China Under the Four Modernizations, Part I* (Washington, DC: Government Printing Office, 1982), 253. See also Walder, *Communist Neo-Traditionalism,* 50–51 and 54.

78. According to Li and Hu, *Liudong renkou,* 340, in 1986 the State Council issued a ruling permitting peasant labor in state-owned textile and silk enterprises, which could be invoked when there were insufficient recruitees in the cities and towns where the firms were based.

79. Officials from the Tianjin Textile Bureau said in a June 11, 1992 interview that beginning in 1991—the same year that the second set of State Council regulations were issued on the employment of peasant contract labor in state firms (see note 78, above), outsiders' wages began to come from the factories' budgets. There continued to be different parts of the budget designated for regular and for temporary, peasant labor, the latter of which they referred to as "off-plan," and yet the amount for the outsiders' wages was still set according to a plan and was still a part of the overall budget.

80. Ding, "Peasant Contract Labor's Wait," 18; interview at Tianjin No. 3 Silk Weaving Factory, June 18, 1992: "Without these girls we couldn't operate our machines"; Li and Hu, *Liudong renkou,* 37; and Wuhan shi, 140: The units are forced to rely on outside labor for the enterprises to go on, because city people won't do it; ibid., 150: There's a fear of heavy jobs with no one to do them"; and ibid., 140, on the building materials trade: "Present workers ask for a transfer, so, to maintain the enterprise, [management] is forced to rely on outsider labor for the firm to go on."

81. Li and Hu, *Liudong renkou,* 346.

82. This point is made in Howard, "Rice Bowls and Job Security," 100.

83. Interview, June 16, 1992.

84. Interview, June 18, 1992.

85. Li and Hu, *Liudong renkou,* 347.

86. *NFRB,* July 16, 1990, 1.

87. Ge and Qu, *Zhongguo mingongchao,* 157. Xinhua News Agency in late 1993 agreed: Foreign company employers often fail to implement the contracts signed with their employees. This is in FBIS, October 28, 1993, 45.

88. Jiang, "The Prominent Role of Unions," 17.

89. See note 78 above.

90. Interview at the Population Research Institute of the Guangdong Social Science Academy, May 11, 1992.

91. Jiang, "The Prominent Role of Unions," 17.

92. For references on this, see a State Council ruling of December 1981 restraining the entry of rural labor into the cities because of the recession then; on the 1989–1990 recession, see Howard, "Rice Bowls and Job Security," 104; Guo Zhengmo, "The Macroeconomic Background and Policy Toward the Present Phenomenon of 'Blindly Wandering' Rural Labor Forces," *Nongye wenti* [Agricultural issues], no. 7 (1989): 20; *MB,* January 29, 1990, translated in FBIS, February 7, 1990, 31; a Xinhua News Agency release about the Guangdong Labor Bureau translated in FBIS, March 9, 1990, 38; and *CD,* April 19, 1990, stating that Beijing will send home more laborers from the rural areas to provide work for the unemployed local residents.

93. On this, see Wuhan shi, 184, which contains a directive from Guangzhou on first ensuring that no one in the city can be hired for a particular position before hiring outsiders; and ibid., 194, a directive from Harbin of October 1987 of the same cast.

94. Interviews on June 11, June 16, and June 18, 1992, respectively.

95. "The Impact of the 'Floating Population' Surplus Labor," *Daxuesheng* [University student], no. 5 (May 10, 1990): 36–38, translated in Joint Publications Research Service, JPRS-CAR 90–054 (August 17, 1990): 44. Thanks to Regina Abrami for sending me this reference.

96. *NFRB,* December 14, 1988, 2.

97. Ge and Qu, *Zhongguo mingongchao,* 133.

98. Strikes by workers in state-owned firms protesting layoffs are reported in *MB,* January 23, 1994, translated in FBIS, January 24, 1994, 32 (which reports that "eventualities" in the second quarter of 1993 were 83.9 percent higher than in the same period in 1992, where "eventualities" refers to collective actions by more than ten persons in the form of strikes, collective slowdowns, sit-ins, etc., concerning the layoff of redundant labor power); in *China Focus,* November 1993 (quoting Ni Zhifu, the head of the All-China Federation of Trade Unions as stating that 13 million workers are jobless or forced to work part-time because of enterprises operating below capacity and that there had been about 400 work slowdowns, more than 200 strikes, and 68 demonstrations involving 500,000 workers in 25 provinces); in *South China Morning Post,* July 8, 1993, reprinted in FBIS, July 8, 1993, 19, stating that in the first half of 1993 there had been 190 strikes

and protests involving 50,000 workers; and in *ZM,* April 1993, 37, translated in FBIS, April 6, 1993, 66–67. A sample report of workers being dismissed in state firms is in FBIS, February 8, 1993, 26 (from Xinhua, February 7, 1993).

99. There are many official and foreign reports of strikes in foreign-funded firms. For a few examples, already in the summer of 1988 Beijing Domestic Service reported, "Since 1986 work stoppages and strikes by temporaries have occurred many times in Shenzhen" (translated in FBIS, August 23, 1988, 41). Two and a half years later, *MB* stated, "Work stoppages and strikes have occurred frequently in Shenzhen and Zhuhai recently. A total of 74 strikes involving nearly 10,000 men took place from June 1989 until the end of 1990, primarily in township and village enterprises and in foreign-capital enterprises" (translated in FBIS, March 30, 1991, 67). Ge and Qu, *Zhongguo mingongchao* 152, speak of strikes against Hong Kong–funded firms; and an AFP article from the autumn of 1993 told of strikes at Korean and Japanese factories, in Tianjin and Guangdong, respectively, translated in FBIS, September 28, 1993, 36. Mention of slowdowns, strikes, and collective hunger strikes appears in the work of the Chinese scholar Jiang Kelin (see Jiang, "The Prominent Role of Unions," 17).

100. The very systematic study by Parish et al., "Nonfarm Work and Marketization," comes to a similar, if much better documented, conclusion.

101. Although the replacement of permanents by temporaries is just what is occurring as urban youth desert the state manufacturing firms.

102. *CD,* March 6, 1993, 2, reprinted in FBIS, March 8, 1993. The article noted that, by the end of 1992, urban employment in China totaled 147.9 million, 2.8 million more than at the end of 1991, but that the number of people holding permanent jobs had fallen by 1.1 million to 76.9 million, with 2.7 million more people working under contracts than the year before, for a total of 18.6 million. The rest were holding temporary jobs. A similar report appeared in the *South China Morning Post,* October 23, 1992, 1, 3. In it the director of the World Economic Forum is quoted as having said, "It appeared that China would attempt to progress by developing the service industry to absorb unneeded industrial workers."

103. Castells and Portes, "World Underneath," 11.

104. Ibid., 33. "Unrestrained capital" gives no welfare benefits; "primary social networks" govern recruitment, so this statement returns us to our two original hypotheses.

9

Work Units and Housing Reform in Two Chinese Cities

Yanjie Bian, John R. Logan,
Hanlong Lu, Yunkang Pan, and Ying Guan

The Chinese system of housing provision is being reorganized as part of the market reform in progress since 1978. Important structural changes in the economy have occurred—the relaxation of central planning controls over investment, production, and distribution of goods; the emergence of a small private sector; and promotion of a much larger collective sector that behaves much like private enterprise (Lee 1988; Nee 1989, 1991; Fong 1990; Walder 1992). As has been the case in most other socialist countries (Szelenyi 1983; Szelenyi and Manchin 1987; Pickvance 1988), work units have played an important role in this system. Work units influenced who would receive housing, often making the final decision themselves. Increasingly over the years, work units also built and managed apartment complexes. This participation gave work units considerable leverage over the lives of their workers. Indeed, it might be argued that housing allocation was more important to employees than salaries, at least before the explosion of income inequality in the past five years (Walder 1992; Logan and Bian 1993; Bian 1994, chap. 8). Therefore the process of housing reform is of momentous concern to work-unit managers.

China's housing reform was initiated by Deng Xiaoping in April 1980. The basic idea was to commodify (but not necessarily privatize) public housing, so

Funding for the work presented in this chapter came from a National Science Foundation grant (SES-9209214) and from a grant-in-aid from the University of Minnesota Graduate School. We thank Deborah Davis for her helpful comments on an earlier draft.

that in the end the state can be released from its responsibility to provide housing as a welfare good. The theory was that the state should be separated from the economy, but the economy, including the real-estate industry, should operate under a "planned commodity" framework, or, in the words of Deng Xiaoping, "a market economy with a Chinese character." Financially, the state foresaw that, after a 1979 tax-for-profit reform in industry, enterprises would increasingly retain large profits, and, as a result, the state would no longer be able to generate sufficient funds for public housing as before. So, housing reform policy was a decision determined largely by the financial reforms in industry.

Dowell (1993), representing the viewpoint of the World Bank, argues that the goal of housing reform is "a commodity system of housing delivery, in which individuals and enterprises purchase units from real estate development corporations." In a report analyzing the first phases of China's urban housing reforms until 1989, economist George Tolley (1991) similarly suggests that a key to the transition from housing as welfare to commodified housing is to "divorce housing from work units" (92; see also Barlow 1988; Yang and Wang 1992). Work units, in a fully commodified system, would play no direct role in housing, but would simply provide the income stream through which employees finance home purchase or rental in the private market.

We present a different scenario here. Regardless of the "official" goal of housing reform, we argue:

1. that housing policies since 1978 have accentuated the direct role of work units in housing,
2. that work units have continued to rely on their control of the allocation process to attempt to reward their own employees, and
3. that there is little reason to expect the commodification of housing to disrupt this aspect of the system's operation.

There is a growing consensus that market reform has preserved some features of socialism, particularly the advantages of many members of the old political class. Party members and factory managers in the former Soviet bloc have discovered that their political connections and control over scarce resources are profitable (Staniszkis 1991; Burawoy and Krotov 1992). Privileged access to housing is one of the key mechanisms of such "commodification of redistributive privileges" in Hungary (Szelenyi and Manchin 1987, 120–21). Observers have pointed to many ways in which the gradual and partial reforms made by Chinese authorities have been absorbed into the existing institutional framework (Lin and Bian 1991; Lin and Hao 1992; Walder 1992; Chen and Gao 1993; Logan and Bian 1993; Shirk 1993; Bian 1994; Bian and Logan 1996; Zhou and Tuma 1994). Analysis of housing reform in China thus offers crucial insight into the changing system of stratification and privilege.

Housing as a Scarce Resource in Urban China

Before the market reform period, Chinese urban centers experienced growing housing shortages due to the bias of the state's investment policy against housing and its policy of maintaining low rents (Sun, Chen, and Li 1991). The proportion of basic construction investment funds allocated to housing declined from 9.1 percent in the mid-1950s to only 2.6 percent in 1970 during the Cultural Revolution. But from a modest 7.8 percent in 1978, the first year of market reform, it reached the height of 25.5 percent in 1991 (Lee 1988; Chen and Gao 1993). In most cities the past decade has seen unprecedented levels of new housing construction. Nationally, the average housing space was in the range of 4 square meters per person from 1950 to 1980, but by 1993 it had risen to 7.5 square meters (State Statistical Bureau 1994, 288).

Because housing remains largely a local phenomenon, subject to the historical, demographic, and political–economic factors in each city, as well as to the policies of the central government, it is useful to explore city differences as well as similarities in the relationship between work units and housing. Because conditions vary greatly from city to city, it is difficult to make generalizations that apply to all of urban China (Wang 1990). The specific cases that we study, Shanghai and Tianjin, are not representative of urban China. They do, however, have some attractions. Both offer a great variety of types and hierarchical levels of work units, differences in local housing policies and reform experiences, and regional variation between south (Shanghai) and north (Tianjin).

In order to assess the housing conditions of individual households, and to relate these to the characteristics of their work units, we rely largely on surveys that we organized in 1993. These include two sorts of surveys: (1) random sample surveys of about 1,050 residents in each city, and (2) surveys of the work units in which they were employed, yielding a total of about 500 cases in Shanghai and 350 in Tianjin. These surveys offer the most recent data for urban China on the characteristics of people's housing, the extent and nature of inequalities in housing among the population, the participation of work units in the housing system, and the progress of housing reform as seen from the perspective of both residents and employers.

A high proportion of respondents indicated dissatisfaction with their current housing situation. In Tianjin, 54 percent indicated that they were "not very satisfied" or "not satisfied," and the percentage is even higher for Shanghai (67 percent). These responses are especially surprising in light of the strong bias toward positive or neutral responses in Chinese surveys, partly because most are conducted by government agencies. A more specific question asked about satisfaction (on a five-point scale) with a set of fifteen characteristics of people's jobs. Only 12 percent in Tianjin and 5 percent in Shanghai indicated that they were "very" or "fairly" satisfied with housing allocation by their employer, compared to more than 30 percent in both cities who were "very unsatisfied" or "not very satisfied." Of all fifteen job characteristics, housing allocation had the lowest or second-lowest satisfaction level in both cities (next to opportunity for promotion or for a salary raise).

Dissatisfaction is rooted in the difficulty that younger people have in getting their own apartments, the small size of apartments (particularly when multiple generations of family members must live together), and the lack of basic amenities such as kitchens and bathrooms. Size and facilities are the two factors that people give most weight to with respect to housing. Given a list of eleven criteria that would affect their willingness to change their current home, the highest proportion of respondents (70 percent in Tianjin and 71 percent in Shanghai) listed increased living space as a factor that they would "consider highly." A majority (52 percent in Tianjin, 69 percent in Shanghai) listed improved housing facilities. Therefore we focus our attention on these two characteristics. (The next most important was proximity to work, listed by close to half in both cities; such factors as convenient transportation, neighborhood environment, and proximity to shopping or other services were ranked much lower.)

Chinese authorities are sensitive to the issue of overcrowding and give priority to finding new housing for those who are in the worst circumstances. But although there was a broad expansion of the housing stock in the 1980s, following the end of the Cultural Revolution, local governments' criterion for identifying "hardship" cases is typically set at around 4 square meters per person. This means that four persons living in a single room about 12 feet square are at the margin of "hardship." In fact, as of 1993 about 15 percent of respondents in each city live in less than that amount of space. The average living space provides about 6 or 7 square meters per person. This compares with national figures that show that average living space per person has increased from 3.6 square meters in 1978, to 6.0 in 1986, 6.9 in 1990, and 7.5 in 1993 (State Statistical Bureau 1994, 288).

Table 9.1 shows that crowding is highly related to dissatisfaction with one's current housing. In Shanghai, the percentage "not satisfied" or "not very satisfied" ranges from about 91 percent among those with less than 4 square meters to only 36 percent among those few who have more than 12 square meters per person. In Tianjin, this relationship is somewhat less pronounced.

A related issue is squeezing more than one generation of family members into a single room. Current standards recognize hardship when members of three or more generations (that is, parents, their adult children, and their grandchildren) share a room. More common is having two generations in one room or three generations in two rooms (the latter, of course, is considered preferable because it allows some privacy at least to one married couple in the household). The majority of respondents in both cities have at least this degree of crowding (55 percent in Shanghai, 50 percent in Tianjin, of whom 9 percent in Shanghai and 5 percent in Tianjin have three or more generations per room). Crowding measured in this way is also highly related to housing dissatisfaction.

Table 9.1

Housing Dissatisfaction (percentage "not satisfied" or "not very satisfied" with their housing condition, by space per person and kitchen and toilet facilities; sample *n* in parentheses)

	Shanghai	Tianjin
Size of housing unit per person:		
Under 4 sq. m.	90.9 (154)	88.0 (166)
4–6 sq. m.	81.9 (365)	76.3 (240)
6–8 sq. m.	65.5 (232)	53.4 (191)
8–12 sq. m.	44.6 (157)	41.1 (219)
More than 12 sq. m.	36.2 (119)	20.2 (193)
Kitchen:		
None	86.8 (174)	83.8 (191)
Shared	85.3 (307)	81.1 (90)
Private	53.3 (546)	45.3 (736)
Toilet:		
Public	80.3 (372)	66.5 (579)
Shared	79.0 (238)	79.7 (74)
Private	51.0 (404)	32.9 (355)

About half of Shanghai respondents and nearly three-fourths of Tianjin respondents reported that they have a private kitchen (typically a closet-sized space for cooking) in their apartment. Some share a kitchen facility with others (as in a hallway), while others have no separate space at all. A private bathroom is less common. In Shanghai, 41 percent have a private bathroom, 23 percent have a shared bathroom, and the remainder (36 percent) must use a chamber pot or public toilet. In Tianjin, only 42 percent have a private or shared bathroom. These figures are much higher than those cited by Whyte and Parish (1984) for the mid-1970s.

These basic facilities, which are taken for granted in major Western cities, are not yet "standard" for a substantial share of Chinese urban residents. Like overcrowding, they are a major source of dissatisfaction (again see Table 9.1). In Tianjin, for example, 84 percent of persons with no kitchen are "not satisfied" or "not very satisfied" with their housing, compared to 45 percent of those with a private kitchen; the figures are 66 percent for persons with no bathroom and 33 percent for persons with a private bathroom. Results for Shanghai are comparable.

Thus, although housing overcrowding is declining and apartments are becoming better equipped, compared to the prereform period, improved conditions are still not yet at the level expected by most urban residents. Many families still live in poor conditions and high-quality housing continues to be an extremely scarce resource in much of urban China.

The Role of the Work Unit in Public Housing

The role of work units in housing has evolved considerably since the foundation of a socialist system in 1949 (Tang 1994). The pattern of home ownership and private rental markets was greatly altered at that time. In the early 1950s, the new government took over all real estate whose owners either had left China because of the Communist revolution or were forced as the subjects of the revolution to turn over their properties including housing. These were single-family homes and rental properties, forming the first noncommercial housing stock owned by the state. In Shanghai, the municipal government was able to include nearly all the housing stock under its direct control and turned it into state-owned rental units (Ye et al. 1993, 114). In Tianjin, some housing was retained by government agencies and other powerful organizations, although the rest became the rental property of the municipal government.

In 1956 and 1958, in accordance with the Socialist Reform of Capitalist Enterprises in Industry and Commerce, a parallel reform was launched to transform small-scale private rental homes into state-owned housing throughout China. Some home owners were forced to sell their "surplus" housing to government agencies or organizations in which they worked. This was repeated during the Cultural Revolution (1966–76), but this time the owners' work units usually took over their homes without compensation. Some of these houses were returned to the original owners after 1978 as part of a government policy to correct wrongdoings of the Cultural Revolution.

Parallel to the state takeover of existing private housing was the state monopoly in land use and housing investments under the umbrella of public ownership. In Shanghai, private funds accounted for 85 percent of total new housing investment in 1950, but declined to 12 percent in 1958, to 6 percent in 1976 (the end of the Cultural Revolution), and to 2 percent in 1990. (The decline in the 1980s occurred in spite of a threefold increase in private investment.) As a result, private housing became a small share of total housing. For example, Shanghai's private housing was 71 percent of the total housing stock in 1950. In 1958, it declined to 32 percent, and it was only 24 percent of the total in 1976. By 1990 private housing had increased in absolute volume, but it accounted for only 21 percent of the total at that time (Ye et al. 1993, 114, 149). The 1990 figure was higher than Tianjin's (14 percent) but close to the 24 percent for forty-one large Chinese cities (Yang and Wang 1992, 89).

Work unit housing comprises the largest share of the public housing stock. As commonly understood in the research literature (Whyte and Parish 1984; Walder 1992; Logan and Bian 1993), this is housing that is owned, managed, and distributed by work units to their employees as an employment benefit. This "traditional" definition, however, identifies only the most visible category of work unit housing. Ownership, allocation, and management are actually separate dimensions of property rights, and they do not necessarily coincide with one another. A full account of work unit housing must include the following categories:

1. *Work unit–managed housing (danwei fang).* This category refers to housing that is managed by a particular work unit, such as a factory, a school, a store, or a government office. When housing is managed by the work unit, it must have been owned and allocated by the work unit. In this sense, this category meets the traditional definition of work unit housing. Historically, large work units in industry, especially those that are managed by central ministries, have this type of work unit housing.

2. *System-managed housing (xitong fang).* The term *system* here refers to the bureaucratic system with which a work unit is officially identified and affiliated. For example, a railroad bureau and its subordinate work units comprise a system. When the bureau develops collective housing projects within the system, it owns, allocates, and manages its housing stock. Although its subordinate work units are allocated apartments from these projects, they neither own nor manage the apartments in which their employees live. The bureau does it all on their behalf. In Shanghai and Tianjin, as in other cities, system-managed housing is a popular type for those systems whose work units are small and scattered throughout the city (e.g., education, commerce, and service sectors). Types 1 and 2 combined are identified as "work unit self-managed housing" (*ziguan fang*) in the official statistics.

3. *Work unit–allocated housing (danwei fenpei fang).* Public housing is often managed by the municipal housing office, regardless of who built or owns it. It was common in Tianjin before 1978 and in both Tianjin and Shanghai after 1978 for housing to be built and allocated to employees by a work unit, but for management to be contracted to the local housing office. In other cases, housing built by the government, the system, or the work unit is owned by the municipal government. Work units are given the right to allocate those housing units to which they are entitled (in terms of needs, financial contributions to municipal housing projects, etc.), but all the housing stock is managed by the municipal government (its housing bureau). This practice predominated in Shanghai's public housing before 1980 (although ministry-run work units operated their own housing). This third category is excluded from the traditional definition of work unit housing as well as from the official classification, although it is especially important in Shanghai and Tianjin.

These distinctions point to two aspects of possible work unit participation in housing. The first is direct ownership and management; the second is allocation of the municipal stock. A third form of participation has become important during the reform period. Previously, even when work units organized housing construction projects and paid for them out of their own budgets, the actual source of funds was the central government. State enterprises (but not collectives) were eligible to receive funds specifically earmarked for housing investment, and the amount of funding was related to the bureaucratic rank and size of the enterprise (Lee 1988; Yang and Wang 1992). Since 1978, there has been a substantial shift in the work unit role, from being a manager of state housing funds to taking responsibility for investment decisions out of their own budgets. Even in Shanghai, where most public housing has historically been managed by the municipality, as early as 1980, more than half (55 percent) of new investment capital for public housing construction was raised by work units. This figure has increased steadily (to around 70 percent in the mid-1980s and up to 86 percent in 1990) (see Ye et al. 1993, 101). At the national level, in 1983 work unit funds accounted for 57 percent of total new housing investment, compared to 26 percent from the state and 17 percent from private individuals (Yang and Wang 1992).

Despite recent trends, in both Shanghai and Tianjin the majority of public housing is owned and managed by the municipality. Comparing the two cities based on residents' reports of the source of their housing, work unit housing is much more important in Tianjin (28 percent of the total housing stock) than in Shanghai (only 15 percent). This difference also appears in the proportion of respondents whose work units have housing complexes (58 percent in Tianjin and 34 percent in Shanghai) or have built new housing since 1980 (50 percent in Tianjin vs. 25 percent in Shanghai).

These figures can be compared to national and city totals reported officially (see Yang and Wang 1992). In urban China as a whole in 1990, 59 percent of housing space was in work unit housing, and there was less in municipal housing (16 percent) than was privately held (24 percent). Beijing had a greater than average predominance of work-unit housing space (68 percent), while Tianjin (39 percent) was lower than average and Shanghai (12 percent) was extraordinarily low. In both the latter cities, municipal housing took up most of the remaining stock; no more than 20 percent was private. Therefore in evaluating the work unit's role in housing, it is especially relevant in these two cities to consider not only the residences that they own and manage but also their influence over the allocation of municipal housing.

Inequality in Housing

Although housing has long been treated as a public good in China, with only a small proportion of the urban housing stock under private ownership, that does not mean that it was equitably distributed. In this respect, China has been remarkably similar to other socialist societies (see Szelenyi 1983). In Tianjin, for example, we find that the top 10 percent of households (these are people with 50 square meters or more) occupy 21.8 percent of the total space, while the bottom 10 percent (those in units of less than 11 square meters) occupy only 3.3 percent of the total space. While these disparities are probably small in comparison with market societies, they are very salient to the people at the top and the bottom of the scale in China.

Inequalities stem in part from allocation policies within work units: Not only seniority and family status, but also workers' formal administrative authority, party membership, political connections, and occupational standing affected the selection of persons lucky enough to be assigned an apartment. They also result from inequalities between work units, especially in the distribution of housing investment: Government agencies and state enterprises have received the bulk of public investment in housing, which they were free to direct toward their own employees (Lee 1988; Walder 1992; Logan and Bian 1993; Chen and Gao 1993; Bian 1994, chap. 8). Both sources of inequality provide insight into the functioning of work units.

Allocation Standards

It is well known among scholars that housing space is allocated according to people's administrative standing. Yang and Wang (1992) report that the standards for work-unit housing in the prereform period called for 42–45 square meters for workers, 45–50 for cadres, 60–70 for cadres at the division level, and 80–90 for cadres at higher levels (*chu ji*). Partly for this reason, housing inequality is also associated with income. The State Statistical Bureau reported that, as late as 1985, households in the top 20 percent of the income distribution had about a third more floor space than other households and were also more likely to have running water, a separate kitchen, and sanitary facilities (cited in Logan and Bian 1993). Another survey showed that a third of households with per capita income of less than 80 yuan lived in crowded housing (i.e., less than 4 square meters per person), but only 8 percent of households with per capita income of 120 yuan or more lived in such crowded housing. Moreover, about 20 percent of cadres below the bureau rank lived in crowded housing, while no cadres above the bureau rank lived in crowded housing. The administrative allocation of housing reinforced a new privileged class (Whyte and Parish 1984; Walder 1986).

Confirming such patterns at the national level, we found that administrators in Tianjin enjoyed nearly twice as much space per capita (24.4 square meters) as low-level manual workers (14.8 square meters), and they were also considerably more likely to have a private kitchen and toilet. There are similar but smaller differences in Shanghai.

Our respondents are aware of such disparities, and only 36 percent in Tianjin and 25 percent in Shanghai consider housing allocation procedures in their work unit "very fair" or "fair." Nonetheless, when asked to rate criteria for housing allocation (for either work-unit or municipal housing) by their importance, respondents reported that the highest weight should be given to criteria reflecting needs (the condition of one's current housing, being married but without separate housing, or being engaged to marry and without separate housing). In addition, Tianjin respondents reported that considerable weight is given to one's age and seniority in the workplace, but these were ranked fairly low by Shanghai respondents. Complementing these findings, in our survey of work unit officials the "condition of current housing" and living in a three-generation household were by far the most important criteria in both cities. On a four-point scale, more than half the work units in both cities reported that seniority in the unit, one's work performance (49 percent in Shanghai), and being married or engaged (and without independent housing) were "very important" or "important" factors.

Curiously, both bureaucratic considerations (position on the waiting list) and political criteria (administrative position or Communist Party membership) were assigned only low to moderate importance by individual respondents. A majority of Tianjin work units stated that the "opinion of work unit leaders" is an important factor. But this factor was generally denied in Shanghai, and work units in both cities stated that such factors as administrative position or party membership were unimportant. A different picture emerged, however, when individuals were asked how various "strategies would work for you in getting a better residence." Use of indirect connections (help from parents, relatives, or friends) is considered to be of value by very few respondents. Direct action, including changing jobs, exchanging with others, and renting private housing, is similarly given little importance. Clearly at the top in both cities are to "maintain a good relationship" with "the leaders in charge" and with "the housing committee" of the work unit. Also rated fairly high is obtaining help from one's direct supervisor or from the work unit leader. These results reflect people's awareness of the political character of allocation decisions.

Allocation criteria are not static but change from year to year. These changes not only correspond to current government policies on what groups should be given priority but, more importantly, reflect the changing political structure within the work unit. Housing has been a sensitive and perhaps the most important reward to workers, and, in most work units we interviewed, leaders must distribute it according to allocation criteria that have been discussed and approved by managers, labor union officials, and the congress of workers' representatives. However, work unit leaders are influential participants. Usually, a task force is appointed by the work unit director to draft or revise a previous document to specify the allocation criteria to be used in the present year. Within the limitation of available housing to be allocated, a key issue to be resolved by the task force is to figure out who should be given a new or bigger apartment. Allocation criteria are set accordingly.

An example of this "backward justification" procedure comes from an interview with a woman who was a member of the task force designated to revise her work unit's housing allocation criteria in 1987:

> One of the many difficult cases that we [the 1987 task force] handled successfully was that of Mr. T. He who was transferred from another work unit two years ago and did not have the five-year tenure that was a necessary condition to

receive an apartment from the work unit. However, he was promised a housing unit when the director persuaded him to transfer. More importantly, Mr. T worked with the director very closely since he came, and the director very much wanted to provide a housing unit to him as promised. We worked hard to find a way to create a new criterion that only Mr. T would qualify for. This should be carefully done because housing was very limited and we must not leave a big hole that would allow other people to qualify. In the end, the new criterion was that 'employees with a degree of graduate school who are recently transferred from other work units (within five years) and whose spouses' residence is in the countryside are eligible applicants and are given the priority.' This was created solely for Mr. T.

Inequalities Between Work Units

Under the traditional system, the main source of investment for public housing came from the state annual budget for basic construction projects—projects to build new productive, commercial, and service facilities. These projects were not exclusively for new establishments. Expansions of existing workplaces made up a large part of this budget. The second source is the state budget for maintaining and renovating existing facilities. This budget was as small as 4 percent of the basic construction budget in the 1950s, but since then had increased to 25 percent in 1978 (State Statistical Bureau 1984, 301). In both budgets, a category for residential housing was created for building public apartments that in principle were to be used by the families of the workers hired to work on the new, expanded, or renovated facilities. The budgets for residential housing development varied from year to year and within each year across projects, depending on political decisions to favor production or consumption. In general, a larger proportion was budgeted for housing development in the basic construction funds than in the maintenance and renovation funds.

State-owned work units were the main recipients of both state budgets and therefore also of housing development funds. But large-scale collectives might also receive these funds because their projects for plant development and renovation were included in state economic plans (Yang and Wang 1992, 71). This investment structure determines that the more investments a work unit receives for constructing or renovating its facilities, the greater the likelihood it will obtain housing development funds from the state. Because more investment means more values built into the facilities and probably more hiring, this investment structure further implies that work units with higher-valued assets or larger numbers of employees received larger housing development funds.

Larger housing development funds did not necessarily mean more or better housing units built for the work units that received these funds. All the work units, whether government agencies, nonprofit organizations, or productive and commercial enterprises, were under the jurisdiction of the government bureaucracy that made all the decisions concerning the use of these (and any other) funds received (see Bian 1994, chapter 2). Work units managed by central ministries, however, were likely to use their housing development funds directly themselves for two reasons. First, central ministries in Beijing could not possibly manage housing construction projects for their work units, located throughout China; these projects had to be operated on a local basis. Second, the work units managed by central ministries tended to have high administrative ranking, which gave them the bureaucratic power to maintain their autonomy from the possible intervention by local governments in their housing development projects. As a result, central ministry–managed work units tended to have independent work unit housing compounds in all the cities, including Tianjin and Shanghai.

Local work units, state and collective alike, were subjected to housing policies of the local governments. In Shanghai, where the housing shortage was a serious problem from 1958 to 1979, Ye et al. (1993, 103–13) documented that central and local work units were subject to a dual system concerning the management of housing development funds. The central work units managed their funds independently from the municipal government, although their housing construction was included in the plans of the municipal housing development. Local work units' housing funds, however, were managed by the municipal government. Under the "six togetherness" principles for planning, investment, design, construction, distribution, and management, the municipal government reacquired all the housing development funds that had been part of their investment in building new or renovating existing work units. Some apartments went to the work units that had contributed large amounts of housing funds to the municipal housing projects, but most of these apartments went to high-ranking civil service cadres whose families also lived below the standard established by the central government (which assigned more space to higher-ranked cadres).

Tianjin, more exemplary of urban China in terms of housing management strategies, used a less centralized model, allowing work units to develop their own housing projects parallel to those of the municipal government. However, except for central ministry–managed work units, few enterprises and institutions developed independent housing projects, but these projects were developed by their government jurisdictions on their behalf. For example, the municipal bureau of education would retain housing funds for the organizations under its direct jurisdiction, used these funds either to build housing compounds or purchase a cluster of apartments from municipal housing projects, and allocated housing units to employees in these organizations as well as the headquarters of the bureau. Education bureaus in the nine city districts would do the same within their districts. Similar practices were replicated in other bureau systems at both municipal and district levels. Allocation of housing built by these various "systems" favored higher-ranked work units, with the result that housing was allocated from higher- to lower-level work units.

In summary, the pre-1978 housing system favored work units that were (1) in the state sector, (2) managed by central ministries, and (3) local, with a higher bureaucratic rank.

Our survey data allow us to compare several aspects of work unit participation in housing: whether they have their own housing complexes (or compounds), whether they have built housing for their employees since 1980, and what share of their workers live in work unit vs. municipal housing. We compare different kinds of work units, based on their size, bureaucratic rank, and economic sector (e.g., government agencies vs. state enterprises or collectives). For these analyses, we use only respondents who are leaseholders and for whom we have information on work unit characteristics.

Table 9.2 reports the relationship between size, rank, and sector and all four housing indicators. We find that almost all of these are significant (as measured by analysis of variance). In both cities, larger work units are more likely to have their own compounds and to have built housing since 1980. At the extreme, 98 percent of the largest work units in Tianjin (those with more than 5,000 employees) have housing compounds and all of them have built housing. The pattern is the same in Shanghai although, as we have seen, the overall percentages are lower. In consequence, larger work units have a lower proportion of their employees in municipal housing and a higher proportion in work unit housing. With only one exception, however—the largest work units in Tianjin—a majority of workers are in municipal housing.

The effects of work unit rank are also considerable, but they are not felt across the entire range of ranks. The main difference is between those at the bureau level or higher and all others. For example, in Shanghai, unranked work units actually are more likely to have housing compounds than those ranked sector or below; but the highest-ranked work units clearly surpass all others.

Finally, the economic sector that the work unit is in has significant effects in Tianjin and, for most variables, also in Shanghai. In Tianjin, it is clearly state enterprises that are most likely to own and build work-unit housing, and enterprises have the highest proportion (though not a majority) of workers in work unit housing. Government agencies stand out at the opposite end. Although they may have recently built work unit housing, they are unlikely (only 23 percent) to have work unit compounds, and nearly all their workers are housed in municipally owned residences. Other types of work units, whether nonprofit organizations, collectives, or the miscellaneous category that we have termed the "new sector," fall in between.

Shanghai presents a similar pattern in terms of the contrast between enterprises and government agencies. There are two unique characteristics for Shanghai. First, nonprofit organizations stand out among the other categories for high participation in work unit (as opposed to municipal) housing. Second, the overall preponderance of municipal over work unit housing results in relatively small sectoral differences in the percentage of workers who are in these two types of housing.

In assessing the sources of work unit differences in housing, we found fairly small differences between Shanghai and Tianjin. Size, rank, and sector all play

Table 9.2

Ability of work Unit Providing Housing by Work-Unit Characteristics
(in percent)

	Work unit complexes	Built housing	% municipal	% work unit
Tianjin				
Size:				
Less than 100	45.0***	46.4***	69.3***	18.2***
101–500	55.9	55.1	71.8	19.7
501–1,000	75.0	69.1	62.4	25.9
1,001–5,000	83.7	90.1	51.5	36.0
More than 5,000	98.4	100	23.1	69.2
Rank:				
No rank	67.6**	76.3***	60.7***	29.8***
Sector or lower	66.7	64.7	68.3	23.8
Division	69.0	67.3	60.2	30.7
Bureau or higher	86.5	94.1	41.0	51.3
Sector:				
Government agencies	23.1***	36.4***	87.1***	6.5***
Nonprofit organization	56.4	60.9	69.9	24.1
State enterprise	80.3	80.1	50.9	38.3
Collective enterprise	59.1	62.2	66.0	14.0
New sector	53.3	28.6	72.2	11.1
Shanghai				
Size:				
Less than 100	7.5***	8.1***	80.8*	7.7***
10—500	22.5	22.4	77.0	7.0
501–1,000	53.0	44.8	77.3	17.3
1,001–5,000	65.1	46.2	70.8	19.8
More than 5, 000	74.3	78.8	57.5	30.0
Rank:				
No rank	51.0***	38.6***	73.8**	14.8***
Sector or lower	29.9	20.3	77.5	8.5
Division	45.6	36.6	75.0	15.0
Bureau or higher	79.5	73.8	54.9	39.2
Sector:				
Government agencies	15.4***	23.1***	92.9	7.1*
Nonprofit organization	36.7	36.3	70.1	20.6
State enterprise	56.5	46.5	71.2	16.0
Collective enterprise	22.5	18.8	76.5	7.8
New sector	22.2	20.0	84.0	4.0

*$p<.1$; **$p<.05$; ***$p<.01$.

important roles in determining how directly work units participate in housing construction and ownership. There are much greater differences between the two cities in the degree to which these factors affect housing outcomes for employees. Let us consider specifically housing space and facilities. Besides the provision of a kitchen and toilet, we also have information on four other facilities: water, fuel, bathtub, and shower. These have been summed into a scale whose values range potentially from zero to ten, as follows: kitchen (0 = no; 1 = shared; 2 = private), bathroom (0 = public; 1 = shared; 2 = private), water (same code as bathroom), fuel (0 = coal stove; 1 = liquefied gas; 2 = piped gas), bathtub (0 = no; 1 = yes), and shower (0 = no; 1 = yes). Table 9.3 provides the average values of these two variables for persons employed by various kinds of work units.

In Tianjin, several of these relationships are significant. Workers in larger work units have only a slight floor space advantage, but larger work units have a considerable advantage in terms of facilities. Work unit rank is consistently and strongly related to both outcomes. Remarkably, employees of nonranked work units have only about 23 square meters of space, compared to about 36 square meters for employees of high-ranking work units. There are also clear sectoral differences in floor space. In this case, however, the advantage is held by employees of government agencies and nonprofit organizations (or the few new-sector units), while both collectives and state enterprises apparently offer less space.

By contrast, in Shanghai few of the differences are statistically significant. There is only a slight pattern of more space and facilities for larger work units. Rank has no effect on space, and the significant relationship with facilities is complicated by the fairly high value for nonranked work units. Government agencies seem to offer more space (though not significant) and facilities than other work units, but otherwise there are no clear sectoral differences.

These varying results for two major cities illustrate the decentralization and local peculiarities in China's housing system. We first thought that the differences could be accounted for by the unusually small share of work unit housing in Shanghai. Privileged work units, after all, are more likely to provide housing in both Tianjin and Shanghai. Perhaps this advantage translates into better residences only for those who live in work unit housing. Indeed, when we look separately at residents of work unit and municipal housing, there is a clear advantage in both cities to those in work unit housing: Their apartments are about 20 percent larger and rate a point or two higher on the facilities scale. But the advantages of larger, high-ranking work units are still apparent in Tianjin regardless of the type of housing. That is, for example, high-ranked work units provide larger and better-equipped work unit housing to their employees, and they also apparently allocate larger and better-equipped municipal housing. These work unit characteristics have little impact in Shanghai on either type of housing.

Another hypothesis that we considered is that much of Shanghai's public investment went toward rebuilding old temporary housing that had been

Table 9.3

**Average Housing Space and Facilities of Residents
by Characteristics of Their Work Unit**

	Space (sq. m.)	Facilities
Tianjin		
Size:		
Less than 100	29.38	5.20[***]
101–500	26.62	5.78
501–1,000	27.57	5.76
1,001–5,000	30.07	6.18
More than 5,000	31.78	7.05
Rank:		
No rank	22.60[***]	.14[***]
Sector or lower	26.82	5.73
Division	29.49	6.09
Bureau or higher	35.96	7.00
Sector:		
Government agencies	33.77[***]	5.65
Nonprofit organization	32.24	6.31
State enterprise	27.56	5.96
Collective enterprise	25.21	5.42
New sector	33.56	5.72
Shanghai		
Size:		
Less than 100	20.52	5.85
101–500	22.30	5.86
501–1,000	22.71	6.51
1,001–5,000	22.73	6.65
More than 5,000	25.91	6.50
Rank:		
No rank	24.13	6.57[***]
Sector or lower	21.38	5.62
Division	23.28	6.86
Bureau or higher	23.48	7.35
Sector:		
Government agencies	26.20	7.57[*]
Nonprofit organization	21.75	6.63
State enterprise	23.05	6.02
Collective enterprise	23.95	5.86
New sector	27.29	6.36

[*]$p<.1$; [**]$p<.05$; [***]$p<.01$.

constructed before 1949. It has been argued that the municipal government favored plans to renovate old residential areas where there was high concentration of working-class families. The municipal government retained ownership, allocation, and management rights to such housing. It was preferentially distributed to the previous residents in the renovated areas and to hardship cases (i.e., two married couples, three generations, or adult siblings of opposite sexes shared a single bedroom; less than 2 square meters per household member). To the extent that these policies were followed, work units would have little impact on housing allocations. But only 17 percent of the housing investment from 1950 to 1971 was used in this way, and a much lower percentage was found for more recent years. Other forces were probably at play.

Our tentative view is that the key factor is the greater degree of centralization of housing allocation within Shanghai, reflecting in part the greater control that the central government exercised over Shanghai compared to other large cities. We note that Shanghai was the most important regional source of income for the central government budget (about one-sixth of total income from 1956 to 1980). It was in the interest of central planners that local and work unit budgets be controlled by municipal authorities. Thus, for example, for many years local work units could not retain any housing investment funds; these funds were controlled directly by the municipal government.

Shanghai was also the only major city (Yang and Wang 1992) where rent levels were kept sufficiently high to cover the maintenance costs of public housing. In fact, there were "surpluses" after expenses for maintenance and managerial costs. From 1949 to 1990, Shanghai's government was able to retain about 30 percent of public rents for new housing projects (5.6 percent), city infrastructure projects (2.2 percent), investment in nonhousing production (6.7 percent), and surpluses that were passed on to the state in the forms of "turnovers" (2.8 percent) and taxes (12.1 percent) (Ye et al. 1993, 113). This does not mean that Shanghai's rents had been maintained at a "market" level. But, compared with many other cities, including Tianjin, rents were a financial incentive for Shanghai's government to exercise a monopoly position in public housing.

The same motivation might have led work units to attempt to gain control. But we note that Shanghai's leadership has traditionally been very responsive to central government leadership, whether under left-wing Communists who were loyal to Mao (Ke Qingshi from the mid-1950s to the mid-1960s and Zhang Chunqiao in 1966–76) or under reformers loyal to Deng Xiaoping (Jiang Zemin in the 1980s). We believe that the centralized housing system that was implemented in 1957 through 1980 was backed by local leaders as a signal to Mao of their efforts to make Shanghai a more socialist place. Thus, newly constructed housing units were allocated to cadres according to their civil service ranks (to meet the national standard), to model workers who were politically loyal and ideologically "purer," and to those families who were in great need of housing (Ye et al. 1993, 103). From 1950 to 1969 (but except for 1961 and 1962), about 95 percent of the new housing stock was distributed to families in housing hardships (Ye et al. 1993, 150). And when housing was allocated through work units, the work units were given little discretion in carrying out municipal policy.

Housing Reform in the Early 1990s

As noted above, China has experimented with the introduction of market mechanisms in the allocation of housing among urban residents. In the redistributive socialist system, housing was treated as a welfare good, with rents that did not even cover essential maintenance costs. Since 1993, rents have been raised substantially, with various forms of subsidies offered to enable residents to absorb the cost. Attempts have been made to commodify housing, promoting acquisition of public housing by tenants, although clearly this has proved to be a more difficult policy to implement. The old housing institutions are not being overturned quickly.

Because enterprises were expected to retain large profits, and these profits would be turned partly into work unit welfare funds (mainly for housing and health benefits) and partly into wages (bonuses and other incentive payments), the first housing reform policy in 1980 was proposed with the slogan that "the state, the work unit, and individuals share the responsibilities" (*guojia, jiti, geren gongtong fudan*) for housing investments, projecting that each would contribute one-third of the investment in new housing projects. Although this specific division proved unworkable, the general principle for a tripartite investment structure was reinforced by the state throughout the 1980s and in its most recent reform directives.

The past decade saw a drastic reduction in state housing funds, but funds from individual families did not grow as projected simply because wages were very low. (The average yearly wage for urban employees was 826 yuan in 1983, compared with the then-projected price of 10,000 yuan for a median quality apartment of 40 square meters [State Statistical Bureau 1984, 331, 455].) From 1986 to 1988, several cities, not including Shanghai and Tianjin, experimented to increase wages proportionally in order for wage earners to pay for increased rents, but this one-time effort proved to be unsuccessful as these increases were happening mainly in the accounting books of one's work unit. The state also tried to sell its housing stock in most cities including Shanghai and Tianjin, first in 1983–85 and then in 1988–89, but given the low wages, few families could afford to own a home. They were not motivated to own a home either, because that would mean losing the privilege to live in a subsidized apartment. When prices were reduced below construction costs to promote sales, distribution was controlled by influential cadres who quickly swallowed nearly all the housing units on the "market" (Yang and Wang 1992, 5–6; similar experiences have been found with other commodities, such as the opening of the stock market in Shanghai and Shenzhen). This type of "commodified housing" was short-lived.

Nevertheless, a significant change in the 1980s with lasting effects was that work units, particularly industrial enterprises, became the most important investor in urban housing. Indeed, work units not only developed their own housing compounds but became the main buyer in the emerging housing market.

Starting in 1991, new housing reforms were initiated by the state. The principal document was the State Council's "Opinions Concerning an All-Around Promotion of Housing Reforms in Cities and Towns" (State Council 1991). The main reform directives are summarized as follows:

1. Raising rents to the simple production level (to cover costs in maintenance, management, and depreciation) by 1995, to the semicommodity level (adding mortgage interest and property tax) by 2000, and finally to the commodity level (adding insurance, land use, and profits) in the long run. Note that, because 70 percent of housing is owned by work units, work units will play an important role in this project.

2. Encouraging residents to purchase their current housing (from their work units or from the municipality). Priority is given primarily to the sale of new housing (to employees of the selling work units) and only secondarily to leasing (also to employees).

3. Establishing "public funds for housing," which are collected by the city government from work units (5 percent of their wage bills) and workers (5 percent of their wages). The workers are the formal "owners" of these funds, but their use is actually controlled by work units.

4. Reinforcing the tripartite investment structure but specifying each role: Work units and individuals initiate and the state assists with supplemental funds.

5. Gradually changing into a "socialized management system of public housing," indicating that the public ownership may not be altered but that residential properties should be managed by "community organizations" or "economic entities that join together the housing offices of work units."

Commodification and Privatization

What have been the actual effects of these reforms in Shanghai and Tianjin? First, rents have risen sharply. Of those who pay any rent, the median monthly rent per household for Tianjin in 1991 was 4 yuan, which rose to 10 yuan in 1993. In Shanghai the median was 5 yuan, rising to 10 yuan in 1993. Rents have become more closely related to floor space. In Tianjin the correlation between housing unit size and rent in 1991 was .46, increasing to .67 in 1993. In Shanghai this correlation rose from .43 to .58 in two years. At least in this respect, rents are now much more closely aligned with apartments' market value.

Raising rents and linking them more closely with the quality of the apartment can in themselves have substantial consequences. They introduce new market constraints on housing consumption and new complications in a system that has traditionally favored certain categories of workers. An example is reported for a major automobile manufacturer (Second Automobile Manufacturer 1992). Housing reform beginning in 1989 has raised rents to a "quasi-cost" level, from less than 1 yuan monthly for a 40–square-meter apartment to more than 50 yuan. Simultaneously, the firm provided all employees with housing subsidies equal to 23 percent of their base salary. In consequence, the firm reports that people have reduced their expectations for newer or larger housing, and they may be more willing to consider purchasing their apartments (at subsidized prices). The hierarchy in housing allocation has also been undermined: Division-level cadres and others have become less likely to apply for larger apartments, even when they qualify for more space under state standards.

Despite the "commodification" of rents, privatization of housing is moving slowly in these cities. Of the ninety private homeowners in the Tianjin sample who did not simply inherit their homes (representing 8.6 percent of the total housing stock), only six had purchased since 1991 and only nineteen had purchased since 1978. In Shanghai, of 126 such homeowners (11.9 percent of the total housing stock), again only 6 had purchased in 1988 or later, with 21 since 1978. Most of these ownerships predate the Cultural Revolution.

Further, only 15 percent of Shanghai respondents and 8 percent of Tianjin respondents report that their work unit has begun to sell housing to employees. And only 3–4 percent of renters plan to purchase their own housing within the next five years.

These findings are reinforced by our work unit interviews. Less than a quarter of work units in either city reported that they had sold any work unit housing to employees, and in only a few instances did this involve more than 1–2 percent of employees. About 20 percent of work units indicated that they had plans to sell commodity housing to employees by 1995 or to buy housing from the municipal housing office to sell to employees. A somewhat higher proportion planned to provide subsidies (sometimes 10 percent, but more commonly around 30 percent of the purchase price) to employees who buy commodity housing on their own: about 20 percent in Tianjin and nearly 30 percent in Shanghai.

In short, we find that housing reform has proceeded quickly in the area of rent increases and specifically in the form of relating rents more directly to housing space. But privatization of the housing stock in these two cities has barely begun.

Shanghai respondents were asked several specific questions about housing reform. An early municipal survey in Shanghai in 1991 showed that 84.6 percent supported the reform (Song 1992). In our survey, however, conducted two years later, the majority stated that they were unfamiliar with the details of the reform policies; only about one in four said they were "very familiar" or "quite familiar" with the policies. Nearly half (43 percent) did not wish to state an opinion about the success of housing reform. Of those who did, views were almost equally divided between people who considered it "very" or "quite" successful (30 percent of all respondents) and those who considered it "not very successful" or "unsuccessful" (27 percent). Asked how housing reform has affected their family's living standard, most replied that it has had no influence (73 percent). Almost nobody believed that it has improved their living standard (2 percent) while an appreciable number (24 percent) said that it has worsened it.

The Marriage of Work Units and Housing

Although the goal to separate housing from work units may be both necessary and attainable in the long run, the task has proved far more difficult than expected (Wang 1992). The current trend is in the opposite direction (Sun 1994; Zhang, Zhang, and Li 1994; Liu and Ma 1994). As work units have become the primary financier for housing development projects, the marriage of housing with work units seems to have become even stronger than ever.

Reforms in the state's financial and fiscal structures in 1979 altered the traditional pattern of housing investment. These reforms gave profit-making enterprises some autonomy to retain their earnings. The previous profit-turnover system is being replaced by a taxation system in which an enterprise is allowed to retain a portion of its profits after taxes. According to government regulations, retained profits should be divided into funds for factory development (40 percent), funds for bonuses (30 percent), and funds for employee welfare (30 percent). A portion of the last category should be designated for housing projects. In principle, these profit-making enterprises are no longer entitled to state housing funds that are used for housing projects for government agencies (*guojia jiguan*) and nonprofit institutions (*shiye danwei*). Yet, the real situation is far more complex. Based on our observations, we distinguish the following situations.

The first is enterprises that have sufficient self-generated funds to build or purchase housing for their employees. Most of these enterprises make profits from which they generate housing funds. However, the designated category of welfare funds (30 percent of retained profits) is not the only source of housing investments. Bank loans are a significant additional source. Earnings from an enterprise's "third sector units," which offer services and are allowed to have independent budgets, are used partly as housing investments. Still another source is the profits retained for factory development, but these profits are invested in employee housing. This last category is popular but not in accordance with state regulations, therefore the expenses in line with this category are unlikely to be found in either work-units' accounting books or formal survey questionnaires filled out by these work units.

One might think that enterprises in this category could generate housing funds independent from state control, representing a significant power shift due to market reform. The situation is not so clear. Walder (1989, 1992) has shown that an enterprise still needs to deal with vertical connections with its government jurisdiction to generate earnings, even though it appears to be an independent economic entity. One mechanism of hidden state control has been a two-price system: Products obtained at a state price are cheaper than those purchased in the market at a negotiated price. So, an enterprise can make profits by obtaining materials at a state-controlled price (through its connections with the government) but selling its products at a higher, market price. The enterprise also can make profits by obtaining tax benefits. Finally, the enterprise needs permission and support from its government jurisdiction to take loans from state banks for both productive and housing projects. In these cases, therefore, "market" resources must be combined with "political" resources in order to invest in new housing.

A different situation is presented by enterprises that continue to receive state housing funds or housing units. Some enterprises are required by the government to sell their products at a state controlled price (low), implying low or no profits for them. Many of these enterprises are in deficit, but these deficits are said to be "policy permitted." Also, many enterprises do not make profits at all, for historical or structural reasons. Enterprises in these situations usually are under contract with the government, receiving special tax and funding treatments. These enterprises cannot generate housing funds by themselves, but they are likely to receive grants or housing units from the government agencies to which they report.

Many small state-owned enterprises make good profits, but their welfare funds are insufficient for housing projects that require large amounts of investments. They have two choices. They may give up their housing projects (if few employees rely on them for housing) and use welfare funds in the forms of benefits in kind (lunches, work clothing, etc.) or bonuses (again, not in accordance with state regulations). Alternatively, they may turn in a portion of these funds to the government in return for an allocation of public apartments. The latter choice may be attractive to those enterprises whose managers want to obtain housing. Less commonly, employees in hardship cases can inform government officials of their housing situations, and their work units may be required by the government to exchange welfare funds for apartments to be distributed to those particular employees.

A third case is nonprofit institutions. Funding sources for housing for employees in nonprofit institutions have been basically unchanged under market reform, with the state remaining as the primary financier or the supplier of housing. In this sense, the traditional pattern still applies to nonprofit institutions. However, there are many exceptions. Some institutions, using their organizational resources or position, can effectively organize income-generating activities. Earnings are used in many forms, such as bonuses, floating salaries, and housing investments. Land-rich institutions may develop joint housing projects with money-rich enterprises. Still other institutions can receive special grants from the government to develop their housing projects.

Government agencies at higher levels continue to have clear advantages over most nonprofit institutions. They are privileged for two reasons. First, officials in high-level government agencies tend to have high civil service ranks and therefore are entitled to more housing space with better facilities. Second, high-level government agencies have direct control over the allocation of public housing and can channel apartments even to ordinary employees in their units.

In addition to advantages based in the traditional housing allocation process, government agencies also benefit from certain changes in the reform period. Real estate development firms, popular in Shanghai and Tianjin since 1990, are likely to be managed by or do business through municipal or district government agencies. For example, the three largest such firms in Tianjin are directed by a senior adviser of the municipal government (a former vice mayor), the construction commission of the municipal government (which is the highest authority for all housing development projects in the city), and the municipal government's real estate bureau, respectively. These firms make high profits that in part become housing funds for these high-ranking government agencies.

Second, many government agencies are the headquarters of bureaus and companies managing profit-making enterprises or nonprofit institutions. In both situations, these bureau or company headquarters commonly "skim off" housing from their subordinate work units. One usual strategy is to ask for processing fees for housing projects of their subordinate work units, which are paid in the form of housing. A more straightforward strategy is to require that a certain percentage of housing must be retained by the bureau or company headquarters after the construction is complete.

A final new situation is that of private enterprises. Many of these do not provide housing themselves; either their employees rely on housing from their previous state employers, or their spouses still work in state firms; in China this has been known as "one family, but two systems" (*yi jia liang zhi*). Some particularly well-financed international joint ventures buy commodified housing. This category has proved to be the mainstay of true "market-priced" housing in the reform period.

Work Units and Privatized Housing

In the long-range vision of a privatized housing market, as noted above, work units no longer play any direct role. An evaluation of the current reform period, however, shows that "privatization" actually reinforces the work unit's centrality. In Shanghai, by early 1995 about half a million households (or about 18 percent of total households) had purchased their current public apartments. Of the total sold housing space, two-thirds were municipal housing and one-third work-unit housing. If this trend continues, the emerging housing system will "legalize" and document in property rights terms the previous system of housing distribution in the following ways.

First, most housing sold through 1996 had been allocated by work units to their employees, favoring high-ranking cadres, party members, older workers, and employees of high-ranking work units. Even with newly constructed housing, the type, size, and quality of housing available to a worker are determined largely by the work unit. Hence the inequalities built into the previous redistributive system are being perpetuated in the commercialization of housing in the new era.

Second, sale prices were extremely low. In an entirely private housing market, only a small number of urban residents could afford housing at current construction costs. Given the present wage levels and the welfare economy, the ratio of recovery-cost rent to average annual urban household cash income was more than 20:1, compared to the ratio between 2:1 and 6:1 in most market economies. The rent required to recover fully the costs of investment in new housing could surpass 70 percent of the average household's monthly income (World Bank 1992). For example, even with a typical discount, a new apartment unit is sold at the equivalent of five to seven years of a worker's salary. Consequently, as Zhou and Logan (1996) point out in their analysis of privatization in Guangdong province, the actual pricing scheme for "commodified housing" is complex. Housing built or purchased by work units is usually sold to workers at greatly discounted prices, with the size of the discount typically proportional to the status of the worker.

Third, the most important feature of the new system of housing commodification is that those buying at discounted prices typically do not receive full title to their properties; what they have purchased is not ownership rights, but use rights. For example, in a state-owned factory in Tianjin, an apartment of some 50 square meters of living space (two bedrooms, a hallway, a kitchen, a bathroom, and two small balconies) is priced at 5,000 yuan, which is a year and a half's salary for an average worker in that factory. Those paying this price do not pay rents any more and are given a certificate of possession that can be passed onto the next generations within the family. However, the apartment is not allowed to be sold or leased to other people by the employees; the legal owner of the apartment is the work unit. What has happened is that this factory has adopted the "sales" mechanism to generate funds for developing new housing projects, without relinquishing its claim on older housing. In other cases the new owner has the right to sell after five years, but must give a first option to the work unit (or municipal housing office, if the apartment had been owned by the municipality) and accept a lower-than-market price.

Discussion and Conclusion

Housing continues to be a scarce resource in urban China, and work units continue to be a key allocator of this resource. The market reform process has altered the work unit's role in housing. Although the state continues to be the main source of housing investment for some sorts of work units, others—particularly state enterprises—have gained new levels of both autonomy and responsibility for housing. Even in "marketized" housing, where consumers purchase new apartments or their previously rented apartment, work units necessarily intervene decisively in determining who has access to what kind of housing, at what price, and the potential transaction of a purchased apartment.

We found some significant differences between Shanghai and Tianjin, and these reinforce the common observation that conclusions can rarely be reached for China as a whole. Work units have historically had a smaller part in the system of housing allocation in Shanghai than in most of China. Although there have been clear differences in how work units obtain housing (some being more active than others in housing ownership or management), centralized allocation standards and procedures have apparently reduced their influence over who gets what. Yet we suspect that this is changing as a result of the reliance on work unit investment in new housing. Tianjin may be more representative of urban China. But it, too, is somewhat unique. And it is well known that the housing reform process, like other aspects of market reform, has proceeded at widely disparate rates in the various regions of the country. In parts of South China, for example, privatization occurred rapidly, and most people now "own" their dwellings in some cities and towns. This is only beginning to occur in Tianjin and Shanghai. As we have indicated, marketization does not necessarily reduce the work-unit role in housing, but it does alter its form.

Through 1993, change in this system could be described as either fast or slow, depending on which aspect was considered. On the one hand, total housing investment levels had skyrocketed, offering considerably improved residential conditions. Work units were operating in new ways as housing entrepreneurs, in some cases even speculating on land or commodified housing but more commonly seeking simply to improve their control of this resource. Rents had recently doubled and could be expected to continue to rise quickly. People were aware of housing reform, and owning a home was understood as a real future possibility. On the other hand, the nexus between housing and work units was at least as strong as before. The characteristics of work units that had previously given them advantages in access to housing mostly continued to do so, and these continued to have an important political component (although "market profitability," which we did not try to measure here, may have become a new consideration in some cases). And work-unit allocation procedures had not changed, insofar as our data could ascertain. We found no changes over time (measured as differences between recently occupied housing units and those that had been allocated before the reform period) in the predictors either of work-unit participation in housing or of who benefited from housing inequalities.

We have seen the following picture of the urban housing system in China: Housing production, distribution, and exchange have begun to be considered a commodity process, and work units of all types have been involved in it. Interorganizationally, work units see one another as producers or consumers of housing as a commodity, and they mobilize their land, economic capacity, and especially their positional strengths in the changing economic and administrative system to compete for housing stock. Within organizations, work units still consider themselves redistributors, allocating their housing resources to their employees according to government regulations; but these regulations are neither redistributive nor market-driven. Rather, both principles are used to imply that housing is a commodity as well as a welfare good. In fact the government has both openly encouraged work units to seek exchange values in selling their housing to their employees, and, at the same time, approved (albeit quietly or silently) having work units reward their favored managers and workers with heavily subsidized work-unit housing. In the words of Deng Xiaoping, we label this emerging system a "market system with Chinese character."

Bibliography

Barlow, Melinda. 1988. "Urban Housing Reforms in China: A First Overview." Working Paper of Urban Development Division of the Policy, Planning and Research Department, World Bank.

Bian, Yanjie. 1994. *Work and Inequality in Urban China.* Albany: State University of New York Press.

Bian, Yanjie, and John R. Logan. 1996. "Market Transition and the Persistence of Power: The Changing Stratification System in Urban China." *American Sociological Review* 61: 739–58.

Burawoy, Michael, and Pavel Krotov. 1992. "The Soviet Transition from Socialism to Capitalism: Worker Control and Economic Bargaining in the Wood Industry." *American Sociological Review* 57: 16–38.

Chen, Xiangming, and Xiaoyuan Gao. 1993. "Urban Economic Reform and Public-Housing Investment in China." *Urban Affairs Quarterly* 29, no. 1: 117–45.

Dowall, David E. 1993. "Establishing Urban Land Markets in the People's Republic of China." *Journal of the American Planning Association* 59, no. 2:182–92.

Fong, Peter. 1989. "Housing Reforms in China." *Habitat International* 13, no. 4: 29–41.

Lee, Yok-Shiu. 1988. "The Urban Housing Problem in China." *China Quarterly,* no. 115 (September): 387–407.

Lin, Nan, and Yanjie Bian. 1991. "Getting Ahead in Urban China." *American Journal of Sociology* 97: 657–88.

Lin, Nan, and Maishou Hao. 1992. "Local Market Socialism: Reform in Rural China." Paper presented at the Symposium on the Great Transformation in South China and Taiwan: Markets, Entrepreneurship, and Social Structure, Cornell University, October 16–18.

Liu, Zeyuan, and Zhigang Ma. 1994. "Work Unit Housing Management in the Reform and Exploration Process: Report and Analysis of the Fifth National Meeting of Work Unit Housing in Steel and Iron Enterprises." *China's Real Estate* 166, no. 10: 27–30.

Logan, John R., and Yanjie Bian. 1993. "Inequalities in Access to Community Resources in a Chinese City." *Social Forces* 72, no. 2: 555–76.

Nee, Victor. 1989. "A Theory of Market Transition: From Redistributive to Markets in State Socialism." *American Sociological Review* 54: 663–81.

———. 1991. "Social Inequalities in Reforming State Socialism: Between Redistribution and Markets in China." *American Sociological Review* 56: 267–82.

Pickvance, Chris. 1988. "Employers, Labor Markets, and Redistribution under State Socialism: An Interpretation of Housing Policy in Hungary 1960–1983." *Sociology* 22: 193–214.

Second Automobile Manufacturer of China. 1992. "Develop the Housing System Reform with Consideration to the Interests of State, Collective and Individuals." *Chinese Real Estate* 4.

Shirk, Susan. 1993. *The Political Logic of Economic Reform in China.* Berkeley: University of California Press.

Song, Shunfeng. 1992. "Policy Issues Involving Housing Commercialization in the People's Republic of China." *Socio-Economic Planning Science* 26, no. 3: 213–22.

Staniszkis, Jadwiga. 1991. *The Dynamics of the Breakthrough in East Europe: The Polish Experience.* Berkeley: University of California Press.

State Council. 1991. "Opinions Concerning an All-Around Promotion of Housing Reforms in Cities and Towns" (State Council Document no. 73, 1991) (Guanyu quanmian tuijin chengzhen zhufang zhidu gaige de yijian [guobanfa (1991) 73 hao wenjian]). In *Compilation of Real Estate Management Documents of Shanghai* (Shanghai shi fangchan guanli wenjian huibian), 543–51. Shanghai: Shanghai Real Estate Management Bureau.

State Statistical Bureau of China. 1981. *Statistical Yearbook of China: 1981* (Zhongguo tongji nianjian: 1981). Beijing: Chinese Statistical Press.

State Statistical Bureau of China. 1984. *Statistical Yearbook of China: 1984* (Zhongguo tongji nianjian: 1984). Beijing: Chinese Statistical Press.

State Statistical Bureau of China. 1994. *Statistical Yearbook of China: 1994* (Zhongguo tongji nianjian: 1994). Beijing: Chinese Statistical Press.

Sun, Qinghua, Shuling Chen, and Cunxian Li. 1991. *Housing Reform and Housing Psychology* (Zhufang zhidu gaige yu zhufang xinli). Beijing: Publishing House of China's Construction Industry.

Sun, Yaowen. 1994. "New Housing System Implemented in Foreign-Invested Firms in Tianjin's Developmental Zones." *China's Real Estate* 165, no. 9: 25.

Szelenyi, Ivan. 1983. *Urban Inequalities Under State Socialism.* New York: Oxford University Press.

Szelenyi, Ivan, and Robert Manchin. 1987. "Social Policy Under State Socialism: Market, Redistribution, and Social Inequalities in East European Socialist Societies." In *Stagnation and Renewal in Social Policy*, ed. G. Esping-Andersen, M. Rein, and L. Rainwater, 102–39. Armonk, NY: M.E. Sharpe.

Tang, Wing-shing. 1994. "Urban Land Development under Socialism: China Between 1949 and 1977." *International Journal of Urban and Regional Development* 18: 392–415.

Tolley, George. 1991. "Urban Housing Reform in China: An Economic Analysis." World Bank Discussion Papers no. 123.

Walder, Andrew G. 1986. *Communist Neo-Traditionalism: Work and Authority in Chinese Industry.* Berkeley: University of California Press.

———. 1989. "Factory and Manager in an Era of Reform." *China Quarterly*, no. 118: 244–54.

———. 1992. "Property Rights and Stratification in Socialist Redistributive Economies." *American Sociological Review* 57: 524–39.

Wang, Yaping. 1990. "Private Sector Housing in Urban China since 1949: The Case of Xian." *Housing Studies* 7, no. 2: 119–37.

Wang, Yukun. 1992. "New Views of Urban Reforms in Urban China" (Zhongguo chengzhen zhufang gaige xinsifei). Supplement no. 2 in *Housing Reform*, ed. Yang and Wang, 291–306.

Whyte, Martin K., and William L. Parish. 1984. *Urban Life in Contemporary China.* Chicago: University of Chicago Press.

World Bank. 1992. *China: Implementation Options for Urban Housing Reform. A World Bank Country Study.* Washington DC: World Bank.

Yang, Lu, and Yukun Wang. 1992. *Housing Reform: Theoretical Rethinking and Practical Choices* (Zhufang gaige: lilun de fanxi yu xianshi de xuanze). Tianjin: People's Press of Tianjin.

Ye, Bochu, et al. 1993. *Residential Housing in Shanghai: 1949–1990* (Shanghai zhuzhai: 1949–1990). Shanghai: Scientific Mass-Learning Press of Shanghai.

Zhang, Qiufang, ed. 1990. *Theories and Practices in Housing Economic Reforms* (Zhuzhai jingji gaige de lilun yu shijian). Beijing: Peking University Press.

Zhang, Xuebin, Hao Zhang, and Zhihao Li. 1994. "Tentative Analysis of City and Work Unit Housing Funds." *China's Real Estate* 163, no. 7: 24–6.

Zhou, Min, and John R. Logan. 1996. "Market Transition and the Commodification of Housing in Urban China." *International Journal of Urban and Regional Research* 20: 400–21.

Zhou, Xueguang, and Nancy B. Tuma. 1994. "The Political Economy of Job Transition in Urban China, 1979–1993." Paper presented at the annual meetings of the American Sociological Association, Los Angeles, August 5–9.

Index